Gender and Qualitative Methods

INTRODUCING QUALITATIVE METHODS provides a series of volumes which introduce qualitative research to the student and beginning researcher. The approach is interdisciplinary and international. A distinctive feature of these volumes is the helpful student exercises.

One stream of the series provides texts on the key methodologies used in qualitative research. The other stream contains books on qualitative research for different disciplines or occupations. Both streams cover the basic literature in a clear and accessible style, but also cover the 'cutting edge' issues in the area.

SERIES EDITOR

David Silverman (Goldsmiths College)

TITLES IN SERIES

Doing Conversational Analysis
Paul ten Have

Using Foucault's Methods
Gavin Kendall and Gary Wickham

The Quality of Qualitative Research
Clive Seale

Qualitative Evaluation
Ian Shaw

Researching Life Stories and Family Histories
Robert L. Miller

Categories in Text and Talk
Georgia Lepper

Focus Groups in Social Research
Michael Bloor, Jane Frankland, Michelle Thomas, Kate Robson

Qualitative Research Through Case Studies
Max Travers

Methods of Critical Discourse Analysis
Ruth Wodak and Michael Meyer

Qualitative Research in Social Work
Ian Shaw and Nick Gould

Qualitative Research in Information Systems
Michael D. Myers and David Avison

Researching the Visual
Michael Emmison and Philip Smith

Qualitative Research in Education
Peter Freebody

Using Documents in Social Research
Lindsay Prior

Doing Research in Cultural Studies
Paula Saukko

Qualitative Research in Sociology: An Introduction
Amir B. Marvasti

Gender and Qualitative Methods

Helmi Järviluoma, Pirkko Moisala and Anni Vilkko

SAGE Publications
London ● Thousand Oaks ● New Delhi

Bruce Johnson acted as English translation editor

First published 2003

SAGE Publications Ltd
6 Bonhill Street
London EC2A 4PU

SAGE Publications Inc.
2455 Teller Road
Thousand Oaks, California 91320

SAGE Publications India Pvt Ltd
B-42 Panchsheel Enclave
Post Box 4109
New Delhi 100 017

British Library Cataloguing in Publication data

A catalogue record for this book is available
from the British Library

ISBN 0 7619 6584 x
     0 7619 6584 8

Library of Congress Control Number available

Typeset by C&M Digitals (P) Ltd., Chennai, India
Printed in India at Gopsons Papers Ltd, Noida

Contents

Preface and Acknowledgements   vii

1   Performing and Negotiating Gender   1

2   Gender and Fieldwork   27

3   Gender and Life Stories   46

4   Gender in Membership Categorization Analysis
    Helmi Järviluoma and Irene Roivainen   69

5   Not only Vision – Analysing Sound and Music from
    the Perspective of Gender   84

6   Research Reporting and Gender   107

Bibliography   118

Index   134

Preface and Acknowledgements

Late in an August evening 2002 we three writers were drinking toasts at the Kolme Kruunua (Three Crowns) restaurant in Helsinki. Nearby in the Senate Square, the mayor of Helsinki had just finished hosting her annual popular music concert. We had planned to treat ourselves with music after finishing a five-year project: the manuscript of the textbook you are holding.

As usual, the final corrections, the printing, and packing the pages neatly to be sent to Sage took far more time than we had planned. We didn't make the concert, but actually we didn't mind. After five years of planning, collecting materials and bibliographical information, writing, re-writing, translating, negotiating, getting inspired, being desperate, arguing and sulking, melting, laughing and editing, we were nearly there.

This book is practical guide for recognizing gender/ing in different kinds of research materials. We show a selection of possibilities to analyse gender as something which is not given, but which is always negotiated and performed. In addition, this book is also a performance, prepared by the three of us – Helmi, Pirkko and Anni – in countless negotiations. Writing itself is always a process, and this book is one important step for us in our thinking and writing about gender. You can read more about our own positions in relation to qualitative gender studies at the end of Chapter 1.

Some kind of narration, however, can be constructed about the history of this book. In 1997 the series editor, David Silverman, contacted his former student, Helmi Järviluoma, suggesting the idea for the book. After pondering alone upon the subject for a short while, she contacted here colleague Pirkko Moisala, and together they started to intensively plan the contents and collect the bibliography. Helmi was able to write some of the book while working as a researcher in the Academy of Finland; and so did Pirkko at the last stage of the writing process – thank you the Academy of Finland. Finally, Anni Vilkko was recruited as a welcome new member of the team. In fact, it is better to say that a new team, or triad, was created. Everybody commented on each other's texts. Examples, exercises and bits and bites of text were transferred between the writers during the writing process. Helmi started with Chapter 2, Pirkko with Chapter 1, and Anni with Chapter 3, and they continued to bear the principle responsibility for writing those chapters. Pirkko and Helmi together drafted the framework for Chapter 5, after which Pirkko took charge of writing the gendered analysis of film and video music, and Helmi added the part on soundscape. Anni and Helmi shouldered the responsibility for Chapter 6, but Pirkko had a large input as well. Chapter 4 was written by Helmi and Irene Roivainen from the Department of Social Policy in Tampere University. Thank you Irene for the inspiring writing sessions. Thanks also go to the journal *Sosiologia* for permission to use some parts of an earlier MCA article by Irene and Helmi.

We would like to thank the friendly and professional staff of Sage Publications, especially Louise Wise, Karen Phillips and Ian Antcliff. Associate Professor Bruce Johnson from the School of English in the University of New South Wales acted as a Translation Editor for us, for which we are very grateful. Without the series editor, David Silverman, the book wouldn't exist. We are thankful for his support and patience. Thanks are also due to Heljä Mäntyranta, Soili Keskinen and Taru Leppänen, the editors of the journal *Nuorisotutkimus*, and to all colleagues, friends and family members from whom we have received encouragement and support during this project.

13.02.03
Helmi Järviluoma, Pirkko Moisala, Anni Vilkko
In the cyberspace between Turku, Lieto and Helsinki

1

Performing and Negotiating Gender

Short history of and overview of gender studies   9
The Study of men and masculinities   11
Sexuality and gender   12
Performativity of gender   14
Masculinity and femininity   16
Gender identity   17
Gender produced by research methods   18
The necessity of positioning   22
Deconstructing the tie between 'feminity'
    and 'qualitive' methodology   23
Conclusion: towards gender analysis   24

This book has grown out of the conviction that gender, the cultural construction of femininity and masculinity, cannot be avoided in any research activity. It is present in all human action and its products, including researchers and their research. Gender is an important criterion in identifying ourselves and is central to the way we perceive and structure the world and events in which we participate. It influences all aspects of our being, of our relationships and of the society and culture around us. Gendered conceptualizations, norms (what is considered to be proper behaviour), values (the personal characteristics that are highly valued) and attitudes (the kinds of prejudices that come into play when we meet a person of a different gender), have a profound effect on both the personal and social, the micro and macro levels of our lives.

Gender must be taken seriously in every kind and at every level of research, from practical choices to methodological questions, as well as at every stage of the research process. This is a conviction which we have formed not only as gendered human beings but also as scholars working in a range of fields, including social politics, musicology, ethnomusicology, sociology and anthropology. In our opinion, the duty of researchers is not only to explore but also to question the cultural patterns relating to gender in all human actions and its products. Ignoring gender in qualitative research is the same as ignoring one of the most fundamental elements in the natural sciences.

In the analysis of qualitative materials, gender can be identified and analysed at all levels: at the individual/personal level (identifications, subject positions), and in the socially constructed and maintained discourses ('texts', ideologies and social institutions). Likewise, of course, in between these levels: how subject positions are negotiated within the prevailing gender systems, and how gender discourses produce individual gender positions.

In research work, gender should be understood as a concept requiring analysis, rather than as something that is *already* known about. The common-sense understanding of gender should be seriously interrogated. What is our common understanding of gender? How is it represented in cultural action and products? Which kind of power structures does it produce? And what are the mechanisms by which we construct our understanding of gender?

The field of gender studies ranges from radical feminist studies to areas without any overt feminist content. Even though women's studies and feminist theories have provided the major contribution to this field, gender analysis has also been conducted from various other political positions. Gender has been an issue both for the political interests of feminism and the intellectual interests of sociology and other sciences. Critical engagement with the contemporary social world in terms of the ways in which the usually asymmetric gender differences are produced, maintained and resisted – that is, critical feminist theory – has not been the only driving force of gender studies. Within sociology, for example, gender has also been examined as the social construction of difference, though without necessarily addressing questions of inequality and power, which are central themes of feminist theory. Only those gender studies which are committed to the struggle against sexism and patriarchal power can be regarded as feminist in nature (Moi, 1990: 18–21).

Institutionally, many study programmes which previously were called 'women's studies' are changing their names to 'gender studies'. While this shift of focus from women to gender might reduce the radical feminist impulses of these programmes, it more comfortably accommodates a broader range of questions regarding gender, such as the construction of masculinity and sexuality, areas of study which have, however, also traditionally belonged to the curriculum of women's studies.

In this textbook, we take the social constructionist approach to gender while simultaneously examining the mechanisms of power included in these constructions. As Deborah Cameron (1996: 84) has emphasized, gender should not be used as an explanation of things, because it is itself a social construction in need of an explanation. In addition to examining gender roles, we should ask what the mechanisms are which create/construct such roles. Thus, gender studies focus on the exploration of how the categories of men and women, masculinity and femininity, as well as possible other gender categories, are socially constructed. What ideas and judgements are attached to them? What are the mechanisms which maintain, support or challenge the prevailing gender system? How is power negotiated in gender constructions?

The concept of 'gender' refers to the social and cultural construction of 'biological' sexes. Our understanding of biology is also based on social and cultural knowledge. Gender and sex are 'created and recreated when practiced and discussed' (Yuval-Davis, 1997: 119). They are closely related, although not because one is 'natural' while the other represents its transformation into 'culture'. They are both cultural categories, that is, they are culturally constructed ways of describing and understanding human bodies and human relationships. Gender and sex affect our identities, our understanding of self and our relationships with others (Glover and Kaplan, 2000: xxv–xxvi.)

The categories of 'men' and 'women' may have some biological grounding in visual, aural and otherwise observable features, but these categories are simple homogeneous groups. The number of conceptualized sexes and genders not varies in different cultures. Categories of 'men' and 'women' are not the only possible sexes, and other categories are acknowledged, for example, transsexuals and androgynes. Our cultural categories of gender are even more numerous and varied. The socio-cultural possibilities implied in being a man or a woman, and what is socially expected of each, vary enormously depending on place, period and personal situation.

According to Linda Nicholson (1994: 101) our comprehension of what a woman is evolves from both differences and sameness. A woman is thus a map of intersecting similarities and differences, an internal coalition. The same may be said of men. Many social factors, such as class, race, ethnicity and age, play essential roles in the construction of gender. The gender of an Indian woman is different from that of a British girl and the gender of an old man differs from that of a teenage boy. A study focusing on gender should recognize the variations that are to be found in particular times and places. Gender 'is more relational rather than essential, structural rather than individual – a property of systems rather than people' (Marx Ferree and Hess, 1987: 17). Gender is a fluid social category, which is always being negotiated anew.

Stereotypical images of women and men, opinions about purported qualities of masculinity and femininity, as well as all beliefs concerning males and females, can be examined as aspects of a gender belief system (see Deaux and Kite, 1987: 97). A gender belief system – or dominant gender schema, as suggested by Devor (1989) – is working on us from the moment we are born. We learn the prevailing sex roles in the course of enculturation (primary learning of our first cultural surroundings) and socialization (the process of becoming a member of a society).

Psychological studies have questioned if socio-emotional differences between male and female babies are assigned by birth – if they are biological – or cultural. If newborn female babies are more sensitive to aural and social stimulus and more able to maintain eye contact with the carer than male babies, as psychological research (Weinberg et al., 1999) has revealed, is this actually a result of differences in mothers' behaviour arising from the child's gender? Lamb et al. (1979: 97) argue that learning to recognize masculine and feminine styles of interaction begins long before a child can conceptualize gender. It also has more impact on their sex-role development than their parents' attempts to shape their gender behaviour.

Gender stereotypes within a culture are pervasive in a baby's surroundings. J. Bridges (1993) made a qualitative analysis of 60 randomly chosen congratulatory cards for parents of newly-born male children, and of 60 cards for those of female children. The study revealed that qualities emphasizing activity (pictures of running, building or wrestling boys), were associated with a male child, whereas passive qualities were associated with a female child. Girls were pictured watching the activities of the male children or sitting in the middle of roses and hearths. Similar kinds of stereotypical thinking were observed in the behaviour of those mothers, who more easily accepted shyness in their daughters' than in the sons' behaviour (Hinde et al., 1993). Through these kinds of gender stereotypes children learn the prevailing gender system. At the age of two months children can differentiate male and female voices (Leinbach and Fagot, 1993) and, at one year they can connect a male voice with a male face and a female voice with a female face (Poulin-Dubois et al., 1994). We learn to make gendered observations in early childhood, but gendering the world and its events around us continues as one of the central modelling systems throughout our lives.

Case 1.1 Agnes, learning to be a woman

A famous and instructive example of the cultural construction of the institutionalization of gender construction is the study by the socio-logist Harold Garfinkel (1967). He studied Agnes, who was a patient sent, in 1958, to the psychiatric clinic of UCLA. Agnes had been born as a boy with boy's genitals, and raised as boy until the age of seventeen. However, at the age of twelve she also had started to get a female shape and breasts.

When Agnes came to UCLA she was nineteen and nothing revealed that she wouldn't 'really' be a woman: she had a shapely figure, she was tall, had pretty features and fine fair hair, and she dressed as a girl. She wanted to have a sex-change operation and was very determined to achieve womanhood.

Garfinkel begun to study Agnes as a 'case' in order to learn about the ways in which gender-identity is produced and refined through observable but subtle practices, which however, are part of institutionalized social interaction. As John Heritage has said, the result of the study was a profound analysis of gender as a constructed social fact (1996: 181).

Agnes had become a very sensitive ethnographer of gender. She was conscious of the connections between behaviour and gender in all kinds of everyday social situations. The key situations were dressing up and applying make-up, and the problems of 'proper female behaviour', i.e. sitting/walking/talking like a woman. It was hard for Agnes to learn not to talk like a man.

Part of the problem was that she had little if any of the same biographical experiences as other girls. She had to achieve womanhood through undetectable, difficult and unending work. Heritage (ibid.: 186) describes Agnes' situation with a metaphorical question: What is it like to build a ship when it is already sailing? Such was the difficulty that faced Agnes in her attempt to construct gender identity through countless socially ordered micro-practices.

For Garfinkel, the constant differentiation between the cultural specificities of men and women was the outcome of study, not the starting point. The reproduction of these institutionalized genders is supported by processes based on moral accountability, which become actualized in everyday reactions towards people, who deviate from 'the natural' gender (see also Kessler and McKenna, 1979).

According to Deborah Tannen (1990: 8), who studied conversational practices of American men and women, gender socialization is so strong that girls and boys grow up in what are essentially different cultures. Even if one declines to adopt these roles and, instead, contests them, this also takes place in relation to the socially acknowledged gender roles. However, all boys and girls do not become socialized in the same way even though they may live in the same environment. This has been strongly confirmed by the so-called constructionist approach to learning (among others Leinbach et al., 1997). A girl growing up primarily among boys may develop physical skills that require strength and speed, whereas another girl in the same kind of male environment might emphasize qualities which usually are called feminine. In opposition to earlier psychological studies, which explored the differences between the genders and assumed homogeneity within each, more recent studies look for differences within genders.

Gender is also a fundamental principle of the organization of social arrangements and action. Almost everything in our surroundings is gendered in one way or another. For instance, we speak of Mother Earth, and *das Vaterland* (the fatherland, *patria*); various cultural practices are taken for granted as being gendered, so that, for example, heavy metal music associates more with masculinity than with femininity. In addition, most often our gendered understandings of the world and its phenomena are hierarchically ordered; certain qualities are accorded more value and respect than others because of the nature of their gendering. Gender, with the power attached to it, is a subject of constant negotiation in our daily social lives. In addition, today's representations of gender in the Western world are often, as Theresa de Lauretis (1987: x) has asserted, produced by a number of distinct 'technologies of gender' such as cinema or advertising. The impact of these mediated images of gender on people's gender beliefs and gender performance cannot be underestimated.

Case 1.2 Masculinity in heavy metal music

Robert Walser (1993) studied gender constructions in heavy metal music demonstrating how it reproduces and inflects patriarchal ideologies and assumptions. To him, 'heavy metal is, as much as anything else, an arena of gender, where spectacular gladiators compete to register and affect ideas of masculinity, sexuality and gender relations' (ibid.: 111). Notions of gender are represented in the texts, sounds, images, and practices of heavy metal. In addition, fans of heavy metal experience confirmation and alteration of their gendered identities through their involvement with the music (ibid.: 109).

Simultaneously when heavy metal replicates the dominant sexism of contemporary society it also is a space in which female fans and female performers can experience power, dominance, rebellion and flirting with the dark side of life, usually designated as male prerogatives (ibid.: 131–2).

Case 1.3 Gendered theory of classical music

In Western classical music, the main theme or melody which is repeated throughout a symphony or other kind of work, is regarded as the masculine theme, whereas, the second theme, the role of which is to challenge the main theme but which, however, remains secondary and doomed to 'lose the game' to the main theme, is called the feminine theme (see, for example, McClary, 1991).

The negotiation of power is part of gender. The feminist branches of gender studies (see, for example, Marshall, 2000: 155) remind us that even though gender can be approached as a discourse, an ideological phenomenon, a fiction or a construction, it also has practical and material consequences for both women and men. Gender is not an 'innocent' social category or an unimportant aspect of our identity. Instead, it may open or close doors in our lives, limit or broaden our possibilities to live our lives to the fullest.

Gender studies is a wide field, which takes as its points of departure various methodological understandings of the term 'gender'. Gender can be regarded as (1) a social variable (what do men do, what do women do); (2) a system (gender order and gender hierarchy; that is, what kind of system do genders create in relation to each other, how genders are hierarchically ordered); (3) a social construction (how gender/s are socially and culturally produced in language, social action and cultural products); or (4) a political tool (how gender ideologies can be reconstructed and changed). Thus, gender analysis is not simply interested in examining what men/women are or do. It examines how the world surrounding us is gendered and how it affects us, our identity, everyday activities, as well as all other products of human behaviour. It studies how gender is taken up, regularized, institutionalized, resisted, contested and transformed.

In this book we introduce different methods for recognizing gender/ing in qualitative research. We show ways in which gender can be analysed in different kinds of research materials, in life stories, interviews and conversations, in sound, music, film and video. We also discuss the roles it plays in fieldwork and research reporting. Our approach to gender is to examine it as a social construction, which involves the whole of the research process. The discussion is supported mostly by feminist theories and studies although we also acknowledge gender studies which are not feminist in nature. However, the driving force behind most gender studies – women's studies, men's studies, the study of masculinities, gay, lesbian, and queer studies – is anti-sexism, the political objective of resisting asymmetrical relationships between and within genders.

Case 1.4 Finnish gender order represented in music

Even though Finland was among the very first countries in the world where women were allowed to vote (in 1907), and despite the fact that women's work outside the home is more a rule than an exception and that the present legislation and social security system attempt to advance gender equality, gendered practices as well as ways of behaving and thinking in Finland are far from representing gender equality (see Anttonen et al., 1994). This obvious contradiction between policies of gender equality and practices of gender inequality creates a particular cultural climate based on the tension of negative gender difference. Negative gender difference is embedded in all aspects of Finnish culture. Even though the state school system (there are few private schools in Finland) gives equal opportunity of education to both genders, and men and women are both highly educated, different social expectations are imposed on different genders. Girls are expected to adopt patterns of care-taking and domestic maintenance. The social norms placed on females emphasize modest, if not withdrawn, and obedient behaviour, whereas boys are expected to grow up to be outwardly active, 'heroically' disobedient, and take an interest in sports.

According to 57 life stories written by music students, the conventional gender roles of today's Finnish culture are already essentialized in kindergarten (ages three to six): in musical plays, for example, girls perform the roles of angels and fairies and are expected to participate in singing, while the boys are bears or shepherds and are not expected to participate in singing. In primary school (ages seven to twelve), these roles continue: girls are expected to play recorders in a group, while boys receive more encouragement and attention from the teacher and play instruments (such as drums) individually. The girls dance to the accompaniment provided by the boys. These gender roles in music were adopted early by the pupils themselves. One of the students remembered how, already at the age of six, she was astonished to realize that a woman could be a conductor or play trumpet. Another believed that any girl who wanted to play drums was boyish.

At secondary school (ages thirteen to fifteen), gender roles in music are stressed even more: 'The girls went to sing in a choir while the boys formed bands to play rock music.' Girls who nevertheless play rock music, choose to play more melodic rock (what the Americans call 'soft rock'), while boys play heavy rock. In music lessons, the boys are given more tasks to do and the more expensive instruments to play: thus, the girls either sing or play recorders, of which there are many in the classroom, whereas the boys get to play the two electric guitars and the only drum set.

The gender roles taught in kindergarten are reinforced by the two distinct musical spheres of boys and girls at primary and secondary schools. The young people themselves actively maintain their adopted gender roles; exceptions to the gender norm are not usually allowed. Girls in exceptional musical roles, such as those wanting to play drums or an electric guitar, were suppressed by ridicule or by having their wishes ignored, while boys in exceptional roles – a singing boy, the few boys taking a music class – were admired and encouraged. However, boys also reported gender limitations: a boy soloist in a female choir was ridiculed and a boy playing piano felt that his 'masculinity' would have been endangered among those peers who did not play music if he had not been competent in sports as well.

The fact that piano playing may compromise the masculinity of a Finnish boy, for example, refers to the possibility that art music, in Finnish music culture, is regarded as a feminine activity. This may be because the gender behaviour expected of Finnish males, heroic defiance and physical activity, does not correspond with behaviour related to art music. As we know, art music demands constant, controlled, obedient exercising, alone and indoors. Due to this gender expectation, rock music, with its creative freedom and group working patterns, works much better to support the masculine image of a boy.

Different kinds of gender categories may also be formed around music. Unusual gender roles become more permissable and acceptable during the later stages of music education: at high schools (ages sixteen to eighteen), conservatories, and universities, gender limitations are no longer as strict as at primary schools. The girls and boys are no longer pushed to follow gender norms. Unconventional gender roles become more or less accepted. 'Feminine boy' and 'masculine girl' were terms often used in the collected musical life stories. Some students claimed and others reported that their teachers had said that it was good for a boy dealing with music to be somewhat feminine: his manliness would give him strength and aggressiveness, but his feminine side would provide him with softer, emotional characteristics, also needed for the proper interpretation of music. In other words, the 'proper' interpretation of music required both genders or 'some kind of bisexuality'. In this case, the term 'bisexuality' was used by the students and their music teachers as a metaphor for whatever kind of behaviour (not necessarily sexual behaviour) that crosses conventional gender lines. However, female students were always said to be lacking masculine strength and the aggressiveness required to perform certain works. The collected stories give the impression that only boys can have both the requisite male and female qualities for the perfect interpretation of music ('only a man can make good music, but bisexuality gives the required sensitivity for interpretation'), while girls will always be lacking power. It seemed that it cannot as easily be imagined that girls/women have the required kind of bisexuality for a valid interpretation of music (Moisala, 2000a).

Short history and overview of gender studies

There is a lack of agreement about the origins of gender studies. Barbara Marshall (2000: 21) states that the distinction between sex and gender was originally introduced in the medical and psychoanalytical literature of the mid-1950s or perhaps even as early as the 1930s by psychologists. While Freud was examining human sexual behaviour in order to increase our understanding of the unconscious regions of mental life, psychologists interested in sexology were exploring the dimensions of human sexual behaviour. The concept of gender emerged originally in the early 1960s, in the area of overlap between sexology and psychoanalysis (Glover and Kaplan, 2000: xviii). Initially, scholars wrote about gender roles, cultural standards regarding 'manly' and 'womanly' patterns of behaviour, which an individual adopts. By that time, it was already understood that a person's sexual preferences and proclivities cannot be deduced from anatomical facts.

Even though not all gender studies are necessarily feminist in nature, feminist studies have provided the strongest foundations and theoretical innovations for gender studies in general. The concept of feminism was already current by the mid-nineteenth century, and many influential feminist writers of the early twentieth century, such as Simone de Beauvoir, still serve as an inspiration to feminist approaches. As an academic field, however, feminist studies first emerged in the 1960s.

De Beauvoir's book *The Second Sex* (1949) analyses the otherness of women in a male-dominated Western culture and examines the images of femaleness constructed by men. She argues that one is not born to be a woman but grows to be one. Because the norm for a human being is always a male, the concept of 'man' refers only to males and to the male world, a woman becomes defined in relation to a man. Thus, a woman is always the Other in relation to a man. Kate Millet (1977: 29–31) was one of the pioneer proponents of the argument that gender is defined by culture; she stated that because the early psychologists regarded gender as psychological, it had also to be cultural. Her book *Sexual Politics* (1977) studied the literary images of women in texts of male writers. Her aim was to show how these male constructions of women failed to correspond to 'real' women. Much of the work of present-day feminist literary studies continues to analyse the images of femaleness and women in literature, however, scholars no longer believe that a 'wrong' or 'right' image of a real woman exists. Rather, the image is regarded as a discursive construction within particular socio-cultural and historical contexts.

The struggle against sexism and patriarchal values, and the attempt to reconstruct the mechanisms which maintain the asymmetrical relations between genders, form the basis of feminist studies. What was previously regarded as 'natural' differences of sex have been de-naturalized and politicized by feminist studies (Marshall, 2000: 10). Today, feminist studies is a multidisciplinary field with ramifications throughout academic research. One can no longer speak of a single feminism, but of various feminisms. The political objective, to promote the position of women, underpins all branches of feminist studies. At the same time, there is a continuing, theoretically stimulating and fruitful discussion about who these 'women' are: are they black, white or Asian?; are they lesbian or straight?; do they come from the so-called Third World countries or from the West?; are they Muslims or Buddhists? 'A woman' should be regarded as an umbrella term, under which gather together different kinds of women, different levels of experience and different identities (Braidotti, 1994: 164). Women's status, rights and the struggle for a better life appear very different from different positions.

The so-called Second Wave feminist movement (see Nicholson, 1997) emphasized gender differences. At first, the gender difference was seen entirely as a tool which the male-dominated society used to oppress women, because women were different, the same rights were not granted to them as to men. Therefore, the early feminists of that period aimed at gender equality by deconstructing gender differences. The political trap in this project was that the measure of equality was defined by the male standard.

The next step in the development of feminist studies was in reaction to this endeavour. As a result of consciousness-raising groups of women established in the 1970s, some feminists began to consider gender differences as positive differences. Women's bodies and different life experiences became sources of positive female identity and power. The same development took place also within men's studies, evolving as a pro-male movement.

Again, these feminist theorizations had two kinds of consequences. On the one hand, they disclosed the existence and value of women's traditions; on the other, they led to a form of ghettoizing of women. The school of French feminism, which evolved around the innovative writings of Hélène Cixous, Luce Irigaray and Julia Kristeva, sought a solution to this problem by critically examining the language in and through which our understanding of genders is constructed. They believe that because stereotypical images of genders are constructed in language, they can also be deconstructed in and through language. The languages of 'speaking (as) women' (*parler femme* by Irigaray) or 'women's writing' (*écriture féminine* by Hélène Cixous) were visualized as locations where both women and men can express themselves free from the logocentric, patriarchal order.

Within feminist studies, it has always been understood that the social construction of 'a woman' and femininity takes place in the frame of gender order, thus, within the gender system in which different genders negotiate and struggle for power. Any given gender role acts in relation to other gender roles within the whole gender system of that particular society. Even though the emphasis of feminist studies has been on women with the political aim of their emancipation, a kind of side effect of feminist studies has been the critical examination of maleness and the social category of man. Feminist theories have served also in other ways as an inspiration and example for studies which began also to see men as a social category.

The study of men and masculinities

Men's studies evolved as a reaction to feminism in early 1970s in the USA. Men's studies – in Europe, called the study of masculinity – are generally characterized by pro-feminism and anti-sexism (Sipilä, 1994). Echoing feminist theories, gender and gender relations are also regarded within men's studies as a product of social interaction. However, the critical driving force of feminism, to break down the suppressing mechanisms of gender order, is absent. How could men, particularly heterosexual men, have similar kinds of interests as women, asks Jorma Sipilä (1994: 18)? Jeff Hearn and David Morgan (1990: 15) state that men, in positions privileged by a patriarchal order, have usually as little need to theorize about their own position as a fish in the water. Men's studies, instead, have illuminated the varieties of masculinities, the asymmetrical relations between them and the mechanisms that support them.

Men's studies and studies on masculinity examine the cultural construction of masculinity. When framed as critiques, they question the social norms and practices, which define the norms and ideals of masculinity. George Mosse (1996), who has explored the construction of the 'manly ideal' in Western society from the late eighteenth century, argues that the 'manly ideal' of the modern era has been partly defined by what it excludes. In particular, any traits regarded as feminine, as well as emotional vulnerability in men, have been regarded as weaknesses.

The discussions within men's studies have echoed feminist theories. Instead of *a* masculinity, we should speak of masculinities. Power is also negotiated among different kinds of masculinities; there are those masculinities, which are marginalized, as well as those which maintain the hegemonic position. The hegemonic, 'ideal' masculinity, which takes different forms in different contexts and situations, does not correspond to the reality of most men and, as in the case of femaleness, the mass media play a central role in the creation of hegemonic masculinity (see Connell, 2000).

Case 1.5 Hegemonic and marginalized masculinity

When Helmi Järviluoma (2000) was studying a Finnish amateur folk music group consisting mainly of middle-aged and older men in a rural town, she realized the positionality of gender discourses: what is regarded as marginal at a certain moment depends on the position of the viewer. The musicians of the *pelimanni* ensemble, which she studied, were marginal in relation to the music college and the town's male choir, which performed 'art' music. The latter represented the hegemonic masculinity of the local musical life. The members of the male choir had 'their chests full of honorary medals', as the *pelimanni* conductor bitterly observed (ibid.: 70).

Järviluoma wanted to resist this hierarchical order of masculinities relating to different genres of music and chose to see the activities of *pelimanni* musicians as a positive way of 'becoming a minority', which escaped the hegemonic order of the majority. For instance, the best-known media figure and symbol of Finnish folk music, the fiddler and composer Konsta Jylhä, could cry on the stage and remain, nonetheless, a 'man of the people'. Julia (1981b: 144) has talked about several artists having the same 'fragile sensitivity'.

Sexuality and gender

Gender and sexuality are distinct but closely linked aspects of being a wo/man; sexuality is always part of the discourse of gender. To learn sexuality is to participate in the process of socialization into the gender order. Desire is a negotiation between the individual and society. Heterosexuality can be seen as a compulsory order, which maintains manly power (Rich, 1980). As Drucilla Cornell (1995: 75) writes, women are inseparable from the ways femininity is imagined and fantasized within the constraints of gender hierarchy and heterosexual norms.

The interconnectedness of gender and sexuality, however, is not a simple matter. In fact, sexuality evokes the same questions as gender: is it a biological and physiological, or a psychological or a cultural issue? However, it is just as important to see the different emphases of the concepts of sexuality and gender. According to Whitehead and Conaway (1986: 1–5), sexuality refers to that sphere of interpersonal behaviour, which is most directly associated with leading to, substituting for or resulting from genital union.

Following Michel Foucault's (1979a) analysis of the discursive explosion of sex during the past two hundred years in the Western world, sexuality has also come to be seen as an explanation for various cultural forms and patterns. Foucault's ideas regarding the genealogy of sexuality have served as an often-cited source of inspiration for much of the work in gender and feminist studies, where, however, they are also widely criticized for male-normativity. What remains is the understanding that sexuality, like gender, is constructed in language and in social interaction and is the subject of power negotiations.

Today's gender studies also include gay and lesbian studies. Their political aim is to promote the position of sexual minorities and to resist homophobic and heterosexist attitudes. Gay and lesbian studies have argued that sexual orientation – like gender – is a culturally constructed category, which guides our thinking and social action. Within gay and lesbian studies, so-called queer theory has renounced fixed dichotomies of any kind of difference, including those of homosexuality and heterosexuality, masculinity and femininity, maleness and femaleness. These studies have demonstrated the situational and performative character of sexuality and sexual identity (Weedon, 1999: 72–4). Thus, the contributions of queer theory are not restricted solely to gay and lesbian studies. It has also demonstrated that conventional gender categories are too simplistic to serve even as an adequate description of the pleasures of the body. How could these categories then be taken as cultural or human universals?

Case 1.6 Bending gender categories in everyday action

Gender-blender is a gender category referring to people who belong to one sex and identify themselves also as belonging to the corresponding gender, however, who perform a mixture of both male and female characteristics. For instance, a *gender-blending* woman may dress like a man and her gestures and style of talking are more easily interpreted as those of a man. The sexual orientation of *gender-blenders* may be either homosexual or heterosexual.

One of the women Holly Devor (1989: 101–2) interviewed for her study on *gender-blending* females felt strongly that, against the measures of the conventional gender order, she seemed more like a man than a woman. She was even therefore considering a sex change operation. Because her sexual orientation was homosexual, she eventually found a lesbian community, which provided her with a gender option of a 'mannish woman'; she could be both a woman and as masculine as she felt.

Performativity of gender

One of the most influential feminist theorists of the recent decade, Judith Butler (1990; 1997) sees gender both as a symbolic form of 'public action' and an identity deriving from the recurrences of that action. She argues that there is no gender identity prior to the expression of gender, rather, that gender identity is constituted by the repetition of performative expressions (1990: 24–5). Butler belongs to those feminist theorists who theorize the body and its relation to gendered subjectivity, and who reject 'sex' as something that is bodily given, to which the construct of gender is added. Butler sees sex 'as cultural norm which governs the materialization of bodies' (1993: 2–3). Gender categories, such as 'man' and 'woman' are representations constructed within cultural institutions. They are thus cultural constructions.

Performance and performativity in Butler's use should not be mistaken as simply some kind of masquerade or an intentional play with gender roles (for instance, choosing to play the role of, to perform, a manly woman). Performativity refers to the performative constitution of gendered conventions. According to Butler (1993: 234), performance as an event (such as a staged performance) has to be separated from performativity, which consists of norms which precede and guide the performance and the performers. Power is always important in gender performance. Gender performance is bounded by the gender system surrounding it, even though it may seem to contest, mask, or oppose conventional gender roles. Therefore, gender performance should be understood not only as a negotiation between an individual and his or her cultural surroundings and its conventions, but as repeated performances of the gender system, with their capacity for change and alteration. 'A performative act is one which brings into being or enacts that which it names, and so marks the constitutive or productive power of discourse' (ibid.: 134).

Gender, like other cultural categories such as ethnicity and sexuality, is performed differently in different situations and locations. Gender performance, like any performance of other cultural categories, takes place as a negotiation between context-bound and situational subjects. The gender system of the culture (including power relations) and personal experiences are involved in the gender negotiation. The performance of gender is not simply the performance of bodies, human beings in action; the concept of performativity is applicable also to language use and other cultural texts, such as the arts. The usefulness of performativity in gender analysis of many kinds of qualitative materials, such as music and film, conversation, literary and interviewed texts and in fieldwork, will be demonstrated later in this volume.

The usefulness of the concept of performativity in gender analysis is manifold. It encourages us to see beyond individual gendered expressions, to see the conventions behind them and at the same time beyond those conventions. It liberates us from the idea of the 'truth' of gender by requiring us to examine gender as a process, in which it creates itself. Butler used the example of drag to illustrate the point: 'Is drag the imitation of gender or does it dramatize the signifying gestures through which gender itself is established?' (1990: xiii–ix). When the naturalness of 'sex' and heterosexuality are questioned, we can no longer claim that gender, as female or male, has any natural meaning. Drag is a way of demonstrating this political point, which, at the same time, also provides a valuable analytical tool.

Case 1.7 Gender performance in a Finnish dance restaurant

Ten members of the Music and Gender Study Group of the International Council for Traditional Music took part in an experiment organized by Pirkko Moisala (see Moisala, 2001) in Helsinki, in 1999, in order to explore the impact of scholars' identities and previous experiences on the observations made during the course of the fieldwork focusing on gender. The experiment set out to determine how gender is negotiated in the dance restaurant Vanha Maestro, paying attention to the following questions: What factors are at play when negotiating gender in a Finnish dance restaurant? How is gender performed and which factors influence gender negotiation? The advice for the fieldwork was brief: make (and record) concrete observations about the interaction between women and men – observe also your own gendered behaviour. How do men/women, musicians and customers, behave and dance? How do they interact with people of the same and different sex? How is the action of musicians gendered? Who has power? How is power negotiated between genders? Also note behaviour which crosses gender conventions. How is your own gender performed in the situation? Observe how it affects the situation and the observations you make.

At first, it appeared to the observers that gender roles and the power attached to them seemed to be obvious and clearly established. Men were the ones who had the initiative and power. They gazed and walked among the women and picked up their partners. On the dance floor, they led the dance. The role of the women was to be the object of the men's eye. They waited, adapted and followed. The ruling norm at the restaurant seemed to follow the traditional Western gender order: men having power and initiative and women being the objects of men's initiatives. On a closer look, the researchers found a variety of different male and female performative styles of negotiating power. There were many men who were not active inviters to dance, nor did they look at the women. And there were women wearing trousers and women who took the initiative to ask men to dance. Several gender patterns were performed on the dance floor: men whose body language exaggerated masculinity and who almost imprisoned the women they danced with, and men who allowed space and freedom to their partners. Some of them would even ask their dance partner to lead the dance if they found themselves unable to do so. The gestures and movements of the dancers varied from women who stressed their femaleness and men exaggerating masculinity, to men and women who moved in a gender-neutral way. One and the same person could perform different gendered styles in different situations. The equal interaction among other men changed in female company into a protective pattern of behaviour, whereas women immediately began to emphasize their femaleness when a man entered their company.

The conventional knowledge of Western heterosexual gender roles is coded into couple dances, in which the woman is supposed to follow the movements of the man. The dance position in these kinds of couple dances limits women's movements, allowing the man to define the space, the direction and speed of the movement. The couple dance, however, is also about partnership and cooperation: dancing partners have to move as a unit, sensing each other's move-ments, otherwise the dance does not work. Thus, couple dance is also a sign of a gender contract and cooperation (Moisala, 2001).

Masculinity and femininity

Central to all gender analysis is the differentiation between being a man and being a woman and the attitudes and ideologies attached to conceptualizations of what is masculine/feminine (see, for example, Moi, 1990). Again, among scholars, there is no agreement as to whether the distinction femininity/ masculinity is natural or cultural. Feminist theorists use concepts of feminine and masculine to refer to social constructions, that is, to gender models based on cultural and social norms, whereas the concepts of manly and womanly (or simply man/woman) refer to the more biological dimensions of sexual differ-ence (ibid.: 18–21). As Glover and Kaplan (2000: 2) state, to be a 'woman' or a 'man' biologically, psychologically and socially, is not necessarily to be thought 'feminine' or 'masculine', qualities which can be ascribed to both cultural and 'natural' phenomena such as sounds, music, colours, cars, animals and sports. They also can be used across gender lines: a man may have 'feminine' qualities and a girl may be said to act in a boyish manner. Yet the attributes 'feminine' and 'masculine' are not completely independent of biologically sexed females and males: 'feminine' always evokes 'woman' and 'masculine' evokes 'man'. Therefore, femininity may be defined as a set of attributes ascribed to biologically sexed females and, similarly, masculinity to biologically sexed males (ibid.: 2).

Femininity and masculinity, and the ways to represent them in the arts and in cultural action in general, vary from one culture to another as well as constantly changing within any particular culture. Therefore, there is no natural way of thinking about masculinity and femininity. The qualities, connotations and attributes connected to 'femininity' and 'masculinity' always depend on the cultural and social situation, time and place. For instance, red is not a feminine colour in every culture and a low voice has not always been regarded as a sign of strong masculinity.

Even though femininities and masculinities are created and sustained as ideational representations, they are always linked in systematic ways to institutionalized forms of power (Oakley, 1998: 134–5). Glover and Kaplan (2000: 4) suggest that it would be more useful to think of femininity in the plural – femininities – and to see femininity as an umbrella term for all the different ways in which women are defined by others and by themselves. The same applies to men.

Gender identity

Gender identity – that is, gender which one 'attributes' to him/herself, her/his gendered self-image – evolves from differences between 'I' and 'others', as well as between 'we' and 'others'. When positioning oneself in the category of 'we' as distinct from 'others', the experienced similarity to people also belonging to the category of 'we', as well as the experienced differences from 'others', are part of the identification process. For example, men find their identity when experiencing sameness with other men and differences from women, as well as when they experience sameness with women and difference from men. Gender identity is naturally only one facet of the total identity. It is constructed and 'lives' in close connection with the other aspects of identity, such as ethnicity, race, age and class.

Identity is not something that is given. We are not born with an identity, rather, it gradually develops in relation to our experiences of social interaction and our cultural surroundings. Through such experiences a person localizes her/himself and is localized into social reality. According to Whitehead and Conaway (1986: 5), gender identity emerges as a result of socially significant experiences in which the individual is categorized on the basis of his or her sex and the gender profile associated with it. Whitehead seems to assume that a person has one, rather static gender identity. Nowadays, however, gender identity is no longer seen as a static entity which is formed in one's childhood and early adulthood. Instead, it is a process never completed, an *identification*. In the words of Stuart Hall (1996: 2), 'Identification is constructed on the back of a recognition of some common origin or shared characteristics with another person or a group, or with an ideal, and with the natural closure of solidarity and allegiance established on this foundation.' The concept of identity which he deploys is not stable and essentialist but instead strategic and positional, constantly in the process of transformation (ibid.: 3–4).

Rosi Braidotti (1994: 159) asserts that gender subjectivity (a conscious and deliberate political position; ibid.: 166) – as well as gender identity (gendered self) – is discursively constructed in three connected domains: differences between men and women, differences among women and differences within oneself. Gender identities and subjectivities are constantly negotiated. The negotiation of gender identity and subjectivity takes place in relation to gender conventions and structures of the culture and society, in various social situations, in interaction with people of the other and the same sex, and as an integral growing process of an individual. Like many other recent theorists, Braidotti emphasizes the fluidity and the process-like nature of gender when calling for 'the nomadic mode ... as an art of existence' (ibid.: 166). Gender negotiation involves various strategies to present gender, to cover or even mask it.

Gender identity, like any other identity, emerges from gendered experiences of sameness and differences, it is situational and it changes through life. Identity and identifications evolving from the relations of difference are historically and socially specific, they are bounded by time, place and their social surroundings.

The concept of identifications emphasizes the flexible character of identity. Our identifications may also be contradictory and paradoxical. One person may have several simultaneous and interconnected but contradictory gender identities, such as an identity as a mother, a daughter and a wife. In addition, distinct sides of gender identity are played out in different contexts; different situations bring out different aspects of our identifications. For example, can a lesbian identity, which refers both to one's sexual orientation and to a political position, be regarded as the most important index of who one is? In some contexts a homosexual woman may have a lesbian identity but in another kind of contexts, the same person may prefer to identify herself as a woman, refusing to reduce her identity to a sexual preference or, she may be assigned such identity despite her unwillingness to identify in that way.

It is also important to notice that gender identity is not the same thing as gender role. Even though these concepts connect with each other, the latter refers to adapted social roles, whereas gender identity refers to what one feels oneself to be. The formation of identities is simultaneously an individual and a social project, which is always undertaken in the context of historically available interrelations (Marshall, 2000: 158–9).

Gender produced by research methods

In our opinion, the essence of research work is questioning and looking systematically and openly for answers to questions. The ultimate goal of research is to provide possible answers to those consciously articulated questions. We cannot expect the answers found to be the final 'truth', nor even provisional 'truths', about the researched phenomena. Rather, they are interpretations arising from an analysis, which, in turn, is conducted systematically on selected material from a chosen theoretical perspective and position. In such disciplinary work, all the choices made and all the stages in the research work must be open to criticism. The reader of the research report has to know which theoretical basis was used, how the material was collected, selected and organized, and which methods of analysis have produced the results of the research in order to be able to judge the validity of the outcomes.

The realities which are translated into research material are always mediated in one way or another. Each study has a theoretical background and methods of analysis, which have determined the choices by which material is collected. Thoroughly considered and articulated frames of reference for the research – methodology consisting of theory and methods of analysis – support, organize and guide the interpretation of the research material. Methods, which are the focus of this textbook, are inseparable from theory and consist of those practices according to which the researcher makes observations. They also include the rules, according to which the observations made can be interpreted. There are no observations untouched by theories and no theories untouched by observations. Methods are not only useful tools for research. They produce the research result. Thus, different methods produce the object of the research – in this case gender – differently.

Gender analysis requires explication of the frame of reference based on a chosen theory of gender. Like any other research, gender analysis demands careful focusing and contextualization. As being present everywhere is a privilege reserved only to gods (Virilio, 1994), gender analysis – like any other research – demands careful focusing and contextualization. In addition, the researcher has to position him/herself, and make an attempt to distance her/himself from his/her gender in order to see the limitations of the chosen perspective on gender.

Gender so pervades us all that one's own gender conventions are easily taken for granted. Like any other ideological construct, gender is embedded in and expressed through daily interactions. As Nancy Bonvillain (1995: 275) has stated, people usually experience their own behaviour as normal and natural rather than as motivated and mediated by cultural constraints. We tend to be unaware of the underlying rationales that influence our actions and responses. That easily blinds our 'analytical eye'. This may be the central paradox of gender studies: in order to be able to question, that is, to analyse, gender, one has to seek to distance oneself from one's own gender system. This distancing, in turn, is possible only insofar as the researcher acknowledges gender within him/herself and in the surrounding culture.

The analysis of gender, particularly, when studying one's own culture, demands that the analyst sees and 'reads' differently from cultural conventions. The old saying about being unable to see the wood for the trees, applies to gender analysis as well. A useful way of seeing differently is to imagine how interpretations would change if the gender in the research material were replaced by another one. This may open the researcher's mind more clearly to the gender conventions also of his/her own culture.

Case 1.8 Stories of how gender chose us

Anni Vilkko: Gender became a part of my research interest almost as soon as I began to read autobiographies for my master's thesis at the end of the 1970s. The material consisted of life stories written by ordinary Finnish women and men, and in my mind they began to fall into those two groups, depending on subtle differences. Women's stories seemed to lead me into more intense acts of interpretation than the men's. Certainly, this was partly because it was easier for me to identify with women's lives, but I also found qualitatively plausible differences. After concluding that women's and men's autobiographical representations differed according to different kinds of emphasis on life events and different ways of writing their autobiographies, I chose women's stories for closer scrutiny.

At that time I was not acquainted with any feminist discussions of autobiography, nor with gender theories at all. I simply wanted to study women's lives and their representation, without thinking of comparing women and men. My goal was to enquire more deeply into women's ways of knowing and performing their lives. Thus, I accidentally found myself taking one of the basic positions in feminist methodology and epistemology at that time; that is, not to focus on comparisons between men and women, because of the fact that men's lives and their representations threaten to constitute a norm against which women's stories are read and evaluated. Such a research frame reinforces women in the status of the other, without producing gender-specific new knowledge (see Vilkko, 1997: 44–5).

Needless to say, differences between men's and women's self-representations became of interest later on, after I had become more acquainted with women's life stories through my dissertation concerning ways of narrating and interpreting women's autobiographical narratives (Vilkko, 1997). Thereafter I started to study ageing, and in particular one of those areas of everyday life, namely the home, where gender and gendered differences are of decisive importance (see Vilkko, 1998).

Pirkko Moisala: When collecting research material in Nepal, in 1975–76 and again in 1985, for my dissertation on Gurung music (Moisala, 1991), I found that gender became crucial in every aspect of the field work. In the Gurung village, I learned much about the gender order of the local people, but no less about that of the Finnish culture in which I grew up. The Nepalese gender order acted as a kind of mirror, which made me more aware of my own gendered behavioural patterns, attitudes and values. As an outsider in that cultural environment, I observed to see how the Gurung genders functioned in relation to each other. At first sight, I, as a young Western feminist, saw only the asymmetry of the Gurung gender order: women did the housework in addition to taking care of the lifestock and helping in the rice fields and, after they married, they were forbidden to perform music in public, whereas the men did not help at home, and monopolized the public sphere. Gradually, I learned to see also the complementary side of the Gurung gender order. The tasks assigned to different genders complemented each other and women also had power in Gurung life, although mostly in different areas from the men.

Subsequently, I have examined how genders are negotiated, performed and represented differently in different kinds of texts. I have explored the way a contemporary woman composer negotiates her gender in media publicity at different stages of her career (Moisala 2000b: 2000c) and how gender is represented in music videos and films. The women may repeat the conventions of prevailing gender system but, every so often, they also parody or contest them. I like to think that music, like any other performing art, provides an interesting site for a variety of gender performances and representations (Moisala, 2000a). I also have been interested in studying what I call musical life stories, stories which people have written about their lives with music. They reveal much about the cultural conventions connected to different genders as well as personal ways to negotiate gendered positions. My latest study applies the theories of Luce Irigaray in music analysis.

Helmi Järviluoma: Gender was one of the contexts I chose – or the theme of gender chose me – when I was collecting and analysing ethnographic material for my doctoral dissertation (Järviluoma, 1997; 2000) among a group of amateur musicians playing folk music and old dance hall music. I examined the ways in which gender nuances were maintained and produced in the ongoing process of local, everyday interactions among the musicians – and how I, as the participating researcher, was part of that category work. I paid particular attention to the aspects of power, gender and ethics of ethnographic fieldwork. I applied the 'membership category analysis', concepts developed by the sociologist Harvey Sacks in studying gender and found them very useful.

My work is affected by ethnomethodology and social constructionism. In my gender analyses it has meant using bottom-up analysis and avoiding treating people as 'cultural dopes', to use the term coined by Harold Garfinkel: instead, I have tried to show how people use norms and categories in constructing, maintaining and contesting genders. However, I am also very much indebted to feminist theories, especially the study of language, conversation and power. I do not consider the 'constructionist' and 'feminist' approaches as opposed but very much as fertilizing each other. In a Foucauldian sense, I prefer to study the power in different kinds of everyday interactions and discourses, without forgetting the link between micro and macro levels of analysis.

The necessity of positioning

The participants in the research in question (i.e. both the researcher and research subjects, whether texts or human beings) collectively maintain, produce, change, and/or resist the conventional gender categorizations of their cultural environment as they negotiate gender between themselves. Researchers can talk about 'femininity' and 'masculinity' or 'men' and 'women' as conceptual categories or cultural models, but only as a point of departure from which to examine the way research subjects construct and use such categories (Järviluoma, 2000). The descriptions people make are partly shaped by these categories; however, the same descriptions may also reshape them. The gender negotiation and performance take place in interaction with people of the other gender and among people of the same gender in everyday activities. Gender identities are produced within these interactions. In addition, gender plays a role in relations of power, relations of production, emotion, attachment and sexual desire (Marshall, 2000: 43).

Research is not solely an activity of the brain. It is conducted by the whole of the human being, including gender. The researcher has his/her own experiences of the gendered world and society. He/she has grown up in a gendered environment, he/she is either a man or a woman, and has a sexual orientation. The researcher therefore participates in the construction of gender in the course of the research as well. Only by becoming conscious of his/her gender position is the researcher able to create some distance from the gendered perspective from which he/she makes the interpretations. Thus, the researcher's self-reflective work is an important part of any research process.

In our opinion, the point of departure for gender studies (as for all scientific work) should be that there is no 'innocent' research. Each study is involved, in its own way, in the social construction of gender. Theory, research and the politics of gender are intimately related. The theoretical stance taken in relation to gender in research has practical consequences. Acknowledgement of the theoretical position as a political position is part of the research process. What are the consequences of this research; how does the researcher justify his/her theoretical and political position? This self-reflection should lead to an explicitly stated position, which is taken into account in the course of the research process. What kind of resources of interpretation – personal and educational, contexts of interpretation, political positioning – does the researcher possess? How do they direct and influence the observing, reading and hearing, that is, analysing gender in the research material?

We believe that the researcher is always a part of his/her study. His/her scholarly background, as well as the political and methodological choices she/he makes define the position from which the study will be conducted, and directs the results of the study. The 'objectivity' of a study evolves from the explicit positioning of the background factors influencing the methodological choices, the perspectives taken, as well as the selection of the material.

Deconstructing the tie between 'femininity' and 'qualitative' methodology

Ann Oakley has written a ground-breaking book on the history and sociology of different ways of knowing called *Experiments in Knowing: Gender and Method in the Social Sciences* (2000). It is of great interest to us in this project that she, who was one of the key figures in the early 1980s' wave promoting qualitative methods, now says that it has actually been a loss to women that the 'experimental methods' have been anathematized by feminist studies.

She argues convincingly that the dichotomy between quantitative and qualitative methodologies today 'functions chiefly as a gendered ideological representation' (ibid.: 3). In this ideology, experimental methods represent the far end of 'quantitative' methods and are also considered to be most masculine. Qualitative methods, or as they were also called in the 1980s, 'soft' methodologies, are seen and heard as feminine. Oakley has conducted a reading through the history of science and social science, and it is within this history that she wants to contextualize these processes of methodological development. She also claims that the context of gendered social relations is crucial if we want to understand methods or methodology (ibid.: 4). Some earlier voices have criticized the stark dichotomizing between 'qualitative' and 'quantitative' (Silverman, 1989; 1993). However, the history of this polarization has not been studied as thoroughly as Oakley does.

One of the key moments was when the second-wave feminists of the late 1960s and 1970s realized that many disciplines were biased. In social sciences this led to developments in which quantitative methods were deemed 'hard', and scholars regarded 'qualitative' methods as the route to knowledge (ibid.: 5). Oakley is candid in admitting that she herself has 'a certain involvement' in the problem: 'I began by singing the praises of "qualitative" research, of in-depth interviewing and observation as ultimately more truthful ways of knowing' (ibid.: 13). Her article, 'Interviewing women: a contradiction in terms?'

(Oakley, 1981) showed that the textbook model of social science interviewing, which considered the interviewer as a cold 'data-collector' and the interviewee as 'data-provider', did not fit in practice, especially in the context of women interviewing women. Notwithstanding critical voices, her work was hailed as creating a new, post-positivist paradigm for social sciences (Oakley, 2000: 14).

What has happened, then, in the late 1990s for Oakley, who is now 'advocating the use of "quantitative" and experimental methods as providing what is often a sounder basis for claiming that we know anything' (2000: 14)? She focuses on the field of women and health research, and she wants to promote an emancipatory social science which aims at reliable and democratic ways of knowing. Here we come to the key point of her 'strange conversion experience' as she herself calls it (ibid.). She does not agree with the contention of many post-modernists and post-feminists that there is something 'bad' about *all* science (ibid.: 297–8).

She argues that we need to rehabilitate and reshape 'quantitative' and also experimental ways of knowing and that they really can be used productively to map women's situations. She presents many illustrations of this. Why, then, are we still writing about qualitative methods? We must note that Oakley is not saying at all that 'qualitative' methods are 'bad' and that we should all abandon qualitative methods in favour of experimental science.

She considers the gendering of methodology as a part of paradigm war, in which we have two contrasting accounts of knowledge: 'What for one side is a set of "facts" is for the other a complex and impenetrable kaleidoscope of heavily constructed social meanings' (ibid.: 25). Oakley has done pioneering work in deconstructing the discourses which tie 'femininity' and 'qualitative' together. The implications for women's studies, social sciences and gender studies are still to be explored. For the purposes of this book we may conclude it appears that some problems can only be addressed by using 'qualitative methodology', just as some require the deployment of 'quantitative' methods.

Conclusion: towards gender analysis

This chapter provided a basic understanding of gender as something which is not a given, but which is always negotiated and performed. It has argued that gender is constantly being maintained, performed, and renegotiated in different social situations and in different locations. Gender can be 'read', interpreted, from all social texts, not only from literature and from the products of mass media, but in social action and interaction, as well from the arts.

Gender should be approached as a construction and a performance. Gender should not only be used as a noun, but adjectivally, or as a verb, *to gender, gendering, gendered* (see Marshall, 2000: 161–2). Gender is 'a construct existing at various levels of abstraction' (ibid.: 62). The task of gender studies is to reveal how gender is presented and represented, performed, regularized, institutionalized, resisted, contested and transformed. These questions should not only be addressed to our research material, but to the whole of the research process, including ourselves, the researchers and our gender negotiation in the research work.

Genders form a system. That is, the gender categories of a culture are conceptualized in relation to each other. The prevailing gender system is adopted and applied by the members of the society and culture in question. In addition, gender is only one of the many ways in which people construct identity. All social categories, such as those regarding gender, sexuality and race, are formed and reformed in different contexts and through processes of struggle over meaning, recognition and distribution (Marshall, 2000: 155). That makes the negotiation of gender into a complex multidimensional process and, therefore, gender analysis requires particular care. The researcher has to recognize the limits of gender analysis. What other social dynamics are at play in gender construction? Because the researcher cannot study the whole of 'reality' through one research methodology or project, only a narrow range of factors can be analysed in relation to gender. Which other social factors are crucial for that particular gender performance?

Gender is discursive, ideological, a fiction, a construction, but it also has very practical and material consequences for both women and men. As Ann Oakley states, 'femininities and masculinities are created and sustained as ideational representations linked in systematic ways to institutionalized forms of power' (1998: 134–5). Because gender is relational, constructed through human interaction and social processes, gender negotiation has to be seen as a situated performance. Gender analysis must therefore be carefully contextualized. What are the time and place of gender performance? What kinds of settings do those circumstances provide for the performance of gender? What has happened before, what is the historical situation? What social and institutional effects are at play in the gender performance? Contextualization, however, does not mean that the total situation of gender performance should be studied. Again, it is the researchers' task to choose those contextual elements, which are most relevant to the research enquiry.

Exercise 1.1 Write your own autobiography from the perspective of gender

Imagine participating in a competition organized by a magazine. The instructions tell you to write your own life experiences from the perspective of gender, from early childhood to the present day, approximately 20 pages. Describe your memories and life events without trying to analyse them; write them as you remember them, as concretely as possible. How did people of different genders act and interact in your home (mother, father, siblings), at school (fellow pupils, teachers of different gender), in your free time (playmates, friends, neighbours), at work? Write about your own gender identity and experiences through your life. When and how did your own gender play a role? Do you remember having observed unconventional gendered behaviour by other people? Write also about events and occasions, which have made you (or somebody else) perform your gender differently.

NOTE: This is an important exercise since the story will be used as material for analysis in later chapters of this book. Therefore, carefully develop your narrative from preliminary sketches to more detailed descriptions. Return to the text several times during the week.

Exercise 1.2 Gender analysis of a text

Choose a newspaper article or exchange your autobiography with that of a fellow student. Your task is to identify and interpret gendered concepts and attitudes, norms and values regarding different genders in the text. Which kind of masculinities and femininities can be identified in the text? Note conceptualizations, norms, values, and attitudes concerning different gender. Which characteristics are assigned to men and to women? Write about the ways in which the author produces his/her own gendered position as well as the gender of the others.

2

Gender and Fieldwork

Positions, postures and bodies in the field	29
The gendered researcher	30
Moving in the field of gender	34
Background of the scholar constructing field observations	34
Joining the mandolin woman on the path of *pelimanni* music	36
Conclusions	43

> Without any pejorativity – quite the contrary – I would say that fieldwork is
> a little bit of 'women's work,' which is probably why women succeed so well
> at it. For my part, I was lacking in care and patience.
>
> Claude Lévi-Strauss in an interview with D. Eribon (1988: 3)

The main focus of this chapter is on the flexible and wide-ranging approaches
to the negotiation of gender taken by both researchers and the subjects of their
research. In the field, various participants perform continuously and situationally different aspects of their gender identity. As proposed in Chapter 1, this
performance can fortify, challenge or even mask gendered features and categories belonging to each of the gender systems at hand. The micro-veins of
power traverse all fields of life, but when analysing gender and fieldwork, it is
especially interesting to study the way power is negotiated between the participants. We will also deal with some of the ethical questions which must be faced
by the researcher of gender.

We are not using gender as an explanation for different 'objective conditions'
but rather as an analytical concept to focus on the construction of gender
in field research. In that context, it would really be more instructive to use
'gender' as a verb (see Chapter 1). The fact that gender is a discursive construct
does not change the fact that gendering has both practical and material consequences for both women and men. The importance of gender should not be
understated, because it is not an inconsequential detail that may be ignored in
research situations. On the contrary, it is a significant topic of research as such
(see van Maanen et al., 1988).

Many have pondered the etymology of the word 'field'. 'In the field' is, after all, where geologists, officers, missionaries, archeologists and natural scientists as well as ethnographers work (Clifford, 1990). De Certeau (1984) asks what do we exclude when we talk about the field? What are the similarities and differences between the kinds of professional knowledge being produced through the spatial practices of the field? In the everyday language of researchers the field is still usually a place, in which the life of 'the Other' is being scrutinized. We find the definition articulated by Roy Turner (1989) still very useful for all the practical purposes of this chapter. Turner considers field to be a certain kind of an *attitude* or perspective, which brings into intersection the interests of the researcher with the lifeworld of the subjects studied. As Järviluoma (1991b) has suggested, sometimes it also useful to think of 'the researcher' in terms of an attitude: 'researcher' as well as 'gender' become actualized in interaction. And it is important to understand that these processes of actualization are themselves amenable to analysis. That is, analysts need not and indeed cannot, step outside the practices they are investigating. Even so, many research reports still try to mask and filter out the corporeal presence and gender of the researcher.

Anthropologists have been interested in gender and fieldwork for longer than sociologists. While sociologists only began such analysis in the 1970s, anthropologists were writing systematically about gender as early as the 1920s and 1930s (Warren, 1988). This, in spite of the fact that the research perspectives of anthropology remained, with a few notable exceptions, very masculine right up to 1960s. It was in the 1970s when the 'male biases' of anthropological explanations and functionalistic fieldwork began to be strongly interrogated, and the reinterpretations of past ethnographies commenced (Assmuth and Tapaninen, 1994: 139). In the late and early 1980s to 1990s several major studies were published (Whitehead and Conaway, 1986; Golde, 1986; Warren, 1988; Bell et al., 1993; Assmuth and Tapaninen, 1994). Of particular value to our study is Carol B. Warren's guide book *Gender Issues in Field Research* (1988), which deals with the ways in which the gender of the researcher affects the relationships in both the field and the final report. She discusses the research preliminaries, the negotiations of one's positions in fieldwork, 'objectivity' and feelings, corporeality and the sexual politics of the field. Another important collection here has been the articles edited by Tony Whitehead and M.E. Conaway, *Self, Sex, and Gender in Cross-Cultural Fieldwork* (1986).

The examples used by Warren derive from the ethnographic practices frequently found in both anthropology and sociology. Warren pays particular attention to the ways in which researchers have tried to control and modify the parameters defined by gender. Ethnographers have different personalities, genders, frameworks and historical situations: it is a myth that all of them could produce the same results. One of the main conclusions of Whitehead and Conaway is that the flexibility of 'gender roles', rather than the gender of the field worker as such is important in field work (Whitehead and Price, 1986: 293).

Thus, one of the main themes of this chapter is the negotiation of gender in the field. We begin with the concept of *posture*, which raises some new possibilites regarding the dynamic, bodily and situational analysis of the established debate over ethnography and gender. We then deal with the differing views of ethnographers regarding the following: to what extent should they adopt the gendered practices, 'postures' and category-bound features of the people or communities studied? The chapter concludes with a case study by Järviluoma (1997; 2000) in which she discusses, among other things, the local construction of gender in ethnomusicological fieldwork.

Positions, postures and bodies in the field

According to Judith Okely (1992: 17), knowledge acquired during the fieldwork is basically a bodily experience. Okeley did not find this 'knowledge' in her field notes, but in a photograph she had taken in the field. In that photograph, she stands together with an important researchee, a gypsy woman. Okely noticed from the photograph that she herself had adopted the same bodily posture as the gypsy woman standing beside her. While adopting her posture, she had also replicated her 'stance' towards life/attitudes of life. Her body 'knew' before her mind, it had re-positioned itself apparently spontaneously. Okely concludes that her body had, in this way, produced and performed a certain kind of (anti-)power relationship between the subject and the object (Merleau-Ponty, 1962: 140–1; Okely, 1992: 17). While we do not believe that there can be an anti-power relationship in the field – no-one can step outside of power – nonetheless, the concept of posture is undoubtedly useful in the examination of gender in the field.

Terhi Utriainen provides an interesting description of her fieldwork experiences in the Olonets, Karelia, in the 1990s (1998), applying Okely's concept of posture when referring to a certain dimension in positioning. In the context of her study, posture refers to the researcher's way of situating her/himself, her/his life experience and situation, style and language in concrete fieldwork situations, as well as in writing (1998: 293). Usually, positioning refers to individual scholars and their need to position themselves. Utriainen's model can also apply to how a group of researchers and researchees might become aware of how they may assume postures, drawing on their life situations and experiences.

Utriainen (1998: 295) describes a late summer evening when the researchers had been walking along the paths of a Karelian village. When they returned to their quarters, a house owned by an old woman, she was already asleep. When the researchers went to their beds, the woman, however, began to ask questions about their lives, such as why they didn't have any children. The room was suffocatingly hot, a different kind of space from the well-ventilated city homes of the researchers. The old woman waited until everyone was in bed before she began to ask intimate questions. This was her home, her space, where she had the power. She was not a passive subject with no other function than to wait for the visitors. For one reason or another, she was irritated, perhaps because of their late evening walk, which had disturbed her sleep. They were all in the same situation, lying down on their beds, in the dark room, microphones undoubtedly out of reach in their bags. The only thing which existed was the voice of the old woman, which they experienced in their bodies. The dialogue between the researchee and the researchers proceeded without any eye contact and, therefore, perhaps more directly, from ear to ear, from one female body to another.

The question of posture relates closely to the relationships of power and the subject–object problematic, one which is much discussed in women's studies. It also connects with the nature and quality of shared knowledge and with the body. At best, the adoption of postures can be seen as a continuous process which includes all the stages in information processing, collecting, analysis, interpretation and presentation (Utriainen, 1998: 294).

The gendered researcher

Ethnographers take various positions regarding the question of the extent to which a researcher should either try to adjust to the social and gender norms of the researchees or, at the opposite extreme, not care about them at all. According to the latter view, the researcher can conduct his or her tasks more freely if he or she maintains a distance between him/herself and the expecta- tions of the researchees. This attitude was articulated in a letter from the field (cited in Smith Oboler, 1986: 42) by the Sextons who studied and lived in Papua New Guinea. They claimed that they did respect the habits of the people among whom they lived with, and wanted to learn from them. The Sextons also insisted that their own habits should be respected by their friends, the researchees. As anthropologists, they considered that their aim was to 'know', not to 'be'.

The opposite position is taken by those ethnographers who try their best to learn and apply the gender norms of the society. This is the attitude Leon and Regina Smith Oboler, adopted in the research project led by Regina. The reason for their desire to adjust to the local gender system (Nandi, Kenia) was their wish to distinguish themselves from the colonial whites. This strategy, however, made it frustratingly difficult for Regina to maintain her identity as the leader of the project. It also placed considerable pressure on Leon (1986: 37). However, since he was a Jewish man and had already been circumscribed, he passed the most significant Nandi test of malehood. On another occasion, he did not shiver when swimming in cold water, which significantly increased his prestige as 'a man'. As these examples reveal, the adoption of the right kind of posture may also happen by pure luck.

Gendered action in the field does not result solely from conscious and rational choice. We often act with our bodies before we think or speak. Colin Turnbull (1986) has studied the way our gestures and behaviour betray us if we act against ourselves. He seeks honesty in the field, and first and foremost honesty towards oneself, which, in his view, is the greatest honesty we can show towards our hosts and hostesses (ibid.: 20). For instance, he acted honestly when politely refusing to sleep with the Ndaka-headman's daughter and, thereafter, his son – the family had both syphilis and leprosy (ibid.: 18-19). Rational understanding is, in the early stages of the fieldwork, often limited and it is important to learn to improvise and to react to others' actions in ways that are, as far as possible in harmony with the local dynamics (ibid.: 20). These are learned through action and interaction.

Many fieldwork guides (see, for example, Warren, 1988), note that cultures tend to have certain gender positions into which scholars and foreigners are placed. For example, the role of an adopted child, of 'men's sister', or a mascot may be assigned to a female fieldworker. Women who do not care for norms or who modify them according to their own needs may be placed in the categories of 'loud' or 'mythic' women, or even of a 'creature' being able to change from one gender to another.

Case 2.1 Negotiating gender in the Himalayas

Pirkko Moisala has conducted ethnomusicological field work in a Gurung mountain village, in Nepal, in a series of visits from 1975–1996. Together with her husband, they were the first white people who had ever stayed in the village, so most of the villagers did not know much about Western cultures. Moisala and her husband chose to openly 'perform' their own culture and gender system, nevertheless, trying to be careful not to offend local values in any way. Several events that followed taught them about the Gurung gender order, and the Gurungs about the Finnish system. For instance, local women used to wash clothes at a well. After the field workers had washed clothes there together, some village males came to advise Matti Lahtinen that he should cease doing so because, otherwise, their own wives would require them to do the same. Thus, there was an imperative of male solidarity, and the division of household work between sexes was the subject of discussion. The Gurung gender order can best be described as hierarchical but complementary; women and men have their respected duties and areas of power but women, in general, have less power and freedom to influence their own lives.

The villagers obviously felt the need to situate the visitors into their own social system in which caste, gender, and age together determine the status of a person. The gender which was assigned to Moisala was that of a young man. She did not observe the duties and norms imposed on women in the local society. As a woman, she should have carried water for the household, and cleaned and prepared the mud floor before her husband woke up. She also should have had bracelets, long hair and a long skirt. In a society, where girls marry and begin to have babies as teenagers, she, as a 21-year-old childless woman, was an odd exception. Consequently, she was greeted and treated as the younger brother, *kancha*, and allowed, for instance, to participate in an all-male meal at weddings. Local girls covered their faces at her presence as if she had been a male stranger. During that visit, it was not possible for her to enter the female world and Gurung females kept their distance.

Nine years later, the gender assigned to her by the villagers was completely different. On that field trip, she took along her son. The villagers called her *didi*, elder sister, and visited her house frequently, sharing openly their life stories and allowed her to record songs, even though it was not proper for a Gurung woman to perform in public and the singing voice of an older woman was regarded as ugly. The male child made her a woman in the eyes of the Gurungs even though this time she was not accompanied by her husband and, again, she did not conform to the proper dress code nor fulfil the duties of a woman. Perhaps these other 'non-womanly' aspects were 'conceded' to a foreign female (Moisala, 1991; 2000).

The gender position of the scholar is negotiated within the prevailing cultural information on sources and actions. The scholars are categorized and interacted with according to those protocols. Many female scholars claim that yielding to the position defined by the culture may eventually provide richer material than opposing it (see, for example, Abu-Lughod, 1987; Utriainen, 1998: 296). 'After all, the social place of women in Western society has traditionally been to stand behind men, out of their sight: as mothers, wives, nurses, secretaries, and servants,' claims Warren (1988: 18). Thus, a female scholar like Warren may be placed into the category of a female servant. As a servant, she could move around in a mental hospital and in court, researching files without any men – who were focused on more 'important matters' – paying any attention to her. In hospitals she, a professor and scholar, was regarded as a visiting nurse student. Male visitors hardly ever were thought to be nurses, instead they were assumed to be psychiatrists.

The scholar can take assumptions to the field about how her/his gender will limit the work which are too narrow. This is illustrated by Laurie Krieger's description of the anxiety with which she approached her fieldwork in Cairo. Because she was afraid of being categorized as a prostitute, she scrupulously followed every rule she knew regarding a woman's role. Gradually she learned the norms and how to obey them and, simultaneously, also how to adapt or work around them. By the conclusion of her fieldwork she could cross many of the barriers she had visualized for herself at the outset (Krieger, 1986: 117, 123).

Krieger (1986) constructs a useful model of the gender expectations in the field. The researcher has to distinguish between (1) those prejudices which the researcher him/herself brings to the field, and the expectations expressed by the researchees; (2) what the local people expect from each other and what they expect from the researcher or anthropologist; (3) those fundamental aspects of gender roles which not even a foreigner can violate, as opposed to those norms which are less important. The researcher has also to learn (4) how to adapt or work with gender expectations so that he/she can collect the necessary research material.

Carol Warren (1988) and Pat Caplan (1988) also describe situations in which tension, conflict and a lack of positive understanding between the researcher and the researchees may provide better information than an overly mutually accommodating relationship. The stay in the field may be more pleasant if the researcher takes a lover, but does this give him or her access to the sources of information?

A conflict may actually prove to be useful, as in the experience of the ethnomusicologist Tarja Rautiainen (1993) when she violated the rules of Cuban music culture by trying to play *batá* drums. Eventually this led her to the study of women's position in Cuba and in her home culture, rather than the study of Afro-Cuban music, which was her first research area. She could position herself both as a scholar and as a representative of her home culture (1993: 3–6, 11). Several female scholars have observed that participation in women's activities does not occur to them or does not feel 'right' (Wax, 1986: 148; Jackson, 1986).

The positioning of a scholar in relation to the subject of enquiry has been actively discussed for a couple of decades. Feminist methodologies have challenged us to acknowledge the political and subjective nature of all kinds of research (Abu-Lughod, 1990). The ideology of objective research has given way to the demand for explicit positioning and self-reflection. The point of departure is that every choice made by the scholar, his/her theoretical background, methodological tool and resources of interpretation, is loaded with ideological and other cultural assumptions. The scholar him/herself is also a part of the research; another scholar working with the same research material is likely to arrive at different interpretations and research results.

In fieldwork, the intertwining of the research and the researcher is particularly obvious. Fieldwork material is collected at a certain time and in certain sociocultural situations in interaction with certain people. It is impossible to imagine a researcher who can maintain an objective distance from the subject of enquiry, and the influence of personal experiences and contexts in the fieldwork, as well as in the writing of ethnography, cannot be denied (see, for example, Barz and Cooley, 1996).

Moving in the field of gender

Nancy Oestrich Lurie has recounted an amazing story about an experience at an Indian gathering which she was attending as a young female anthropologist. A drunken young man from another camp made unwelcome advances towards her, when a large, ferocious Indian youth from the camp where Lurie was doing her study, took the offender by the collar and with one hand 'lifted him off the ground and shook him, wagging a reproving finger in his face with the other hand:"Lishen you, she's no girl. She's an anthropologisht!"' (Lurie, 1972; Wax, 1986: 145) The categories of 'girl' and 'anthropologist' seem to exclude each other, and furthermore, Lurie's profession seems to locate her as non-approachable in sexual terms (see further, Chapter 4).

Most non-Western societies are used to strangers. However, it is not always easy to categorize a female researcher as a 'woman', as in the example from Nepal reported by Pirkko Moisala (see also Dee, 1975). Category mobility, in Moisala's case from 'the younger brother' to 'a woman/mother', is one of the keys to understanding the negotiation of gender and of sexuality in the field. In this connection, Colin Turnbull uses the term 'role-mobility' (1986: 18): he has observed how the researcher can be moved from one role to another either during one field trip or during several consecutive trips (ibid.: 21-6). Over several field trips Turnbull was repositioned by the Zairean Mbuti hunter–gatherers from 'a child' into 'a youngster' and finally to 'a grown-up' and 'an old man'. During the first period of fieldwork he did not know much about life by the local standards, and he was also unable to feed himself: obviously he was 'a child'. By the next visit he was considered 'an adolescent', thus sexual, allowed to sleep in groups either around the fireplaces or in the bachelor sheds. During the next visit Turnbull was accepted as an adult man, who was allowed to live in celibacy if he so wished. In the final journey he was categorized as belonging to 'the old men', and he became once again in a way free of gender. This 'role cycle' was only possible thanks to a series of visits to the field, and it is important to remember that he was moved from one category to another: he was not able to make these moves of his own accord.

Background of the scholar constructing field observations

In the fieldwork experiment already referred to earlier in Chapter 1 (see Case 1.7), conducted in a Finnish dance music restaurant, researchers were also encouraged to observe their own gender performance. Self-reflection was expected to play an important role in the observations, and the intention was also to conduct participant observation. The setting was fruitful for this kind of experiment because the participants came from various national, ethnic, social and scholarly backgrounds. They were female, from different countries, and their ages and academic profiles ranged from a PhD student in her early thirties to a senior full professor approaching her retirement. One of them was disabled and one Asian-American, the rest were white Europeans and Americans. Sexual orientations were not discussed even though it may well have had an influence on the observations made, particularly because the dance restaurant plays out a heterosexual norm. Customers come to the restaurant Vanha Maestro, one of the best-known dance restaurants in Helsinki, to find either short- or long-term company, to spend an evening with companions or simply to dance, often also with one's own partner or spouse. Food is not served in the restaurant; it is only for dancing, socializing and drinking. This kind of dance restaurant setting was familiar to everyone in the group of observers. With the exception of the youngest observer, they all had previous experiences of dance restaurants, although from different cultures and different times.

People are always dressed up for the evening and when the orchestra is playing, the dance floor is full. Women are dressed in an older style of glittering, provocative clothing: dresses and high heels and plenty of make-up. The men wear white shirts and jackets. Everyone has dancing shoes. The dress code is also socially controlled. A woman belonging to the group of researchers taking part in the experiment, who was wearing regular walking shoes, was asked by a stranger pointing at her shoes, if she was really hoping to dance. Another, who was dressed in a scholarly 'gender-neutral' style – in jacket and trousers – was scrutinized so intently by both women and men that she hardly dared to walk through the hall. A woman without make-up was stared at with astonishment. The dress code of men was even stricter and more uniform, and the researchers saw no deviations from it.

In the discussions following the dance event, it became obvious that the past experiences and histories as well as the current identity factors – such as age, ethnicity, race, world-view, body, and feminism – of the researchers affected the observations made and the negotiation of gender in the dance restaurant. The older participants who had gone to similar kinds of dances in their youth perceived the situation as a desirable opportunity for communication between the sexes and as a positive performance of maleness and femaleness. The Asian-American scholar observed details relating to race and ethnicity, and a student studying competitive dancing of disabled people made observations about how her own disability was perceived by other customers.

The theoretical stances taken by the observers also framed the observations made. The feminists noticed the power inequities between the sexes whereas non-feminists did not observe these. Proponents of theories of gender performativity were more sensitive to the distinctions in gender performance than those whose attentions were underpinned by theories emerging during the first wave of women's studies; they tended to observe roles more straightforwardly in terms of women versus men. The character of observations reflected also the level of prior fieldwork experience, particularly the capacity to balance distance from, and participation in, the event. Fieldwork experience equipped the researcher to observe the situation, including her own gender performance, from a theoretical point of view, whereas the lack of it made the observations more or less detached.

The role of the scholar enabled the observer to establish some distance from the situation, to play 'a fly on the wall', but at the same time the restaurant with its 'staged' gender roles made the researchers become aware of their own gender performances. The conspicuous gender codes of the situation forced them to re-identify their own gendered selves. They all reacted to the situation as women who are socialized into the Western dance culture: they were waiting to get an invitation to dance and felt disappointed and discouraged if they did not, because a dance invitation means acceptance as a 'woman'. A feminist was even afraid that her feminism would show and deprive her of opportunities to dance. Many of the researchers did not even dare to look at the men. The youngest one was an exception, and she received the greatest number of dance invitations; she experienced a sense of power and had the courage to take the initiative to ask men to dance. When she did so, she felt that she 'helped the poor guy out'. Power does not always lie in the hands of the male, but, instead, is always negotiated anew.

The gender experiences of these observers demonstrate how gender relates to various other identity categories, such as age, ethnicity, previous mental and physical experiences, appearance, as well as to educational, social and cultural backgrounds. Each of the observers looked for familiar models through which to categorize and identify her observations. The observations made of the dance evening grew out of the observer's gendered identity. Field observations are always bounded by the researcher's own physical and gendered identities, which are renegotiated in every social situation. When studying an event to arrest, sample and analyse it, the researcher intervenes with his/her own performance, and makes the event into his/her own story. While performing ourselves, we construct multiple performance events. That is how we imaginatively create the world and its events. In this process, the boundaries between insiders and outsiders are blurred: we relate to the events through our identities and past experiences and create our own, different readings of an event (Moisala, 2001).

Joining the mandolin woman on the path of *pelimanni* music

Towards the end of the 1980s one of us, Helmi Järviluoma, joined a *pelimanni* musicians group, a mid-Finnish rural amateur musicians ensemble playing folk and traditional dance music. She had become interested in ethnomethodology (see Chapter 1 and Chapter 4). She wanted to study the Finnish folk music movement at grassroots level, and was frustrated with interview methods, through which she had struggled to get to know what folk music meant to people.

Finally, it seemed that the only way to understand the meanings of music was through ethnomethodological ethnography, where the ethnographer is interested in the everyday methods that the members of a certain community use when producing the social order, which is a result of human interaction (Dingwall, 1981; Garfinkel, 1984/1967). She joined a *pelimanni* musicians group consisting of 25 members, and reformulated her research problem. How did this group construct and maintain itself through its social practices? What kind of category work did it do, what kind of boundaries are drawn both within the group, and in relation to groups outside? How, when and why do the different dimensions of the group's identity become actualized? She was interested in the detailed and observable practices through which the musicians brought their reality into being. (Järviluoma, 1997; 2000).

During her first attendances at group rehearsals Järviluoma noticed that the males were in the majority. There were only two women actively participating in the group, though occasionally some other female musicians participated. Interestingly the subject of gender was evident right from the start when the researcher played with and observed the group, and tape-recorded the rehearsal discussions.

Järviluoma was a 28-year-old female researcher in a group dominated by late middle-aged and elderly men. By the second rehearsal the conductor of the ensemble had categorized the researcher as 'the princess'. Järviluoma reflected on this categorization both on her own and in study groups: 2 what do the categories of, on the one hand 'princess', and, on the other, 'researcher' actualize. The princess in some way negates the kinds of activities usually associated with the identity of 'researcher'. She is a 'fairytale creature', whose knowledge is not threatening to the knowledge of musicians, but conversely the knowledge of the musicians is not threatening to the princess. She has to be treated with respect. At the same time, those who characterize her as 'princess' become categorized as 'gentlemen'. This was evident in the fact that the group avoided rough jokes when the female researcher was present. It became apparent that 'the princess' was some kind of a mascot, when Järviluoma was assigned to another, more mature category, when she returned to the group 6–7 years later. Now, she was called by her first name, Helmi, and the new young 14-year-old keyboard player was called 'the princess'.

The fact that during her main field research period Helmi Järviluoma was categorized as princess by the musicians she was studying contrasts interestingly with the fact that she did not actively seek to foreground her 'feminine' side (see also Chapter 4). The category 'researcher' is, like that of 'woman', something being continuously socially constructed and maintained in practice. When Järviluoma participated in the group, she foregrounded the features appropriate to the 'researcher' aspect of her identity, not 'motherhood' or even 'musicianship'. Patricia Ticineto Clough talks in her book *The End(s) of Ethnography* (1992; see also Bell et al., 1993) about the ways in which researchers try to construct for themselves a coherent gender identity. Järviluoma continually had to negotiate between feminine and masculine categorizations: while the conductor of the group insisted on describing her in feminine terms (princess, wife), she herself tried to suppress these aspects of her identity while conducting her research.

In the same set of data compiled by Helmi Järviluoma, there is another scene which is very revealing in relation to the gender categorization and identity practices of rural Finland and its researcher (Järviluoma, 2000; see also Chapter 4). She noticed that it was the women of the group who always prepared coffee for the breaks. Out of the 23 men only two participated in coffee-making. In 50 per cent of the cases the only two women in the ensemble made the coffee by themselves, in the other 50 per cent it was one of the women, Anna, together with a man. The conductor of the group made coffee on his own on one occasion.

Järviluoma became interested in the thoughts of the women regarding the fact that they could lose so much practising time because of the coffee break. Anna, for example, would almost without exception leave the rehearsal hall half an hour before the break and go to the kitchen, pour the coffee for the men, then gather up and wash the cups. Some years later, when neither was any longer participating in the ensemble's rehearsals, Järviluoma interviewed Anna. The ensemble had been extremely important to Anna and she had been a member for almost 20 years. She felt that she had been very bold in joining, since at the time she could not play any instruments at all. In fact, 20 years later, when Järviluoma was doing her research as a member of the group, Anna still did not play her instrument much at all: when playing her mandolin, she only moved her right hand.

Nevertheless, she obviously felt that she was a full-blooded *pelimanni* musician, and a full member of the group. She participated in all the group activities and was the first to volunteer to sell tickets for concerts. It is possible to interpret her participation in the kitchen work and other voluntary work ancillary to performance as giving more *legitimation* to her membership of the group. But the question remains as to why Anna had not involved herself more in playing her mandolin – after all, 20 years was certainly enough time to gain competence. One answer, however morally or ethically questionable it may be, is that she was a useful and legitimate member of the group only as long as she put the interests of the men above her own.

In interviewing Anna, Järviluoma was extremely sensitive to the delicacy of the topic, and especially so because Anna had fallen seriously ill just before the interview, being diagnosed with Alzheimer's disease. The interview had to be conducted with her husband present, although he sat at a distance from the two women. Anna took pleasure in reminiscing about her time as a member of the music ensemble, and she remembered those 'old times' with affection, but on some occasions she would look at her husband, who answered several questions for her.

Case 2.2 Negotiating gendered ethics in an interview situation

We have retained here a few transcription symbols conventionally used in conversation analysis. They show among other things, how some areas of conversation are marked as sensitive:

$	smiling or laughing voice
#	squeaking voice
(0.5)	pause in tenths of seconds
[	overlapping talk

Helmi: Sometimes I then (.) was watching #erm# watching the things that (0.2) you did in that group so, well, there were two people who made coffee (0.5) it was you and (–) Mikko Lehtonen ((male)) (0.5)

Anna: It happened a long time ago

Helmi: $Ye-a-h-h$

Anna: ((*laughs*))
((removal))

Helmi: And I (–) sometimes listened when Mikko complained that can't *any*one else here (0.2) $make coffee$

Anna: Yes

Helmi: So I thought about whether you found it tiring (0.5)

Anna: Well no

Helmi: $tiring$ that coffee making

Anna: #erm# but on the other hand it was because one had to wash the dishes then so that took nearly the whole time (*laughs*) nearly #erm# others went to play but #erm# it didn't make any difference to me (–)

Helmi: Ym (0.3) well I sometimes thought about the fact that one *lo*ses *practis*ing time

Anna: So one *does* lose(.) does lose but (1.0) on the other hand one already got some (.) $practising done too$ [(((*laughs*))

Helmi: [$yea.ah$ $ yes$ (0.4) yes

Anna: for a long time

In this interview extract there is a lot of laughter. The laugh means different things at different points in the discussion: sometimes Anna's words reminded the researcher of the long duration of the research project. Sometimes laughing is a way of easing the discussion of the subject at hand, delicate not only because of the reference to a now-dead member of the group (Mikko), but also to alleviate the possibility that Anna might hear the researcher's comments as criticism. The researcher softens her own account of the 'kitchen situation', partly by always starting from her own point of view on the matter.

Järviluoma also reports that she had heard Mikko complaining about his coffee-making duties. She defines her position interestingly as that of a 'third person', who happens to be a man, rather than as someone actually present in the interview situation. By reporting Mikko's speech she avoids the impression that she personally is taking a critical position. This way she is 'preserving solidarity' with Anna. In the way she reports Mikko's grievance, however, the researcher discloses her own position: she is observing the situation so-to-speak over Mikko's shoulder, and it is her voice that is heard in the smiling tone ($make coffee$). Anna's first answer is, 'Well no', but she seems to take the researcher's points, and talks about how long it took to do the washing up. However, she generously stresses that she really did not mind. Because she was a member of the group for so many years she felt that, even with lengthy 'coffee- making' breaks, she still accumulated enough practice time.

We have to remember that it is the researcher who raises the issue. She does not bring it up from the perspective of gender, but begins from the membership category (see Chapter 4) of the *pelimanni* musicians group. Thus it is consistent that Anna does not choose to speak from a gender perspective either, but as a member of the ensemble. The ensemble is similar to groups like 'family' or 'gang' in the sense that belonging to them presupposes some kind of loyalty and sense of belonging. *Pelimanni* women of the group could well have formed a 'team' internal to the group as well, but such a membership category does not exist in Anna's repertoire, and she does not choose an overtly gendered speaking position. Anna's comments can be read as showing her loyalty to the group. She does not arrange her activities into strict hierarchical order; it is through the researcher's questions that the hierarchical positioning intrudes into the discussion. On the contrary, Anna is contesting the hierarchies by emphasizing that the (male) director of the ensemble also made coffee at times. She creates a new sub-category for the ensemble: the coffee-makers. If the director is a member of the coffee-makers, it can be seen as an important and select group. Thus Anna constructs herself as part of an important activity.

Anna considers herself to be bolder than the other women since she came to the male-dominated ensemble without having played her intrument before. She considers herself to be independent, but attends to others' needs at the same time. What kind of effects does this sense of responsibility towards others have on Anna, and on women musicians in general? The division of labour in the Finnish countryside, at least for the elderly or people in their late middle age, often duplicates the foregoing model: the kitchen is the women's space. From one point of view we could ask: in whose interests would it have been had Anna become a virtuoso mandolin player at the expense of her woodwork hobby, her membership of the school administrative delegation, her grandmotherly duties? Should we as researchers wave the flag of enlightenment and declare that our reading of the situation is the right one: that is, that this is against the spirit of human progress and that the whole group should be ashamed of its behaviour?

Case 2.3 Emotional presuppositions in girl's studies

The Finnish youth sociologist Jaana Lähteenmaa (2002) has recently problematized some of the presuppositions of feminist girl studies. She has launched the concept of 'emotional presuppositions', meaning the suppositions which already exist before the research has started, which are partly recognized, partly linked to unconscious emotions, and which define and restrict the research questions, the areas studied and the interpretations formed.

She has problematized the powerful emotional presupposition of even the most recent girl studies: that the aim of the feminists is to save the girls, to empower them. But to save them from what and to empower them to do what? She does not try to downplay, for example, the value of the 1970s' Birmingham Centre girl studies: it was necessary to pay attention also to the cultural practices of girls, when up to that point, boys had represented the whole of the 'youth culture'. However, the imperative of emancipation involved a double standard where girls were concerned: they were not only supposed to rebel against capitalist society but also against the patriarchy. Their bedroom fan culture was not seen to be especially creative.

Lähteenmaa derived great inspiration from the Birmingham Centre girls scholars in the early 1980s: she wanted to free Finnish girls from the chains of patriarchy which prevented them from playing rock. The problem was that most of the girls that she interviewed, scrupulously using contemporary feminist in-depth interview methods, said they did not want to play rock. They had many other things to do. Gradually the researcher understood that if she, as a researcher, wanted to do a favour for the girl fans, she could do so by introducing the creative aspects of their fan culture into the public debate. Even so, her research also generated a range of valuable data and raised significant questions. Why is it, for example, that girls playing drums is still considered to be inappropriate?

From another point of view, however, there are obvious disadvantages in the fact that we women are expected to divide and fragment our attention. It is not unequivocally a virtue. A woman should at least have the opportunity, for example, to develop her expertise on her favourite instrument, as indeed many women do. The endless taking care of others is a honey trap. (See also Cohen, 1991; Näre and Lähteenmaa, 1991: 329–35).

When it comes to research ethics, it seems that returning to the field after the analysis of tapes, field diaries, and other data, and following up the issues with the people being studied, is important. Järviluoma's study was enhanced when she also took into account the 'mandolin woman's' own interpretations of her rich life in *pelimanni* music.

On the one hand, the people studied have to meet 'strangers' who transgress or try to transgress familiar gender boundaries. On the other, feminist researchers end up meeting women who do not always conform to a researcher's expectations of what is appropriate and emancipative. Faye Ginsburg (1993) was studying a right-wing American anti-abortion movement and had to ask herself how she, as a feminist, should respond to this kind of women's movement, whose members actually claim to be working on behalf of women. Elizabeth Lawless confronted similar problems when she studied female preachers in the USA. As a feminist, she felt obliged to interpret her data in a way that showed that in the case of one particular, preacher, male oppression, in the form of her husband, had restricted her career (Lawless, 1992: 307). Later, however, even though still wanting to sustain her interpretation, she deeply regretted that she had not shown her interpretations to the preachers before publishing the book. In particular, the preacher mentioned above had her own interpretation which challenged the researcher's reading. Lawless believes that her book would have been better if both interpretations had been included. (ibid.: 308–11; see also Koskoff, 1993; Ribbens and Edwards, 1998).

David Silverman (1993c: 199–201) has argued, however, that from the point of view of validation it is not necessary to have the findings endorsed by the members of the group studied. According to Silverman, it is the duty of the researcher to make her or his result available to the people studied and let them draw their own conclusions from them. Often the researchees use the results in such creative ways far beyond the researcher's imagination.

The question has also been raised as to whether the claim that a researcher should be empathetic is to be accepted uncritically. This claim is often advanced in integrative ethnography, in which the sequences of ethnographic observation are related to the whole of culture (Baszanger and Dodier, 1997: 8). In order for the researcher to form an understanding of the view-points and listening-points of the other, there is an initial phase of questioning in field-work, which

> is itself embedded in a certain tradition, that of the interpreter ... While it is paramount for a fieldworker to be attentive to the expectations and role projections of the people being observed, this is less in order to achieve an empathetic attitude than because the interrelations themselves and, finally, the fieldworker and the work done on his/her experience are the preferential instruments of observation. (ibid.: 12, 13)

Conclusions

The epigraph to this chapter perpetuates the myth of the superior abilities of women in fieldwork. Lévi-Strauss also denies that this is a pejorative comment, but in doing so, reaffirms it as such (Jackson, 1990; Caplan, 1988). This recalls an attitude referred to in Chapter 1 (see also Heinämaa, 1999; Oakley, 2000): it is often thought that women are better at qualitative research because they are 'more co-operative and empathetic'. Yet it is clear that the difference between good field workers does not correspond to the distinction between men and women. Lévi-Strauss's claim is unsound.

Carol Warren (1988) laments the fact that the interactional sequences described by researchers lack information about the semiotic process, through which the interactions are produced as knowledge – analytic categories, field notes and ethnographies. The texture of connections between experience and the production of knowledge still reproduces and maintains mythologies about the 'place of women' in field work. Above, we have tried to re- and de-construct the positions of researchers, the situated languages and styles, and the gendered category work in the process of 'writing culture', by reference to certain ethnographic episodes.

In fieldwork situations the interlocutors continuously construct interpretations of each other's talk and behaviour. The participants construct the interpretations together: thus the meanings are culturally and socially available to all of them. The members of a study perform situationally different aspects of their gender identities. Sometimes, the postures familiar to one's 'sex' do not feel familiar, and the researcher may oppose them – sometimes without consciously being aware of it. As in the case of Järviluoma, this awareness only emerges when *analysing* the data later: only at that point did she begin to understand the ways in which 'the researcher', 'the gender of the researcher', 'the researched' and their gender were constructed in interaction.

This is an example of the researcher 'interrupting' (see Silverman and Torode, 1980) her data. The material is 'interrupted' at some point in the analysis. The researcher forms her own interpretations, and goes back to the people she has studied in order to present those interpretations to them as sensitively as possible. It may then appear that their interpretation is different. Do we have to select the *right* interpretation?

In the case above, Järviluoma used the interview to illuminate the ways in which one of her research subjects, a female participant in the ensemble, constructed meanings in relation to her actions. Later the researcher carefully analysed situationally the postures assumed in the interview, not only the situations that arose, but how they were negotiated. Even if the interviewee was ill, she could in subtle ways take 'power', and was able to enhance the picture which the researcher had formed according to her observations and theories about the 'status' of women in the group studied.

Researchers cannot ignore the norms of the groups they are studying, but nor must they always totally submit to them. Both the researchers and the people studied use norms: their actions cannot be reduced to norms. The unity of the researcher with the field can well constitute a *dialogic* unity: not univocal, and accepting many different views.

Being in the field
Pasturing oneself in a landscape, field constructed by my research
Smelling, tasting, touching, listening
observing
being moved and transformed
by the Others
To whom I am as much the Other
In this constant negotiation of Othernesses
we find, define and redefine our positions.
                                        (Pirkko Moisala)

Exercise 2.1 Analysis of gender through participant observation

Choose a place or instance where social interaction occurs between women and men, or alternatively, between members of the same sex in a gay environment (café, restaurant, meeting, club). Observe also your own activities and feelings. During one session, record concrete, down-to-earth observations about the interaction between people. Avoid abstractions and generalizations at this level, for example, do not just say 'she was interested in him' but tell us the gestures, movements and mimes through which you can tell this: 'she glanced at him several times, smiled at him and went to talk him, and sat on the chair next to him'. How do the men/women behave and talk? How do they interact with people of the same and different sex? What happens when people of other sex enter the space? Who/which gender has power in the situation? How is power negotiated between people? Make observations about activities that cross gender conventions. What is your own gender performance in the situation? How does it affect the situation and the observations you make?

Exercise 2.2

Read again Case 2.1. Negotiating gender in the Himalayas. Analyse and discuss the ways in which Moisala negotiated and renegotiated her gender in interaction with the Gurung people in Nepal. Then discuss the way notions of gender differ between your own culture and the Gurung, and the differences in research ethical questions that these imply.

Notes

1 Here we are referring to a Foucauldian view of power as micro-veins, outside of which no-one can step (Foucault, 1980: 59–60, 89–99; see also 1979b).

2 One important group who discussed this extract of data was the interdisciplinary circle of method studies working in the Department of Social Policy, University of Tampere, Finland, in the 1990s, initiated following a course led by Professor David Silverman.

3

Gender and Life Stories

Lifetime, narrative identity and coherence   47
The reader and narrative models for a life story   49
Representations of gendered lifetime   50
Reading autobiographies, looking for gender   52
Autonomous male, relational female subjects   54
From emancipatory confession to performance   59
Conclusion   64
Notes   68

A text about life, whether we call it a life story or an autobiography or some other name, always refers to a life lived, to gendered life events and to a gendered bodily subject, producing a narrative of that life. The text on which life is inscribed has a body, a narrated gender, which connects cultural and personal issues and ideas in a narrative of a self.

The receiver of the text is the embodied reader or listener, the other. Gender is constructed in interpretative reading acts by using elements referring to lived gender, cultural gender and the gendered reader's perceptions of the text.

The study of life stories in research practices is a challenging problem because of the amplitude and all-encompassing nature of the life narratives. Here the idea of a life story is used in a very broad sense, including both literary autobiography and oral narratives, and these terms are used interchangeably. One defining feature for our purposes, however, is that the life story has a temporal dimension – it is characterized by movement through time. We also intend to limit our discussion generally to forms of self-narration, and to exclude from the discussion life stories narrated by another person. We recognize, however, that the distinction may be ambiguous.

In this chapter we discuss the relations between gender and life story from the point of view of *reading and interpreting gender*. The main idea is to locate *gendered strategies of narrating a life*, by reading research where gender and gendering practices play a conspicuous role. The studies we look at consider literary autobiographies as well as self-narratives told by ordinary people.

First, we introduce some basic coordinates of autobiographical storytelling from the narrator's point of view. We will consider lifetime, narrative identity and coherence as well as culturally specific modes of narration, with reference to autobiographies written by Finnish women.[1] We shall also propose ways of reading gender in representations of self. The second part of this chapter will then focus on theories and changing perceptions regarding life narrative and gender.

Lifetime, narrative identity and coherence

We perpetually tell ourselves and others narratives of our lives. These versions of life incorporate personal stories about events, choices, fateful moments, important experiences and meaningful life course transitions. Each successive account, reflection and moment of storytelling adds new issues to the story: they strengthen or revise old interpretations, transfigure the composition and plot the story anew. The shapeless mass of life events becomes ordered in a series of everyday story-tellings, and the cumulative outcome of that succession is the story of a life.

At the heart of the story is our life in time, its progress and continuous change. By reminiscing, identifying, repeating and evaluating, we bring coherence to the changes in our life. The questions of continuity and discontinuity have always been focal points in research in the field of autobiographies. When a woman states, for example, that she is entering a qualitatively new phase in her life, by connecting past and present and creating expectations concerning her future, she constructs new order in her life. This narrative linkage, where stages of life are woven together, aims at producing a narrative identity, which is at the core of making one's life story.

The following quotation from the opening of an autobiography illustrates some features of self-narrative practices:

> My first home was a grey log farmhouse in the heart of Central Finland. The sauna was grey, and so were the storehouse and the stone cowshed. From the house you first crossed a patch of lawn, then went down beside a bit of the hay field towards the birch wood that came right up to the sauna, stretching out towards the pasture.
>
> It was on a bench in the grey sauna house that I was born. The path to the sauna was the start of my path through life, the pieces of which I have begun putting together to form some sort of coherent order. In summer the path always felt soft and warm to my bare feet, though sometimes when running I would stub my toes on a stone. It is as if the memory of the path has engraved indelible traces on the soles of my feet.

With these words an ordinary Finnish woman of 53 (the life story was written in 1991) begins her written autobiography. This passage of orientation, where the writer metaphorically 'shakes hands' with the reader (Vilkko, 1994: 271), introduces us to the author and invites us to follow the stages of her story.

Here, the writer uses a basic recollection to set the story of her life in motion: an early memory of walking down the path to the sauna, while at the same time generalizing the significance of this memory.

The writer first tells us a few facts about the early stages of her life. She describes the scenery: the farmyard of her childhood home surrounded by outhouses, and the path down to the sauna, beyond which stretches the world outside the yard. Next, she approaches the farmyard and mentions that she was born in that very sauna. 'The path to the sauna was the start of my path through life' evokes the journey back to the house along that path, the countless times she travelled that path thereafter, and the metaphorical start to life.

The recollection of how the path felt carries the writer closer to her path. By using the words 'always' and 'sometimes' in this context, she reveals that she is not speaking of the memory of a single, unique event, but of the sum of numerous indistinguishable occasions. The memory of walking that path is the memory of recurring events interwoven to form one single impression that has become engraved on her bodily memory. Here the storyteller is conferring value upon this particular memory by assigning it a special meaning in her life: it is inextricably woven into her narrative identity. The path remembered is also felt, it is more than just thought.

Her recollection of the path to the sauna becomes a generalization for life narration. Without the sauna and the path there would be no narrator recalling and writing about how the sauna path continued. As the story-teller writes: 'It was on a bench in the grey sauna house that I was born. The path to the sauna was the start of my path through life, the pieces of which I have begun putting together.' From the value assigned to the path springs also a metaphor for writing about life. In her role as autobiographer, this writer is putting together some of the pieces of her life, as she describes the act of writing. She puts pieces together – facts and personal memories of her life – to achieve 'some sort of coherent order'.

If one is asked, if gender is present in this short citation above, the answer might be that there are hardly any specific properties informed by gendered or gendering expressions, structures or themes. Or are there? When we as readers know that the writer is a woman, we may then begin to discover evidence of that gender in the text. This knowledge may produce conscious or unconscious interpretative inferences, that link biological sex to the style of the story and particularly to the expression of bodily inscribed experiences. Some researchers of autobiography have stated that women often define themselves 'in terms of their body' and tend to be 'emotional in describing their embodied lives' (Gergen and Gergen, 1993: 202, 198). In other words, the autobiography of a woman or a man constructs life in a way which connotes gender in one way or another. In this brief passage, it is arguable that the 'embodied' character of the recollection is an indirect manifestation of gender.

The Reader and narrative models for a life story

The image of the path, briefly introduced above, is a familiar and often used metaphor in autobiographical story-telling. It gives us a glimpse of how the lifetime can be conceptualized in our culture. The shared experience is a sound basis for the creation of mutual understanding. Culturally shared metaphors for the course of life generalize experience and link individual life to life in a specific culture. Here the notion of the 'sauna', as a starting point for life, gives a characteristically Finnish cultural colour to this common, transcultural trope of life as a journey.

In every culture particular narrative forms and models are used when stories about life are told. Intensely charged metaphors not only disclose the way in which the writer articulates her/his life experience, but they also communicate this strongly to the reader. During our life we develop familiarity with the cultural conventions of self-representation. We 'know' how life is to be narrated and how the story ought to appear (see Vilkko, 1994). The coherence of a life story is based on the cultural models through which we direct the reader's eyes towards our life events and which we use as a resource in telling our lives. In the next extract this aspect of autobiography is conspicuously challenged:

> I wish to express my sympathies to the reader of an autobiography and to the scientist on whose shoulders falls the task of attempting to detect some significance in the trivial blabberings of the narrator. Even I regard the effort of putting my life down on paper as an absurdity and the entire passage through life as petty fumbling: Not much of a journey but what is done is done.

In this quotation written by a 58-year-old Finnish female teacher in the first paragraph of the final sequence in her autobiography, her knowledge of the demands her culture makes for consistency is modulated into an exaggeration of narrative incoherence. These clauses of a story function as a macro-evaluation of the life that has been lived as well as of the story narrated. Here the writer is 'bidding farewell' to the reader, and that marks a return to the present time, to the moment of writing (Vilkko, 1994: 271). The autobiographer regards the act of writing the story as a *negotiation* with the cultural expectations she believes the reader connects with autobiography. The writer refers to a norm of attempting to construct a vision coherent enough to be called an autobiography. This conception of narrative coherence in autobiography can be understood as a cultural meta-narrative, which demands attention and commentary if the story-teller deviates from the script. Here the writer creates a self-deprecating vision of a course of life and the structuring of its events, stating that the narrative composition parallels her 'fumbling' life.

Her conclusion is addressed to the readers of the life narrative in order to negotiate the value of the self-representation. This lightly self-demeaning conclusion gestures to a distance between life and its representation, asking the readers to intersubjectively interpret and judge the truth of the autobiography. The writer playfully undermines one of the most basic assumptions in self-referential narration, namely that it is a meaningful individual activity. In her case, she declares, that assumption is absurd. But more than this, the text signals that autobiographical story-telling is fundamentally a *social action*. Even if the writer refers to her personal life, she at the same time stresses the fact that the life represented in autobiographical writing is not just a private matter. The story is not a story until a reader makes sense of it. There is 'some significance in the mere blabberings' that must be discovered by others. The interactive process between the written text and the reader should be seen as fundamental in the constitution of autobiography. This rhetorical juxtapositioning of the autobiographer and the reader justifies the ambiguities in the interpretative process: the story may be incoherent and fragmentary, but now it points to the future readings and imagined interpretations of it. The story is made up anew in the act(s) of reading.

In order to recapitulate her life story, the autobiographer makes use of the vocabulary, tropes and models provided by the surrounding culture. 'Not much of a journey but what is done is done' is a robust phrase. In the Finnish cultural register it can be understood as a gendered expression, more frequently used in masculine than feminine discourse.[2] Whatever the connotations, familiarity with the conventional models generates a life narrative which makes sense. It meets the requirements of the social world but, at the same time, it enables the production of a particular, personal and unique story. The alert reader faces the intriguing question of negotiating the role of a 'manly' style in this singular autobiography of a woman. Is it just the personal tone of this individual, characteristic of her daily interaction with others? Or more generally: does a woman always negotiate her gender and reconfigure her discourse, when she performs the story of her life in the public sphere, which is often dominated by masculine values (see e.g. Smith, 1987: 19)?

Representations of gendered lifetime

The next extract is written by a 64-year old Finnish woman. Her life is described through an unambiguously gender-specific cultural model of life representation:

> You would at first think it would be easy to write about a woman's life. This is not so. I could compare a woman's life to, say, a big basket of scraps. Absolutely enormous. Full of fabrics of all colours. Larger and smaller pieces. Neatly cut, relatively long strips and pieces cut on the cross. The patchworker wants to go through them all, many times, before she begins to plan her work. The work as a whole, the colours and qualities are important to her.
>
> What is it like, then, to be a woman born to the colourful basket of her own life? You can't sort your scraps, either the colours or the qualities. Rough, ordinary grey frieze and

shimmering silk may find themselves side by side. What do you do then? You can't sort out the qualities because that's how they were in your basket. You're afraid of the next bits: will they be more suitable or even less? You nevertheless grow curious: you eagerly rummage through your whole life basket from top to bottom! To add to it all, you are impatient!

One important element of those narrative acts which perform the life story, is the images and the figures of speech individuals employ. In writing a life story the author generates a fresh insight into her life. While making use of well-worn metaphors which are common in story-telling, the author also creates new metaphors. A life lived becomes denser when told, a narrative represents life by giving it shape and order.

In her analysis of Finnish women's autobiographies Anni Vilkko (1994) studied the metaphors of life as a cultural resource to bring coherence to the narratives and the lives women are narrating. The use of imagery drawn from the cultural pool is governed by 'more than cool reason', to use the title of Lakoff's and Turner's work (1989) on poetic metaphors. When we write, our culture writes through us, but in ways and through images that we make our own, through conscious and unconscious decisions that reflect personal experience. (Vilkko, 1994: 275).

Classified into three categories, the first class of metaphors linked life with a cycle (for example, a circle, semi-circle, the circular course of nature: morning and night, spring and autumn, a season for blooming and a season for withering away). The second class was analogous to the concept of life course and emphasized the image of life as a meaningful journey by combining nature and human activity (for example, an episode having a beginning and an end, a path, the auto-biographer as a wanderer). The third class focused on the act of bringing shape and order to disparate and confusing elements. These metaphors mainly drew on activities of cultural production and clarify the process of autobiographical narration itself (threads in fabric, a cloth on the loom and the weaver; a rag rug, a patchwork quilt; a jigsaw puzzle, etc.) (see Vilkko, 1994: 273–4).

Each metaphor discloses some aspects of reality while it masks others (see Lakoff and Johnson, 1980: 10–13). These three categories present us with three different structuring principles: life as cyclic, life as a linear continuum, or life as discrete events seeking coherence. These images are traditional, transcultural and, in most cases transcend gender. But in the third class the majority of the activities and the artefacts produced traditionally belong to the woman's world. Moreover, while this imagery differs significantly from the other two, it also references traditional and familiar activities, at least in the world of women. This category promises a particular autobiographical language which is *gender-specific*. Even though these metaphors are poetic and may be remote from daily speech, they are not solely a matter of rhetoric but are deeply engaged in models of social performance which are associated with women's lives, irrespective of their individual ability to sew, spin or weave (see Vilkko, 1994: 275–6).

These womanly metaphors of cultural activity and products also reveal the multi-layered character of the past and the interlacing of past and present. This aspect of both life and its representation being heavily entangled in the same imagery is not equally present in the cyclic and the continuum metaphors. The figure of patchwork reveals the process of weaving life lived into its representation. As a construction, it is part of the elementary logic of autobiographical storytelling. As a metaphor, it is an image which is seldom employed as the image of life and life-writing of male authors. Would men choose, for example, the metaphor of a jigsaw puzzle, instead of patchworking? And one could also ask if this image is more familiar to older rather than younger women.

Case 3.1 Reading gender-specific practices in autobiographical texts

Nancy K. Miller has written extensively on autobiography in the field of feminist literary criticism. In her article 'Arachnologies: the woman, the text, and the critic' (1988) she touches upon the ideas and imagery of women's life-writing. She discusses the metaphor of weaving, following the Greek myth of Arachne, who was a famous weaver but was transformed into a spider and to a continual act of spinning in consequence of her disobedience against the gods. According to Miller, what commends Arachne as a model for feminist poetics is the way she provides a trope for the life-writing of a woman that is intertwined with the life itself. Arachne is punished for the subjective, autobiographical quality of her art, for her point of view. She is doomed to lose her subjectivity and her mastery over the textile to be produced, doomed to repeat with her body the never-ceasing act of spinning, without ever more being able to create subjective representations. This means that there is no life narrative separate from a life (Miller, 1988: 77, 80–3).

Miller points here to a method of reading and interpreting women's autobiographical texts, which she calls the practice of 'over-reading', which is needed when analysing non-canonical works and women's writing (a poetics of 'under-reading'). She suggests that readers should focus on the moments in texts which, while representing writing, may reveal gender-specific rules and practices of textual production. Weaving as a metaphor represents an autobiographical subject choosing how to write a life and deciding what is a culturally appropriate way of representation. Here we find a representation of writing, entangled with its material (ibid.: 77, 81).

Reading autobiographies, looking for gender

You bend your life course to a narrative
your narrative identity in the core of it
you reminiscence, remember, collect, construct, write

aiming at a coherent figure
aspiring to fill the gaps (which are especially of importance)

As a singular – unique – you are not at all alone
– negotiating yourself is a social act –
you use language to communicate
    conventions to assist
        metaphors to distinguish the essence
            models towards which to contrast yourself

When you are ready (until next time, maybe next night in dreams)
you evaluate
this version of life
    what did you write about
    how did you do it
then you allow it to rest
    also a reader in your mind
    another, whom you trust with the interpretation.
                                                    (Anni Vilkko)

The methodological approaches are bound to the social and historical time and place of their production, and they also signal a tight connection to the values of that moment. Knowledge *about* and knowledge *in* autobiography are particularly meaningful in researching life narratives and narrating practices. The practices of life narratives and narration may be a *topic*, a phenomenon which performs gender with its norms of expression. Or autobiography may be treated as a *resource* of knowledge, where the practices of 'doing gender' can be discovered in personal and unique stories of life. This latter model takes the researcher a step further in analysing autobiographies: autobiography is not just research material among other data, but also a set of practices which produce knowledge in accordance with its own protocols, implicating the reader in this process (see Stanley, 1993: 43–5).

Autobiographies are also located in time and history. They are as much concerned with the socio-historical period they are being told in, as with the ways of speaking or writing in that period, as they articulate the personal events of the life lived and the thoughts of the experiencing subject. Gendered 'real lives' in autobiographies (resource) may turn out to be the products of gendering norms of expression. The text on which life is inscribed may be made up of such themes (topic) which are associated with gendered subjects.

In the past 25 years there has been extensive discussion of gender-specific differences in autobiography and other self-narrative practices. The field of autobiographical studies is interdisciplinary by nature, but there are also more or less established theoretical orientations among the disciplines: psychologists have centred on the self (*auto*), sociologists and social sciences have focused more on the lived life (*bio*) while literary criticism has concentrated on written texts (*graphe*) (see Ray, 1998: 117). As far as gender-specific aspects of autobiography are concerned, feminist critics, mostly in literature and in social research, have raised the most significant questions, and often in parallel with each other. The answers vary considerably, but there are some general arguments which have had great impact on the discussion and definition of the gendered nature of autobiographical self-representations.

Autonomous male, relational female subjects[3]

The debate on gender and autobiography initially began with feminist literary critics noting that theories of literary autobiography ignored women as auto-biographers. The feminist writers argued that the theoretical premises of the genre were grounded in the autobiographies of famous male authors such as Augustine, Montaigne, Rousseau, Goethe and Darwin. These narrative norms and conventions for self-representation tend to marginalize women as writers of their lives. According to Sidonie Smith's (1987: 54) review, the female self in autobiography was characterized as self-effacing, oriented to private life, sensitive to others' needs, relational and subjective, anecdotal and fragmentary in composition. The male self-narratives were read as self-centred, self-assured and independent, linearly organized and oriented towards public life and socially notable personal achievements. The life-writing practices as well as the stories of women did not meet the requirements and norms of a genre demarcated in such terms.

In arguing that the male autobiographical canon had overlooked women's autobiographical life writing, literary critics were not calling for canonical legitimacy for women. The master convention was understood as gender-biased. It situated women's autobiographical writing as secondary to men's writing. What would have been more appropriate was to recognize that there are some female self-representational practices, and to reveal how women make sense of their lives when narrating it. The goal was to develop historically situated, gender-specific practices to write and read autobiographical narratives (see Kosonen, 1995).

One way of overcoming the restrictions imposed by the masculinization of the genre was to enlarge its borders by incorporating into it other forms of autobiographical story-telling than just literary autobiographies. For example, diaries, journals, letters, life story interviews, oral histories, poetry and autobiographical novels were studied by feminist literary critics and social scientists (Stanton, 1984; Benstock, 1988; Brodzki and Schenk, 1988; Heilbrun, 1989; Interpreting Women's Lives, by Personal Narratives Group, 1989). Many scholars regarded these minor forms of autobiographical writing or oral practices as more familiar to women as well as more often employed by women than by men. This diversification to incorporate the forms of women's autobiographical storytelling brought literary critics and sociologists closer to each other and made the field more interdisciplinary. In feminist sociology and social sciences, oral life stories, produced in life story interviews (often called 'in-depth interviews' of 'ordinary' people) became one of the main methods of studying gendered lives. In feminist practices this model of intensive conversation was often embodied in the exchange of personal experiences between interviewer and interviewee.

Case 3.2 Biography vis-à-vis autobiography

Liz Stanley's sociological theory of 'auto/biography' refers to the statement that there is not much difference between one's autobiography and a biography written by someone other than the subject of the life lived. These categories of knowing overlap. The notion of 'auto/biography' indicates that while reading other people's life narratives, a researcher inescapably produces, consciously or unconsciously, her/his own story as well (Stanley, 1992; see also Marcus, 1994; and Marcus, 1996: 188–9, 194).

In the first phase of autobiographical criticism the gendered life narratives were read through and against the life lived (*bio*), emphasizing the normative events and transitions of women's life course and the significance of their social relations. Some studies located differences between women's and men's autobiographies in terms of their separate life worlds; that is, not only in dissimilar points of view on similar lives but in divergent interpretations of the world (Kolodny, 1986). The private and personal were regarded as women's realms, while men attended to public domains and their achievements there. Other studies explained women's autobiographies as a direct reflection of women's predetermined, subordinated position in patriarchy (Jelinek, 1980; 1986). The subordinate social status of women was regarded as a valid explanation of the narrating as well as reading practices of an autobiography. The reported fragmentary and incoherent, non-linear way of expressing the self in a narrative form – compared to the coherent and linear self-narrative characterizing men's reflection – was explained by referring directly to womanly life practices. The ways to narrate were thought to mirror the woman's experiences as a daughter, as a wife and as a mother. Each of these confines the women to the status of addressing the needs of others (ibid.:).

The critics emphasized particularly the role of others (especially family members) in governing the everyday lives of women (Mason, 1980; Stanton, 1984; Jelinek, 1986; Brodzki and Schenk, 1988; Friedman, 1988; Heilbrun, 1989; Gergen, 1992). In relation to this, some investigations disclosed that women habitually narrate their lives in relation to someone else's life events, locating themselves 'between the lines' or 'backstage' (Fahlgren, 1987). The 'significant others' involved are often (famous) husbands or fathers, who would as autobiographers narrate themselves as independent subjects and masters of their lives. Another variation was the tendency of women to represent themselves as passive objects rather than active subjects. This relates to the assumption that female autobiography centres on human relations and the private sphere, due to women's subordinated position. There is a pattern in which a female life is narrated as if the woman, even if occupying a distinguished position, had deliberately remained a passive bystander.

This pattern was questioned by theorists arguing that it might have prevailed at the end of nineteenth century, but was no longer valid (see Heilbrun, 1989: 24–5). The main point was that this model of interpretation does not distinguish the life lived (*bio*) and its representation (*graphe*); it overlooks the fact that the narrated self in autobiography always has a referential relation to the author and her real life outside the text (Smith, 1987: 17–18; Vilkko, 1991: 119).

However, these arguments concerning the location of gender differences in female and male self-narratives became linked to the notion that women are *relational* in their self-narrative practices, compared to men's *autonomous* life-writing (Mason, 1980; Friedman, 1988). This simplistic polarity became a widely accepted, foundational view for the study of autobiography in women's studies in literary criticism as well as in social sciences. The categories 'relational' and 'autonomous' functioned as an influential model for those empirical findings which, one way or another, suggest differences based on gender. This model offers a 'natural' explanation for the order of things in autobiographical narratives, anchored in the thematics of gendered lives told by autobiographers.

Case 3.3 Gender difference in identity constructions

For instance, when studying ageing and life course, Nouri and Helterline (1998) found the traditional gender difference in autobiographical narratives of elderly men and women (life history interviews of 30 people, 70 years of age and older, born before 1920). According to their observations, gender emerged as an important dimension in the thematics and story lines of self-representations. Men constructed their identities as individual heroes, very seldom mentioning their marriages or the birth of their children. Women, on the contrary, constructed their narrative identities in relationships to God or significant others, discussing in particular detail their marriage and children.

The researchers considered the dissimilarity in topics and story lines to be mirroring a gender difference. They regarded these results as an outcome of old age and of a specific generational pattern of meanings: the elderly people participating in the study belonged to a generation that has always regarded gender as a 'naturally gendered' biological reality, having never had any cause to question these scripts of their life stories. However, the authors wonder if the next generation of the elderly people will be more sensitive to the gendered elements in narratives of their lives (see Nouri and Helterline, 1998).

The polarity 'relational' vs 'autonomous' has been contested by referring to a central aspect of all autobiographical practice. This practice is intersubjective and intertextual by nature, and furthermore, relationality does not operate exclusively in women's self-representations (Smith, 1987: 18; Vilkko, 1991: 119; Miller, 1994; Hyvärinen, 1998). Another line of reasoning contesting this reductive gendered model of autobiography refers to those female auto-biographers who perform a life story as just as self-centred as those of the male stereotypes (Stanley, 1992: 133; Somers and Gibson, 1994: 56–7). The most important critique, however, has come from some feminist theorists who emphasized that relationality and autonomy should not be regarded as oppos-ing, gender-bound features in autobiographical storytelling, but instead, that the categories should be treated as viewpoints of the reader (Miller, 1994: 5–18; Somers and Gibson, 1994: 56–7; Somers, 1994). Every autobiographer discusses and reproduces her or his self in relation to others; the important point is how the others are represented, what role they play in the narrative and what the nature of the relationships between the narrated self and the represented others is. Gender cannot be considered as a stable and given element of autobiography. It is always produced in the acts of reading and interpreting.

Case 3.4 The role of significant others

Nancy K. Miller, who in her article 'Representing others: gender and the subjects of autobiography' emphasized the importance of reopening 'the discussion of gender identity and the forms of auto-biography' (1994: 4), has also analysed the canonical male autobio-graphies with particular attention to the role of significant others in autobiography. In Augustine's *Confessions*, for example, she found the relational pattern of self, not only in relation to God, but 'more entangled with the other who is his mother than critics have some-times wished to see' (ibid.: 19).

This reconfiguration of gender relations in reading practices, described above, demonstrates that the study of autobiography always circles around the theoretical and methodological issue of how to read life narratives, and that this issue is entangled with discussions of gender. Feminist readings of autobiography have mainly been interpretations of female selves in female life-narratives, and in this project men's autobiographical representations have merely served as a kind of reflective surface – and often very stereotypical ones – against which to shape the female self-narratives. Attempts to find ways of reading both female *and* male texts were made as early as 1980 by Mary Mason, who introduced the distinction between 'relational' and 'autonomous' into autobiographical criticism. She hesitated to adopt gender difference as a starting point in research, when actually her goal was to read women and men in their auto-biographical texts side by side (Mason, 1980: 27). 'Relationality' and 'autonomy' as categories of ways of reading gendered narratives do not deny or exclude the idea of gender as a valuable category of analysis. The focus is still on gender-bound reading, which means awareness of the fact that the protagonist of a text is (for example) female and the reader's interpretations are gendered (see ibid.: 266–7).

This recognition of gender-bound reading has accompanied the critique of essentialism. The direction is towards a more nuanced reading, where differ-ences in women's and men's life representations could be compared and inter-preted more sensitively, emphasizing variations in representational styles. Using Miller's idea of '*the styles of relation*' (1994: 18), we can ask, for example, how the other is positioned in self-narrative. Can we qualitatively or quantitatively mea-sure the gender-based distinction? Are these distinctions fixed or changing? What are the social and cultural dynamics which could be changing the con-ventions and modes of self-representations?

Case 3.5 Constructions of 'home'

When reading autobiographical 'home histories' of elderly women and men written in the 1990s Anni Vilkko (1998) found that 'home', typi-cally regarded as a woman's domestic and relational site, was dis-cussed in different terms and degrees by men and women. Similarities and dissimilarities between women and men are both quantitative and qualitative. It is notable that women write about themes relating to home much more often than men, in whose texts the topic is some-times even difficult to find: they are inclined to emphasize spheres out-side the home. Women and men also identify the home in different ways. Women focus on the interiors of their homes and the actions taking place within them to a greater extent than men. Men, on the other hand, are more inclined to cross the boundaries between the interior and the exterior, concentrating on the outward appearance of the buildings, technical details, the yard, or the scenery. These differ-ently signified domestic sites were interpreted as different areas for the formation of socio-cultural gender identities, not gendered spheres in themselves (Vilkko, 1998: 30–1, 68).

In autobiographies by men, home largely appears as a question of arranging the living of a family; acquiring the residential space – often building a house by himself – and assessing its suitability for living, emerge as central considerations. Women, on the other hand, take part in planning and acquiring a home, but more than this they tend to 'make the home': they settle down and decorate apartments, and in their autobiographies they place central events of life within the walls of the home. Thus, 'inside of the world', as Raimondo Strassoldo writes of home (1993: 38), appears differently to writers of different genders, as if seen from different directions. A common denominator in descriptions of home for both sexes, however, is the family. Home, family and the proximate human relationships are all thematically linked in the descriptions, despite the differences in emphasis.

The differentiated manifestations of gender in the narration of unfolding phases of life are more nuanced. Both women and men describe extensively, and in a similar manner, their childhood homes. The places lived in during one's childhood are intensely experienced, and are thus almost inevitable material for one's memories. The difference between descriptions of inside and outside spaces, mentioned above, however, is also manifested in childhood. In the autobiographies of the post-retirement adults referred to in this study, the places lived in during adolescence are, on the other hand, hardly dealt with at all. Founding a family signals a return to the gender-based differences in the meanings of home in autobiography. It is during this phase of life that the descriptions of home by women and men differ from each other most radically. Women write extensively on the topic, concentrating on the indoor spaces, whereas men write very little of home and concentrate on their working life. With regard to the subject of home, retirement age as a stage of life brings the two genders closer to each other, and the events described in autobiography are situated more and more at home and indoors. (see Vilkko, 1998).

Thus, some topics in autobiography do not neatly fall into gender categories, but change situationally and historically.

The emphasis on choices made by the researcher in autobiographical criticism is consistent with feminist methodology's insistence on subjective modes of interpretation and conscious positioning of the self in interpretation. One manifestation of reader-bound interpretation is the interest shown by feminist researchers in reading women's self-narratives reflexively, in terms of their own autobiographies. This means that a researcher brings her own lived experience one way or another into her research practices. They have also recognized unequivocally that their own life histories affect their interpretation (see Stanley, 1992; Miller, 1995).

From emancipatory confession to performance

Even if the researchers themselves had reservations concerning gendered constructions of narrative identity (Mason, 1980: 27), in the mid-1980s many feminist researchers agreed that there was a difference between male and female autobiographical representations, wherever it was located. Moreover, they were ready to *politicize* the conception of asymmetrical gender systems. They emphasized that other marginal communities apart from women exhibit practices of self-representation that are historically and locally situated, and which relate to significant others and to influential collectives, including not only repressive ones. The hegemonic male-dominated, individualistic values were declared to be elitist, and valid only for the self-representations of Western men in positions of socio-economic privilege. The dominant conventions of self-talk were considered to have overlooked the significance of socio-culturally bounded group identities and collective experiences of women and minorities. Thus the underlying social practices, which produce differences in gender identities, had been under-estimated or ignored (Friedman, 1988: 34–5; Sommer, 1988).

Women had, therefore, ideological and political as well as psychological reasons to disavow the male individualistic paradigm of autobiographical theory. It was suggested that the idea of 'relationality' was to be understood in norma-tive and ideological terms, as a value more desirable for women than autonomy (see Somers and Gibson, 1994: 56–7).

This political and ideological perception was based on the idea of the *eman-cipatory* function of self-narratives. To emancipate, to give a voice to the silenced and to communicate the experience of 'real life' to the audience were, among others, the driving forces in promoting life narrative practices in research in general, and in feminist studies of women's autobiography in particular. These ideas were reinforced by central premises in feminist epistemology, that is, that the personal experiences of women should be heard at every stage of the research process.

Not all researchers agreed with these prescriptive approaches to the study of gender differences in autobiographical representations. For example, Susan Stanford Friedman (1988) criticized the male values and norms of auto-biographical theory and posited a difference between male and female self-representations. However, in the analysis of life narratives she dealt with women's ceaseless *negotiations* with the norms of self-expression and the discussions between privatization and collectivity, between individuality and relationality (see Friedman, 1988).

One approach to the question of women's relationship with the traditional conventions of autobiography was to think of female autobiographers as posi-tioned to interrogate those norms and constraints of this genre. Women inter-face with the cultural conventions and negotiate the rules, insinuating their own stories through the major narrative (Smith, 1987: 17–20; Vilkko, 1991: 118, 120; Gergen, 1992). This interpretation emphasizes subjective *agency* (*auto*), manifested through decisions about conventions regarded as repressive (Miller, 1980, 1995). Gender rules are maintained, over-ruled, or modified for indivi-dual purposes. Researchers had observed that some female autobiographers openly exploit the master rules of autobiography; they play with female cultural conventions of confession as well, ironizing them and thus transcending the genre pacts (Brodzki and Schenk, 1988: 9–12). Liz Stanley considered this negotiation as elementary praxis in all feminist autobiography, which, according to her, is 'reflexively concerned with its own production' (1990: 62), mixing at the same time genres and styles of expression to find its own character.

This conscious disclosure of the gendering of the norms of self-narrative undermines them, transforms the modes of narrating and makes the construction of narrative identity more flexible. It also signals an emerging awareness of the generic conventions of autobiography and of their power. On one hand this transition is emancipatory, in enabling the subject to resist the power of dominant conventions and to represent the self 'in her own way'. On the other, the subject realizes that the life narrative is not just spontaneous confession, but a conscious activity. The authenticity of original experience is not guaranteed simply by reflecting on the experiences. The representation (*graphe*), either oral or literal, becomes increasingly important as a component of autobiographical truth.

The moment of losing innocence regarding the chronicling of experiences refers to the 'linguistic' or 'narrative turn' in autobiographical storytelling (Rorty, 1967; Ricoeur, 1984, 1985; Hyvärinen, 1998). This way of thinking foregrounds the role of language in establishing the order of things. Social reality is produced in language, and the uses of language construct the world around us. Language in autobiographical story-telling is thus not just an instrument, and we cannot see through it to the 'real' life events narrated in life stories. The role of the narrating subject (*auto*) in actively constructing her identity in autobiographical practices is central.

Shifting the focus from traditions to agency can be understood as a step toward postmodern or late modern ideals of self-identity. Postmodernity disavows the universalizing norms of self-representation. Along with the conception of multiple, disconnected identities, fragmentation as a distinctive feature of female autobiography has also been called into question. The theory of a new postmodern autobiography acknowledges incoherence and fragmentation as features of all autobiographical narratives, whether male or female. In literature and fiction especially, postmodern autobiographers break with conventions. As Päivi Kosonen (2000) has noted, authors such as Marguerite Duras, Nathalie Sarraute and Georg Perec create a sense of discontinuity by using narrative modes such as anecdotal and non-linear writing, incoherence in discourse and meta-narration concerning the legacy of autobiographical truth. This pattern of autobiography rests on the perception that the experiences are intrinsically disconnected and irretrievable. Thus the attempt to create a coherent and meaningful life course through autobiographical reflection is futile: the truth retreats from the reflecting subject. The new model of autobiographical truth, according to such authors, is characterized by disconnected, scattered and fragmentary textual conventions of performance. Thus the late-modern autobiographer is zig-zagging between the old and the new register to narrate a life, searching for possibilities to recite it in another way, that guarantees the openness of the text (Kosonen, 2000).

There is a link between emphasis on agency in autobiographical self-representation, and the discussions of gender identity in 1990s' feminist theorizing, particularly that of Judith Butler (1990, 1993). The most influential development in recent feminist autobiography studies has been the examination of autobiography as *performance*. Performance and *performativity*, as principal characteristics of self-narrating practices, invoke a subject definitively in motion. There is no interiority prior to the self-narrative; the autobiographer creates her identity in self-narrative practices. The subject is processing her gender identity in her life narrative and in real life – she is *doing gender* all along the line. Gender itself is performative, according to Butler (1993: 20). This dynamic notion of agency means, for example, that there is no reason to think that a woman is essentially or through socialization, fragmentary, passive or relational. The increased interest in the life narratives of women from different ethnic groups and sexual minorities has also underlined the fact that the fundamental issue and premise in researching women's self-narratives are seldom a gender-based homogeneity (see Marcus, 1996: 192–3; Smith, 1998).

Case 3.6 Performativity as a means of reading subjectivity

Performativity, according to Judith Butler, 'must be understood not as a singular or deliberate "act", but, rather, as the reiterative and citational practice by which discourse produces the effects that it names' (1993: 20). A Finnish sociologist, Marja Kaskisaari (2000), has argued for performativity as a way of reading and interpreting gendered subjectivity in autobiographical self-representations. She argues that subjectivity is created and recreated through processual acts by reiterating and citing the autobiographical practices with their norms. By applying the idea of autobiography as a 'place' for a modern subject to become emancipated in and through confession, the reflecting subject may presuppose some kind of interiority as a guarantee of individuality. But, as the author argues, a place opened up for a subject is a place of the other, in terms of the prerequisites and conditions of autobiographical reflection. A subject is always questionable and unformed. This conception of autobiographical reasoning disavows the potential of such autobiographical truth which is not situational, not located in time of reflection. For Kaskisaari this performative approach to self-reflecting narratives has been applied specifically to examine lesbian subjectivity within the prevailing heterosexual discourses and order (see Kaskisaari, 2000: 75–85).

The emphasis on performativity and on choices made by the self-conscious subject also suggests that the *time perspective* of autobiographical practices has been framed anew. Above all, the very idea of a life narrative as simply retro-spective, a 'natural' configuration, has been called into question. Notwith-standing their retrospective direction, autobiographical practices are anchored in the present and oriented to the future. Life narrative is not defined only by the questions of how I became the person I am now. The questions – how am I?, in what direction is my life changing? or how would I like to change my life? – are as important as the retrospective ones. Accentuating the present and the future as perspectives and orientations in autobiographical narration signifies that autobiographical texts should be examined also as a project, activity and process (Marcus, 1996; 191–2; see also Kaskisaari, 2000).

Case 3.7 Temporality in life stories

The conception of multiple levels of temporality in the practice of self-referential story-telling has been affirmed afresh in psychological research connected to gender-specific perspectives by Katri Komulainen (2000). She studied Finnish women's (aged 17 to 44) educational life stories and closely examined their gendered inter-pretations of life. She called the oral interviews 'independence nar-ratives', in which women interpreted changes in their lives and composed their life stories by constructing a bridge from the past to the present. Komulainen used the concept of 'key rhetoric' (Hyvärinen, 1997) rather than, for example, plot, choosing to study the vocabulary and metaphors which embody the moments of change in the lives of the interviewees. The author concluded from her results that gender differences in life stories are temporal dif-ferences within the self; she found 'a hierarchical split between the past (dependent) self and the present (independent) self'. Life story, in this case, is a 'future-oriented retrospection' (Komulainen, 2000: 449–59).

These general views, which shed light on both gender and life narrative, point in the same direction as sociological theorizing on reflexivity in the 1990s. There the practices of self-reflecting narration are regarded as significant in relation to the idea of the self as a reflexive project across the changes and ruptures of modern society (see, for example, Giddens, 1991, 1994; Beck, 1992). According to the theory of late modern individuality, every subject is positioned in a reflexive relation to contemporary modern institutions and is continuously constructing the narrative of self-identity. The emphasis is on new demands and challenges set by a post-traditional social order, not on the potential formation of an individualistic or self-contained personality. Reflexivity is a response to the fact that coherence and continuity in individual life can be created only by engaging with the opportunities for transformation presented by dynamic social environments. These transformations relate to, for example, generational relations, living or home spaces, social networks and life course transitions, among many other issues. Mastery over social change lays the foundations of a dynamic self-identity. For example, various life course transitions, when individuals are separated from their previous positions within a social structure and moved to new ones, may cause confusion in a person's social identity and thus stimulate reflexivity (see Giddens, 1991; 1994).

Case 3.8 Transitional moments of life

Laurila and Vilkko (2001) studied the death of a husband as a transitional moment in which a wife moves into a new gendered social category of a widow. In autobiographical narratives of widowed women, this new gender identity was described as a shock, as women realized that the word 'widow' now referred to them. They felt negatively stigmatized by that word. Importantly, the women were highly aware that the gendered connotations of the term 'widow' referred to a lower social position, a B-class citizen, only-a-half person and unfortunate (see also van den Hoonaard, 2000: 92).

One of the women generalized the gendered categories of widowed women at the time she was widowed (at the age of 37 in 1958): 'A single woman was a despised old maid and married women were categorized according to their husbands' occupations. A widow was a pitiable in-between.' She continues with another fragment, giving an example how oppressive the status of a widow can be. When she travelled abroad for the first time in her life and had to acquire a passport, she needed an extract from the parish register. In this extract her title was 'the widow of an engineer'. This happened in 1971, when she was 50 years old and had lived as a professional woman supporting her family alone for 14 years, yet 'still I was a mere continuation of my husband!', she exclaims – and adds that this made her a feminist. The subject here is constructing her narrative identity as an independent woman by setting bounds to the prevailing gender system, by resisting it and defining herself as a feminist.

Conclusions

The narrative identity is an identity continuously under consideration. Identity work is based on and also generates the practices of autobiographical narration, which extend beyond the borders of the traditional representations of the genre. The uses and forms of autobiography thus become more pluralistic and endlessly varied, which was also one focus of the discussions in the previous chapters. One implication of this multiformity is that the life story of a subject need not follow the pattern of the cultural gendered narratives traditionally offered to us – not even as its counterpart or mirror in the negotiation of self-representational qualities. The classic (male) autobiography suggested a model of individual growth and demanded continuity and coherence as structuring principles. The idea was to find retrospectively a coherence which employs the narrative of an identity. The story of life, as whole and continuous, linearly progressing from one event to another, has been contested by referring to the fragmentation of life itself, but also by stating that identity is narrative by nature. Narrativity is quintessentially dynamic. When striving to possess life, we create identity by narrating, and through narratives. Our consciousness of life and identity are narratively constructed in their forms (Bruner, 1986; McAdams, 1993).

This idea of lifelong identity work posits the life story also as a means of coping. The goal is to create coherence from the demands of changing life situations. These acts of 'narrativizing' experiences may function, for example, by generating fresh and working life metaphors, bringing new insights into a subject's life. These practices concentrate on narrating the life of a subject anew, striving for a coherent vision, even if admitting that this happens only situationally and on a small scale. They are widely used in therapeutic professional and semi-professional practices. We produce our life stories in oral story-telling in normal situations and in research interviews, in face-to-face situations as well as in groups with others. There are many socio-historically grounded forms of self-talk which have emerged in the contemporary world (such as, for instance, reminiscence groups and narrative therapy), where an individual's comprehension of his or her life course, and particularly of its transitions, ruptures and gaps, are pieced together. Instead of coherent forms and patterns, this self-referential narration produces the process of meaning-making and reflection, which directs itself to intense, often momentous experiences and puzzling over the pieces (see Vilkko, 2001).

In general, structuring life by autobiographical story-telling is a vivid, living body of practice in late modernity. Narrativity reflecting life has burgeoned. Autobiography is by no means the main generic form of self-narrative practices. Autobiographies and biographies, memoirs and reminiscence, as well as artistic forms other than literature – for instance, cinema, photography and the visual arts – all make constructive use of autobiographical modes. At the same time the uses of self-referential narration have percolated down through the social hierarchy, to any singular individual, irrespective of social status or expressive competency, as for instance the ability to express him- or herself in writing. These practices cite and reiterate (Butler, 1993; Kaskisaari, 2000) the idea of confession as a form of narrative activity, regarded traditionally as particularly appropriate for women. They rely on the potential of personal story-telling to communicate the experience to others, not just oneself. And it is just this speaking to others, which makes this pattern of self-narrativity so successful and significant (see Vilkko, 2001).

In research regarding life-reflecting narratives there has been a shift from the documentary life history to the emphasis on a constructive act of reflection. Using the terminology used here, theorizing on autobiography in late modern society has shifted from *emancipatory* (realistic) to *performative* (discursive) ways of approaching life narratives (see Kaskisaari, 2000). The multiplicity of forms and uses radically tests theoretical discussions of autobiographical narratives. Researchers have to critically revisit the phenomenon 'autobiography', the way its text are read, and the role played by gender.

Exercise 3.1 Analysis of a life story narration

Consider the following three extracts from the autobiography of a woman aged 59 (in 1991), describing an episode in her 'home history' (Vilkko, 1998). To what extent are gender and gender systems audible in the autobiography? Can you identify a silenced gender? Discuss the reasons for silencing gender. Which genders can you identify in the text? Which roles do these genders play? How are these genders presented? How does the author present her gender? Does the gender presentation of the author differ from one place and stage of life to the other? In which ways?

(1) We were in our new home already by the next evening. I was delighted to arrange things in the kitchen. There was nothing other than the metal-framed bed and the child's bed to be put into the room. The older girl slept between us. The chamber was large and airy, and even the kitchen was of a good size. We had running water, the kitchen range looked very dignified, it had plenty of room for all the pans and kettles. A sink unit, a draining cupboard: we had nearly entered heaven. The stove in the room used wood, and my husband immediately started calculating how much this would cost. I was annoyed that he should start to count out all the expenses on our very first day. I was well aware that things were difficult for us, but this first evening should have gone by without the perpetual topic that was more than familiar for us; we could have just been happy and let things work out by themselves. I worried about the empty room, too, although I tried to ignore it. I hung mother's old curtains on the window so that the room looked like someone was living there and no one would come enquiring about it [if the apartment were still free]. I found some rags for the kitchen window as well.

(2) There should be some furniture in the chamber as well, such a pretty room should not be empty, it sort of does injustice to the room. Of course this would mean buying by instalment, after all, we had survived it before. I was very ambitious as far as furnishing was concerned, a home ought to look homely, although not necessarily expensive. I finally fell asleep and on the next day I felt cheery and enthusiastic after the gloomy calculations. My two healthy hands and enthusiasm were the best of assets.

... I was fixing the closets, organizing ours and the children's clothes. Now we had two closets instead of just one. How a single closet could make one happy, not to mention the numerous other additions. The kitchen range heated the water for both the dishes and washing up, where the old place had but one measly ring. I was very satisfied with the kitchen, it had everything I needed; our earlier furniture turned out to be a good buy, it looked good with the light green kitchen walls.

I was happy despite all the scarcity, just as glad as the moment allowed me to be.

(3) The set of furniture we had found was carried in next day. A sofa, two armchairs, a small table and a cupboard for the linen. I had decided to acquire more linen as well, little by little. The dream of going to work was so strong in me that I knew I would acquire the missing bits and pieces.

The lady from downstairs came over to wonder at the new furniture, although it was quite ordinary. The cover was of red plush with a new and clean smell to it. The room looked truly stylish; if we could just get new curtains and carpets it might actually be just splendid. The walls also seemed to lack something, but I had better forget about that for the time being, this was quite enough.

My husband was strangely quiet. Did he have regrets about this deal? I started to feel guilty. Had I acted too hastily with the apartment and these furnishings, had I after all demanded too much? I tried to tell myself that these were just basic things, that there was nothing unnecessary or unrequired. We would have to pay the bill for two years, but that would not be too great a task. Anything further should be given up, definitely.

I kept going to the room door to marvel at it all. My husband was sitting on a brand new armchair, holding the baby who was plucking at her father's ears and laughing. I took the older girl on my lap and sat on the other chair.

'Isn't it fine? Now there is room for playing, they don't have to be underfoot all of the time.'

'It's good to sit here anyway.'

That was his point of view, and a good one, too.

Exercise 3.2 Analysis of your own autobiography as a story

Analyse the autobiography you wrote for Exercise 1.1 How did you present your own gender in the text? To whom did you write the story? How did that affect the way you presented your gender? How did the form of the story, i.e., written, affect the way of presenting your gender?

What kinds of gender roles have you learned at home, at school, at different places and stages of your life? How has your own gender performance changed over the years? How have age and different places and contexts affected it? Were the observed and experienced gender roles complementary and/or oppositional? What have you learned about gender fluidity; in other words, about the various combinations of the categories feminine, masculine, woman, man?

Notes

1   These life stories are unpublished stories, gathered for research purposes, and stored in the Folklore Archive of the Finnish Literature Society; collection 'Satasärmäinen nainen' (Women with a hundred angulars and wheels) (1991).
2   This expression is often used by men, for example, when they characterize their part in the Second World War, meaning that it was no fun but you did your best.
3   The following two chapters owe much to 'Johdanto (Introduction)' in Hyvärinen, et al. (1998: 7–25). For further reading, see also Smith and Watson, (2001) and Smith and Watson (1998: 3–52).

4

Gender in Membership Categorization Analysis

Helmi Järviluoma and Irene Roivainen

Gendering membership categorization   70
What is MCA?   72
Basic concepts   73
MCA and foreign categories   81
Conclusions   82

In their everyday speech and justifications, people move in a power field consisting of two charged strategies: *categorization* and *particularization*. On the one hand, we are able to distinguish someone we have met from the category in which we have previously placed them, or alternatively, we avoid right away placing them in any given category (Billig, 1987: 131). On the other hand, it would be downright absurd to claim that we do not categorize (ibid.: 131); we place people and things in general categories. With all their incompatibility, these two crucial strategies of interaction are complementary and simultaneous.

In this chapter we present a review of membership categorization, a review of the manner in which, when speaking, we continuously relate ourselves and others to various categories. Depending on the context, we are 'researchers', 'mothers', 'friends', 'women', 'Northerners', or even 'musicians'. Our everyday knowledge of people is to a great extent organized into categories, and into activities and features which characterize these.

The practices of categorization have been and are continuously discussed in various disciplines, not least in the different schools of philosophy, social psychology and cognitive sciences. Harvey Sacks, a sociologist perhaps better known as the elaborator of conversation analysis, developed a 'toolkit' for studying membership categorization practices (1966; 1972a; 1972b). He called it the Membership Categorization Device (MCD), referring to the membership category groupings and their rules. Here, we use the somewhat more accessible term membership category analysis (MCA) (Hester and Eglin, 1997) and have also tried to simplify the sometimes complicated Sacksian terminology.

In the following, we discuss the ways in which the MCA 'apparatus' can be used when analysing the construction of gender in different types of texts. Following an outline of the central concepts of MCA, we discuss categories as local, shareable and routinized constructions of conventional lay knowledge and we identify features shared by MCA and conversation analysis. We include concrete examples to illustrate the use of MCA, and conclude with an excercise.

Gendering membership categorization

People possess everyday knowledge, which is constantly being refined, about the organization of gendered categories. What are the categorization practices and devices in their everyday activities? We believe that Sacksian category analysis is useful in studying the construction of gender, and do not think it should be dismissed because of its 'masculinity' (Järviluoma, 2000). MCA sounds very 'masculine' if we think of the way many French feminists have abandoned labels, namings and isms on the grounds that these tie the labelling to a phallogocentric desire to stabilize, organize and rationalize our conceptual world. However, we incline to the position articulated by Toril Moi (1990: 175–6): she considers it important not to banish logic, conceptualization and rationality as 'non-feminine' but instead try to develop a society in which these virtues will not be categorized as masculine. (Heinämaa, 1999).

Furthermore, MCA must be seen in the context of its theoretical tradition. Sacks did not design it in order to reproduce rigid categorizations. On the contrary, his approach tried to show how these categories are constantly being constructed and maintained through everday interactions, and to show the subtle and complex ways in which culture works (Watson, 1994; Silverman, 1998, 74–97).

Typically, postmodern societies produce endless streams of messages, images and signs. In order to understand society, we have to be able to decipher cultural codes and different social 'languages'. We need to explore how ideas of gender are created and reconstructed through a variety of texts (Cameron, 1996: 31). But it is in language in particular that people are able to call into question a previously posited world. The practices of conversation are rich, and language users are able to describe the world with great flexibility and variety.

Membership categorization analysts do not regard the categories – and the rules governing their application – as cognitive prototypes inside people's heads or as inflexible conceptual grids which people would automatically impose when categorising. Categorization is a *culturally methodical* (procedural) social activity (Watson, 1994). The categories are interpreted as collective phenomena and as cultural resources: this is a map which people use to navigate their way in the interactive situations they find themselves.

As Carolyn Baker (1997: 132) puts it: 'Tracing members' use of ... categories and devices in any settings, including interview settings, is a means of showing how identities, social relationships and even institutions are produced.'

Case 4.1 Assumed gender categories

Carolyn Baker observed the following scene: a woman, a young boy holding a screwdriver, and a man entered a bakery. The woman behind the counter greeted them and then addressed the child as follows: 'Have you been helping Daddy?' There was a pause that I distinctly remember because, as an observer-analyst of the scene, I had time to consider the gender assumption being made: that Daddy was being helped rather than the mother. The woman customer then said: 'This is not Daddy.'

Gender differentiation is internalized and affected by language. It is less often recognized, however, that the internalization of gender differentiation is also affected by meta-language, i.e. the systems through which we speak about language (for example, the categories of grammar) (Cameron, 1996: 122–3). Words, and thus categories, are liable to change since people do not learn simply, or even normally, their meanings from dictionaries. They learn, maintain and construct the meanings in practice, when using categories. However, we must remember that some people have more power than others to influence other people's usage of language. They have greater resources through which to circulate meanings (ibid.: 141). Many English teachers still insist that their students use the 'generic' pronoun 'he'; and *The New York Times* refuses to use the female title Ms (ibid.). An associated reason why categories are resistant to change is that the 'renovations' do not have access to a 'free market' of language, since the institutionalized gatekeepers such as the education system, administration, media, grammar, linguists are not easily bypassed (ibid.: 142–3).

Case 4.2 Generic pronouns

In the English language the generic use of the pronoun 'he' has only been standard practice for less than 200 years. When reading Jane Austen one notices that the plural form of the pronoun, 'they', is used as generic far more often than the prounoun 'he': 'If someone's stolen my pen, will they please return it' (Cameron, 1996: 122). It is the Harvard linguists who assembled a mass of obscure theoretical assumptions based on the hypothesis that grammar is a 'natural' autonomous structure, unaffected by people's practices. The hypothesis is faulty (ibid.).

Not only institutions, but ordinary communities of people act as gatekeepers – situational categorizations (see later) can become routine categories only after they have passed 'the preventive censorship' or collective control of the community (Knuuttila, 1992: 151). One reason why MCA is useful in the critical study of gender is that it raises awareness of the subtle forces of culture, not only for continuity, but also for change. Both the general public and people in powerful positions maintain, produce, or resist the discourses of femininity and masculinity in the course of their everyday activities. Deborah Cameron claims that we should resist the tendency to understand 'masculine' and 'feminine' as natural categories, and realize their status as restrictive and unequal structures (1996: 122–3). In the meantime, when we still have to live with the prevalent use of these categories, we may scrutinize how people use them and create gendered nuances in their everyday lives. We can talk about femininity and masculinity as conceptual categories or cultural constructs as a point of departure for critical analysis (see also Wieder, 1974: 40–50).

What is MCA?

Press headlines often exploit the idea of categorization. Arresting headlines are often constructed out of conflicting or confusing categories. In the Finnish newspaper headline 'Cleaner fell down lift shaft in insurance company' there is clearly a tension between the role of an insurance company in promoting safety and the fact that it obviously failed to do so on its own premises. Some time ago, 'A minister in nude pictures' was used as a headline to boost sales of tabloid papers in Finland.

Case 4.3 Juxtapositioning categories in headlines

An example provided by J.R.E. Lee (1984) is 'Girl guide aged 14 raped at Hell's Angels convention'. This headline promotes curiosity as to how a Hell's Angel and a girl guide could converge in a news headline. What kind of conventional knowledge underpins this puzzling juxtapositioning of categories? It is only on further reading of the article that we discover that the girl guide was kidnapped.

After the first reading it is necessary to consider the organization of the headline categories which refer to persons. What kind of everyday knowledge is linked to the inter-category relations; what kind of features essential to the categories – activities, motives, causes, beliefs – are linked to them? (Hester and Eglin, 1992: 233). Here we have two morally opposed categories: 'innocent victims' and 'evil-doers'. Together they form a grouping, namely 'the parties in a rape' (Lee, 1984: 70). We then need to attend to the function of the words: in this case the immediate activity, the context of interaction, which is also partly shaped by the words, is the reading of the newspaper (Hester and Eglin, 1992).

The theoretical foundations of membership categorization analysis are derived from phenomenology, from social constructivism by Berger and Luckmann (1975) and from several approaches in cognitive psychology. In practice, MCA enables the *systematic* coding of even a large set of data. It is a link in the chain of other data-driven analytical methods like discourse analysis (DA) and conversation analysis (CA). On the one hand, it may be linked to the other two with regard to the data size and level of detail (Silverman, 1990). On the other, the approaches of MCA in part respond to a different set of questions, even though they belong to the same methodological family. Rod Watson (1994) has attempted to address the questions raised by contemporary discourse analysts regarding MCA and claims that conversation and categorization analysis are inevitably intertwined.

Following Sacks, MCA concepts were further developed by, among others, Lena Jayyusi (1984), Carolyn Baker (1984; 1997), Rod Watson (1987; 1994; 1997) and David Silverman (1993; 1998). MCA analysis has been applied to an extremely broad range of data and texts. It has been used to study texts from the Bible to fiction, from telephone and other everyday conversations to film dialogue (Silverman, 1993b; cf. McHoul, 1987). As further examples, MCA has been used to study different categorizations within 'stage of life' (Baker, 1984; Nikander, 2000), and by Lena Jayyusi to study communicative praxis as moral order (1984; 1991). Other research areas have included medical sociology (Peräkylä and Silverman, 1990; 1991; Silverman, 1994), step families (Ritala-Koskinen, 1993), and music and identity (Järviluoma, 1991b; 1997; 2000). Watson (1987) has studied how categories are combined in order to stigmatize or to praise, and, in addition to Schegloff (1972), Drew (1978) and Roivainen (1993; 1995; 1999) have investigated definitions of location and locality.

In the following we will review the central concepts of MCA. The review is partly based on our earlier writings (Forsberg et al., 1991; Järviluoma and Roivainen, 1997). The apparatus constructed by Sacks includes more detail than we can present here, and for a more detailed summary, see Silverman (1998: 74–97).

Basic concepts

Membership category, standard pair and category-bound features

Membership categorization analysis starts out from the observation that a significant proportion of the knowledge needed in our everyday interaction is organized as *membership categories* – we listed some examples of these in the second paragraph of this chapter. In simplified terms, people are identified by being placed in categories.

Peter Eglin and Stephen Hester (1992) use the following headline to illustrate categorization: 'Engagement was broken – Temperamental young man gassed himself". The almost 100 per cent probability is that we will interpret this to mean that it was the fiancée of the young man who broke off the engagement and that the young man was so unhappy that he killed himself. We adopt this reading in spite of the fact that the headline could be read in a number of other ways – not the least because the word 'engagement' has several different meanings (ibid.: 243).

Here, the membership category 'young man' is used, but we read the man as representing the category 'fiancé'. This is because mention of an engagement highlights the standardized relational pair or to put it more simply, *standard pair*, fiancé–fiancée. Such pairs (e.g., husband–wife, parent–child, colleague–colleague) belong together 'logically' and are linked to a multiplicity of rights and duties. As soon as one member of the pair is mentioned, the other one becomes present by inference.

The basic *category-bound feature* of the fiancé–fiancée pair is the fact that they are engaged to be married. In our minds, this pair is linked with such features as wearing rings and being in love. Thus, engagement has a 'grammar' of its own, just as suicide has. The 'temperamental' 'fiancé' may commit suicide on losing his fiancée as part of the 'grammar' of suicide (Eglin and Hester, 1992). Membership category and the features and activities related with it are mostly selected simultaneously (co-selection). Whenever features are formulated, explicitly or implicitly, as conventionally accompanying some category, we may talk of them as being category bound. The concept of a 'category-bound feature' is an extension by Lena Jayyusi (1984) of Sacks's concept *category-bound activities*, which also continues to be useful, even if narrower in scope. Where features are presented in discourse as having been situatedly produced through their tie to some category, we may talk of them as being *category-generated features*.

Membership categorizations and membership groupings with their rules (MCDs)

Jayyusi (1984: 20) usefully distinguishes membership categories from *membership categorizations*. Categories (such as 'conductor', 'musician', 'mother', 'vandal') are already available as a matter of course in everyday categorization activity. In contrast, categorizations are not pre-existent, but require construction, often on the model adjective + category ('nice woman', 'skilled musician', 'withdrawn child', 'a hippie type'). Thus, Jayyusi's term 'membership categorization' denotes the situational construction of types: 'Categorization refers to the work of members in categorizing other members or using "characterizations" of them, whereas the former [Category] refers to the already culturally available category concepts that members may, and routinely do, use' (ibid.).

Members of a community know that certain membership categories and categorizations seem to go together naturally (Sacks, 1966: 15–16). They form *membership groupings*: 'These collections constitute the natural groupings of categories, categories that members of society feel "go together"' (ibid.). Sacks expressly points out that the groupings he has analysed were not constructed by him as a researcher from his own experience: the fact of a category belonging to a certain grouping is always visible and audible in the data.

The crux of Sacks's analytical problem is: What are the rules of membership categorization? How do people in their everyday interaction select the correct category grouping? (Jayyusi, 1984: 212). The membership groupings with their rules or toolkits were called by Sacks (1966; 1972a; 1972b) 'Membership Categorization Device', or MCD. The present authors belong, among other groups, to the device 'family' which, in addition to 'mother', also includes the categories 'granny', 'daughter', 'child', 'father'. As 'researchers' we belong to the device 'occupation', along with 'teachers', 'lawyers', 'masons' and 'consultants', and so on. We may also be grouped according to our stage in life – we do not belong to the categories 'child' or 'senior citizen', but, rather, to 'the middle-aged'. However, as Nikander has pointed out, we could be both 'middle-aged' and 'little girls' if we look at how age categorization in conversation 'works to manage the practical business of identity work' (Nikander, 2000: 335).

Among the devices mentioned, the first one, 'family' may be regarded as a duplicative organization (Sacks, 1972b). This implies that some of the membership devices clearly form a team or a unit. When looking at a certain population, therefore, we do not count the number of mothers and fathers, but that of 'complete families', 'fatherless families', etc. Sometimes devices with a duplicative organization only contain one membership 'slot' for each category: for instance, in a republic, there can only be one president in office and – at least until fairly recently – there could only be one mother in a Finnish family.

Sacks found certain systematically repeated rules of application used by people when categorizing. *The economy rule* (e.g. Sacks, 1972a) guarantees that in a specific situation a single category from one MCD grouping, chosen from a large pool of possible options, may suffice to describe a person, as in the following example of Angrosino. This holds true despite the fact that every one of us can be categorized in countless appropriate ways – that is, we belong to many membership groupings. Additional categorizations are not always needed, but they may, of course, be used depending on the situation.

Case 4.4 Economy rule – one category is enough

When Michel Angrosino (1986: 70) started his field research in Trinidad, it was enough for the host community to know him as an unattached man: 'As far as my new friends were concerned, I might well be a student and a white person from the United States and an anthropologist – but I was still a man, an unattached man, and deep down they all knew that that could mean only one thing.' In this community, any man was considered to be guilty of infidelity until he was proven to be not guilty.

The *consistency rule* implies that when one person has been identified as belonging to a category, often the next person, for example, in a social conversational situation, is characterized by using the same category. When somebody presents her or himself in terms of, let's say, profession, it is likely that the following self-presentations fall into the same membership grouping. According to Sacks, this is related to a desire for functionality.

This is an example from a set of data by Helmi Järviluoma, dealing with the gender categorization and identity practices of a group of Finnish rural amateur musicians (see also Chapters 1 and 2; Järviluoma, 2000). The ensemble consists of 23 men and from one to three women, mostly between 50 and 70 years old.

Case 4.5 Field diary, Helmi Järviluoma, Virrat 1988, 33–7. Names 'translated' into English

1. Anna left quite early and I realized quite soon she had gone to make coffee. A little later on, the other woman left as well. After a fairly long time she game back saying that it was 'coffee time'. At first, the players paid no attention to her. Then they repeated the piece, then we all went to have coffee.
2. The men were sitting at the table, women pouring coffee.
3. Everybody goes, one after the other and washes up their cups. Andrew in front of me is joking: 'I cannot wash the dishes. I have to see how Bill does it.' Daniel continues: 'Haven't you washed the dishes since you came out of the army?' 'No, I didn't do it even then, I just knocked my mess tin a bit.' Sylvia (the other woman) took the cups from under men's noses and washed them. The women came to the rehearsals later on (after the second piece?). By accident, even I nearly stayed with them to clean up.

We can at least extract the membership categories of 'women', 'men', 'musicians' and 'researcher' from the example above. It is particularly revealing here to see how Järviluoma is constructing herself as 'a researcher' in the situation. As the last line suggests, she was thinking that it does not belong to the work of 'a researcher' to wash more than her own cup and clean up after the coffee break. Pouring the coffee and washing up the dishes seemed to her to be category-bound activities of 'women'. She could put them into hierarchical relationship to the activities bound to the category of the 'musicians'.

In fact, in participating in the group's activities she had to constantly choose the category-bound features that foreground and maintain the 'researcher' dimension of her identity instead of, say, 'a mother'. She refused to build herself up as feminine as Anna and Sylvia did. She used her cultural knowledge in exactly the same way as the participants in the situation to create the social order. Category-bound activities or features of a music researcher include such things as observing the players performing, taking photographs of them and recording their music and talk, not pouring coffee.

In the example, Andrew is bringing up an MCD, the army, that consists – or at least used to consist – almost exclusively of men. In general, his joking (3) about washing the dishes can well be seen as 'doing masculinity' (cf. Coleman, 1990: 196). Andrew washes his cup competently, but he is making an effort to make it seem (or at least sound) clumsy. He is questioning his ability to wash up. To use Wil Coleman's example (ibid.), a man is doing masculinity, when he 'is asked by a female friend to hold her bag, where that bag is seeable as "a woman's bag", that man may make a deliberate effort to hold it in such a way as to show that it is not his bag, and despite appearances ... he is and remains "a proper man"'. Daniel, when asking his question about washing dishes in the army, is (1) on the one hand showing that he understands what Andrew is talking about, but (2) on the other hand he is slightly disrupting Andrew's masculine joking. In the army, men are bound to get involved in 'women's category-bound activities'. For Daniel it is evident that all men have in at least one stage of their lives been required to wash dishes so that it could conceivably happen again later.

Anna does not assign priority to the category of musician. Instead, from inside the group, we find here a *qualitatively specified standard pair* 'men-performing-duty' and 'caring-and-helping-women'. Standard pairs are often specified in this way (Cuff, 1980: 45–6): we not only speak about mothers and children, but we talk about 'loving mothers and happy children' or 'indifferent mothers and neglected children' (Forsberg et al., 1991). Pairs often mask a moral order which is disclosed only when somebody contests expectations – as Järviluoma notably did in Case 4.5, by violating the moral order of being female.

Membership categorization as local routinized knowledge

The empirical basis of the membership devices lies in the 'natural grouping' into categories carried out by the members of a community. The early version of MCD has consequently been characterized as a mixture of naturalism and ethnomethodology (Schegloff, 1989: 202). In terms of its basic idea, MCD may appear as a naturalistically closed and rigid set of codes, in that it differentiates the categories used to classify people into membership categories and further into membership devices.

When using gender categories we speak of, for example, 'the opposite sex' or 'a chick' (Sacks, 1992: vol. 1:60; see Edwards, 1997); 'lady', 'girlfriend', 'prostitute' or 'gentleman' (Sacks, 1972; see Silverman and Peräkylä, 1990: 305–6). In studying the spontaneous grouping into categories by the members of the community it could be said that we are dealing with knowledge which is 'natural' in a situational and epistemological rather than in a ontological sense. We are dealing more with local, shareable and *routinized* constructions of conventional lay knowledge than with pre-given sets of cultural codes. Categories are common currency in community interaction for practical purposes (Keesing, 1987: 373–7; Eglin and Hester, 1992: 16). This interaction in itself requires the openness of membership categorization.

The conclusions on MCA made by Lena Jayyusi, Rod Watson, Peter Eglin and Stephen Hester bring the double bond of routine and situatedness described above into sharper relief. Jayyusi distinguishes the culturally fairly stable *membership categories* from the more situational *membership categorizations* (see 'Basic Concepts' above). She also divides category features into 'natural', category-bound features, and situational, category-generated features. (Jayyusi, 1984: 36–7, 212–13). Another example of the double bond is the distinction by Eglin and Hester and Watson into *natural* and *situational* membership categories (see Eglin and Hester, 1992). In natural categorization, membership categorizations or groupings (such as 'family') are taken as routine and given, in which case the speakers only need minimal contextual information to be able to combine categories into groupings. In situational categorization, such self-evident possibilities of combining categories cannot be assumed, especially if the topics are not familiar or if the conversation is extremely context-bound in its content (Watson, 1994). In a way, therefore, natural and situational collections appear to refer to the stability and shareability of everyday knowledge. Shared cultural understanding and context determine to a great extent the degree of givenness of categories.

The issue may be considered from several angles. For instance, it would be possible to make a distinction, following Aaron Cicourel, by seeing the (natural) membership categories as residing in the cultural deep structures, while membership categorizations or situational membership categories would be procedural knowledge, which is closer to 'the surface' (Cicourel, 1983; Knuuttila, 1994a). Michael Billig, on the other hand, would only speak of categorization when the focus is on the resemblance of the object to be categorized to other objects. He would use the concept of particularization to emphasize the unique features of the object (1987: 140).

This anti-mentalist map was characteristic of Harvey Sacks's research approach (Watson, 1997: 4). He regarded as collective phenomena even such mental predicates, ostensibly characterizing the individual, as 'to understand' and 'to prefer'. In fact, it is only possible to speak of 'understanding' and 'not understanding' after we know what these signify in a given culture. Similarly, prioritizing things depends on previous agreements and is related to cultural hierarchies of preference (ibid.).

Eglin and Hester claim (1992: 12) that the ethnomethodological conception of MCA stands in marked contrast to decontextualized models of membership categorization. However, the study of mentalities and ethnomethodology have noticeably approached each other in recent years (cf. Knuuttila, 1994a; 1994b;

Edwards, 1997). Similarly, we think there is reason to relax the strict distinction between the – cognitively oriented – mainstream of categorization research and membership categorization analysis, which is closer to ethnomethodology. In fact, even Sacks's 'apparatus' contains the idea of stability of categories.

Both CA and MCD?

At worst, the categorization theories in social psychology describe the categorizer as a rather boring creature – perhaps even as 'an organism' with a one-dimensional drive to categorize 'information' (Billig, 1987: 124). Michael Billig attempts to open up this one-dimensionality by suggesting that categorization and particularization or specification are closely intertwined: our ability to categorize presupposes the ability to particularize (ibid.: 133). Billig doubts whether there exists a language so far impoverished that its users would want, or be constrained, to describe the world rigidly, in one way only.

Case 4.6 Combining CA and MCA in analyzing identities

Helmi Järviluoma's analysis (1997) dealing with the categorization and identity practices of a group of amateur musicians uses the tools of both categorization analysis and conversation analysis. It appeared that for the musicians in the group, highlighting another dimension of their identity is by no means a dramatic event, rather, it is part of their everyday life (see also Peräkylä, 1990: 28). Pirjo Nikander used both MCA and CA (2000) when exploring the implications of a discursive view of age categorization and age identity. Her task was to produce 'empirically grounded observations on the communicative practices through which age identity and age categories are applied, modified, and challenged in talk'. Nikander talks about age identity, but her words can also be applied to gender: this approach is useful when studying gender categories and the ways in which they function 'as flexible sense-making resources for the participants' (ibid.: 337), and how gender identities become locally and interactionally defined and negotiated.

Membership categorization analysis and conversation analysis may thus be seen as complementary rather than mutually exclusive approaches. It is true that in his later life Harvey Sacks moved away from the analysis of categorizations to a greater emphasis on the analysis of speech activity sequences (cf. Silverman, 1993a; Watson, 1997). However, it would be an exaggeration to claim that Sacks changed from categorization analysis to conversation analysis in 'mid-flight', so to speak, and that consequently his earlier work was superseded (cf. Watson, 1994).

Conversation analysts often, albeit implicitly, point out that their shoes fit Harvey Sacks's footprints better than others. One reason for this provides food for thought for conversation analysts: if 'speech–external' categories are really considered to be relevant to the organization of conversation, then conversation is no longer a completely autonomous or discrete system. Sacks, however, never said this (Watson, 1994). He dedicated several lectures to describing how people elaborate their conversational contributions so that they are oriented to recipients-as-categorized.

One of the most obvious categories thus analyzed by Sacks is the 'caller-called' pair in telephone conversations (Sacks, 1992: 361). The 'caller' and the 'called' are turn-generated categories. They are generated, maintained and spread through turns. These turn-generated categories were analyzed by Sacks by means of a much scantier and less cumbersome arsenal than before.

Case 4.7 Turn-taking, age and gender

The organization of turn-taking may also depend on age categories, for instance. Sacks refers to the famous study of Burundi speech by Ethel Albert. In the rhetorical speech of the Burundi, a category-based turn-taking was prevalent. The person categorized as the most senior spoke first, thereafter the next in seniority, and so on. However, status categories confuse the seniority categories in that princes could take their turn before the aged, if the latter belonged to the common folk. Thus, a person speaking at a given point in a conversation may have been heard to speak as the representative of a given category, such as 'nephew'. A similar organization of turn-taking is also familiar in our culture.

Gender categories are also involved: Burundi women – just like servants – only spoke when spoken to (cf. Watson, 1994). It is a pity that Sacks chose an example of turn-taking from such a highly patriarchal society as the Burundi. After all, he could have cited the studies on Sioux Indians among whom it is the elderly women who are respected, feared and privileged to deliver moralistic speeches at ceremonies (Wax, 1986: 137). Also, among the Munduguru, Yolanda and Robert F. Murphy noted a similar phenomenon (1974: 105–6): 'An old woman may sit where she pleases, and men will actually defer by making room for her. She may talk on whatever subject interests her, and if this requires that she interrupt the men, then so be it.'

Overall, Sacks's later work may be seen as a minimalist version of his earlier MCD apparatus. He still discusses the rights, duties and activities related to categories, but he no longer considers it necessary to involve the entire theoretical apparatus (Watson, 1994). The formal analysis of categorization activity can clearly be distinguished through the emphasis on *form* related to Sacks's sequential analysis.

Possibly conversation analysts threw out the baby with the bathwater when excluding categorization analysis from their work. Watson (1994) compares this theory of changing viewpoints with Toulouse-Lautrec's famous sketch: on the one hand, it shows the head, shoulder and necklace of a young Parisian woman, but if the necklace is taken to be a mouth, it appears to depict a hook-nosed old woman instead of the young one. So, a radical methodological turn is counter-productive if it drives the researcher to relinquish a detailed, form-oriented or sequential analysis of categorization, or if he or she considers that categories have no sequential implications.

Our 'boring' and one-track categorizer appears as a much more creative user of language, with many more skills of situational navigation, if we combine the analysis of categorizations with the analysis of conversation sequences or with other specific analysis.

MCA and foreign categories

There is undoubtedly a significant difference between applying MCA to data from one's own language area and culture, as opposed to data collected from a completely foreign culture. However, it is not impossible that one might also succesfully apply MCA to the latter. After all, it is the realization that the categories brought to the field may differ significantly from those held by members of the field community that forces fieldworkers to address their own biases. As Whitehead and Conaway (1986) put it: 'The resolution process may begin internally as the fieldworker tries to understand why members of the host community react to him or her as they do; it may begin externally as he or she searches for local categories that foster an understanding of the indigenous culture.'

Case 4.8 Furthering understanding through categories

When Regina and Leon Smith Oboler studied the Nandi in Kenya (1986: 42), it took some time for them to realize that there are two important membership categories in Nandi: being polite (*ketalait*) and being rude (*kingelel*). It seemed to Regina Smith Oboler that the usual response of a Nandi to a violation of a norm depended very much on his/her general feeling towards the person involved. If it is negative, the explanation for the behaviour is 'that is a very rude person'. If it is positive, the behavior will be reinterpreted in such a way that it does not really constitute a violation of a norm. Similarly, Harvey Sacks (1992) has talked about the way in which categories are bent – the 'stage-of-life' category of an adult male is often modified by saying: 'Boys will always be boys'.

Furthermore if we look at Chapter 2, we can, in addition to what has been said about the event in that connection, hear it as a category negotiation – or rather, a contest. As said earlier, a drunken young man made unwelcome advances to the young woman anthropologist Nancy Oestrich Lurie; another young Indian man read his action to be that the other man was categorizing Lurie as 'a girl' – a category implying both her gender and stage of life. He furiously contests the category 'girl' by stressing her professional category and, thus, particularizing her as an anthropologist. Interestingly enough, this seems to make her non-approachable sexually.

Conclusions

Harvey Sacks and MCA occupy a pivotal position in naturalism, ethnomethodology and constructionism. It would be a pity if MCA were to be regarded only as a rigid and technical method: in its Sacksian application it always involves a strong element of interpretation. The data does not have a 'pure' voice, but must always be interpreted in context and as context.

Frequently, lay categorizations are not observed analytically by researchers. Even when they are, we often label these as erroneous or at least as secondary versions of the truth, as compared to research. Thus, we come to deny the everyday social world and ultimately the basis of scientific knowledge. MCA is an excellent compass for the researcher who wants to navigate in this world of everyday significations.

MCA includes both categories bearing collective significations and categorizations which change constantly in interaction. The rules of typification are characteristic for interpersonal communication, but equally typical is the breaking of categories and creating new significations.

In a way, the fact that we categorize all our lives could be described as the Kantian 'dream of forms'. We squeeze the content of the world into forms, and imagine that these forms compose the world as such. Alternatively we could accept that we live in the 'awake-world' of forms, and, thus far, MCA is only able to chart this awake-world. The unconscious 'truth' is 'only occasionally visible or audible in symptoms, dreams, phantasies, jokes, as the riddles of texts and the multiplicity of interpretations' (Ihanus, 1995: 97; Järviluoma, 1997: 55). MCA and CA analysts could, however, be the pioneers of a holistic research approach to the study of gender. Already, we analyse laughter, ironies, word games, hesitations among other language features, which refer to the unconscious without revealing it.

**Exercise 4.1 Membership category analysis of
conversational field data**

Identify gendered (a) categories; (b) MCDs; (c) category features and
category-bound activities; (d) a standard pair.

The midde-aged men of the *pelimanni* ensemble studied by Järviluoma
are at the annual meeting of their association. During the year, women,
aged between 20 and 35 years old, have joined or re-joined the group.

>   A = the head of the association (one of the male musicians);
>   B = the conductor (male). P = Pause. [= Overlapping talk.

1 *A:* It's great that we have more of the fair sex (P) now ...
       we have more girls
2   than than normally, generally, we have only one and
       now's there's four (P)
3   and (P) it's great that Hillevi has come back to the gang
       after being some
4   years [away
5 *B:* [the *pelimanni* group's appearance has become better
6 *A:* much better
7   (*several persons laughing*)
8 *A:* And so we can state that we others grow old gracefully.
       This is a marvellous gang. That's it and now to the
       meeting ...

Exercise 4.2 Membership analysis of your own autobiography

What kind of gendered categories can you identify in your own life story
(Exercise 1.1)? Analyse your story using MCA concepts.

5

Not only Vision – Analysing Sound and Music from the Perspective of Gender

Positioned perceiver – the learned and gendered
    meanings of sound   85
Interpreting the meanings of music   89
Sounds and music as gendered discourse   90
The study of music videos and film music   93
Methods of analysing image and music   95
Reading gender out of material combining images and music   97
Studying gendered soundscapes – some useful
    conceptual models   98
Sounds, space, gender   102

What's in Music?

Music is not just sounds, but
cultures, values, attitudes
whispering to my mind
Not only men or women singing
But, sounds that are
either masculine or feminine.

In the music,
I hear my upbringing and my culture,
the gender structure of my mind.
          (Pirkko Moisala)

In this chapter we focus on how gender categories are performed and reshaped in film soundtracks and music videos. We will also refer to the other soundscapes of our surroundings. We wish to stress the importance of the analysis of sound and music, since they are usually neglected in ethnographic and media studies. In emphasizing sound we do not ignore the fact that human beings use all the senses they have at their disposal. We are multi-sensory beings. However, in the modern era it is the eye, vision and visual aspects of experience which have been foregrounded in the study of culture – this kind of ocularcentrism needs to be challenged. Sound is important in the qualitative study of gender, since learning gender roles not only means visible aspects of those roles: we learn gender through the total sensorium.

Students in disciplines other than musicology are often unconcerned by the idea of analysing music and sound. However, we emphasize the fact that these are not the exclusive domain of musical experts: all of us are sonologically competent. Everybody is able to perceive and understand, to talk and write about sounds, and of course able to develop listening and analytic skills. It is characteristic of bourgeois musical culture to make some people feel inferior regarding their ability to discuss music. A select group assigns to itself the authorized cultural capital to talk about music, and its members make much of the special skills needed to interpret it. As Peter Martin, applying Bourdieu, has suggested, 'Differences which are social in origin are presented, particularly through the ideology of formal education as though they were "natural". In this way, the vast majority of people come to believe that they are not "musical"' (1995: 69).

It has also been noted that music has a gendered position in our culture, which may well be one of the reasons for music being the 'step-sister', the Other, of music video and film studies. Composer Richard Wagner is often cited as authorizing such a model: he saw music and lyrics as coming together in opera in an act of love, in which poetry is the masculine and music the feminine partner: music demands 'the fertilizing semen' of the libretto (see Glass, 1983). Musicologists have claimed that the male hegemony is crucially visual (Shepherd, 1991: 156–9), to which the corporeality of music appears threatening. As Susan McClary puts it, there is always the likelihood of music itself in Western culture being regarded 'as the feminine Other that circumvents reason and arouses desire' (1991: 79).

We have been hearing sounds and music ever since we were in the womb. We are able, if only we are willing, to speak about them. Often we are not fully aware of all the things we know, especially those which are very close to us. Everyday sounds and music in everyday life belong to this category – such as TV advertising jingles, music in aerobic classes or the different sounds of men's and women's shoes on different floors. We know more than we think about the gender of music and sounds. We need to make them 'anthropologically strange', and to train our ears and our ways of listening. Musicologists have a specialized way of framing their analyses, but we all have other competencies, no less relevant, whether we are students of folklore, sociology, media studies, literature, or anthropology.

Positioned perceiver – the learned and gendered meanings of sound

In the process of civilization, in the interplay of exchanging meanings intersubjectively, we have learned to inscribe some things as masculine, some as feminine. As we learn a culture, becoming enculturated, we internalize these categories, including the sense of the appropriate sonic behaviour of a girl and a boy. As suggested above, we are 'sonologically competent', which means, we have an understanding of the meanings of sounds in our culture. Ola Stockfelt described (personal communication, quoted in Järviluoma, 1996) how young people who do their homework with the television on know, without looking at the TV, whether the main character on the screen is a male or a female and what is happening (so-called *secondary listening*). Sounds envelop us constantly. We do not necessarily have to focus on the sound (conduct *primary listening*) in order to decode their meanings.

Case 5.1 Shared meanings of music revealed by an experiment

The unpublished research by Philip Tagg and Robert Clarida provides persuasive evidence regarding the shared competence of Westerners concerning the meanings of music. The researchers asked TV and film music audiences to describe the associations which certain examples of music evoked in them. While the answers varied greatly, when grouped statistically, a significant degree of coherence could be identified. Kassabian, who worked in 1989 together with Tagg and Clarida on the project, compared the nominated associations with the *Selected Sounds Mood Music Catalogue*. She observed that in 27 per cent of respondents, associations regarding women occurred when listening to TV and film melodies which accompanied pictures of the countryside, and similarly, women were most often located in the categories of 'pastoral' and 'romantic' in the *Selected Sounds Mood Music Catalogue*. (Kassabian, 2001: 19–20). This observation led her to the conclusion that the intentions of the producers of film and mood music, as well as the listener's way of decoding these meanings, showed a significant level of correspondence with each other. In other words, she argues that beneath individual variations in responding to mood music and film music, there is some kind of a common competence, an ability to 'read' meanings of music. All people do not read musical meanings in the same way or as fluently. Music reading ability varies from one person to another but importantly, it does not require the ability to read music notation.

The perceiver of music – including the researcher – has her or his own personal history of music. The perception of music is influenced by the convergence of both the shared listener competence, as well as the listener's individual relationship with the music. The musical history of the perceiver, referred to by Marcia Herndon and Norma McLeod (1981) as 'musical storage', functions as a kind of a filter in every new musical experience. Music becomes interpreted through the previously learned, engendered cultural and individual patterns. Kassabian (2001) theorizes that music preconditions the psychological attachment of the perceiver to the movie. Music connects the perceiver to the processes of producing and reproducing meanings and ideologies, which, in their turn, are interwoven with the identifications of the perceiver. Identifications come into being through negotiation of a range of social factors (gender, ethnicity, sexuality, race, social class, age).

Kassabian emphasizes accordingly (2001: 62), that memories, emotions and identifications, desire and agency are implicated in the perception of popular music, because of the listener's prior relationship with it, coloured as that is by cultural meanings. She notes (ibid.: 64) that audiences do not leave their past outside the movie theatre. It is not only popular music which evokes memories, emotions and subject positions and which guides the listener to different subject positions, as Kassabian (ibid.) claims. This is the case for every kind of music. Listening to music – and sounds in general – always involves socially grounded identifications, incorporating gender.

Case 5.2 Race and gender as aspects influencing the perception of a video

The enquiry by Brown and Schultze (1990) into the perception of a video by Madonna, 'Papa Don't Preach', revealed how the race and gender of the viewer, as well as his or her feelings towards the artist, influenced the interpretation of the video. While black reviewers saw the video as a description of a father–daughter relationship, white reviewers saw it as a video about teenage pregnancy.

The concept of 'perceiver' as theorized by Kassabian (1997: 269–70) is useful when examining the human perception of films. The perceiver is not the same as the 'real' movie-goer. Nor can it be reduced to the textuality of the movie, as previous film studies have done. The perceiver, defined by Kassabian, is a theorized perceiver who can represent different identity categories, races, genders, social classes and sexual orientations. What is common to all perceivers is simply the process of perception, in which all the elements of the film – dialogue, plot, vision, music and sound effects – are equally involved. Kassabian claims that the perceiver, while listening to and watching a movie, unconsciously and consciously produces differences between his or her own subjectivity and the subject positions provided by the film. The central point is that the perceiver of music finds the meanings of music according to her/his personal (musical and gendered) history and identifications; the interpretation of music and film depends upon the textual and inter-textual competence of the perceiver (ibid.: 267–78). Music supports or resists the possible affiliations of the perceiver with the subject positions provided by the film. However, the power of music resides not only in its connection with visual images such as film. All forms of music have the ability 'to shape the ways we experience our bodies, emotions, subjectivities, desires, and social relations' (McClary, 2000: 7). Music – and sounds in general – are central forces in the construction of self.

One further consideration underpins the examination of the perception of music and sounds: the same music can mean different things to the same person in different situations. As music sociologist Tia DeNora proposes, 'music comes to have recognizable social "content" in and through its perceived participation in these (and other) realms' (2000: 13). She uses music played in aircraft to illustrate the dynamic relationship of music with social life; music evokes, stabilizes and changes the parameters of both the collective and individual subjectivity.

Case 5.3 'In-flight' music

Music sociologist Tia DeNora (2000: 10) asks how travellers are made to feel safe on a particular flight, apart from simply trusting in flight traffic controls in general. DeNora claims that music is a key element in inspiring confidence in passengers.

She flew in March 1999, from London to California, noting the in-flight music programme. The boarding was 'accompanied' by an 'ambient music video' – what she calls, 'True North', in which images of lakes and glaciers – cool and muted greys, greens and blues – were accompanied by slow, low-pitched melodies and whale song. When the moment of take-off came, the mood of the music and sounds altered:

> The safety video began with decisive, upward-sweeping and clearly defined trumpet music which then faded to the background as the firm and friendly (male) voice described what the passengers should do in the event of an emergency. The brass regained full volume when the presentation was about to end and the plane taxied out to the runway for take-off. (ibid.: 11)

Both the visual and the aural parameters of the video have been carefully selected in order to try to invoke 'preferred ' or appropriate action frames (ibid.: 13). In the example above, the soundscape was intended to reduce anxiety – even the fanfare, Aaron Copland's 'Fanfare for the Common Man', 'moves at a stately moderato pace' (ibid.). At the same time, however, the fanfare was an attention-seeking gesture. Trumpets are associated with heraldry and the military (precision, technology, logistical expertise) (ibid.: 11).

Trumpets are also associated with masculinity: the ethnomusicologist Curt Sachs describes in his *History of Musical Instruments* (1968) 'the virile trumpet' as one of the most masculine of all instruments in the world – in some cultures a woman can be killed after touching the exclusively male trumpet. In Western countries the education of a bourgeois girl is aimed at 'pleasantness', and blowing a trumpet did not fit this ideal (cf. Öhrström, 1987: 192). In Finland, this ideal was still active in the 1930s (Järviluoma, 1986). Blowing a horn or a trumpet is inappropriate for a girl, and like loud talking and laughing of women, is negatively sanctioned in many cultures.

In the in-flight music, a male voice followed the trumpets. How would we experience the trumpets, if a friendly female voice followed them? Would the military attention-seeking gesture change to a more androgynous signal, like an orchestra of angels?

Interpreting the meanings of music

The most recent music research attempts to find methods to interpret social, including gendered, meanings of music. It explores what music means, and how we can access these meanings. Music has meanings in many ways: there are conventionalized associations evoked by a musical style; a piece of music may also awaken personal memories, and specific musical parameters such as melody, rhythm, harmony and timbre, as well as the style of performance, voice production and the movements of the performers, connect with certain meanings. Like any other human artefact, music is assembled from various elements and intersected by multiple cultural codes. The meanings of music and sound are found in inter-textual relations. They are context-specific and changeable; the same music carries different meanings to different people. It is impossible to point to one 'true' meaning of music. The meanings of music are not simply inherent in musical sounds, nor do they reside wholly outside them, but in the space between, in the meetings between sounds and their listeners (receivers). Different people – and the same people in different situations – read different meanings into music. However, at the same time there are some shared ways in which most Western people read musical meanings, including gendered meanings.

The first field in music research to become interested in the social meanings of music was ethnomusicology which, originally, studied non-Western musics and Western folk musics. In the study of the music of foreign cultures, it is difficult to remain unaware of the central role of culture and society on the formation of musical sounds. Western art music and its study, however, are still influenced by the ideology of autonomous musical works, the idea of music as a phenomenon independent of its social context. In popular music studies one of the most fruitful approaches has been to study the ways in which the musical and social elements are articulated together.

As Peter Martin (1995: 24) puts it, while it seems clear enough that music does convey meanings, it has proven very hard to define them, or to find out how the meanings are communicated. Being a social constructionist, Martin stresses that meanings are not inherent, nor intuitively recognized, 'but emerge and become established (or changed or forgotten) as a consequence of the activities of groups of people in commonsense, taken-for-granted ideas about how it ought to sound. In every culture, some conventional patterns of organized sound become accepted as normal and even natural' (1995: 57).

Tia DeNora (1986: 90) similarly argues that musical communication cannot be understood as a system in which messages pass unambiguously from a 'transmitter' to a 'receiver'. Listeners always have an active role in making sense of sounds. She argues that (ibid.: 93) it is in fact the very ambiguity of music which makes it possible for both ordinary listeners to construct meaning for it, and for those with institutional power to try to impose authoritative meanings on music.

Music also has the power to change the meanings of the visual. Claudia Gorbman (1987: 16–17) has illustrated how a scene of a movie is changed if its music is altered: changing a major mode to a minor makes the scene sadder, adding a tuba creates a humorous effect and a faster tempo accelerates the events and creates optimism.

Sounds and music as gendered discourse

One of the dimensions of social meaning produced by images and music, and those media which combine the two, is gender. Anahid Kassabian (2001: 29–36) has examined the study by Tagg and Clarida, mentioned above, in relation to gender. Particular aspects of the music of television title tunes were clearly associated with women – for instance, harmoniousness and the countryside; and certain aspects with men – force, urban environments and guns. Kassabian noticed that the associations corresponded to the early feminist theory dichotomizing 'nature/women' versus 'culture/men'. The 'pastoral' musical examples in the study by Tagg and Clarida were instrumental music, harmonious, flowing *in legato*, and with simple rhythms. These musical characteristics are also mentioned by Kalinak (1982) as connected to 'the musical ideal wife', and heard by Claudia Gorbman (1987) as the female romantic 'good object' of 1940s' movie music.

Kathryn Kalinak (1982) observed the ways in which the stereotypical images of women, the fallen woman and the ideal wife, in the Hollywood movies of the 1940s and 1950s were accompanied by music. The ideal wife was illustrated by upward melodies played by violins and flutes accompanied by simple rhythms and wide harmony, whereas the fallen woman was coloured by dotted rhythms, chromatic melodies and saxophone solos in blues and jazz styles.

In music research, gender perspective has had many formations. During the first wave of feminist music studies, which is described by the ethnomusicologist

Ellen Koskoff (2000: x) as the *women-centric* research phase, scholars retrieved and studied the work of female composers and artists who had been neglected by earlier music historians, ethnomusicologists and popular music researchers. The second phase can be called the *gender-centric* phase, during which researchers moved into scrutinizing 'music creation and performance as contexts for reinforcing, changing, or protesting gender relations' (ibid.). The third and current phase has focused on the ways in which *musical and social structures* are embedded within each other. Recent feminist music research is underpinned by the postmodern turn in feminist theory, gay and lesbian studies, cultural and performance studies, semiotics and psychoanalysis (Koskoff, 2000).

Today, gender is studied in all forms of music. Susan McClary (1991: 2000) considers Western 'art music' to be ideologically charged through conventional ideas and values held as self-evident – including conceptions concerning gender and conventional sex roles. In popular music studies, gender research focused initially on sex roles: what the men and the women do in and with music, as well as on the lyrics. The gender aspects of the music and the other sounds were relatively neglected until the 1990s when an increasing number of researchers turned their attention to how music is gendered, how masculinity and femininity and the borders between them are constructed.

Case 5.4 Representations of women in popular music

Venice T. Berry (1994: 184–5) considers popular music to be an area of culture which is dominated by men: the gender roles are constructed from a patriarchal listening point/view point. Berry refers to extensive research literature which tends to suggest that woman in popular music is either the ideal saint, a bitch, a whore, a sinner or a victim, and often she is dead (see also Clément, 1989).

The representations of women in popular music vary somewhat with the sub-genre. Rubey (1991), who studied rock music videos of the early 1990s, found that women were mostly objects of violence or aggression, and sex. They were represented condescendingly and rarely as professionals of any sort. The status of women in country music videos seems to be defined according to the women's ability to catch and keep a man. Blues videos represent women as the objects of sexual misuse. Heavy metal videos are generally considered to be most sexist of all, with sadistic overtones. In the videos analysed by Rubey, the 'good' women act only as silent, invisible, or as powerless victims. Characters shown as strong and sexual female beings are made to seem seducers and betrayers (1991: 870–83).

While heavy metal has mainly provided identity models for young white males, rap music has fulfilled a corresponding function for black people. Both, however, represent women in surprisingly similar ways. Berry (1994) considers the image of women in rap music videos as sexist: women are treated with contempt and disrespect. In the worst case, women are objects of sexual, physical and verbal abuse. Berry (1994) has analysed, in addition, the music videos of four pioneering women rap artists: Salt 'N Pepa, MC Lyte, Queen Latifah and Oaktown 3 5 7. Confining her attention to the visuals and the lyrics, she finds that women in videos of those bands are presented as embodiments of black feminist power and energy.

As Holly Kruse (1999: 99) claims, one should not schematically generalize about gender, which is negotiated in relation to other categories of identification, such as race, ethnicity, social class, generation, disabilities and sexuality. Thus, the analysis of gender should examine how these other categories are related.

Case 5.5 Positive gender performance of black women in a music video

Janet Jackson's early 1990s' video 'The Rhythm Nation Compilation', produced a new kind of language of desire and a new position for a female viewer (and listener) (Rubey, 1991: 894–5). At the beginning of the video the directors comment on them, constructing Jackson as a creative, intelligent professional, someone who aims at promoting the status of black people, especially women. The video begins with the words 'We're a nation with no geographic boundaries – pushing forward a world rich of colour lines'. In a stylized factory setting we see a young black man, with tears in his eyes, watching the dancing Jackson and her companions. The lyrics call on people to act collectively to improve social conditions. 'Lend a hand to help your brother do his best – Let's work together to improve our way of life'. The choreography suggests self-control and military discipline. Jackson and the other dancers are dressed in identical black uniforms: they move in unison and in the same rhythm, dancing like robots, with stiff square arm movements. The factory environment, the black-and-white scenery and the choreography hinting at Asian martial arts, underline the atmosphere of remorseless determination. Jackson is also dressed in a uniform and is performing asexually and almost anonymously in front of, but as one of the members of the group (Rubey, 1991).

Various gender stereotypes in popular music are, however, far too simplistic to survive gender analysis. One anthology in which the writers go beyond the obvious stereotypes is *Sexing the Groove* (Whiteley, 1997). They unmask the deeper gendered power structures of rock, as well as the mechanisms which marginalize women, and reveal complex and multi-faceted performances of gender, which deconstruct stereotypes and heterosexuality. The anthology *Sex Revolts* (Reynolds and Press, 1995) foregrounds the radicalism of gender performances in rock, whether they are misogynistic, idealizing women or defining space for female rockers.

All music produces gendered meanings, but in different ways. Each musical genre has created its own gender conventions, which can be decoded by those who have familiarized themselves with that genre. As Kassabian (1993) claims with regard to film music, the analyst must above all take into account the musical genre and its gendered associations and connotations.

The study of music videos and film music

Music and picture – the aural and the visual – are always closely related. It is not only in art forms such as film, theatre, musicals, opera, and dance that they are intertwined, but also in the minds of the perceivers. Waiting rooms, shopping malls, gyms, slalom slopes, techno raves, multimedia programmes, films, jazz clubs, concert halls, music videos as well as jogging with headphones are all experiences in which the visual and the aural are inseparable. In fact, music and sounds are nearly always experienced in situations where the visual plays an important role.

Gender is one of the social categories produced by music as well as images, and the media combine the two. Superficially, it may be thought that gendering is more obvious in images than in music. However, the performance of gender in music, sound and image is multi-faceted and often subtle. It is especially challenging to read gender in texts which combine images and music.

Films and music videos possess their own traditional conventions in combining music and image. In a music video, the visual image functions to market a musical piece as well as the performer/s. In principle, it is a music-driven medium. The most famous of its predecessors is perhaps Disney's *Fantasia*, but short music clips were also made by American bands in the 1940s and the 1960s produced rock movies, most notably those of the Beatles (see Ruud, 1988: 33–49). The music video is usually of the same duration as the sound recording but apart from simply providing a visual accompaniment to the music, the visual presentation has other functions as well. It constructs a public image of the performer or the band, so that the visual content is not determined solely by the musical piece but by the whole marketing package: the performers of music, their career and lifestyle image. There are many categories of musical videos. The genre is a significant factor determining visual style. The American media scholar Ann Kaplan (1987) divided music videos into five groups: (1) the romantic visual treatment of melodic tunes; (2) filmed nihilistic heavy metal videos, often in live concert situations, in which women are represented as objects of the male gaze or even violence; (3) classical videos narrated in the style of Hollywood films; (4) postmodern videos that use pastiche as a stylistic device; and (5) socially aware and critical videos. It is, of course, possible to typify videos in many other ways, and new styles are emerging constantly. However, it is important to take into consideration the chosen video genre as one of the contexts of interpretation.

Dan Rubey (1991) compares the watching of music videos to radio listening: they are not intensively watched but serve more as a background to other activities. The analysis of the content of videos reveals their complexity. Rubey (ibid.: 877–8) claims that the viewers unconsciously or consciously decode several different signs: the genre of music and style, the emotional experiences evoked by the video, the lyrics of the song, the narrative borne by the lyrics or the images, the choreography, performance style, costume, fashion, the physical characteristics of the performers, gestures, staging, performance settings, camera work, colours. The fan constructs a narrative from all these elements. Music videos have taken imagery from advertisements, mainstream and experimental movies, and documentations of performances. The inter-textuality of music videos increases the range of interpretations.

Holly Kruse (1999: 93) claims that video analysis has concentrated too exclusively on the visual data, text and plot, while neglecting music. This has led to a privileging of certain readings. Going further, she argues that it is not enough to analyse the lyrics, musical structure, sound and picture. One has also to take into account the practices of the institutions and economies of popular music, and their effect on the production, marketing and reception of popular music.

The main distributor of music videos, multinational MTV, tends to perpetuate the masculine model of popular music. The music videos of the 1980s constructed women as sex objects. In the 1990s, MTV began to promote videos challenging this tradition, more frequently videos presenting women in active roles, and unconventional gender models (Kruse, 1999: 91–2). Kaplan (1987) also argued that videos of female artists in the 1980s, such as Madonna and Tina Turner, were critiques of the objectifying male gaze, and models of a new female gaze under which men were made the objects of women's desire. While such videos are now familiar in the repertoire of music video channels, however, the same channels still show videos of rap and heavy metal, in which women are the targets of men's sexuality or even violence. Video channels also currently present a wider variety of ethnic performers than hitherto. Rap videos, in particular, have brought more black performers to video channels.

Rubey argues (1991: 902) that music videos offer more space for experimentation and creativity than the traditional TV programmes and movies. They improve the viewer's visual literacy. Between blacks and whites there is a broad spectrum of different skin colours. The same applies to women and men who also can possess and represent several different gender positions. The experimental nature of music videos provides an opportunity to represent and think differently about these social categories.

Two categories of music use in Hollywood movies can be distinguished: films in which the music has been composed, and films whose soundtrack is compiled from separate pieces, which are either pre-existing or composed for the particular film (Kassabian, 2001). According to Kassabian's theory, the former kind of movies offer *assimilation identifications* for the receiver, which are demarcated and controlled according to dominant ideologies. The assimilation identifications assume that the receiver distances herself or himself from every-day reality and identifies with the stereotypical model offered by the movie. For example, the older Hollywood movies offered the identification model of the white heterosexual male, defending the ideology of liberty, and the model of the white, ideal wife sacrificing herself for the sake of the family.

The movies using compiled, separate pieces of music, offer more varied and flexible models, so-called *affiliation identifications*. According to Kassabian's research (2001), Hollywood movies in the 1980s and 1990s have increasingly used musics which offer affiliation identifications. Kassabian claims that this reflects a transition in American culture. Today's movie-goers are not willing to identify with models that are remote from their own everyday realities or with models offered from top down. Sexual, ethnic, disability and gender groups which were previously marginalized, demand today that films offer identifica-tions also for them.

Methods of analysing image and music

All film music researchers recognize the difference between *on-screen sound*, i.e. a sound, the source of which can be seen in the image, and *off-screen sound*, i.e. the source of which comes outside the image; the *diegetic* sound evolving from the story, and the *non-diegetic* sound born outside the story. The French film music scholar Michel Chion (1994) has specified further several ways in which image and music can be combined in films. Although he does not examine in detail the interpretation of cultural meanings in movies, gender interpretations included, he provides some models of the relationship between image and music, which are useful when analysing gender. According to Chion (1994: xxv–xxvi), there is no 'natural' way to combine image and music in films. He argues that a medium combining image and music is perceived in a special way. That is, visual images combined with sound are perceived differently from the way they would be without it, and the visual image in turn adds a significant dimension to the perception of music. Music and image give some sort of addi-tional value to each other. Music which always is connected to time influences the visual perception of movement. The sound can also either reinforce or con-test the visual.

Chion argues (1994: 81) that music differs from the other sounds of the movie as well as the images in the sense that it is freer from time and place. In our opinion, however, it can stretch itself over large historical and spatial distances only inside the film, in relation to the other aspects of the plot. For a perceiver of the film, music is always bounded with its cultural contexts, including its gendered meanings.

Also useful for the gender analysis of audio-visual media are some of the different ways of listening identified by Chion (1994: 25). The analyst can voluntarily direct her or his own listening and choose either (1) *causal listening*, that is, observing cause and effect relationships between music and image; (2) *semantic listening*, that is, interpreting the cultural codes; or (3) *reduced listening*, which concentrates only on the sound. Again, Chion seems to assume that 'abstract' sounds as such, without any cultural meanings can be perceived. We, however, claim that 'pure' reduced listening is not possible because sounds cannot be perceived without some sort of semantic meanings connected to them by the listener. The first two methods, however, are of particular use in the analysis of the gendered meanings. For instance, causal listening may help the analyst to observe how music and image together construct certain gender representations, and semantic listening focuses the listener to interpret representations of gender in music. A particularly useful method for gender analysis is *commutation*, which involves the substitution of different music over the visuals. How does different music change the gender interpretation of the scene? This may further open the mind of the analyst to observe the gendered connotations of music.

The role of music varies throughout any given movie. Sometimes its purpose is to act as a background context for the image, at other times it becomes the focus of attention. Kassabian (2001: 56–60) identifies three functions of film music: *mood, identification* and *commentary*. In a sense, all the music in a movie contributes to atmosphere, but mood music refers specifically to music which closely relates to the emotional tone of other elements in the film. Identification music is a musical idea connected to a certain element of the film: a character, a turn of the plot, a situation, a place or an object. Commentary music either reinforces or contests a scenario. It may well be useful to examine which kind of gender is evoked by mood music, how different elements of the film, its characters and scenes are gendered by music and how gender connotations evoked by music comment upon different scenarios of the film. A particular person, place or object of the film is also often accompanied throughout the movie by the same musical theme, which is called a Leitmotif. Which kind of gender is constructed by it?

One further method of analysing music and image is presented by Nicholas Cook (1998). He argues that music and image must be interpreted in conjunction with each other because they are part of the same experience. Therefore, he begins his analysis transcribing music and image into the same 'score', this produces instructively detailed observations about the complementarity of music and image. Writing a 'score' forces the analyst to listen and see the film in a more detailed way, which in turn evolves in a richer analysis. In our opinion, the musical part of the 'score' does not necessarily have to consist of notes. Instead, it may simply consist of verbal descriptions of music and sounds.

It seems that to date we have relatively few models for the analysis of images, words, sounds and music, and even fewer for cultural and gendered interpretations of a multimedia entity. The concepts of Chion and Kassabian help us to study the relationships between images, music and plot. The method suggested by Cook encourages us to make detailed transcriptions as the first stage of the analysis and Kassabian's concept of the perceiver emphasizes the importance of the position and background of the perceiver/analyst.

Reading gender out of material combining images and music

The gender analysis of music videos, films and other audio-visual media seeks to explore the ways in which they construct gender. This takes place at many levels, never solely on the basis of music, or images, or sounds, or words. Any analysis of only one component remains inadequate as an account of the experience of the perceiver. Femininity and masculinity in music are produced through a range of effects, including sound colour, instrumentation, rhythmic, melodic and other musical elements. In addition, the conventions of a certain musical genre and the position of the 'reader' affect the way gender is read. When music is intertwined with images, dialogue and plot, it needs to be read as part of this often ambiguous mutual complicity.

To analyse the gender construction of a film or video, the steps below would be followed:

1 Making the preliminary narration. Write down your first impressions of the gender performances in the film/video and make your own preliminary 'story' of its gendered content. These first impressions may have a crucial role in forming your research question/s.

2 Defining the theoretical framework, method of analysis and the research question/s. On the basis of the narration you can then select an appropriate theoretical framework and set of analytical concepts, and the analytical method. It is important to know the material well in order to find the relevant research questions.

3 Making the detailed transcription. Provide a detailed transcription of the research material, its images, sounds, and text. Since this is to help in making detailed observations, the selection of visual and sonic elements to be incorporated into the transcription will be based on the theoretical framework, research questions and the central analytical concepts. It is important to note that the transcript already is the first stage in the process of analysis and not simply a neutral presentation of the research material.

4 Analysis of the transcription. The analysis and interpretation of the transcription try to answer the research question/s. At this stage it may be useful to make a preliminary test analysis, which helps to refine the method, transcript, or even

the research question. With the help of the test analysis, it is possible to check whether the transcript is detailed enough for analysis of the data, if the method is appropriate, and which questions the analysis will be able to answer.

The research question directs the analysis and the repertoire of analytical concepts demarcate it. Furthermore, the analysis is underpinned by the chosen theories of gender. The chosen theoretical context may, for example, direct attention to the relationship between the image and music; how music reinforces or contests the gendering presented in the image, and vice versa. Alternatively, you can consider the cultural meanings of gender difference produced by the combination of images and music, including what shades of gender differentiations are absent.

5   From the data-driven perception towards the theory-based interpretation. The fifth phase moves from the data-driven analytical perceptions towards a theory-based interpretation. The interpretation is guided not only by the theoretical framework and specified analytical concepts but also by the contexts which are chosen to inform the analysis and positions from which the interpretation is made. The relevant contexts can include the economic and social conditions, art category and tradition, film/music genre, publishing channel and the background information regarding the performers. It is also important to note that gender is an identity factor which comes into being in relation to other factors like race, ethnicity, nationality, age and social class. Other identity factors constitute special contexts for gender performance. In addition, other texts can be used in the interpretation. The basic premises and meta-theory, the choices made by the researcher, her or his position, the theoretical framework and the contexts of and resources for interpretation need to be explicated in a scholarly project.

The foregoing selective review of film music and music video literature introduces some useful approaches to gender analysis of film and video. The current literature, however, provides few analytical tools for the total constellation of sound, music, text and images which constitutes the total site of the perceiver's physical and cognitive experience. Whether we are aware of it or not, we are all, however, experts in the everyday practices of decoding the gender differentiations in the media. The task of the researcher is to unmask these coding mechanisms. We finish the chapter by moving from sound in film to gender and the everyday soundscape.

Studying gendered soundscapes – some useful conceptual models

If music is poetry, then the sound environment is prose. If music is words, then the sound environment is body language. If music is an aria, then the sound environment is a recitative. If music is a polished statement, then the sound environment means everyday babble, where the morality and structure of society are being mediated and worked out, where they become concrete.

(Ola Stockfelt, 1994)

Sound and image have important similarities, even if they are different media, claims Theo van Leeuwen (1999) in his useful introduction to basic semiotic approaches to studying speech, sound and music. One of the similarities is perspective. Undoubtedly, the study of the perspective of sound and image reveals different presentations and representations of gender.

Perspective hierarchizes elements 'of what is represented by placing some in the foreground, either literally, as in a landscape, or figuratively, as on the cover of a book, which may have letters in the foreground and a photograph in the background, or as in the soundtrack of a film, which may have dialogue in the foreground and music in the background' (Leeuwen, 1999). From the point of view of gender it is revealing to analyse the way music is sometimes brought into the foreground to express the inner emotions of the main characters, as for example in *The Piano* (1993) and *Amélie* (2001).

Case 5.6 Mood music in the film by Jane Champion, *The Piano*

Theo van Leeuwen has noted that in a climactic scene of Jane Campion's movie *The Piano* the conventional figure-ground schema of Hollywood films is reversed. Usually, music creates the mood in the background: as if emotion ought to be 'held back', as less important than the action and dialogue.

In one particularly strong scene music becomes figure, in particular the motif connected to Ada's (Holly Hunter) emotions of longing and loss. In this scene the mute Ada's husband Stewart (Sam Neill) cuts Ada's playing finger with an axe. The music overrides the sounds of the rain, the screaming and the sounds of the chopping, which are in the background 'as if her inner world has, for her, and hence also for us the audience, more reality and more relevance than the outside events, however cruel and oppressive they may be' (Leeuwen, 1999: 19).

In many Hollywood film classics music is foregrounded at points at high emotion, for example, in one of the most famous scenes in cinema, the bathroom scene in *Psycho*. However, it is not the inner emotions of the girl in the shower that are foregrounded in *Psycho*.

The study of perspective is also important in gendered study beyond film, in the study of *soundscape*: our acoustic environment or the total field of sounds – noise, music, sounds of nature, people or technology (Schafer, 1977). In the terminology of soundscape studies as developed by the World Soundscape Project led by R. Murray Schafer, the concepts *figure* and *ground* are referred to as *signal*, and *keynote sound* respectively. Signal is sound with meaning, which we have to listen to consciously. While we might not necessarily be conscious of the keynote sound or the 'ground' of the environment, it nevertheless has profound effects on our mental and physical state. Nowadays different *lo-fi*-hums and rumbles are ubiquitous (Schafer, 1977). In *hi-fi-soundscape* we can easily distinguish the separate sounds, while in *lo-fi-soundscape* sounds blur into each other (see further: Schafer, 1977; Augouyard and Torgue, 1996; Truax, 2000; Järviluoma and Wagstaff, 2002).

Case 5.7 Pitch level and authority

Pitch level is an interesting gendered aspect of sound, both when it comes to the speaking voice and singing. According to van Leeuwen (1999), the same radio journalist spoke in a low, authoritative voice when reading the news on a certain radio station, while on another, youth-oriented station her voice was much higher. In Western societies women lower the pitch of their voices in order to gain authority. Van Leeuwen suggests that men speak in a higher pitch to gain the same effect.

Often it is the contrary that is said to be the case: if men raise the pitch of their voices, they are feminized and lose authority. The language researcher Deborah Cameron (1996) has asked, whether it is correct to associate low voice with authority and the high voice with the lack of it, or is this just sexist prejudice, which considers the special features of women's speech as a 'lack', confirming their inferiority. She takes the latter position (1996: 99).

Case 5.8 Women and the microphone

Anne McKay (2000) refers to Walter Ong's suggestion that the technology of voice amplification helped to open the acoustic public realm to women, who were formerly 'silenced' by virtue of a natural vocal deficiency, reinforced by custom and lack of training. McKay gives less credit to the technology, conceding that while it transformed the character of public speech (men and women were able to speak more intimately), the microphone did not increase the authorization of women to speak publicly (2000: 26; see also Johnson, 2000).

The study of sound and gender is methodologically challenging. The experiencing of sounds – and music (Negus, 1996: 3-4) – is profoundly human, but at the moment we try to share this experience with someone else, we are tied to language and culture.

In the following discussion, we deploy soundscape terminology to study the gendered relationships between signals and keynote sounds, in some scenes from the novel *MotherKind* by author Jayne Anne Phillips (2000). One way to 'listen' to the gendered environment is to read poems and novels. Some authors use the auditive sense in extremely subtle ways, some are more visually or olfactorily oriented. One of the 'ear-oriented' female writers is the American Jayne Anne Philips. In this novel she often describes both the 'real' and the fictive soundscapes heard by the main character, Kate.

Kate has just had a baby and started to take care of her mother who is ill with cancer, and occasionally also her husband's two sons by a previous relationship. Earlier she had been travelling in India, Sri Lanka and Nepal leading a bohemian life and writing poetry. Now, her life is filled with endless caring and mothering.

In the following extract she is at home, with her stepson, Jonah falling asleep against her. The intercom is turned on, humming, in readiness to signal that the baby Alexander has awakened:

> Jonah's head dropped against her. The intercom breathed its airy hum. The hum grew softer, more constant, moving under and around her. The sound was a presence, rhythmic and afloat. She could see the backpack sticking up on the empty beach, but she was too far away to see Alexander inside it. Still, there were no dogs near him, no lions or tigers or bears, and the pack was upright, just as she'd left it. Where there green flies? Were they biting him? She strained to hear a cry and heard the sea. (2000: 245)

The humming sound of the intercom constitutes the keynote sound of this soundscape. Even if Kate is half-asleep, she is ready to be alert, since the keynote of the intercom can at any moment turn into a signal, a meaningful sound. It is also significant that the voice of a newborn baby is loud and piercing (see Tagg, 1994): it demands action from the care-taker, in this case the mother. At this moment there are as yet no signals, and the humming enfolds Kate, its 'presence, rhythmic, afloat' resembling the sounds of the womb, the *chora*. The whole book is full of descriptions of the endless listening 'tasks' that Kate has to perform as a mother: she has to tell the difference between the ordinary and alarming sounds.

In her fitful sleep Kate relives an event in her real life, in which she had to leave her baby boy in a back bag on the empty beach while she was rescuing her stepson from drowning. She can't see any dangerous wild animals, but the essential signal, the possible cry of the baby is masked by the sound of the ocean. The hum of the intercom becomes the hum of sea, preventing her from using her 'primitive ear', *l'oreille primitive*, a concept of the composer Pierre Schaffer (1966) referring to the ear of the 'first human beings'. It was in a constant state of alertness to wild animals and a menacing environment.

The tension Kate experiences between her desires and her life is often described through the sounds that are present in her domestic environment. For example, there are many sections in the book, in which Kate's ambiguous attitudes towards the ever-present hums and rumbles are described. Whose space is being defined by the ventilation hums? She considers herself as a bird in a gilded cage, captive to endless tasks and responsibilities, as signalled by the intercom. She would prefer to fulfil her duties without the soft hum of the intercom. In her earlier life 'she'd always regarded the various droning generator boxes of her neighborhood as ugly and morally questionable, emblematic of the resource-hogging, financial-might-is-right West. Moral responsibility: wasn't it one of the meanings of fortitude' (Phillips, 2000: 241). She has mental pictures and sound memories of India, but '[S]he wouldn't get back there, not for years, not until she was someone else entirely' (ibid.: 243). Now she just wanted 'to sit in roaring air-conditioning until the moisture on her face turned cool and tingly. She really did want to sleep, her senses shrouded in motor hum. If she turned the intercom on full volume, a sharp cry would wake her' (ibid.). As in other writings by mothers, fatigue dominates the consciousness (see Jokinen, 1996: 26). The other sound she hates is the humming of her mother's hospital bed: '"There. Is that high enough? Shall we brush your teeth?" The bed hummed. Kate hated its engine sound and calibrated efficiency even as she was grateful for the mechanisms that raised head or foot by smooth degrees' (ibid.: 249). The hum of the bed and the intercom as well as the howling air-conditioning represent 'blessed noise'. That is how the noise of a loud agricultural machine was described by a Finnish female farmer (an interview by Pöyskö and Vikman, see Pöyskö, 1994). The sound of the machine was deafening but the farmer consider it as 'blessed' since it had made her work so much easier. The *lo-fi*-environment is the price, which even Kate is ready to pay for the mechanisms helping her endless tasks as a carer.

Phillips' writing is replete with sensory descriptions, memories, bodily experiences and thoughts. It can be considered as 'speaking (as) woman' (Irigaray, as interpreted by Whitford, 1991: 50–1) – the language (*langage*) or practices that open up possibilities for women to construct social and symbolic space as female, knowing subjects, producers of truth and culture. Writing is a way to give a body, language, to the enjoyments and pains of motherhood (cf. Jokinen, 1996: 24).

Sounds, space, gender

Soundscape researchers not only associate music with power, but also everyday background hum (Stockfelt, 1994). It's not only the high volume soundscape of 'cock-rock' that can be regarded as a wish to manifest power (see Tagg, 1994). It is said that the steam engine could in technological terms have been less noisy, but its noise level was raised in order to make it more authoritative. To a significant extent, people construct their identities and spaces through the sounds of work and leisure (Stockfelt, 1994). Frequently, this construction is gendered.

Case 5.9 Gendered construction of place through sound

The Swedish musicologist Ola Stockfelt has recounted an instructive story about the gendered construction of place through sound. One evening he was in the bedroom of his flat trying to get his baby girl, a couple of months old, to sleep. Meanwhile, a group of young male neighbours gathered under his bedroom window with their motorcycles, revving the motors very loudly. Stockfelt was furious, and later he realized it was because of the gendered story the noises narrated: they were strong, masculine sounds, he felt, violently coming into his space, where he was supposed to protect his child. The baby apparently was more afraid of the father's fury than of the sounds themselves (Stockfelt, 1994).

It seems reasonable to assume that everybody is entitled to a place in the world, in which they can decide what sounds are to be heard. Sonic power and physical space are unevenly distributed in our world, and this imbalance frequently matches gender demarcations (see, for example, Keightley, 1996). Thus, it is important to listen carefully to the sonic environment.

As mentioned earlier in this chapter, there are relatively few methodological models for the cultural and gendered interpretations of multimedia, and even fewer for doing gendered analyses of soundscapes. In the reading of genders, spaces and soundscapes, however, there are methods and conceptualizations developed by writers on architecture (see, for example, Dyrssen, 1995).

Feminist architectural scholars have long emphasized that it is the sensate users of space who need to be at the centre of scholarly attention (Saarikangas, 2002). The meanings of space are confirmed only in use, in the relationship between the user and the space. Kirsi Saarikangas (2002) takes the idea further in asking: who is actually the 'author' of the space? In one sense, the subjects using the space become the makers of it. The meanings of a lived space are created in the relationship between the way it is used, and its past and present cultural contexts. It is not enough to study the experience purely in terms of visuality. It is the multisensate bodies moving in the space which confirm it, but at the same time the space encourages and discourages certain forms of conduct, many of which are gendered acts, positions, gestures, sounds. How are sounds, lights and smells moving in the space? How does the user moving through the space perceive the spatial perspectives? (ibid.).

A useful concept here is dialogue. Space can be seen as a system of places: a place is space that has become something special through the meanings connected with it. When we move, the places become activated, we enter into dialogue with the places (Stenvos, 1992). Sound and music are important elements in this dialogue. We must not suppose that music and dance simply 'reflect' spaces. As Martin Stokes has argued, they offer the means by which the hierarchies of space can be negotiated and changed (Stokes, 1994: 4–5; see also Blundell et al., 1993; DeNora, 2000). Music, dance and sounds cannot be separated from the spatial practices and processes they are part of, but on the other hand, it would be reductive to simply consider them as their reflections.

When studying gendered lived spaces, it is thus necessary to interpret the sounds situationally. The new methodological developments in soundscape studies stress that we need to study the subjective and shared meanings of sounds, *in situ* and dynamically (Tixier, 2002). It is not only the case that there are gendered differences between persons in the ways they interpret sounds, but we have to also take into account the fact that we never hear the same sound twice, even if the physical vibrations are the same (Stockfelt, 1994). In fact, following Augoyard, we could say that we never hear sounds as such but sound effects (or as Björn Hellström has translated the concept: *sonic effects*) (*l'effets sonaires*) produced by spatial, perceptive and cultural 'distortions' (Augoyard, 1999: 123; Augoyard and Torgue, 1996; Hellström, 2002).

Gender is useful in the analyses of the dynamics of listening and hearing sonic effects. It helps us further in considering the multiple ways in which people both consciously and unconsciously *use* sounds in creating their meaningful lived spaces, rather than just passively succumbing to the sonic circumstances as victims of 'noise'.

Exercise 5.1 Analysis of an advertising jingle

The controversial American ethnomusicologist Alan Lomax and his colleague, the anthropologist Conrad Arensberg, accumulated massive data (a total of 3,525 songs from 233 cultures) on different singing styles throughout the world, and compared the styles to the structures of the societies that had produced them. Lomax made a number of interesting Durkheimian claims relating to the issue of gender. For example, the societies in which one finds the highest occurrence of polyphonic singing are gatherers, early gardeners and horticulturalists, where women bring in the major or equal share of the food. 'In such societies women are not so likely to be shut away from the public center of life; not so often are they passive witnesses of social events, but active participants at or close to the center of the stage' (Lomax, 1968: 167).

Lomax goes so far as to comment on the pitch and voice colour, making inferences about their connections to the societal structures. He describes the voice quality of oriental bardic singers as 'generally tense, high, thin, feminine and placatory' (Lomax, 1970: 64) and the 'nasal resonance and throaty burr' of the American Indian singer as 'expressive of a full-blown and unrepressed masculinity' (1970: 66; both quoted in Martin, 1995: 132). Peter Martin (ibid.: 133) has argued, 'Such conclusions, it may be suggested, tell us more about the conventional representation of gender in modern American society than about the songs and their place in the cultures from which they have been arbitrarily plucked.' In fact, Lomax did test all the songs with American students, and Peter Martin's point that this material could in fact be used to study the gender representations of the 1960s' young, educated generation, has considerable force. But if we are interested in an understanding of gender and song-culture, it is through a detailed and intensive ethnography, not via decontextualized trait lists that we gain the best result (see Feld, 1984).

However, qualitative analysts can use Lomax's analysis in order to invigorate our imagination, which is exactly what we ask you to do in this exercise. As van Leeuwen (1999) has noticed, the interactive structure of the leader–chorus–antiphony singing model which Lomax found in authoritative, patriarchal societies can be found in many con-temporary advertising jingles. The leader is someone who can act as a role model for the 'target' audience. In many forms of contemporary popular music 'the leader is a male singer and the chorus a group of female "back up" vocalists, which enacts (from the point of view of the musicians) and represents (from the point of view of the audience) a relationship of male dominance' (van Leeuwen, 1999). However, if jingles are directed at children, the solo singer is most often another child, 'the "opinion leader" of the peer group or a "grown-up person singing" in a "funny clown's voice", with a choir of children responding' (ibid.: 73).

Your task is to do the following:

1   Record a set of advertisements on a videotape.
2   Analyze the interaction of voices in one of the advertisements, the solos and choirs, the nasality, the high-pitched and low-pitched voices, the perspective between voices and other sounds, and reflect upon how these different voices construct, maintain or challenge our present gender stereotypes.

Exercise 5.2 Analysis of a music video

Record a music video, make a preliminary narration of it, identify its dominant features. Transcribe chronologically its content, for instance, separating the following aspects: (1) things you can hear in music (instruments, repeated patterns, male/female singers, etc.); (2) characters and their actions; (3) spaces and angles of the picture; (4) extra effects (sudden cuts, hologram pictures, etc.); (5) scenes; and (6) clothing, decorations.

Analyse the video with the help of the detailed transcription aiming at answering this main research question: What kinds of gender/s are constructed by the video? Pay attention also to these subsidiary questions: How are the genders presented and performed? Is there a difference between the roles/movements/gestures of men and women; observe performed gender ambivalence ('third gender') or neutrality ('fourth gender')? How are masculinity and femininity performed in music (instruments, sound qualities, rhythms)? What are the gendered aspects of the scenes in the extract; how and where are the different characters situated and how do they move in the space? What about the visual effects, setting and clothing? Do music and image reinforce or contest each other? Which aspects of gender are stressed, deconstructed, ironized or caricatured?

Finally, discuss how the genders constructed by the video correspond to the gendered image of that particular musical genre and with the gender order most familiar to you. What were your own reactions when watching the video? Why did you react in that way, that is, define your own gendered position.

Exercise 5.3 Does soundscape have gender?

1   Keep a sound diary for a week. Write down the gendered sounds you hear in your total everyday environment – whether they are human sounds, technological sounds, music or media sounds, sounds of nature. Pay particular attention to the sounds that seem to you to be 'feminine' or 'masculine'. Why do they? Do you hear ways of producing sounds that are common to men, or to women? How do women/men or boys/girls construct their own place or even power using different sounds?
2   Discuss in small groups, whether in your own culture(s) there exist sounds that are considered to be 'men's sounds' or 'women's sounds'. Are there sounds that you couldn't even imagine being produced by the opposite sex?

6

Research Reporting and Gender

Locating myself into my own text   108
Searching for feminine styles of writing   111
Experimental representations   113

> Clutching her pencil, she wonders how 'the discipline' will view the writing she wants to do. Will it be seen as too derivative of male work? Or too feminine? Too safe? Or too risky? Too serious? Or not serious enough? Many eyes bore in on her, looking to see if she will do better or worse than men, or at least as well as other women.
>
> (Ruth Behar, 1995)

Throughout the chapters of this book we have been exemplifying ways to analyse gender as socially constructed and performed interaction. 'Science' can be heard and seen as socially constructed and performed interaction. So too, the idea of an acceptable 'scholarly research report'.

One of the lasting crucial debates regarding good research reporting has been the relationship between 'subjective' and 'objective' writing, and this question has traditionally been gendered (see Fox Keller, 1985). In this chapter we consider the different sides of this problem. First, we talk about the rhetoric of 'objectivity' in social science reporting. Then we focus on the ways in which the 'subjective' and the feminine can and have been brought into the debate. Do we have to choose between these two modes? Finally, we show some of the ways in which hybrid forms or experimental writing may be used in qualitative research.

Within the sciences there is to be found a deeply rooted mythology in which the objectivity, rationality and spirit are considered to be 'masculine' as opposed to the 'feminine' subjectivity, emotions and nature (ibid.: 11). Even the sociology of sciences tacitly maintains these borderlines: public vs private, impersonal vs personal, masculine vs feminine. Thus this mythology reinforces the autonomy of science. Science and gender form networks of differentiation and connectedness (ibid.: 12). The tacit reinforcement of the autonomy of science masks the fundamental context-boundedness of the fact that all scholarly activities are both deeply personal and social.

Often, the most 'objective results' of science have another side to them, which reveals the most personally constructed impersonality. The 'unsigned' picture the scientist has drawn, in fact, has a signature (ibid.: 14). The objectivist ideology claims from the outset that it is anonymous and disinterested, and thus uncontaminated by personal bias. The subject is shut outside and a veil is thrown over the everyday practices of the scholars. The claim that the 'scientific is personal' may be regarded as a logical extension of the feminist claim that the personal is political (ibid.: 13).

The key word here is rhetoric. The cool remoteness of a scholarly paper, especially a scientific one, is one kind of rhetoric: 'It is this apparent lack of style that gives scientific accounts their authority' (Back, 1998: 286). As Latour and Woolgar (1979) have said, the goal for most natural and social science writing is to achieve 'literary inscription': to write in such a way that a given argument will be accepted as true; that the argument has *facticity*. Les Back has argued that some feminist empiricists see objectivity as a useful tool for many feminist political goals. If we consider 'objectivity' solely as a masculine virtue, we lose the benefits of this rhetoric (Back, 1998).

Locating myself into my own text

Researchers do have many ways of incorporating the narrator into their texts. Leena Eräsaari (1995) has summarized these, following the generalized models articulated by the narratologist Rimmon-Kenan (1983).

It is clear that the narrator always has a voice. At the level of the text the question is: how does the narrator/scholar use different forms and degrees of narrator's 'visibility' in her or his text? Some narrators act as participants in the researchers' stories, some remain detached. The degree of visibility or 'audibility' of the narrator's voice in the text theoretically varies from total absence to full visibility, but in practice, there is no such thing as total invisibility (Eräsaari, 1995: 65). Eräsaari connects the visibility of the narrator to reliability. The researcher can try to reduce her or his participation in the text if that disclosure of participation makes the story sound unreliable. She or he can try to do this even in cases in which they have conducted participatory observation 'in the field'. On other occasions, reliability may depend on the visibility of the participation on the part of the researcher. Under those circumstances the scholarly narrator tries to convince the reader that she or he has really been 'there' (ibid.: 69).

Most scholarly fields have for at least a century enjoined distance, objectivity and abstraction. People have been troubled if personal stories have been inserted into 'the analysis of impersonal social facts', writes the anthropologist Ruth Behar (1996: 12). Behar and some other feminist writers agree with the ethno-psychiatrist Devereux, who as long ago as the 1960s was very much concerned with humanizing scientific research through more explicitly subjective approaches so that it would become more objective. By admitting the subjective element, we are recognizing the reality of the research dynamic, rather than attempting to falsify it. This, arguably, produces a more objective account of what really takes place (Devereux, 1967, as quoted in Behar, 1996: 28–9.)

In the field of Women's Studies, many writers have actively resisted the scientific conventions of representation, where the voice of an author is hiding behind 'the objective', often using the passive voice. Feminists have strategically encouraged this counter-discourse in order to create new, *gender-bound voices* and modes into the scientific professional practices. Thus, in Women's Studies the *personal and autobiographical mode of speaking* is now the most popular and widely used mode of representation, interwoven with the research topic and professional representations concerning the results of a study. This research discourse, which demands the explicit presence of a writing subject, has often been characterized as feminine.

The question of how to incorporate the autobiographical and the personal into research prose is currently a matter of vigorous debate in ethnography, anthropology and sociology. In anthropology the so-called 'literary turn' emerged in the mid-1980s, with the publication of *Writing Culture* (Clifford and Marcus, 1986). Based on postmodernist and textual criticism, it argued for the self-evident but neglected fact that the main work of anthropologists is in fact *writing*.

Women anthropologists, however, were provoked by the fact that they had been excluded from the book on the basis that their texts failed to be both feminist *and* textually innovative. As Ruth Behar (1995: 5) has put it: 'To be a woman writing culture became a contradiction in terms: women who write experimentally are not feminist enough, while women who write as feminists write in ignorance of the textual theory that underpins their own texts.' *Writing Culture* included work by only one female writer, historian Mary Pratt. But she asked a very good question: how is it possible that such interesting people as anthropologists write such extremely dull books (Pratt, 1986; see also Behar, 1995: 4)? Partly in reaction to *Writing Culture*, Ruth Behar and Deborah A. Gordon edited a remarkable collection of innovative essays called *Women Writing Culture* (1995).

Gradually, the 'literary turn' infiltrated the social sciences until it became an accepted element in all qualitative research writing to incorporate the voice of an active subject.

Ruth Behar (1996) connects the audibility of the voice of the scholar in research writing to the issue of emotions. She talks about 'writing vulnerably', arguing that when one writes vulnerably, people respond to the text vulnerably. It generates emotions in readers. Behar puts the question of whether emotions enhance or compromise intellectual understanding, and answers: 'Emotion has only recently gotten a foot inside the academy and we still don't know whether we want to give it a seminar room, a lecture hall, or just a closet we can air out now and then' (1996: 16). How to go about the problem of writing emotion into our more or less autobiographical narratives we fit into our scholarly texts, without draining emotion from the ethnography?

While it is not easy to write 'objectively', as though at a distance, Behar emphasizes that vulnerable writing requires yet greater skill. To locate oneself in one's own text, as in the epigraph to this chapter, does not entail a full-length autobiography. Rather, it requires a clear understanding of 'what aspects of the self are the most important filters through which one perceives the world and, more particularly, the topic being studied' (ibid.: 13). Usually, in ethnographies the intellectual and emotional connections between the observer and the observed have not been thought through adequately. Thus the problem is not so much the fact that a personal voice has been used but the fact that it has not been used well enough: 'a personal voice, if creatively used, can lead the reader, not into miniature bubbles of navel-gazing, but into the enormous sea of serious social issues' (ibid.: 14).

The presence of a writing subject in research texts has awakened critical voices concerning the degree to, and the manner in which a researcher can be present in her or his writing. In the field of feminist literary criticism, for example, Nancy K. Miller (1991) has called for more nuanced conceptualizations of locations and positions of the author in her or his text. Concerning the degree and mode of presence she asks if the autobiographical and the personal are same things in criticism (ibid.: 1). She argues for the right to be explicitly autobiographical, however, the level of self-disclosure may vary. Self-representation may take the form of self-narrative, where this act of writing may constitute a political act. It may also be an attempt to explicate the relations between the personal and the theoretical other. To be personal does not inevitably require autobiography. Instead, personal presence may, for example, be *intensive engagement* with the issue under investigation (ibid.: 1991: 1–4, 24–5).

Finnish sociologist Eeva Jokinen (1998) extends Miller's conceptualization by defining three different forms of authorial presence in the research text. A scholar may be (1) *autobiographically present* by representing her or his lived experience in the context of the research text, implicating herself or himself in the issues studied. Commitment to the study implies intensive presence in the text. (2) *Being personal* in research reporting means striving to intensify the relationship between the researcher and the implied reader who is always constructed during the act of writing. To produce the implied reader in the text involves manipulating the real readers into the role of the implied reader, inviting them to engage with it. Jokinen adds a further aspect to Miller's definition of autobiographical and personal presence. (3) This is expressed through the word '*positional*', by which she means a researcher's self-disclosure of her or his theoretical position in relation to her or his imagined or real audience (ibid.: 188–91).

Searching for feminine styles of writing

Two significant strands of feminist thought may be distinguished as 'American' and 'French' (Keränen, 1993: 41–87). At the beginning of this chapter we quoted a feminist who represents 'American feminism', Helen Fox Keller. Marja Keränen (1993: 41–87; see also Eräsaari, 1995: 53) has characterized this American school of feminism through its emphasis on the marginalization of women in the sciences. Their response is to attempt to change the disciplines through a greater focus on areas and methodologies which reflect 'typically' female interests. On the other hand, according to Keränen, the 'French' strand follows structuralist theories which assert that there is no life outside language. Language, text and science are analysed as an integral part of human thinking and action. Unlike the 'American' approach, they deny the possibility that women can step outside language or science. Rather, they try to re-read and reinterpret the central texts that have created our culture.

The American approach tries to get from the outside to the inside of the discourse, and to change masculine ways of writing in science. One way of doing this is to talk as 'I', acknowledging the feminist position that the personal is the political. This localizing and positioning of oneself has also been criticized. Philosopher Sara Heinämaa (1993) argues that it is impossible to position oneself fully: defining a position leads to the localizing of the positioning, which in turn leads to the positioning of the localizing of the positioning – in other words, to endless reflection. No single researcher can negotiate this endless process. Heinämaa prefers the French idea of the endless process. In the spirit of Luce Irigaray, she suggests that it is better to tell riddles, to hint obliquely and through metaphors, rather than to clarify your points in hegemonic terms. Rather than flatter their intelligence with the illusion of comprehension, sustain incomprehensibility to the point of provocation (Heinämaa, 1993).

While Anglo-American feminists have examined the social construction of gender, the French feminists have focused on language. They aim at deconstructing the patriarchal power structures in language and, in addition, search for feminine styles of writing, a kind of counter language. The main figures of French feminism, Luce Irigaray, Hélène Cixous and Julia Kristeva are often called the priestesses of 'writing the body'. Although some of their shared ideas concerning language and subjectivity will be discussed, it is as important to acknowledge the differences between these theorists. What is common to Cixous, Irigaray and Kristeva is their assertion that women have failed to assume the subject position in language, and they envisage a linguistic space where gender divisions might disappear. A key source for French feminist philosophy was structuralist psychoanalyst Jacques Lacan who argued that women will always be at a disadvantage in language, because the organizing principle of language is the opposition between the masculine phallic presence and the feminine lack (Nye, 1998: 157).

Cixous, Irigaray and Kristeva thus saw that the masculine is the only possible subject position in language within the patriarchal symbolic system. Language, the symbolic, is 'logocentric' (Cixous, 1974), the masculine imaginary transformed into the social. French feminists began to seek a position for women in language, which would escape the symbolic order and which would be self-defined, symbolically and socially represented by and for women. In their opinion, it is necessary for women to represent themselves as subjects of language, because our patterns of thinking and understanding are coded in and by our language. 'Language determines the ways in which we perceive gender and come to know ourselves as gendered beings and the ways in which society perceives gender and creates gendered subjects' (Humm, 1994: 110). Systems of language are also systems of power; language is thus a means of maintaining patriarchal power.

In their views regarding the specifics of women's language, Kristeva, Cixous and Irigaray manifest significant differences, which we will now review. Julia Kristeva links linguistics to the materiality of the body. In that respect, she follows Freud's aim of materializing the unconscious. For Kristeva, psyche and body are textually joined, and she therefore focuses on psychosexual determinants of textual practices. Kristeva seeks the feminine language in the 'semiotic', in the pre-Oedipal language, which occurs between the mother and the child. She uses psychoanalysis to articulate this 'semiotic' discourse, which occurs *before* the symbolic, formal language of society. This, however, does not mean that the semiotic is completely abandoned when moving into the symbolic. Rather, it is simultaneously present as a subtext in the symbolic discourse (Humm, 1994: 100–2), where it can be found as absences, contradictions, irregular rhythms, and ruptures, in place of emotion. The 'masculine' logics and linearity are challenged by the 'feminine' rhythmic and cyclical sensuality (Kristeva, 1981a).

Hélène Cixous and Luce Irigaray also use psychoanalysis, but in a more radical and arguably more feminist way. They use a psychoanalytical approach to formulate a discourse which expresses women's physiology and sexuality, aiming at changing phallocentric language and order (Humm, 1994: 94–6). 'Speaking (as) woman' (*parler femme* by Irigaray 1985a and 1985b) and 'writing the feminine' (*écriture féminine* by Cixous, 1975) seek such spaces and forms of language, to open up new horizons for our understanding of the world, including sexual difference. Cixous suggests direct links between women's desire and language, *écriture féminine*, which could be 'found in metaphors of female sexuality and women's genitals and libidinal differences' (Humm, 1994: 16–17). In Hélène Cixous' words, 'Life becomes text starting out from my body. I am already text. History, love, violence, time, work, desire inscribe it in my body' (1991: 52).

Irigaray's many sided studies on language use have demonstrated how speaking is never neutral (2002). She questions if there are 'within the logical and syntatico-semantic mechanisms of accepted discourse, an openness or a degree of liberty that would permit the expression of sexual difference' (ibid.: 255) and searches for feminine modes of speaking, *parler femme*. She aims at rewriting language by exploring the ways in which female sexuality can create new forms of knowledge. She further argues that as long as the accepted discourse is based on sexual indifference, how can we know anything about the 'masculine' either, or about what the language of the male sex might be (Irigaray, 1985b: 128). Thus, *parler femme* 'implies a different mode of articulation between masculine and feminine desire and language' (ibid.: 136). In all, Irigaray stresses the sexuation of discourse and culture, which all too often are presented as asexual.

Nothing definite can be said about what 'speaking (as) women' or a sexuated discourse might be, because they do not exist. Some guiding thoughts may, however, be picked up from Irigaray's texts. Research evidence shows that the speech which we might comprehend as feminine is dialogical and contextual, connected with the concrete world. It does not pretend to be 'objective' but, instead expresses subjectivities. It is fluid and it rejects binary hierarchies, such as subject/object dichotomies. (Whitford, 1991a: 4–5). 'Feminine syntax' would involve nearness, proximity, but in such an extreme form that it would preclude any distinction of identities, any establishment of ownership, thus any form of appropriation.' (Irigaray, 1991: 136). In essence, a sexuated mode of speaking includes two, instead of one.

The styles of writing deployed by these theorists reveal much about their approach to language. Irigaray's work varies from the traditional or more or less conventional philosophical texts of her early writings to poems and interviews addressed to a general readership – all her texts, however, are firmly grounded in the Western (and more recently also Eastern) philosophical tradition. The reader is challenged to construct the meanings when reading her texts. According to Margaret Whitford, editor of *The Irigaray Reader* (1991a), it is exactly this creative power of imagination which is found when reading Irigaray, because her aim is to 'produce writing that cannot be reduced to a narrative or a commentary, but that calls for an interlocutor' (Whitford, 1991: 13–14). The reader is *seduced to respond creatively* to Irigaray's text and, therefore, 'the response is often as much to do with the reader as with Irigaray' (ibid.: 1991, 14).

Experimental representations

I must be ready to put my world into words, and to offer it to the other.

(Emmanuel Levinas, 2001)

Leena Eräsaari (1995: 71) has asked if the objectives defined by Cixous, Kristeva and Irigaray are unattainable, both aesthetically and psychologically. She believes not: French feminism has proven to be fruitful for her and for many others: 'It sounds like an impossible idea that the *jouissance* of the text and the feminine or poetic writing could be realised within the "periphery" of Finnish Academia – and, on top of that, within research on bureaucracy. Nevertheless, it it the best idea I can think of' (ibid.: 72). Eräsaari has studied bureaucracy in social work.

French feminists exemplify a broader spectrum of feminist and postmodernist critiques of traditional qualitative writing practices. Laurel Richardson (1998: 354) has referred to all these new writing forms as *experimental representations*. They violate prescribed conventions and transgress the boundaries of social science writing genres. One reason why Richardson advocates experimental writing is that it is 'a practical and powerful way to expand one's interpretive skills and to make one's "old" materials "new"' (Richardson, 1998: 354). She encourages students to try these different forms of writing, even if one chooses to write a final paper in a conventional form. This is because for her writing is also a way of 'knowing': a method of discovery and analysis. It is exactly through exploratory writing in different ways that we discover new aspects of our topic and our relationship to it. Writing is not only 'writing up' research, as many students are taught to conceptualize it. Writing is a way of researching, a method of inquiry. Furthermore, the meaning of qualitative research resides in the reading process, and thus it has to be read, not scanned. (ibid.: 345–7).

Richardson identifies five types of experimental writing, which she groups under the heading of *evocative representations*: (1) *narrative of the self* is a highly personalized and revealing text 'in which an author tells stories about his or her own lived experience' (ibid.: 355–6). In these stories accuracy is not the main point, but the narratives of the self allow the 'field-worker' to exaggerate, swagger, and to relive the experience.

Case 6.1 Narrative of the self: Leena Eräsaari and *The Mask of a Creep*

Leena Eräsaari, a former social worker, wrote her book in 1990 combining a general critique of bureaucracy with her personal experience of the difficulties of operating in and adapting to a bureaucratic organization. As a researcher of bureaucracy and social work, Eräsaari later said that she had to follow her own footsteps backwards, to the place where she began, to 'descend to crawling on all fours' (1995: 49). In this sense, her situation was different from anthropologists who try to learn to 'stand on their own two feet' within a new culture that is hitherto unknown. Eräsaari was, on the contrary, trying to find a way to move away from her self-explanatory self-evident experience of 'a native'.

There were two reasons for her choosing the mode of autobiographic *confession*. One was that feminist confessional literature authorizes the manifestation of high levels of emotion. She wanted to find a form which would accommodate her despair, anger and hatred. As she says, there are no legitimate ways of expressing emotions within (social) science. The other reason was that it enabled her to focus on particular kinds of significant detail.

The book was given an ambiguous reception, including silence, and confusion regarding its genre. From others, particularly publishers and their referees, she received anonymous 'expert' reviews, often suggesting ways in which the manuscript *could* be turned into a scientific publication. The book was finally published, but it never really gained the status of 'a real ethnography' among Finnish scholars. In any event, Eräasaari reported that writing an autobiography helped her in many ways to grow up both as a scholar and a person. She learned how to distance herself from her experiences in social work and also gained self-esteem while fighting to get her book published.

The other forms of evocative representations listed by Richardson include (2) *ethnographic fictional representations*, in which writers define their work as fiction. She suggests that this may be a good way for the writer to 'listen' to the material from different angles (Richardson, 1998: 356). (3) *Poetic representation* makes us consider the role of the *prose trope* in constituting knowledge: if, following Richardson's advice, we just try, for example, writing sociological interviews as poetry, it will help us to problematize reliability, validity, and 'truth' (ibid.). (4) *Ethnographic drama* is 'a way of shaping an experience without losing the experience' (ibid.: 357), and it can give voice to something which has remained unspoken. An interesting, postmodernist form of evocative representation is (5) *mixed genres*, in which the researcher uses, and crosses the boundaries of, many different literary, artistic and scientific genres (ibid.: 357–9).

There have already been anthropologists 'mixing genres', and their work has often been suspect in scholarly circles. For example, Ruth Benedict was accused of writing too well, since her anthropology read like poetry (Babcock, 1995). Margaret Mead is often trivialized in spite of being perhaps the most famous anthropologist of our century. Between 1925 and 1975 she published more than, 1300 books, biographies, articles and reviews. Her reputation as a serious scholar was affected by her image as a 'popularizer', who, as a public intellectual, wrote for a non-academic readership, engaging with public issues of her time. Her writing was even ridiculed as the ethnography of the 'Rustling-of-the-wind-in-the-palm-trees school' (Lutkehaus, 1995).

Writers who opposed the flat impersonal voice of Papa Franz Boas as the norm of ethnographic discourse include Ella Cara Deloria and Zora Neale Hurston. The last mentioned 1930s' American ethnographer has been described by bell hooks as being 'at the cutting edge of a new movement in ethnography and anthropology that has only recently been actualized'. Hurston was writing in multiple voices: as an ethnographer, writer, and member of the community. Her storytelling style, writing through the 'spy-glass of Anthropology' was ground-breaking (see Hérnandez, 1995).

It was not only women but also 'native' and 'minority' anthropologists who have been excluded from the canon of 'experimental writing'. It is oddly assumed that experiments in writing are not likely to come from 'people of color or those without tenure' (Behar, 1996: 8). It was the publication of *This Bridge Called My Back* (Moraga and Anzaldúa, 1984) that triggered the most painful of all crises in the North American feminist movement, by observing that 'Other Women' had either been excluded from its project of liberation, or had been included 'matronizingly'. In order to democratize women's access to writing, the book therefore included diverse forms of fiction and essays. Similarly, *Women Writing Culture* includes 'biographical, historical, and literary essays, fiction, autobiography, theater, poetry, life stories, travelogues, social criticism, fieldwork accounts, and blended texts of various kinds' (Behar and Gordon, 1995: 7).

A useful example of the *mixed genre* type of evocative representation is Margaret Wolf's book *A Thrice-Told Tale* (1992) in which she recounts the same event, which happened thirty years earlier in a village in Taiwan, in three different ways: as fictional story, as field notes, and a social science paper. All these stories had different genres and styles, and, most interestingly, different 'outcomes'.

Why is it, then, that – with these few exceptions – ethnographers so often write dull books which are 'killed by science'? Mary Pratt (1986: 38–41) has observed that in order to be ethnography, the writing has to fulfil two conditions. First, the researcher has to present her or himself working in the field. The other is that this presence of the researcher has to be erased from the end result, the report. The minimum requirement is that the researcher–narrator must not be present too obviously. When a book is not considered to be an ethnography (as in the case of Leena Erräsaari above), the reason can often be found in its failure to fulfil these conditions.

It must be noted that male students and scholars can also experience ambivalence and anxiety when they contemplate the paths of scholarly (and other) 'masculine heroes' before them (Lehtonen, 1995). Like the only male writer in the collection *Women Writing Culture*, Laurent Dubois (1995), they may well ask, 'Has my story already been written?' But it is a more fundamental anxiety than this 'anxiety of influence' that hovers over women who write (Behar, 1996: 15), and their experimentation: the anxiety of authorship itself. Ruth Behar attributes this to the fact that they were the 'daughters', receiving the tradition from stern literary 'fathers' who viewed them as inferiors (ibid.). Hélène Cixous has linked the same phenomenon to the guilt that a woman who intends to write feels about her desire to master the language. That's why she has to imagine away her own involvement into this desire for mastery.

Anni Vilkko (1997) has used the metaphor of 'shaking hands with the reader' when talking about the opening sequences of the autobiographies she has studied. Now you are about to close this book. Instead of shaking hands with you, we wave goodbye. As a farewell we say: you can only learn writing through writing. You can 'seduce' your readers and find the intensity in your writing through practising, being open-minded and exploring different literary genres and different ways of writing gender', as a way of conducting qualitative research.

Exercise 6.1 Positioning your own gendered self

Write a new first chapter in your gendered life story using the third person. Use experimental writing and write intensely in order to 'seduce' the reader to continue to read your story. You can choose to write it as a short story, a poem, or a dramatic dialogue.

Exercise 6.2 Discussing gender narratives

Discuss your old and new stories in small groups. How have the exercises in gender analysis affected your perception of your own gender image? What about your ideas regarding gender? Have they changed? In which ways? Why?

Bibliography

Abu-Lughod, Lila (1987) *Veiled Sentiments: Honor and Poetry in a Bedouin Society.* Berkeley, CA: University of California Press.

Abu-Lughod, Lila (1990) 'Can there be a feminist ethnography?' *Women and Performance: A Journal of Feminist Theory,* 5 (1): 7–27.

Angrosino, Michael V. (1986) 'Son and lover: the anthropologist as nonthreatening male', in Tony Larry Whitehead and Mary Ellen Conaway (eds), *Self, Sex, and Gender in Cross-Cultural Fieldwork.* Urbana, IL: University of Illinois Press. pp. 64–83.

Anttonen, Anneli, Henriksson, Lea and Nätkin, Ritva (eds) (1994) *Naisten hyvinvointi-valtio* (Women's Welfare State) Jyväskylä: Vastapaino.

Assmuth, Laura and Tapaninen, Anna-Maria (1994) 'Antropologian naisongelma' (The problem of women in anthropology), in Tapio Nisula (ed.), *Näköaloja kulttuureihin. Antropologian historiaa ja nykysuuntauksia.* Helsinki: Gaudeamus.

Augoyard, Jean-François (1999) 'The cricket effect', in Henrik Karlsson (ed.), *From Awareness to Action,* No. 89. Stockholm: The Royal Swedish Academy of Music, pp. 116–25.

Augoyard, Jean-François and Torgue, Henry (eds) (1996) *A l'Ecoute de l'environnement.* Marseilles: Editions Parenthèses.

Babcock, Barbara (1995) 'Not in the absolute singular', in Ruth Behar and Deborah A. Gordon (eds), *Women Writing Culture.* Berkeley, CA: University of California Press. pp. 104–30.

Back, Les (1998) 'Reading and writing research', in Clive Seale (ed.), *Researching Society and Culture.* Thousand Oaks, CA: Sage, pp. 285–96.

Baker, Carolyn (1984) 'The Search for Adultness: Membership work in Adolescent-Adult Talk'. Human Studies 7, pp. 301–323.

Baker, Carolyn (1997) 'Membership categorization and interview accounts', in David Silverman (ed.), *Qualitative Research: Theory, Method and Practice.* London: Sage, pp. 130–43.

Barz, Gregory and Cooley, Timothy (eds) (1996) *Shadows in the Field: New Perspectives for Fieldwork in Ethnomusicology.* Oxford: Oxford University Press.

Baszanger, Isabelle and Dodier, Nicolas (1997) 'Ethnography: relating the part to the whole', in David Silverman (ed.), *Qualitative Research: Theory, Method and Practice.* London: Sage, pp. 8–23.

Beck, Ulrich (1992) *Risk Society: Towards a New Modernity.* London: Sage.

Behar, Ruth (1995) 'Introduction: out of exile', in Ruth Behar and Deborah A. Gordon (eds), *Women Writing Culture.* Berkeley, CA: University of California Press.

Behar, Ruth (1996) *The Vulnerable Observer: Anthropology that Breaks Your Heart.* Boston: Beacon Press.

Behar, Ruth and Gordon, Deborah A. (eds) (1995) *Women Writing Culture.* Berkeley, CA: University of California Press.

Bell, Diane, Caplan, Pat and Jahan Karim, Wazir (1993) *Gendered Fields: Women, Men and Ethnography*. London: Routledge.

Benstock, Shari (ed.) (1988) *The Private Self: Theory and Practice of Women's Autobiographical Writings*. Chapel Hill, NC: University of North Carolina Press.

Berger, Peter and Luckmann, Thomas (1975) *The Social Construction of Reality: A Treatise in the Sociology of Knowledge*. Harmondsworth: Penguin.

Berry, Venice (1994) 'Feminine or masculine: the conflicting nature of female images in rap music', in Susan C. Cook and Judy S. Tsou (eds), *Cecilia Reclaimed: Feminist Perspectives on Gender and Music,* Urbana, IL: University of Illinois Press, pp. 183–201.

Billig, Michael (1987) *Arguing and Thinking: A Rhetorical Approach to Social Psychology*. Cambridge: Cambridge University Press.

Blundell, Valda, Shepherd, John and Taylor, Ian (1993) 'Editors' introduction', in *Relocating Cultural Studies: Developments in Theory and Research*. London and New York: Routledge.

Bonvillain, Nancy (1995) *Women and Men: Cultural Constructions of Gender*. Englewood Cliffs, NJ: Prentice-Hall.

Braidotti, Rosi (1994) *Nomadic Subjects: Embodiment and Sexual Difference in Contemporary Feminist Theory*. New York: Columbia University Press.

Bridges, J. (1993) 'Pink or blue: gender-stereotypic perceptions of infants as conveyed by birth congratulation card', *Psychology of Women Quarterly*, 17: 193–205.

Brodzki, Bella and Schenk, Celeste (1988) *Life/lines: Theorizing Women's Autobiography*. Ithaca, NY: Cornell University Press.

Brown, Jane D. and Schultze, Laurie (1990) 'The effects of race, gender, and fandom on audience interpretations of Madonna's music videos', *Journal of Communication*, 40: 88–102.

Bruner, Jerome (1986) *Actual Minds, Possible Worlds*. Cambridge, MA: Harvard University Press.

Butler, Judith (1990) *Gender Trouble: Feminism and the Subversion of Identity*. London: Routledge.

Butler, Judith (1993) *Bodies that Matter: On the Discursive Limits of 'Sex'*. New York: Routledge.

Butler, Judith (1995) 'For a careful reading', in Seyla Benhabib, Judith Butler, Dricilla Cornell and Nancy Fraser, *Feminist Contentions: A Philosophical Exchange*. New York: Routledge.

Butler, Judith (1997) *The Psychic Life of Power: Theories in Subjection*. Stanford, CA: Stanford University Press.

Button, Graham (1977) 'Comments on conversation analysis', *Analytic Sociology*, 1 (2): 1009–14.

Cameron, Deborah (1996) *Sukupuoli ja kieli: Feminismi ja kielentutkimus*. Tampere: Vastapaino (orig. *Feminism and Linguistic Theory*. Macmillan, 1985, 1992).

Caplan, Pat (1988) 'Engendering knowledge: the politics of ethnography (Part 2)', *Anthropology Today*, 4 (6): 14–17.

Chion, Michael (1994) *Audio-Vision: Sound on Screen*. New York: Columbia University Press.

Cicourel, Aaron V. (1983) *The Reproduction of Objective Knowledge: Common Sense Reasoning in Medical Decision Making*. San Diego: University of California Press.

Cixous, Hélène (1974) *Prénoms de personne*. Paris: Seuil.

Cixous, Hélène (1975) 'The laugh of the Medusa.' Trans. by Keith and Paula Cohen. *Signs* 1976 1 (4): 875–93.

Cixous, Hélène (1991) *Coming to Writing and Other Essays*, edited by Deborah Jenson. Cambridge, MA: Harvard University Press.

Clément, Catherine (1989) *Opera, or, The Undoing of Women*. London: Virago Press.

Clifford, James and Marcus, George E. (eds) (1986) *Writing Culture: The Poetics and Politics of Ethnography*. Berkeley, CA: University of California Press.

Clifford, James (1990) 'Notes on (field)notes', in Roger Sanjek (ed.), *Fieldnotes: The Makings of Anthropology*. Ithaca, NY: Cornell University Press, pp. 47–70.

Cohen, Sara (1991) *Rock Culture in Liverpool*. Oxford: Clarendon Press.

Coleman, Wil (1990) 'Doing masculinity, doing theory', in *Men, Masculinities and Social Theory*. Jeff Hearn and David Morgan, (eds), London: Unwin Hyman, pp. 186–202.

Connell, R.W. (2000) *The Men and the Boys*. Oxford: Polity Press.

Cook, Nicholas (1998) *Analysing Musical Multimedia*. Oxford: Clarendon Press.

Cornell, Drucilla (1995) 'What is ethical feminism?' in Seyla Benhabib, Judith Butler Drucilla Cornell and Nancy Fraser (eds), *Feminist Contentions: A Philosophical Exchange*. New York: Routledge.

Cuff, E.C. (1980) *Some Issues in Studying the Problem of Versions in Everyday Situations*. Occasional Paper no. 3. Manchester: University of Manchester Press.

Deaux, Kay and Kite, Mary E. (1987) 'Thinking about gender', in *Analyzing Gender: A Handbook of Social Science Research*. Newbury Park, CA: Sage Publications.

de Beauvoir, Simone ([1949] 1986) *The Second Sex*. New York: Penguin Books.

De Certeau, Michel (1984) *The Practice of Everyday Life*. Berkeley, CA: University of California Press.

Dee, Leila (1975) 'Woman's worlds – three encounters', in André Béteille and T.N. Madan (eds), *Encounter and Experience: Personal Accounts of Fieldwork*. Delhi: Vikas Publishing House PVT LTD, pp. 157–77.

de Lauretis, Theresa (1987) *Technologies of Gender: Essays on Theory, Film and Fiction*. Bloomington, IN: Indiana University Press.

DeNora, Tia (1986) 'How is extra-musical meaning possible? Music as a place and space for "work".' *Sociological Theory* 4 (Spring): 84–94.

DeNora, Tia (2000) *Music in Everyday Life*. Cambridge: Cambridge University Press.

Devereux, George (1967) *From Anxiety to Method in the Behavioral Sciences*. The Hague: Mouton.

Devor, Holly (1989) *Gender Blending: Confronting the Limits of Duality*. Bloomington, IN: Indiana University Press.

Dingwall, Robert (1981) 'The ethnomethodological movement', in Geoff Payne (ed.), *Sociology and Social Research*. London: Routledge.

Drew, Paul (1978) 'Accusations: the occasioned use of members' knowledge of "religious geography" in describing events', *Sociology* 12: 1–22.

Dubois, Laurent (1995) ' "Man's darkest hours": maleness, travel, and anthropology', in Ruth Behar and Deborah A. Gordon (eds), *Women Writing Culture*. Berkeley, CA: University of California Press, pp. 306–21.

Dyrssen, Catharina (1995) *Musikens rum. Metaforer, ritualer, institutioner. En kulturanalytisk studie av arkitektur i och omkring musik* (The Space of Music: Metaphors, Rituals, Institutions). Arkitektur, byggnadsplanering. Gothenburg: Chalmers Technical University.

Ebron, Paulla and Lowenhaupt, Tsing Anna (1995) 'In dialogue? Reading across minority discourses', in Ruth Behar and Deborah A. Gordon (eds), *Women Writing Culture*. Berkeley, CA: University of California Press, pp. 390–411.

Edwards, Derek (1997) *Discourse and Cognition*. London: Sage.

Eglin, Peter and Hester, Stephen (1992) 'Category, predicate and task: the pragmatics of practical action', *Semiotica*, 3/4: 243–68.

Eräsaari, Leena (1990) *Nilkin naamio: sosiaaliraportti* (The Mask of a Creep: A Social Report). Helsinki: Tutkijaliitto.

Eräsaari, Leena (1995) *Kohtaamisia byrokraattisilla näyttämöillä* (Meetings in Bureaucratic Scenes). Helsinki: Gaudeamus.

Eribon, Didier (1988) 'Levi-Strauss interviewed', *Anthropology Today*, 4(6): 3–5.

Fahlgren, Margaretha (1987) *Det underordnade jaget. En studie om kvinnliga självbiografier* (The Subordinate Self: The Study of Womanly Autobiographies). Stockholm: Jungfrun.

Feld, Steven (1984) 'Sound structure as social structure', *Ethnomusicology*, xxviii (3): 383–409.

Forsberg, Hannele, Ritala-Koskinen, Aino, Järviluoma, Helmi and Roivainen, Irene (1991) 'MCD-analyysillä moraalisen järjestyksen lähteille?' in Hannele Forsberg et al. (eds), *Sosiaalisia käytäntöjä tutkimassa*. Tampere: University of Tampere, Dept. of Social Policy Tampereen yliopisto, sosiaalipolitiikan laitos, tutkimuksia Sarja A, no. 1, pp. 111–21.

Foucault, Michel (1979a) *The History of Sexuality, Vol. 1: An Introduction* (trans. Robert Hurley). Harmondsworth: Penguin.

Foucault, Michel (1979b) *Discipline and Punish: The Birth of the Prison*. New York: Vintage Books.

Foucault, Michel (1980) *Power/Knowledge: Selected Interviews and Other Writings 1972–77*. Ed. by Colin Gordon. New York: Pantheon.

Fox Keller, Evelyn (1988/1985) *Tieteen sisarpuoli* (Reflections on Gender and Science). Tampere: Vastapaino.

Friedman, Susan Stanford (1988) 'Women's autobiographical selves: theory and practice', in Shari Benstock (ed.), *The Private Self: Theory and Practice of Women's Autobiographical Writings*. London: Routledge, pp. 34–62.

Garfinkel, Harold (1967) 'Passing and the managed achievement of sexual status in an intersexed person, part 1', in H. Garfinkel (ed.), *Studies in Ethnomethodology*. Englewood Cliffs, NJ: Prentice-Hall.

Garfinkel, Harold (1984) *Studies in Ethnomethodology*. Cambridge: Polity Press.

Geertz, Clifford (1995) *After the Fact: Two Countries, Four Decades, One Anthropologist*. Cambridge, MA: Harvard University Press.

Geertz, Clifford (1989) *Works and Lives: The Anthropologist as Author*. Stanford, CA: Stanford University Press.

Gergen, Mary M. and Gergen, Kenneth J. (1993) 'Narratives of the gendered body in popular autobiography', *The Narrative Study of Lives*, 1: 191–218.

Gergen, Mary (1992) 'Life stories: pieces of a dream', in George C. Rosenwald and Richard L. Ochberg (eds), *Storied Lives: The Cultural Politics of Self-Understanding*. New Haven, CT: Yale University Press, pp. 127–44.

Giddens, Anthony (1991) *Modernity and Self-identity: Self and Society in the Late Modern Age*. Cambridge: Polity Press.

Giddens, Anthony (1994) *Beyond Left and Right*. Cambridge: Polity Press.

Ginsburg, Faye (1993) 'The case of mistaken identity: problems in representing women on the right', in Caroline B. Brettell (ed.), *When They Read What We Write. The Politics of Ethnography*. Westport, CT: Bergin & Garvey.

Glass, Frank W. (1983) *The Fertilizing Seed: Wagner's Concept of the Poetic Intent*. Ann Arbor, MI: Hanoncourt.

Glover, David and Kaplan, Cora (2000) *Genders*. London: Routledge.

Golde, P. (ed.) (1986) *Women in the Field: Anthropological Experiences*. Berkeley, CA: University of California Press.

Gorbman, Claudia (1987) *Unheard Melodies: Narrative Film Music*. Bloomington, IN: Indiana University Press.

Hall, Stuart and du Gay, Paul (1996) *Question of Cultural Identity*. London: Sage.

Hearn, Jeff and Morgan, David (1990) 'Men, masculinities and social theory', in Jeff Hearn and David Morgan (eds), *Men, Masculinities and Social Theory*. London: Unwin Hyman, pp. 1–18.

Heilbrun, Carolyn G. (1989) *Writing a Woman's Life*. New York: Ballantine Books.

Heinämaa, Sara (1993) 'Paikka tutkimuksessa. Henkilökohtaisen paikanmäärityksen vaatimus naistutkimuksessa' (Place in research: the claim for personal positioning in women's studies), *Naistutkimus-Kvinnoforskning*, (1): 22–35.

Hellström, Björn (2002) 'The sonic identity of European cities: a presentation of the work conducted by the Swiss-French researcher Pascal Amphoux', in Helmi Järviluoma and Gregg Wagstaff (eds), *Soundscape Studies and Methods*. Helsinki: The Finnish Society for Ethnomusicology Publications.

Heritage, John (1984) *Garfinkel and Ethnomethodology*. Worcester: Polity Press.

Heritage, John (1996) *Harold Garfinkel ja etnometodologia*. (Harold Garfinkel and Ethnomethodology). Helsinki: Gaudeamus.

Hérnandez, Graciela (1995) 'Multiple subjectivities and strategic positionality: Zora Neale Hurston's experimental ethnography', in Ruth Behar and Deborah A. Gordon (eds), *Women Writing Culture*. Berkeley, CA: University of California Press, pp. 148–65.

Herndon, Marcia and McLeod, Norma (1981) *Music as Culture*. Norwood: Norwood Editions.

Hester, Stephen and Eglin, Peter (eds) (1997) *Culture in Action: Studies in Membership Categorization Analysis*. Washington, DC: International Institute for Ethnomethodology and Conversation Analysis.

Hinde, R., Tamplin, A. and Barrett, J. (1993) 'Gender differences in the correlates of preschoolers' behavior', *Sex Roles*, 28 (9–10): 607–22.

Holland, Dorothy and Quinn, Naomi (eds) (1987) *Cultural Models in Language and Thought*. Cambridge: Cambridge University Press.

Humm, Maggie (1994) *A Reader's Guide to Contemporary Feminist Literary Criticism*. New York: Harvester-Wheatsheaf.

Hyvärinen, Matti (1997) 'Rhetoric and conversion in student politics: looking backward', in T. Carver and Matti Hyvärinen (eds), *Interpreting the Political: New Methodologies*. London: Routledge, pp. 18–38.

Hyvärinen, Matti (1998) 'Lukemisen neljä käännettä' (Four turns of reading), in Matti Hyvärinen, Eeva Peltonen and Anni Vilkko (eds), *Liikkuvat erot: Sukupuoli elämäkertatutkimuksessa* (Differences in Motion: Doing and Reading Gender in Biographical Research). Tampere: Vastapaino, pp. 311–36.

Hyvärinen, Matti, Peltonen, Eeva and Vilkko, Anni (1998) 'Johdanto' (Introduction), in Matti Hyvärinen, Eeva Peltonen and Anni Vilkko (eds), *Liikkuvat erot: Sukupuoli elämäkertatutkimuksessa* (Differences in Motion: Doing and Reading Gender in Biographical Research). Tampere: Vastapaino, pp. 7–25.

Ihanus, Juhani (1995) *Toinen: kirjoituksia psyykestä, halusta ja taiteista.* Helsinki: Gaudeamus.

Irigaray, Luce (1993) *The Three Genders: Sexes and Genealogies.* Transl. Y. Gillian and C. Gill. New York: Columbia University Press.

Irigaray, Luce (1985a) *Speculum of the other Woman.* Transl. by Gillian C. Gill. Ithaca, NY: Cornell University Press.

Irigaray, Luce (1985b) *This Sex Which Is Not One.* Transl. by Catherine Porter with Carolyn Burke. New York: Cornell University Press.

Irigaray, Luce (1991) *The Irigaray Reader,* edited by Margaret Whitford. Oxford: Blackwell Publishers Ltd.

Irigaray, Luce (2002) *To Speak is Never Neutral.* Trans. by Gail Schwab. London: Continuum

Jackson, Jean E. (1986) 'On trying to be an Amazon', in Tony Larry Whitehead and Mary Ellen Conaway (eds), *Self, Sex, and Gender in Cross-Cultural Fieldwork.* Urbana, IL: University of Illinois Press, pp. 263–74.

Jackson, Jean E. (1990) 'Fieldnotes as a symbol of professional identity', in Roger Sanjek (ed.), *Fieldnotes: The Makings of Anthropology.* Ithaca, NY: Cornell University Press, pp. 3–33.

Järviluoma, Helmi (1986) *Musiikki, liikkeet, hillikkeet* (Music, Movements, Restraints). Tampere: University of Tampere.

Järviluoma, Helmi (1991a) 'Kenttä tutkijan asenteena', in Pirkko Moisala (ed.), *Kansanmusiikin tutkimus. Metodologian opas.* Helsinki: Sibelius-Akatemia ja VAPK.

Järviluoma, Helmi (1991b) 'Kentän paikallinen tuottaminen: "Tutkijan" ja "pelimannien" kategoriatyöskentelyn analyysia' (Local construction of field), in Hannele Forsberg et al. (eds), *Sosiaalisia käytäntöjä tutkimassa.* Tampere: Tampereen yliopisto, sosiaalipolitiikan laitos, tutkimuksia Sarja A, no. 1, pp. 139–61.

Järviluoma, Helmi (1996) 'Nuoret äänimaisemoijina. Paikan ja tilan äänellisestä tuottamisesta' (Young people as soundscapers. The construction of place and space via sound), in Leena Suurpää and Pia Aaltojärvi (eds), *Näin nuoret. Näkökulmia nuoruuden kulttuureihin.* Helsinki: Finnish Literature Society, pp. 204–29.

Järviluoma, Helmi (1997) *Musiikki, identiteetti ja ruohonjuuritaso. Amatöörimuusikkoryhmän kategoriatyöskentelyn analyysi* (Music and Identity at Grassroots Level). Tampere: Acta Universitatis Tamperensis 555.

Järviluoma, Helmi (2000) 'Local construction of gender in a Finnish PELIMANNI musicians group', in Beverley Diamond and Pirkko Moisala (eds), *Music and Gender,* Urbana, IL: University of Illinois Press.

Järviluoma, Helmi and Wagstaff, Gregg (eds) (2002) *Soundscape Studies and Methods.* Helsinki: The Finnish Society for Ethnomusicology Publications, University of Turku.

Järviluoma, Helmi and Roivainen, Irene (1997) 'Täsenkategorisoinnin analyysi kulttuurisena metodina' (MCA as a cultural method), *Sosiologia,* 34 (1): 15–25.

Jayyusi, Lena (1984) *Categorization and the Moral Order.* London: Routledge & Kegan Paul.

Jayyusi, Lena (1991) 'Values and moral judgement: communicative praxis as moral order', in G. Button (ed.), *Ethnomethodology and the Human Sciences.* Cambridge: Cambridge University Press, pp. 227–51.

Jelinek, Estelle C. (1980) *Women's Autobiography: Essays in Criticism*. Bloomington, IN: Indiana University Press.

Jelinek, Estelle C. (1986) *The Tradition of Women's Autobiography: From Antiquity to the Present*. Boston: Wayle Publishers.

Johnson, Bruce (2000) *The Inaudible Music: Jazz, Gender and Australian Modernity*. Sydney: Currency Press.

Jokinen, Eeva (1998) 'Keskustelua' (Discussion), *Janus*, 6 (2): 188–91.

Jokinen, Eeva (1996) *Väsynyt äiti. Äitiyden omaelämäkerrallisia esityksiä*. (The Tired Mother: Autobiographical Representations of Motherhood). Helsinki: Gaudeamus.

Kalinak, Kathryn (1982) 'The fallen woman and the virtuous wife: musical stereotypes in *The Informer, Gone with the Wind*, and *Laura*', *Film Reader* 5: 76–82.

Kaplan, Ann (1987) *Rocking Around the Clock: Music, Television, Postmodernism and Consumer Culture*. New York: Methuen.

Kaskisaari, Marja (2000) *Kyseenalaiset subjektit. Tutkimuksia omaelämäkerroista, hetero-järjestyksestä ja performatiivisuudesta* (Questionable Subjects: Studies on Autobiographies, Heterosexual Order and Performativity). Jyväskylä: SoPhi.

Kassabian, Anahid (1993) 'A woman scored: feminist theory and the pop music sound-track', *Studies in Symbolic Interaction*, 15: 51–68.

Kassabian, Anahid (1997) 'At the twilight's last scoring', in David Schwarz, Anahid Kassabian and Lawrence Siegel (eds), *Keeping Score: Music, Disciplinarity, Culture*. Charlottesville, VA: University of Virginia.

Kassabian, Anahid (2001) *Hearing Film: Tracking Identifications in Contemporary Hollywood Film Music*. New York: Routledge.

Keesing, Roger M. (1987) 'Models, "folk" and "cultural", paradigms regained', in *Cultural Models in Language and Thought*. Dorothy Holland and Naomi Quinn (eds), Cambridge: Cambridge University Press, pp. 369–93.

Keightley, Keir (1996) '"Turn it down" she shrieked. Gender, domestic space and high fidelity', *Popular Music*, 15 (2): 149–78.

Keränen, Marja (1993) *Modern Political Science and Gender: A Debate Between the Deaf and the Mute*. Jyväskylä: Jyväskylä Studies of Education, Psychology and Social Research 103.

Kessler, J. Suzanne and McKenna, Wendy (1979) *Gender: An Ethnomethodological Approach*. Chicago: University of Chicago Press.

Knuuttila, Seppo (1992) *Kansanhuumorin mieli. Kaskut maailmankuvan aineksina*. Helsinki: SKS (Finnish Literature Society).

Knuuttila, Seppo (1994a) 'Mentaliteetti, mieli ja merkitys', in Seppo Knuuttila, *Tyhmän kansan teoria. Näkökulmia menneestä tulevaan* (Theory of the 'Dumb Folk'). Helsinki: SKS (Finnish Literature Society).

Knuuttila, Seppo (1994b) 'Etnometodologia suullisen perinteen strategiana ja tutkimu-sotteena', in Seppo Knuuttila, *Tyhmän kansan teoria. Näkökulmia menneestä tulevaan*. Helsinki: SKS (Finnish Literature Society).

Kolodny, Annette (1986) 'Map for rereading: gender and the interpretation of literary texts', in Elaine Showalter (ed.), *The New Feminist Criticism: Essays on Women, Literature and Theory*. London: Virago Press, pp. 46–62.

Komulainen, Katri (2000) 'The past is difference – the difference is past', *Gender and Education*, 12 (4): 449–62.

Koskoff, Ellen (1993) 'Mirian sings her song: the self and the other in anthropological discourse', in Ruth Solie (ed.), *Musicology and Difference: Gender and Sexuality in Music Scholarship*. Berkeley, CA: University of California Press, pp. 149–63.

Koskoff, Ellen (2000) 'Foreword', in Pirkko Moisala and Beverley Diamond (eds), *Music and Gender*. Illinois: University of Illinois Press.

Kosonen, Päivi (1995) *Samuudesta eroon. Naistekijän osuus Georges Gusdorfin, Philippe Lejeunen, Paul de Manin ja Nancy K. Millerin autobiografiateorioissa* (From Sameness to Difference: The Role of the Female Author in Theories of Autobiography by Georges Gusdorf, Philippe Lejeune, Paul de Man and Nancy K. Miller). Tampere: Tampereen yliopisto. Yleinen kirjallisuustiede. Julkaisuja 27.

Kosonen, Päivi (2000) *Elämät sanoissa. Eletty ja kerrottu epäjatkuvuus Nathalie Sarrauten, Marguerite Durasin, Alain Robbe-Grillet'n ja Georges Perecin omaelämäkerrallisissa teksteissä* (Lives in Words: Lived and Narrated Discontinuity in the Autobiographical Texts written by Nathalie Sarraute, Marguerite Duras, Alain Robbe-Grillet and Georges Perec). Helsinki: Tutkijaliitto.

Krieger, Laurie (1986) 'Negotiating gender role expectations in Cairo', in Tony Larry Whitehead and Mary Ellen Conaway (eds), *Self, Sex, and Gender in Cross-Cultural Fieldwork*. Urbana, IL: University of Illinois Press, pp. 117–27.

Kristeva, Julia (1981a) 'Women's time', *Signs*, 7 (1): 77–92.

Kristeva, Julia (1981b) 'From one identity to an other' in *Desire in Language: A Semiotic Approach to Literature and Art*. Oxford: Blackwell, pp. 124–47.

Kruse, Holly (1999) 'Gender', in Bruce Horner and Thomas Swiss (eds), *Key Terms in Popular Music and Culture*. Oxford: Blackwell, pp. 85–101.

Lähteenmaa, Jaana (2002) Tyttöjä pelastamassa – mistä ja miksi? (Saving Girls - From What and Why?) in Sanna Aaltonen and Päivi Honkatukia (eds) *Tulkintoja Tytöistä* Helsinki: Finnish Literature Society.

Lakoff, George (1987) *Women, Fire, and Dangerous Things: What Categories Reveal about the Mind*. Chicago: The Chicago University Press.

Lakoff, George and Johnson, Mark (1980) *Metaphors We Live By*. Chicago: The University of Chicago Press.

Lakoff, George and Turner, Mark (1989) *More than Cool Reason: A Field Guide to Poetic Metaphor*. Chicago: The University of Chicago Press.

Lamb, Michael E., Owen, Margaret T. and Chase-Lansdale, Lindsay (1979) 'The father-daughter relationship: past, present and future', in Claire B. Kopp and Martha Kirkpatrick (eds), *Becoming Female: Perspectives on Development*. New York: Plenum Press.

Latour, Bruno and Woolgar, Steve (1986/1979) *Laboratory Life: The Construction of Scientific Facts*. Princeton, NJ: Princeton University Press.

Laurila, Sirkka and Vilkko, Anni (2001) 'Experience of widowhood in later life', paper presented at the symposium 'Ageing but Coping: Women as Workers and Widows', University of Helsinki, Helsinki, August.

Lawless, Elizabeth (1992) '"I was afraid someone like you … an outsider … would misunderstand": negotiating interpretative differences between ethnographers and subjects,' *Journal of American Folklore*, 105 (417): 302–14.

Lee, J.R.E. (1984) 'Innocent victims and evil-doers', *Women's Studies International Forum*, 7: 69–73.

Leeuwen, Theo van (1999) *Speech, Music, Sound*. Basingstoke: Macmillan.

Lehtonen, Mikko (1995) *Pikku jättiläisiä. Maskuliinisuuden kulttuurinen rakentuminen* (Small Giants: The Cultural Construction of Masculinity). Tampere: Vastapaino.

Leinbach, M. and Fagot, B. (1993) 'Categorical habituation to male and female faces: gender schematic processing in infancy', *Infant Behavior and Development*, 16: 317–32.

Leinbach, M., Hort, B. and Fagot, B. (1997) 'Bears are for boys: metaphorical associations in young children's stereotypes', *Cognitive Development*, 12: 107–30.

Levinas, Emmanuel (2001) *Totality and Infinity: An Essay on Exteriority*. Translated by Alphonso Lingis. Pittsburg, PA: Duquesne University Press.

Lomax, Alan (1968) *Folk Song Style and Culture*. New Brunswick: Transaction Books.

Lomax, Alan (1970) 'Song structure and social structure', in M.C. Albrecht, J.H. Barnett and M. Griff (eds), *The Sociology of Art and Literature*. New York: Praeger.

Lurie, Nancy Oestrich (1972) 'Two dollars', in Solon T. Kimball and James B. Watson (eds), *Crossing Cultural Boundaries: The Anthropological Experience*. San Francisco: Chandler, pp. 151–63.

Lutkehaus, Nancy C. (1995) 'Margaret Mead and the "rustling-of-the-wind-in-the-palm-trees school" of ethnographic writing', in Ruth Behar and Deborah A. Gordon (eds) *Women Writing Culture*. Berkeley, CA: University of California Press, pp. 186–206.

Marcus, Laura (1994) *Auto/Biographical Discourses*. Manchester: Manchester University Press.

Marcus, Laura (1996) 'Border crossings: recent feminist auto/biographical theory', in S. Leydesdorff, L. Passerini and P. Thompson (eds), *Gender and Memory: International Yearbook of Oral History and Life Stories*, vol. IV. New York: Oxford University Press.

Marshall, Barbara L. (2000) *Configuring Gender: Explorations in Theory and Politics*. Peterborough, ON: Broadview Press.

Martin, Peter (1995) *Sounds and Society: Themes in the Sociology of Music*. Manchester: Manchester University Press.

Marx Ferree, Myra and Hess, Beth B. (1987) 'Introduction' in *Analyzing Gender: A Handbook of Social Science Research*. Newbury Park, CA: Sage Publications.

Mason, Mary (1980) 'The other voice: autobiographies of women writers', in James Olney (ed.), *Autobiography: Essays Theoretical and Critical*. Princeton, NJ: Princeton University Press, pp. 207–35.

McAdams, Timothy (1993) *Stories We Live By: Personal Myths and the Making of the Self*. New York: Morrow.

McClary, Susan (1991) *Feminine Endings: Music, Gender and Sexuality*. Minneapolis: University of Minnesota Press.

McClary, Susan (2000) *Conventional Wisdom: The Content of Musical Form*. Berkeley, CA: University of California Press.

McHoul, A.W. (1987) 'An initial investigation of the usability of fictional conversation for doing conversation analysis', *Semiotica*, 67 (1/2): 83–104.

McHoul, A.W. and Watson, D.R. (1984) 'Two axes for the analysis on "Commonsense" and "formal" geographical knowledge in classroom talk', *British Journal of Sociology of Education*, 5 (3): 281–302.

McKay, Anne (2000) 'Speaking up: voice amplification and women's struggle for public expression', in Caroline Mitchell (ed.), *Women and Radio: Airing Differences*. London: Routledge.

Merleau-Ponty, Maurice (1962) *Phenomenology of Perception*. London: Routledge.

Miller, Nancy K. (1980) 'Women's autobiography in France: for a dialectics of identification', in Sally McConnel-Ginet, Ruth Borker and Nelly Fuhrman (eds), *Women and Language in Literature and Society*. New York: Praeger Publishers, pp. 258–73.

Miller, Nancy K. (1988a) *Subject to Change: Reading Feminist Writing*. New York: Columbia University Press.

Miller, Nancy K. (1988b) 'Arachnologies: the woman, the text, and the critic', in Nancy K. Miller, *Subject to Change: Reading Feminist Writing*. New York: Columbia University Press, pp. 77–101.

Miller, Nancy K. (1991) *Getting Personal: Feminist Occasions and other Autobiographical Acts*. New York and London: Routledge.

Miller, Nancy K. (1994) 'Representing others: gender and the subjects of autobiography', *Differences: A Journal of Feminist Cultural Studies*, 6 (1): 1–27.

Miller, Nancy K. (1995) 'Our classes, ourselves: maternal legacies and cultural authority', in Mae G. Henderson (ed.), *Borders, Boundaries and Frames: Essays in Cultural Criticism and Cultural Studies*. New York: Routledge, pp. 145–70.

Millet, Kate (1977) *Sexual Politics*. London: Virago.

Moi, Toril (1990) 'Feministinen, naispuolinen ja naisellinen' (Feministic, womenly and feminine) in Pirjo Ahokas and Lea Rojola (eds), *Marginaalista muutokseen, feminismi ja kirjallisuudentutkimus* (From Marginal to Change, Feminism and Literary Studies). Turku: Turun yliopiston offsetpaino.

Moisala, Pirkko (1991) *Cultural Cognition in Music: Continuity and Change in the Gurung Music of Nepal*. Jyväskylä: Gummerus.

Moisala, Pirkko (1993) 'Kenttätyön merkitys etnomusikologiassa. Otteita nepalilaisesta kokemuksesta' (The meaning of fieldwork in ethnomusicology), *Musiikin suunta*, 1: pp. 13–26.

Moisala, Pirkko (2000a) 'Gender performance in music', *Women and Music: Journal on Gender and Culture* vol. 3, 1999: 1–17. University of Nebraska Press.

Moisala, Pirkko (2000b) 'Decentering the term woman composer', in Martina Homma (ed.), *Frau Musica (Nova): Komponieren heute/Composing today*. Sinzig: Studio Verlag, pp. 83–94.

Moisala, Pirkko (2000c) 'Gender negotiation of composer Kaija Saariaho in Finland: Women composer as nomadic subject', in Pirkko Moisala and Beverley Diamond (eds), *Music and Gender*. Illinois: University of Illinois Press, pp. 166–88.

Moisala, Pirkko (2001) 'Gender performance in a Finnish dance music restaurant: reflections on a multicultural fieldwork experiment', *Croatian Journal of Ethnology and Folklore Research*, 38 (1): 7–19.

Moisala, Pirkko and Diamond, Beverley (eds) (2000) *Music and Gender*. Urbana, IL: University of Illinois Press.

Moraga L. Cherrie and Anzaldha, Gloria E. (eds) *This Bridge Called my Back: Writings by Radical Women of Color*. New York: Kitchen Table, Women of Color Press.

Mosse, George L. (1996) *The Image of Man: The Creation of Modern Masculinity*. Oxford: Oxford University Press.

Murphy, Yolanda and Murphy, Robert F. (1974) *Women of the Forest*. New York: Columbia University Press.

Näre, Sari and Lähteenmaa, Jaana (1991) 'Moderni suomalainen tyttöys: altruistista individualismia' (Modern Finnish girlhood: altruistic indidualism), in *Letit liehumaan*. Helsinki: SKS, pp. 329–37.

Negus, Keith (1996) *Popular Music in Theory: An Introduction*. Cambridge: Polity Press.

Nicholson, Linda (1994) 'Interpreting gender', *Signs*, 20 (1): 79–105.

Nicholson, Linda (ed.) (1997) *The Second Wave: A Reader in Feminist Theory*. New York: Routledge.

Nikander, Pirjo (2000) ' "Old" versus "little girl": a discursive approach to age categorization and morality', *Journal of Aging Studies*, 14 (4): 335–58.

Nouri, Marilyn and Helterline, Marilyn (1998) 'Narrative accrual and the life course', *Research on Aging*, 20 (1): 36–65.

Nye, Andrea (1998) 'Semantics', in Alison M. Jaggar and Iris Marion Young (eds), *A Companion to Feminist Philosophy*. Oxford: Blackwell Publishers, pp. 153–61.

Oakley, Ann (1981) 'Interviewing women: a contradiction in terms?' in Helen Roberts (ed.), *Doing Feminist Research*. London: Routledge, pp. 30–61.

Oakley, Ann (1997) 'A brief history of gender', in Ann Oakley and Juliet Mitchell (eds), *Who's Afraid of Feminism? Seeing Through the Backlash*. London: Hamish Hamilton, pp. 29–55.

Oakley, Ann (1998) 'Science, gender and women's liberation: an argument against post-modernism', *Women's Studies International Forum*, 21 (2): 133–46.

Oakley, Ann (2000) *Experiments in Knowing: Gender and Method in the Social Sciences*. New York: The New Press.

Öhrström, Eva (1987) *Borgerliga kvinnors musicerande i 1800-talets Sverige*. Gothenberg: Skrifter från Musikvetenskapliga institutionen 15.

Okely, Judith (1992) 'Anthropology and autobiography: participatory experience and embodied knowledge', in Judith Okely and Helen Callaway (eds), *Anthropology and Autobiography*. London: Routledge.

Peräkylä, Anssi (1990) *Kuoleman monet kasvot*. Tampere: Vastapaino.

Peräkylä, Anssi and Silverman, David (1990) 'AIDS counselling: the interactional organization of talk about "delicate" issues', *Sociology of Health and Illness*, 12 (3): 293–318.

Peräkylä, Anssi and Silverman, David (1991) 'Owning experience: describing the experience of other persons', *Text*, 11 (3): 441–80.

Personal Narratives Group, (1989) *Interpreting Women's Lives: Feminist Theory and Personal Narratives*. Bloomington, IN: Indiana University Press.

Phillips, Jayne Anne (2000) *MotherKind*. London: Jonathan Cape.

Potter, Jonathan and Wetherell, Margaret (1989) *Discourse and Social Psychology: Beyond Attitudes and Behaviour*. London: Sage.

Poulin-Dubois, D., Serbin, L., Kenyon, B. and Derbyshire, A. (1994) 'Infants' intermodal knowledge about gender', *Developmental Psychology*, 30, 436–42.

Pöyskö, Maru (1994) 'Aspects of soundscapes in cowsheds' in Helmi Järviluoma (ed.), *Soundscapes: Essays in Vroom and Moo*. Tampere: University of Tampere Dept. of Folk Tradition, Publ. 19; Institute of Rhythm Music Publ. A2, 71–89.

Pratt, Mary Louise (1986) 'Fieldwork in common places', in James Clifford and George Marcus E. (eds), *Writing Culture: The Poetics and Politics of Ethnography*. Berkeley, CA: University of California Press, pp. 27–50.

Rautiainen, Tarja (1993) 'Matkalla Kuubassa' (Travelling in Cuba), *Musiikin suunta*, 1, pp. 3–12.

Ray, Ruth (1998) 'Feminist readings of older women's life stories', *Journal of Aging Studies*, 12 (2): 117–27.

Reynolds, Simon and Press, Joy (1995) *The Sex Revolts: Gender, Rebellion, and Rock 'n' Roll*. Cambridge, MA: Harvard University Press.

Ribbens, Jane and Edwards, Rosalind (eds) (1998) *Feminist Dilemmas in Qualitative Research*. London: Sage.

Rich, Adrienne (1980) 'Compulsory heterosexuality and lesbian existence', *Signs*, 5 (4), pp. 631–60.

Richardson, Laurel (1998) 'Writing: a method of inquiry', in Norman K. Denzin and Yvonna S. Lincoln (eds), *Collecting and Interpreting Qualitative Materials*. Thousand Oaks, CA: Sage, pp. 345–70.

Ricoeur, Paul (1984–1988) *Time and Narrative*, 3 vols. Chicago: University of Chicago Press.

Rimmon-Kenan, Sholomith (1983) *Narrative Fiction: Contemporary Poetics*. London: Methuen.

Ritala-Koskinen, Aino (1993) *Onko uusperheestä perheeksi?: Tutkimus uusperheen kulttuurisesta kuvasta suomalaisten naisten ja perhelehtien konstruoimana.* Jyväskylä: Jyväskylän yliopisto, perhetutkimusyksikön julkaisuja 4.

Roivainen, Irene (1993): *Lähiö ja sen asukkaat murroksessa: Tutkimus hervantalaisista teollisuustyöntekijöistä.* Tampere: Tampereen yliopisto, sosiaalipolitiikan laitoksen tutkimuksia, A-sarja 5.

Roivainen, Irene (1995) 'Kun ongelmalla on osoite', in *Sosiaalityö, asiakkuus ja sosiaaliset ongelmat*, Arja, Jokinen, Kirsi Juhila and Tarja Pösö (eds), Helsinki: Sosiaaliturvan keskusliitto, pp. 78–98.

Roivainen, Irene (1999) *Sokeripala metsän keskellä. Lähiö sanomalehden konstruktiona.* Helsinki: Helsingin kaupungin tietokeskuksen julkaisuja 1999: 2.

Ronkainen, Suvi (1999) *Ajan ja paikan merkitsemät.* Tampere: Vastapaino.

Rorty, Richard (1967) *The Linguistic Turn: Essays in Philosophical Method.* Chicago: Chicago University Press.

Rubey, Dan (1991) 'Voguing at the carnival: desire and pleasure on MTV', *The South Atlantic Quarterly*, 90 (4): 871–906.

Ruth, Jan-Erik and Vilkko, Anni (1996) 'Emotion in the construction of autobiography', in Carol Magai and Susan H. McFadden (eds), *Handbook of Emotion, Adult Development and Aging*. San Diego: Academic Press, pp. 167–81.

Ruud, Even (1988) *Musikk for oyet, om musikkvideo* (Music for the Eyes, about Music Videos), Osterås: Gyldendal norsk förlag.

Saarikangas, Kirsi (2002) *Asunnon muodonmuutoksia: puhtauden estetiikka ja sukupuoli modernissa arkkitehtuurissa* (Metamorphoses of Dwelling: The Aesthetics of Purity and Gender in Modern Architecture). Helsinki: Suomalaisen Kirjallisuuden Seura.

Sachs, Curt (1968) *The History of Musical Instruments*. London: Dent.

Sacks, Harvey (1966) The search for help: no one to turn to. Unpublished PhD dissertation. Berkeley: University of California, Dept. of Sociology.

Sacks, Harvey (1967) 'The search for help: no one to turn to', in E.S. Shneidman (ed.), *Essays in Self-Destruction*. New York: Science House, pp. 203–23.

Sacks, Harvey (1972a) 'An Initial Investigation of the Usability on Conversational Data for Doing Sociology', in David N. Sudnow (ed.), *Studies in Social Interaction*. New York: Free Press.

Sacks, Harvey (1972b) 'On the Analysability of Stories by Children', in John J. Gumperz and Dell Hymes (eds), *Directions in Sociolinguistics: The Ethnography of Communication*. New York: Holt.

Sacks, Harvey (1974) 'On the analysability of stories by children', in Roy Turner (ed.), *Ethnomethodology*, Aylesbury: Penguin Books, pp. 216–32.

Sacks, Harvey (1989a) 'Doing things with names', *Human Studies*, 12 (3–4), 349–50.

Sacks, Harvey (1989b) 'Lecture Six. The M.I.R. Membership Categorization Device', *Human Studies*, 12 (3–4), 271–81.

Sacks, Harvey (1989c) *Human Studies*, 12 (3–4). Special Issue: Harvey Sacks: Lectures 1964–1965.

Sacks, Harvey (1992) *Lectures on Conversation*, Ed. G. Jefferson, introduction by E. Schegloff, 2 vols. Oxford: Basil Blackwell.

Sacks, Harvey, Schegloff, E.A. and Jefferson, Gail (1974) 'A simplest systematics for the organization of turn taking in conversation', *Language*, 50: 697–735.

Sanjek, Roger (ed.) (1990) *Fieldnotes: The Makings of Anthropology*. Ithaca, NY: Cornell University Press.

Schafer, R. Murray (1977) *The Tuning of the World*. New York: Alfred A. Knopf .

Schaffer, Pierre (1966) *Traité d'objets musicaux*. Paris.

Schegloff, Emmanuel A. (1972) 'Notes on a conversational practice: formulating place', in David Sudnow (ed.), *Studies in Social Interaction*. New York: Free Press, pp. 75–119.

Schegloff, Emmanuel A. (1989) 'Harvey Lectures Sacks 1964–1965. An Introduction/ Memoir', *Human Studies*, 12 (3–4), 185–209.

Schegloff, Emmanuel A. (1992) 'Introduction', in Harvey Sacks *Lectures on Conversation*: ed. G. Jefferson. Oxford: Basil Blackwell.

Shepherd, John (1991) *Music as Social Text*. Cambridge: Cambridge University Press.

Silverman, David and Torode, Briah (1980) *The Material Word: Some Theories of Languasge and its Limits*. London: Routledge & Kegan Paul.

Silverman, David (1985) *Qualitative Methodology and Sociology: Describing the Social World*. Aldershot: Gower.

Silverman, David (1987) *Communication and Medical Practice: Social Relations in the Clinic*. London: Sage.

Silverman, David (1989) 'Telling convincing stories: a plea for cautious positivism in case studies', in B. Glassner and J.D. Moreno (eds), *The Quantitative-Qualitative Distinction in the Social Sciences*. Dordrecht: Kluwer.

Silverman, David (1990) Mentoring notes for 'Advanced course in qualitative research methods', unpublished, 25–27 September.

Silverman, David (1993a) 'The machinery of interaction: remaking social science', *The Sociological Review*, 4 (41), 731–52.

Silverman, David (1993b) 'Unfixing the subject: viewing "Bad Timing"', in C. Jenks (ed.), *Cultural Reproduction*. London: Routledge.

Silverman, David (1993c) *Interpreting Qualitative Data: Methods for Analysing Talk, Text and Interaction*. London: Sage.

Silverman, David (1994) 'Describing sexual activities in HIV counselling: the cooperative management of the moral order', *Text*, 14 (3), pp. 427–53.

Silverman, David (ed.) (1997) *Qualitative Research: Theory, Method and Practice*. London: Sage, pp. 130–43.

Silverman, David (1998) *Harvey Sacks: Social Science and Conversation Analysis*. Cambridge: Polity Press.

Sipilä, Jorma (1994) 'Miestutkimus: säröjä hegemonisessa maskuliinisuudessa' (Men's Studies: disruptions in the hegemonic masculinity), in Jorma Sipilä and Arto Tiihonen (eds), *Miestä rakennetaan, maskuliinisuuksia puretaan* (Constructing Men, Deconstructing Masculinities). Tampere: Vastapaino, pp. 17–37.

Smith, Sidonie (1987) *A Poetics of Women's Autobiography*. Bloomington, IN: Indiana University Press.

Smith, Sidonie (1998) 'Performativity, autobiographical practice, resistance', in Sidonie Smith and Julia Watson (eds), *Women, Autobiography, Theory: A Reader*. Madison, WI: London: The University of Wisconsin Press, pp. 108–15.

Smith, Sidonie and Watson, Julia (eds) (1998) *Women, Autobiography, Theory: A Reader.* Madison, WI: The University of Wisconsin Press.

Smith, Sidonie and Watson, Julia (2001) *Reading Autobiography: A Guide to Interpreting Life Narratives.* Minneapolis: University of Minnesota Press.

Smith Oboler, Regina (1986) 'For better or worse: anthropologists and husbands in the field', in Tony Larry Whitehead and Mary Ellen Conaway (eds), *Self, Sex, and Gender in Cross-Cultural Fieldwork.* Urbana, IL: University of Illinois Press, pp. 28–51.

Somers, Margareth (1994) 'The narrative constitution of identity: a relational and network approach', *Theory and Society*, 23: 605–49.

Somers, Margareth and Gibson, Gloria (1994) 'Reclaiming the epistemological "other": narrative and the social constitution of identity', in Craig Calhoun (ed.), *Social Theory and the Politics of Identity.* Oxford: Blackwell.

Sommer, Doris (1988) ' "Not just a personal story": women's "testimonios" and the plural self', in Bella Brodzki and Celeste Schenck (eds), *Life/Lines: Theorizing Women's Autobiography.* Ithaca, NY: Cornell University Press, pp. 107–30.

Stanley, Liz (1990) 'Moments of writing: is there a feminist auto/biography?', *Gender and History*, 2 (1): 58–67.

Stanley, Liz (1992) *The Auto/biographical I: The Theory and Practice of Feminist Auto/biography.* Manchester: Manchester University Press.

Stanley, Liz (1993) 'On auto/biography in sociology', *Sociology*, 27 (1): 41–52.

Stanton, Donna C. (1984) *The Female Autograph: Theory and Practice of Autobiography from the Tenth to the Twentieth Century.* Chicago: University of Chicago Press.

Stenvos, Anne (1992) Kesto ja järjestys, Tilarakenteen teoria. (Duration and Order. Theory of Spatial structure.) Helsinki: Teknillinen Korkeakoulu.

Stockfelt, Ola (1994) 'Cars, buildings and soundscapes', in Helmi Järviluoma (ed.), *Soundscapes: Essays in Vroom and Moo.* Tampere: University of Tampere Dept. of Folk Tradition, Publ. 19; Institute of Rhythm Music, Publ. A2, pp. 19–38.

Stokes, Martin (1994) 'Introduction', in Martin Stokes (ed.), *Ethnicity, Identity and Music: The Musical Construction of Place.* Oxford: Berg pp. 1–25.

Strassoldo, Raimondo (1993) *Tilan sosiaalinen rakenne* (Place as a Social Construction). Tampere: TKKK, yhteiskuntasuunnittelun laitos. Julkaisuja 21.

Tagg, Philip (1994) 'Subjectivity and soundscape, motorbikes and music', in Helmi Järviluoma (ed.), *Soundscapes: Essays in Vroom and Moo.* Tampere: University of Tampere Dept. of Folk Tradition, Publ. 19; Institute of Rhythm Music Publ. A2, pp. 48–66.

Tagg, Philip and Clarida, Robert (n.d.) Ten little title tunes. Unpublished manuscript. Liverpool: Institute for Popular Music Research Report.

Tannen, Deborah (1990) *You Just Don't Understand: Women and Men in Conversation.* New York: William Morrow and Company.

Tedlock, Barbara (2000) 'Ethnography and ethnographic representation', in Norman K. Denzin and Yvonna S. Lincoln (eds), *The Handbook of Qualitative Reseach* (2nd edition). Thousand Oaks, CA: Sage, pp. 455–86.

Ticineto Clough, Patricia (1992) *The End(s) of Ethnography.* Newbury Park, CA: Sage.

Tixier, Nicolas (2002) 'Street listening', in Helmi Järviluoma and Gregg Wagstaff (eds), *Soundscape Studies and Methods.* Helsinki: The Finnish Society for Ethnomusicology Publications, University of Turku.

Truax, Barry (2000, orig. 1984) *Acoustic Communication.* Norwood, NJ: Ablex Publishing Corporation.

Turnbull, Colin M. (1986) 'Sex and gender: the role of subjectivity in field research', in Tony Larry Whitehead and Mary Ellen Conaway (eds), *Self, Sex, and Gender in Cross-Cultural Fieldwork*. Urbana, IL: University of Illinois Press, pp. 17–27.

Turner, Roy (1989) 'Deconstructing the field', in Jaber F. Gubrium and David Silverman (eds), *The Politics of Field Research: Sociology beyond Enlightenment*. London: Sage.

Utriainen, Terhi (1998) 'Occupying a space as eyes and body: comments on the diversity of fieldwork, the postures of knowledge, and summer experiences in an elderly women's village in Olonets Karelia', in Satu Apo, Aili Nenola and Laura Stark-Arola (eds), *Gender and Folklore: Perspectives on Finnish and Karelian Culture*. Studia Fennica Folkloristica 4. Helsinki: Finnish Literature Society.

van den Hoonaard, Deborah K. (2000) 'Women's experiences of widowhood as expressed in autobiographical accounts', in Jaber F. Gubrium and James A. Holstein (eds), *Ageing and Everyday Life*. Oxford: Blackwell Publishers, pp. 87–102.

Van Maanen, John, Manning, Peter K. and Miller, Marc L. (1988) 'Editors' Introduction', in Carol A.B. Warren, *Gender Issues in Field Research: Qualitative Research Methods*. Vol. 9. Newbury Park, CA: Sage Publications, p. 5.

Vilkko, Anni (1991) 'Kätellä hansikaskädellä. Naisomaelämäkerran tulkitsijan positiosta' (Shaking hands with one's gloves on: the position of the reader of women's autobiographies), *Naistutkimus – Kvinnoforskning*, 4 (4): 6–16.

Vilkko, Anni (1994) 'Homespun life: metaphors on the course of life in women's autobiographies', *Cultural Studies*, 8 (2): 269–77.

Vilkko, Anni (1997) *Omaelämäkerta kohtaamispaikkana. Naisen elämän kerronta ja luenta.* (Autobiography as a Meeting Place: Reading Women's Life Narratives). Helsinki: SKS.

Vilkko, Anni (1998) 'Kodiksi kutsuttu paikka. Tapausanalyysi naisen ja miehen omaelämäkerroista' (A place called home: analysing home histories in women's and men's autobiographies), in Matti Hyvärinen, Eeva Peltonen and Anni Vilkko (eds), *Liikkuvat erot. Sukupuoli elämäkertatutkimuksessa* (Differences in Motion: Doing and Reading Gender in Biographical Research). Tampere: Vastapaino, pp. 27–72.

Vilkko, Anni (2001) 'Elämänkulku ja elämänkulkukerronta' (Life course and its narration), in Eino Heikkinen and Jouni Tuomi (eds), *Suomalainen elämänkulku* (The Finnish Life Course). Helsinki: Tammi, pp. 74–85.

Virilio, Paul (1994) *Katoamisen estetiikka* (The Aesthetics of Disappearance). Helsinki: Gaudeamus.

Walser, Robert (1993) *Running with the Devil: Power, Gender and Madness in Heavy Metal Music*. Hannover: Wesleyan University Press.

Warren, Carol A.B. (1988) *Gender Issues in Field Research: Qualitative Research Methods*. vol. 9. Newbury Park, CA: Sage Publications. (Second edition 2000).

Watson, Rod (1987) 'Interdisciplinary considerations in the analysis of pro-terms', in G. Button and J.R.E. Lee (eds), *Talk and Social Organization*, Clevedon: Multilingual Matters, pp. 261–89.

Watson, Rod (1997) 'Ethnomethodology and textual analysis', in David Silverman (ed.), *Qualitative Research: Theory, Method and Practice*. London: Sage.

Watson, Rod (1994) 'Catégories, séquentialité et ordre social', *Raisons Pratiques*, 5, 151–85.

Wax, Rosalie H. (1986) 'Gender and age in fieldwork and fieldwork education: "Not any good thing is done by one man alone"', in T.L. Whitehead and M.E. Conaway, (eds), *Self, Sex and Gender in Cross-cultural Fieldwork*. Urbana, IL: University of Illinois Press, pp. 129–50.

Weedon, Chris (1999) *Feminism, Theory and the Politics of Difference*. Oxford: Blackwell.

Weinberg, M., Tronick, E., Cohn, J. and Olson, K. (1999) 'Gender differences in emotional expressivity and self-regulation during early infancy', *Developmental Psychology*, 35 (1): 175–88.

Whitehead, Tony Larry and Conaway, Mary Ellen (eds) (1986) *Self, Sex, and Gender in Cross-Cultural Fieldwork*. Urbana, IL: University of Illinois Press.

Whitehead, Tony Larry and Price, Laurie (1986) 'Summary: sex and the fieldwork experience', in *Self, Sex and Gender in Cross-Cultural Fieldwork*. Urbana, IL: University of Illinois Press, pp. 289–304.

Whiteley, Sheila (ed.) (1997) *Sexing the Groove: Popular Music and Gender*. London: Routledge.

Whitford, Margaret (1991a) 'Introduction', in Luce Irigaray, *The Irigaray Reader*. ed. Margaret Whitford. Oxford: Blackwell Publishers Ltd.

Whitford, Margaret (1991b) *Luce Irigaray: Philosophy in the Feminine*. London: Routledge.

Wieder, D.L. (1974) *Language and Social Reality: Approaches to Semiotics 10*. The Hague: Mouton.

Wolf, Margaret (1992) *A Thrice Told Tale: Feminism, Postmodernism and Ethnographic Responsibility*. Stanford, CA: Stanford University Press.

Yuval-Davis, Nira (1997) *Gender and Nation*. Thousand Oaks, CA: Sage.

Other sources

'Anna's' interview, tapes and transcriptions, HJ's archive.

Caplan, Pat (1987) Lectures in the course 'Gender and anthropological field work', Dept. of Sociology and Social Psychology, University of Tampere.

Heinämaa, Sara (1999) Lecture in the lecture series 'Women's studies and qualitative methodology', Turku, 20 September.

KPK Field diary, Helmi Järviluoma 1988, HJ's archive.

KPL Y 9627 Dept. of Folk Tradition, tape archives, HJ, University of Tampere.

Index

advertising jingles 104–5
affiliation identifications 95
age 56, 79, 80
Agnes, learning to be a woman 4–5
aircraft music 88–9
American feminism 111
Anglo–American feminists 111–12, 116
Angrosino, Michel 75
Anna (mandolin player) 38–40, 42, 76, 77
anthropology 28
Arachne 52
army situation 77
assimilation identifications 95
assumed gender categories 71
'auto/biography' theory 55
autobiographies 20, 46–68, 83
    'auto/biography' theory 55
    autonomous male 54–9
    coherence 49, 51, 65
    emancipatory confession 59–61
    exercise 25
    feminist performance 62–4
    gender-specific differences 52–60
    mode of speaking 109–10
    models 49–50
    relational female 54–9
    women ignored as autobiographers 54
autonomous male in autobiography 54–9

babies 3–4, 101–2
background hums 102
background music 86, 96, 99
Baker, Carolyn 71
Behar, Ruth 108–9
belief systems 3
Billig, Michael 79
biographies 55
    see also autobiographies
biological sexes 3
Birmingham Centre girl's studies 41
bisexuality 9
black women 92
bodily posture 29–30
Bonvillain, Nancy 19
boys 4, 5, 7–9

Braidotti, Rosi 18
Bridges, J. 4
Burundi society 80
Butler, Judith 14, 15, 62

CA see conversation analysis
Cameron, Deborah 2, 72
case studies
    Agnes, learning to be a woman 4–5
    assumed gender categories 71
    bending gender categories in everyday
        action 13–14
    biography vis-à-vis autobiography 55
    combining conversational analysis and
        membership category analysis in
        analyzing identities 79
    constructions of 'home' 58–9
    economy rule – one category is enough 75
    emotional presuppositions in girl's studies 41
    field diary, Helmi Järviluoma 76
    Finnish gender order represented in
        music 7–9
    furthering understanding through
        categories 81–2
    gender differences in identity
        constructions 56–7
    gender performance in Finnish dance
        restaurant 15–16
    gendered construction of place through
        sound 103
    gendered theory of classical music 6
    generic pronouns 71
    hegemonic and marginalized masculinity 12
    juxtapositioning categories in headlines 72
    masculinity in heavy metal music 6
    mood music in the film by Jane
        Champion The Piano 99
    narrative of the self: Leena Eräsaari and
        The Mask of a Creep 114–15
    negotiating gender in the Himalayas 31–2
    negotiating gendered ethics in an
        interview situation 39
    performativity as a means of reading
        subjectivity 62
    pitch level and authority 100

case studies *cont.*
   positive gender performance of black
      women in a music video 92
   race and gender as aspects influencing
      the perception of a video 87
   reading gender-specific practices in
      autobiographical texts 52
   representations of women in popular
      music 91
   shared meanings of music revealed by
      an experiment 86
   significant others, role 57
   stories of how gender chose us 20–2
   temporality in life stories 63
   transitional moments of life 64
   turn-taking, age and gender 80
   women and the microphone 100
categories 2–3, 13–14, 25, 37, 69–83
category-bound features 74
causal listening 96
Champion, Jane 99
childhood homes 59
Chion, Michel 95–6, 97
Cixous, Hélène 111, 112, 116
classical music 6
coffee-making 38–40, 76
coherence 49, 51, 65
commutation 96
conceptual soundscape models 98–102
confession 59–61, 114
congratulatory card study 4
consistency rule 76
constructionist approach 5
constructions of 'home' 58–9
contextualization 19, 25
conversation analysis (CA) 73, 79
conversational style 5
Cook, Nicholas 96, 97
cooperation, couple dance roles 16
corporeal, bodily 29–30
couple dances 15, 16, 21, 34–6
critical feminist theory 2
cultural aspects 3, 10, 17
  see also music
cycle as life metaphor 51

DA *see* discourse analysis
dance 15–16, 21, 34–6
de Beauvoir, Simone 9, 10
definitions 3, 6, 72–7
DeNora, Tia 88, 90
Devor, Holly 13–14
diegetic sound 95
discourse 90–3
discourse analysis (DA) 73

drag artists 15
'dream of forms' (Kant) 82
dress codes 35
drum playing 8, 33

economy rule 75
Eglin, Peter 78
elitism in music 85
emancipatory confession 59–61
emotion 41, 109–10
enculturation 5
The Ends of Ethnography (Patricia Ticineto
    Clough) 37–8
engaged couples 74
Eräsaari, Leena 108, 113, 114–15
ethics 39
ethnographic fictional representations 115
ethnography 36–42, 116
ethnography books 116
ethnomethodological ethnography 36–42
ethnomusicology 89
everyday life 13–14, 85
exercises
   analysis of an advertising jingle 104–5
   analysis of gender through participant
      observation 44
   analysis of a life story narration 66–7
   analysis of a music video 106
   analysis of your own autobiography as
      a story 68
   autobiography from the perspective
      of gender 25
   discussing gender narratives 117
   does soundscape have gender? 106
   membership analysis of your own
      autobiography 83
   membership category analysis of
      conversational field data 83
   positioning your own gendered self 117
expectations, field workers 30–3
experimental representations 113–17
*Experiments in Knowing: Gender and Method
    in the Social Sciences* (2000) 23

family 59, 75
fan culture 41
femininity 4–5, 16–17, 23–4, 111–13
feminism 11, 111
   critical feminist theory 2
   literary studies 115–17
   research 2, 11, 42
   studies 2, 4–5, 10, 11, 42
fieldwork 27–45
   anthropological/sociological 28
   and category/role-mobility 34

fieldwork *cont.*
　　dance study 34–6
　　dialogic 39
　　and feelings 41
　　feminist researchers 42
　　field as an attitude 29–30
　　gender expectations in the field 30–3
　　and gender norms 35, 36
　　and gender roles 28, 34
　　gendered researchers 30–3
　　place of women 43
　　posture concept 29–30
　　researcher's background 34–6
　　role-mobility 34
　　and sexual politics 6, 38, 40
　　and 'writing culture' 109
film music 93–8
Finland 7–9
folk music *see pelimanni* folk music group
foreign categories 81
Foucault, Michael 13
French feminism 11, 111
Freud 112

Garfinkel, Harold 4, 5, 22
gatekeepers of language 71
gay and lesbian studies 13
gender
　　analysis 16–17
　　belief system 3
　　blending 13–14
　　categories 2–3, 13–14, 71
　　conceptualisation of 16–17
　　constructions 5
　　difference 2, 52–60
　　discourse of 90–3
　　hierarchy 40
　　identity 17–18
　　limitations 8, 19, 22
　　negotiation 6, 21, 22, 24, 27–45
　　norms 1, 7–9, 12, 16, 30, 33
　　order 7–9
　　performance 14–16, 24
　　representation of 5
　　roles 15–16, 21, 34, 55, 57
　　schema 3
　　social construction of 3
　　stereotypes 4, 90–3
　　subjectivity 62, 107
　　technologies of 5
gender-blenders 13–14
gender-bound voices 109
gender-centric research on music 91
gendered researchers 30–3
gendering membership category 70–2

generic pronouns 71
Ginsburg, Faye 42
girls 4, 5, 7–9, 41
Gurung mountain village 20–1, 31–2

'hard' methodologies 23–4
heavy metal music 6, 8, 91–3
hegemonic masculinity 12
Hester, Stephen 78
heterosexual norms 12, 16
Himalayas 31–2
history 9–12, 28
'home' constructions 58–9
homosexuality 13–14, 18
honesty towards oneself in fieldwork 31
Hurston, Zora Neale 115

identifications 17–18
identities 4–5, 17–18, 22, 47–8, 56–7, 79
images and music 93–8
in-flight music 88–9
interpretation 42
interruption of data 43
interviews 23–4, 39, 54–5
Irigaray, Luce 111, 112, 113

Jackson, Janet 92
Järviluoma, Helmi 12, 21–2, 28, 29, 36–42, 76
Jokinen, Eeva 110
journey as life metaphor 51

Kaplan, Anna 93
Karelian village 29–30
Kaskisaari, Marja 62
Kassabian, Anahid 87, 90, 93, 95, 96, 97
Kate (*MotherKind*) 101–2
'key rhetoric' concept 63
keynote sound 100
kitchen duties 38–40, 76–7
knowledge, local routinized 77–9
Komulainen, Katri 63
Krieger, Laurie 32–3
Kruse, Holly 92, 94

Lähteenmaa, Jaana 41
language 11, 61, 70, 71, 111–12
Lawless, Elizabeth 42
lesbian identity 18
life narratives *see* autobiographies
limitations 8, 19, 22
listening 86, 90, 96
local gender norms 30
local routinized knowledge 77–9
locating myself into my own texts 108–10
Lomax, Alan 104–5

male autobiographies 54–9
male-dominated culture 10
mandolin woman (Anna) 38–40, 42, 76, 77
'manly ideal' 11, 12
marginalized masculinity 12
Marshall, Barbara 9
Martin, Peter 89–90
masculinity
   heavy metal music 6, 8
   hegemonic and marginalized 12
   Membership Categorization Devices 77
   power 9
   qualities definition 16–17
   rationality 70, 107
   study of 11–12
   values in feminine discourse 50
The Mask of a Creep 114–15
Mason, Mary 58
MCA *see* membership category analysis
MCD *see* Membership Categorization Device
Membership Categorization Device (MCD)
      69, 75
   army 77
membership category analysis (MCA) 12, 69–83
   areas of study 73
   basic concepts 73–81
   Category-Bound Features 74
   consistency rule 76
   definition 72–7
   economy rule 75
   foreign categories 81–2
   language 70
   local routinized knowledge 77–9
   membership categorizations 12, 69–83
   membership groupings 74–7
   Standard Pair 74, 77
men's studies 11–12
metaphors in life narratives 48, 51–2
methodology 1–2, 18–22
microphones 100
Mikko 39–40
Miller, Nancy K. 52, 57, 110
mixed genres 115, 116
Moisala, Pirkko 15, 20–1, 31–2, 84
mood music *see* background music
MotherKind (Jayne Anne Phillips) 101
MTV 94
music
   aircraft music 88–9
   analysis 84–106
   associations 90
   background 86, 96, 99
   blues 94
   classical 6, 85
   country 12, 36–42, 76

music *cont.*
   elitism 85
   films 93–8
   gender categories 6, 7–9
   gender roles in dance 15–16, 21
   Gurung music 20–1, 31–2
   heavy 6, 8, 91–3
   heavy metal 6, 8, 91–3
   instrument-playing gender norms 7–9, 33
   interpretation 89–90
   methods of analysing 95–7
   pelimanni music group 36–42, 76
   popular 6, 8, 90–3
   rap 91–2
   rock 6, 8, 91–3
   space construction 102–4
   videos 93–5
   Western art 89, 90, 91
   women's stereotypes 90–3
'musical storage' 86–7

Nandi 81–2
narrative identity 47–8, 61, 64–5
narratives 54, 114–15, 117
   see also autobiographies
narrators 108–10
'natural' category-bound features 78
negotiation of gender 6, 21, 22, 24, 27–45
newspaper headlines 72, 73–4
Nicholson, Linda 3

Oakley, Ann 23–4, 25
objectivity 107–10
Okely, Judith 29
others, role in autobiographies 55, 57

Papua New Guinea 30
parler femme 113
particularization 69
passivity 56
patchworking life metaphor 50–2
path to the sauna 48, 49
pelimanni folk music group 12, 36–42, 76
perceiver concept (Kassabian) 87
performance 15–16, 22, 62–4
performativity 14–16, 24
personal speaking mode 109–10
perspective of sound 99
Phillips, Jayne Anne 101
The Piano (Jane Champion) 99
pitch level and authority 100
place, construction through sound 103
poetic representations 52–3, 84, 115
political aspects 2, 10, 11
popular music 6, 8, 90–3

positioning 22–3, 29, 117
postmodern autobiography 61, 65
posture concept 29–30
power 6, 9, 15
'princess' categorization 37
psychoanalysis 112

qualitatively specified standard pairs 77
quantitative methodologies 23–4
queer theory 13

rap music 91–2
rationality 70, 107
reduced listening 96
relational nature of women's
    autobiography 54–9
research methods 1–2, 18–22
research reporting 107–17
researchers 19, 22, 27–45
rock music 6, 8, 91–3
role-mobility 34
routinized knowledge 77–9
Rubey, Dan 94

Sacks, Harvey 69, 70, 74, 75, 79–82
sauna path 48, 49
scientific objectivity 107–8
The Second Sex (Simone de Beauvoir) 10
Second Wave feminist movement 10, 23
secondary listening 86
self-awareness 19, 22
self-image 17–18
self-location in own text 108–10
self-narration see autobiographies
self-positioning 117
Sexton study 30
Sexual Politics (Simone de Beauvoir) 10
sexuality 12–14, 113
shared meanings of music 86
signal sound 100
significant others 57
Silverman, David 42
'situational' category-bound features 78
Smith Oboler, Regina and Leon 30, 81–2

social constructionist approach 2
social sciences 23–4
socialization 5
socio-emotional differences 3–4
'soft' methodologies 23
sounds and music 84–106
space, construction through sound 103
standard pairs 74, 77
Stanford Friedman, Susan 60
Stanley, Liz 55, 61
storytelling see autobiographies
subjectivity 62, 107
surrounding world features 5

Tannen, Deborah 5
'technologies of gender' 5
temporality in life stories 46, 47, 63
This Bridge Called My Back 116
time aspects 46, 47, 53, 63
transitional moments of life 64
transsexuals 3
trumpets 8, 88–9
turn-taking 80
Turnbull, Colin 31, 34
Turner, Roy 28

unconscious, materializing 112
Utriainen, Terhi 29

Vanha Maestro dance restaurant 15
videos 87, 92, 93–5, 97–8, 106
Vilkko, Anni 20, 49, 51, 52–3, 58–9, 64, 116–17

Wagner, Richard 85
Walser, Robert 6
Warren, Carol B. 28, 32, 33, 43
weaving as life metaphor 47, 50–2
Whitehead, Tony 17
widowhood 64
women-centric research on music 91
women's autobiographical narratives 46–68
Women's Studies 2, 109
Writing Culture 109
writing research reports 107–17

The Art of Teaching Peacefully

Michelle MacGrath

David Fulton Publishers
London

To David and our sons
Mark and Peter.
And to teachers and students everywhere.

'Having eyes, but not seeing beauty; having ears, but not hearing music; having minds, but not perceiving truth; having hearts that are never moved and therefore never set on fire. These are the things to fear,' said the headmaster.

Tetsuko Kuroyanagi, *Totto-Chan, The Little Girl at the Window*

David Fulton Publishers Ltd
Ormond House, 26–27 Boswell Street, London WC1N 3JD

First published in Great Britain by David Fulton Publishers 1998

Note: The right of Michelle MacGrath to be identified as the author of this work has been asserted by her in accordance with the Copyright, Designs and Patents Act 1988.

British Library Cataloguing in Publication Data
A catalogue record for this book is available from the British Library

ISBN 1-85346-560-7

Typeset by Helen Skelton, London
Printed in Great Britain by BPC Books and Journals Ltd, Exeter

Contents

Foreword   v

Introduction   vii

Acknowledgements   x

1 Calm in the Classroom   **1**
   Introduction   1
   Elements that help create ordered
      procedures and a calm environment   2
   Disruptive behaviour: getting an understanding   10
   Owning authority   21
   Teaching points   27

**2 Improving Behaviour through Building Confidence
   and Self-esteem**   **29**
   Helping pupils succeed   30
   Avoiding demoralisation   42
   Constructive criticism   52
   Building confidence and self-esteem   58

3 Developing Relationships with Pupils   **62**
   The value of working at relationships   62
   Communication breakdown: a cycle of mistrust   62
   Towards a solution   65
   Facilitating cooperative relationships among pupils   75

4 Teaching, Conflict and Power   **80**
   A teacher's choice: to take up the challenge, or not?   80
   Power relations and teaching   85
   Ways of developing the home position   86
   Times when conflict is more likely   88
   Teaching points   90

5 Anger   **92**
Why consider anger?   92
Points to consider when dealing with angry pupils   93
Choosing to keep your temper – a technique   95
Helping pupils to manage their anger   96
Teaching points   98

6 Skills   **105**
Negotiating skills   106
Listening and teaching   113
Teaching points: using listening in teaching   117

7 Facilitating New Behaviour   **121**
What may help a change in behaviour   121
Specific requirements for the process of change   123
Some common issues which might undermine change   128
Teaching points: introducing the idea of choice   130

8 Cultivating Calm: Managing Stress Peacefully   **132**
'I've got enough to do. Why tackle stress?'   132
What is stress?   132
Why some people suffer more from stress than others   133
Pupils and stress   133
An approach to minimising stress for teachers   135
Reverse the process   136
Review attitudes and working practices   137
Cultivate calm   143

Appendix I: Specific Learning Difficulties (SpLD)   146
Appendix II: Cultural Attitudes Towards Children   153
Appendix III: Quiz on Anger   154
Appendix IV: Communication Skills   155
Appendix V: Talking not Fighting   158
Appendix VI: Changing Behaviour Questionnaire   160
Appendix VII: Possible Indications of Stress   161
Appendix VIII: Relaxation Techniques: Using Focused Imagination   162
Appendix IX: Checklist for Cultivating Calm   164

Bibliography   165

Index   166

Foreword

Relationships are the core of teaching. The author of this book considers deep, underlying aspects. Michelle MacGrath explores and evokes the positive, sensitive, realistic approach to teaching which makes it such a rewarding profession, enabling children to become successful students: the art of teaching peacefully. We often highlight the potential and actual stresses in teaching. Here is a perceptive, detailed, humane and immensely practical exploration of how to create true peacefulness through peaceful, skilled approaches.

By quoting actual verbal exchanges and including a range of effectively imagined ones, and by describing classroom scenes and the looks and actions of teacher and taught, Michelle MacGrath brings the real classroom and real teacher–pupil interchanges to our minds. She analyses these scenes against an understanding of the depth of human thoughts and feelings, and prompts the reader's own judgement and decisions.

An important underlying theme is that 'the pupils most likely to disrupt are those who feel least sure of themselves, are most frightened and who have the lowest self-esteem'. Thus, seeking peace for learning requires the teacher to find approaches which give to the pupil clarity and certainty about behavioural expectations and which raise self-esteem. This book gives major support to help the teacher develop attitudes, techniques and procedures to help that.

The author's focus on defining limits for pupils' actions is more than a mere technique: it grows from sensitive and realistic psychology. The sections, for instance on 'ground rules', 'ending lessons' and 'how to sit quietly and listen' are models of real help to teacher readers. What can be painful and technically difficult matters, such as working with pupils with 'under-developed skills of self-expression and listening', are practically explored and useful steps are set out.

Michelle MacGrath says of her own early days of teaching that the fact that she 'felt far from peaceful ... sometimes inflamed conflicts'. While none of us have complete control over our own feelings, the author's clear and perceptive analyses of the many doubts and crises which teachers experience offers imaginative and practical help. She prompts echoes for many of us of our own uncertainties, and shows ways of using those feelings positively to improve our teaching. She both evokes for me my own memories of teaching and my observation of teachers now, both those straight from training and, equally importantly, those experienced teachers freshly considering their work and ways of further improving their effect on the pupils.

Michelle MacGrath has added significantly to the small literature on what the basis of teaching in a school is really about, whatever the subject or the tutorial role. She brings observation and experience together with psychology and human sympathy to produce a deeply moving and practical set of recommendations on this most central art of teaching peacefully.

Michael Marland
CBE MA FRSA

Introduction

Teaching came as a profound shock to me. During my first year I was frequently in despair and awaited Monday mornings with cold dread. The pressure of work was relentless with never enough time to complete everything to my satisfaction. In addition to delivering the curriculum, marking, report-writing, parents' evenings and facilitating learning, there were the tasks of establishing and maintaining discipline and building relationships with pupils. I felt far from peaceful and, as I later realised, sometimes inflamed conflicts which, with greater experience, I could have avoided. This made life all the more difficult and stressful. Uncomfortable as my initial teaching experience was, it was not, I have since learned, uncommon.

This is a book of ideas and practicalities. It is an attempt to suggest a way of thinking and working that can promote a more relaxed, calm and, therefore, effective approach to teaching which can help reduce conflict in the classroom.

Most teachers encounter at some time pupils who seem rude, arrogant, angry and apparently impossible to teach. Many of these will be young people struggling to find their way in the process of growing up. Some will have particular problems to overcome. Yet however difficult these pupils seem to teach, in any school there are usually a few teachers who manage to get through to them at least a little, experiencing less antagonism and less disruption to lessons than their colleagues. What is their secret? Are they some of those so-called 'born teachers' or are they simply very skilled and experienced? Having analysed their approach, this book puts across skills which can help at times of potential conflict. It also suggests a style of classroom management which will encourage wanted behaviour and help all pupils, even those with some learning and literacy difficulties, to achieve more.

The question of emotions and relationships cannot be ignored since teaching is, at a fundamental level, about relating to other people. How teachers and pupils feel about their daily experience in school and about each other is crucial if the former are to flourish in their work and the latter in their education. Real improvements in the quality of learning come about when discipline is firm yet respectful and learning is, in the main, enjoyable. This is possible only when teachers are highly skilled, supported, at ease with their work and able to relate positively with the young people in their classes.

This book provides a new approach since its emphasis is not so much on behaviour management as on the cultivation of cooperative behaviour through skilful classroom management techniques, strategies to make work accessible to all, effective communication and the development and maintenance of positive relationships with pupils. It considers power relations in the classroom and how teachers can use these to their advantage. It also deals, in some detail, with how change is possible. The approach is one which includes consideration of the physical, emotional and mental wellbeing of both pupils and teachers.

The first three chapters focus on encouraging cooperative behaviour. This is emphasised since it is clearly preferable to avoid disruption or conflict than to have to deal with them, however effectively. The significance of creating structures and routines to minimise potential disruption is stressed and many practical suggestions are given. In addition, the book aims to give teachers an alternative view of disruptive behaviour and conflict and of the pupils who tend to become involved in them. Such changes in perception can, in themselves, facilitate an approach which reduces the incidence of conflict and manages it constructively should it occur

If pupils have an interest in their education and get something positive out of school they are not only more motivated to learn but are less likely to become involved in aggressive confrontations. Consequently, the incidence of conflict can be reduced considerably and behaviour can be improved by employing techniques for helping pupils achieve and feel good about themselves through that achievement. An improved self-esteem and positive relationships with teachers can reduce the incidence of conflict considerably.

The next two chapters deal more directly with conflict and anger. In Chapter 4 the issue of power within the classroom is discussed and it is proposed that a stance is desirable which is neither aggressive nor diffident, one which enables the teacher to exercise authority confidently while showing respect towards the pupils. Such an approach is, in turn, more likely to earn pupils' respect and cooperation. Techniques for achieving and maintaining this middle ground are found throughout the book.

The question of anger is considered in Chapter 5 and strategies are proposed for dealing with it on the spot in ways which are likely to calm rather than inflame the situation. A programme of work is included for use with pupils. The aim of this is to increase their understanding of anger and its process and to suggest alternative ways of handling it.

Much conflict arises in classrooms, playgrounds and staffrooms through misunderstandings resulting from underdeveloped skills of self-expression and listening. By widening their repertoire of communication skills, teachers can be more flexible and effective in relating to a range of pupils. This can also help them in exercising other teaching skills and in establishing and maintaining the limits and rules essential for efficient classroom management. Through learning communication and other relevant skills pupils equip themselves with alternative ways of managing disagreement rather than resorting to violence.

Chapter 7 focuses on what is needed to help pupils change their behaviour and what might hinder progress.

The final chapter acknowledges the stress teachers may sometimes experience when facing anger, aggression and many different demands on their time, expertise and energy. It proposes techniques for managing stress and frustration as well as strategies for building inner resources, cultivating calm, unwinding and relaxing. This is important because, when stressed, it is difficult to employ the approach outlined earlier in the book. There is an appendix which includes some relevant additional material and some worksheets which can be copied for use with pupils.

Individual teachers are, of course, a part of the organisation of the school and can be supported by whole-school discipline policies, management structures, colleagues and so on. However, when facing a class of some thirty pupils it is sometimes easy, suddenly, to feel very alone! The school day can often seem rushed and pressured. There is not always enough time to ask for help, advice or support. Nor is it always possible. At times of low confidence it is even easy to imagine that everyone else in the school is quite sure of what they are doing and experiences no difficulties. At such times, too, this book might be of assistance. So, if you would like to give more to the pupils in your class while enjoying the benefits of teaching peacefully, read on ...

Acknowledgements

Many people have helped write this book by generously giving ideas and support. Heartfelt thanks to my partner, David Mann, for his encouragement and sustaining love and to our sons, Mark, for his inspiration, and to Peter. I would especially like to thank Michael Marland for his interest and support and for writing the foreword. In addition I would like to thank Valerie Phillips for her wisdom and model of calm and Susan House for discussions and material. Thanks also for their help and support to Susan and Peter Bloomfield, Tony Brown, Don Clarke, Lucy Davies, Anne Dickson, Chantal Howell, Liz Kyberd, Vladimir Levi, Dorothy Lewis, Linda Marsh, Janine Mather, Susannah McInerney, Lesley Morris, Anne Murray, Khaleghl Quinn, Linda Reade, Jiffy Sandison, Juliette Stephenson, Felicity Yates and all the pupils and colleagues with whom I have worked.

Thanks to Mikaela Davies for her poem and Gillian Backhouse for her section on specific learning difficulties. Both retain the copyright for their work.

Thanks to the following for permission to quote from: *Star Woman*, Lynn V. Andrews, Warner Books; *Frogs into Princes*, Richard Bandler and John Grindler, Real People Press; *A Woman in Your Own Right*, Anne Dickson, Quartet Books; *The Fire Dance*, Emaho, Shailendra Publishing; *A Little Edge of Darkness*, Tanya F. Faludy and Alexander F. Faludy, Jessica Kingsley Publishers; *Pedagogy of the Oppressed*, Paulo Freire, Penguin; *Totto-Chan, The Little Girl at the Window*, Tetsuko Kuroyanagi, Kodansha International; *The Craft of the Classroom*, Michael Marland, Heinemann; *The Sickening Mind*, Paul Martin, HarperCollins; *Driving Fear Out of the Workplace*, Daniel K. Oestreich and Kathleen Ryan, Jossey Bass; *Stand Your Ground*, Kaleghl Quinn, Orbis Publishing; *Effective Classroom Control*, John Robertson, Hodder & Stoughton; *Maverick*, Richard Semler, Century Business; *The Stress of Life*, Hans Selye, McGraw-Hill; *Autobiography of a Yogi*, Paramahansa Yogananda, Self-Realization Fellowship.

CHAPTER 1

Calm in the Classroom

True education can never be crammed and pumped from without; rather it must aid in bringing spontaneously to the surface the infinite hoards of wisdom within.

Rabindranath Tagore,
quoted in Paramahansa Yogananda, *Autobiography of a Yogi*

Introduction

Schools are places often filled with noise, bustle, excitement, movement and conflict. It can often be quite difficult to remain calm and reduce conflict rather than adding to it. Yet the benefits are obvious for teachers and pupils alike. This book is about ways you can develop the art of teaching peacefully. This includes an ability to:

- create a calm and ordered environment which will facilitate learning and improve behaviour;
- reduce the incidence of conflict;
- manage conflict effectively if it should occur;
- help everyone to learn and achieve;
- help pupils to manage anger and resolve conflict peacefully;
- manage one's own anger and develop ways of remaining calm.

This chapter considers strategies for making it easier for pupils to cooperate than to disrupt. It is probably true to say that, in general, the pupils most likely to disrupt are those who feel least sure of themselves, most frightened and who have lowest self-esteem. As we shall see in subsequent chapters, pupils who readily resort to aggressive or disruptive behaviour are likely to feel extremely vulnerable within themselves. *The presenting behaviour may at first glance, however, appear to be the very opposite of what is generally considered vulnerable, that is to say, it may be aggressive, boasting and noisy, and so on.*

The reasons for these insecurities may be numerous. They may be connected with learning difficulties, with a fear of getting things wrong in school, a fear of feeling different or of not being accepted by peers, or they may be rooted in life outside school, or in the past. They may be unconscious. Nevertheless, a rule of thumb will be that *the safer the class and school environment, the less disruptive behaviour is needed.* In other words, the *more at ease* a pupil feels within a class, the less likely he or she will be to resort to disruption in order to feel a little safer. The likelihood of conflict will likewise be reduced.

What, then, might pupils need in general to feel more comfortable and safe? Obviously there will be individual differences. However, many will be likely to feel more at ease if they:

- know what to expect, that is to say, they know what will happen in the day, class and school rules and sanctions;
- experience only manageable amounts of change and the unexpected (what is acceptable will vary hugely);
- have an ordered environment in which things have their place;
- feel valued and encouraged;
- have support from and feel accepted by peers;
- have support from and feel accepted by teachers;
- have their own 'territory', for example, their own desk, locker or tray, the same seat on the same table, etc.;
- have a specific role and understand what that is (enthusiastic, organised learner, for example, messenger, student, helper to collect video, etc.);
- have work tasks which they can complete successfully;
- understand the work.

These needs can perhaps best be grouped in three sections:

1. Ordered procedures and a calm environment.
2. Work at an appropriate level, necessary help and equipment available.
3. Positive, supportive relationships with teachers and peers.

The second and third points are dealt with elsewhere, particularly in the next two chapters. This chapter will focus on the first point above. The aim is to set up structures so that there is little need and few opportunities for disruption and cooperation is an easier and more attractive option.

Elements that help create ordered procedures and a calm environment

Elements that help create ordered procedures and a calm environment include:

- routine procedures, for example:
  - having pupils mentally and physically prepare for the lesson outside the classroom;
  - a procedure for entering the class, sitting down and preparing to work;

– a clear beginning to the lesson;
– a strategy for giving things out and packing away;
– an ordered procedure for leaving the class, by table, by row, etc.;
• a seating plan;
• a quick start to a lesson;
• as little to-ing and fro-ing as possible within and between lessons;
• asserting limits: rules and expectations;
• rewards for good behaviour;
• consistent sanctions for poor behaviour;
• training in how to sit quietly, listen, etc.

Let us consider some of these in more detail.

Preparation: the lesson begins outside the classroom

There is a way of being that is appropriate for talking with friends and playing in the playground, and one that is appropriate for thinking and working in the classroom. Often pupils carry their playground frame of mind, body posture and manner into the classroom. This wastes time and invites disruption and conflict. Ensuring a class is prepared for the lesson outside the classroom can, therefore, be extremely helpful.

Pupils learn that passing through the doorway of the classroom marks the dividing line between recreation and study. How they stand will be crucial here. Trying to engage pupils in academic work when they are in a posture associated with play or chat will be very difficult. The appropriate body posture will predispose them to a working frame of mind: it is the particular 'tool' required for school work, the internalised equivalent of an external uniform. Outside the classroom they stand up straight, relaxed, alert, quiet and, above all, still.

Considering the pupils' intention for the lesson is also useful: what do they intend to do and hope to achieve? Rather than aimlessly drifting into the classroom, their minds still on games, conversations and arguments of the playground, pupils can be trained to focus consciously on the lesson ahead. They may be set a question about the last lesson, have to remember two or three things they learnt, think about something for the coming lesson, etc., depending on the age of the pupils. Whatever they do, it must be in silence.

Entering the classroom, preparing for and beginning work

I have observed Year 7 pupils lining up quietly, entering a classroom in silence, sitting down, getting out folders and starting work without any instructions from the teacher who stood silently by watching. I have seen the *same class* pushing, shoving and shouting in a straggling line, entering in a disorderly fashion, rushing for specific seats and sitting down amid a general loud hubbub. The atmosphere was far from a working one. These were the same pupils. Why did they behave so differently in these two instances? I would suggest that the first example was possible because:

- the pupils knew exactly what to do and what was expected of them;
- a specific procedure had been taught;
- pupils were aware of individual sanctions that would follow poor behaviour;
- they had the opportunity of winning a class reward by generally good behaviour (a few minutes given over to puzzles at the end of the lesson, which they enjoyed);
- each lesson started in the same way;
- the teacher was ready and waiting for them outside the class;
- the pupils lined up in a quiet, orderly fashion outside the classroom;
- the pupils knew where to sit;
- the pupils had some work in which they could instantly get involved.

Obviously, all these conditions might not always be possible. The teacher might be coming from a different room and the class might be waiting outside for him or her. Nevertheless, the arrival of the teacher could become the signal for quiet which would be established before entering the room. Techniques could be adapted, as appropriate, for use with older pupils. It might not always be possible for the pupils to have work they could start immediately. However, it could be possible that they know to get out any equipment needed before sitting up straight prepared for work, or the teacher could have a short exercise waiting on the board.

Asserting limits: rules and expectations

Limits are a way of making it emotionally and, indeed, sometimes even physically safe in the classroom. They are a means through which authority invested in the role of teacher or in the particular person as teacher is established and maintained. If clear and respectful but firm and creatively enforced, they can be used to help avoid confrontation, improve relationships and encourage desirable behaviour.

Having clear limits is extremely helpful in classroom management and in feeling greater ease as a teacher. Without such boundaries many pupils feel uncontained. This can be particularly frightening for some whose behaviour is then likely to become more extreme in order to 'push' the teacher into setting limits. For many new and unconfident teachers, which limits to set and how to put them across can be an area of special difficulty. Some schools will have clear policies on behaviour and sanctions and this can help individual teachers in enforcing rules since they have the support of the whole staff. Yet not all possible situations can be covered in detail by policies and there will always remain times when teachers have to set their own limits.

Setting very clear limits does not necessarily mean you have to be bossy or confrontational or have lots of rules. *It is rather a question of an internal clarity of what is acceptable and what is not and an assurance and confidence in putting that across.* Boundaries can be enforced in a non-confrontational yet firm way which reinforces the fact that the pupil accepts the teacher's authority to be in charge of the process in the classroom. This may involve some quick thinking about what the essence of the instruction is and a compromise in order for both parties to save face.

For example, a girl in Year 2 was asked to throw away some scraps of paper she was still holding after clearing up time. She refused. Taken aback, since this pupil usually complied, the teacher thought with speed. Realising that the pupil might want to show the scraps to her parents, she suggested the girl gave her the paper to look after until the end of the day when she could take them home. In this way, the teacher thought of a *third solution* through which confrontation was avoided while her authority was maintained in the eyes of the rest of the class. The pupil concerned was also able readily to accept the teacher's authority since she could do so without backing down. Both were in fact satisfied: the pupil did not throw the paper in the bin; the teacher ensured that no one on the mat was holding scraps of paper. Both had saved face. If the teacher had assumed that the pupil was trying to defy her or if she had become fixed on the idea that the paper had to go into the bin, rather than that the girl no longer held it while on the mat, the incident would probably have ended in conflict.

Thinking through beforehand which limits are sacrosanct and which are flexible can be helpful since we then speak from a position of certainty which will inevitably be communicated in our manner. However thorough we might be in this preparation, there are nevertheless likely to be times when we have to question and reassert our limits on the spot.

It is also useful to question what is the essence of the limit. In this example, it was that the girl was not holding the paper rather than that she threw it in the bin. In the heat of the moment it is easy to get stuck on one demand as the only possible course of action, we must be obeyed or else, particularly if we assume the pupil is deliberately defiant. More often than not, *to begin with* he or she has another agenda, as in this case. If, however, the teacher instantly treats the pupil as if defiant when he or she was not intending that, defiance out of indignation might ensue. The role of a teacher's expectations and assumptions are discussed in more detail in Chapter 3.

Many limits are suggested in this chapter. In general, however, there are some helpful guidelines. For example:

• Prioritise what is crucial for you and the smooth running of the class, differentiating between the essential and the non-essential, and establish these limits *with conviction*. A few precise, yet necessary rules tend to be more effective and easier to apply than a number of more insignificant ones. If a rule is not essential, it is generally best not to introduce it since it provides another potential battleground.

- If the pupils are aware of the rules and understand the need for them, more will abide by them. Conversely, if the rules seem to serve no good purpose other than reinforcing the teacher's position of power and pupils are punished for transgressing them, then huge resentment, disaffection and further conflict can often result.

  With some classes it may also be appropriate to involve pupils in establishing a code of rules. The teacher could, for example, get the class to brainstorm what rules they need in order to learn most effectively, the teacher adding whatever he or she considers essential if these points are omitted. This could become the class code. Reasonable sanctions for the infringement of these rules could also be discussed and agreed, within the parameters of any whole-school discipline policy.

- Setting one general limit can often avoid a large number of smaller ones, for example, introducing a seating plan to limit where pupils may sit can eliminate the need to restrict chatting amongst friends, arguing over seats, etc. Insisting that pupils prepare themselves for work outside the door and enter the classroom in a manner conducive to learning can minimise the number of other limits needed to get the lesson off to a speedy start.

- Emphasising the desired behaviour rather than the undesirable one when enforcing a limit can be more effective, for example, 'Quiet now!' rather than 'Stop talking!'

Not all pupils will have the same standards of behaving well. It therefore needs to be articulated clearly what exactly your expectations are for behaviour in the corridor, in class, in relating to the teacher, and in relating to each other, and so on. A list of rules and expectations could be placed in the classroom. A whole-school approach would be helpful.

Another aspect of limits is that they change. That is to say, what we can or cannot tolerate, enjoy and take on will vary from time to time. The need to reassess the limits we are imposing is signalled by feelings of discomfort. If we are feeling burdened, irritable, stressed or generally unwell much of the time, it may be helpful to consider if it is time to start saying 'No' in some areas internally or externally. Over years of teaching our limits may change quite radically.

In the classroom, saying 'No' can place a safe boundary that helps everyone and maintains sufficient structure within which the lesson can proceed. There is sometimes confusion about allowing pupils freedom of creative expression and establishing a tight structure with clear rules and expectations, for fear that the latter might impose upon and restrict the former. It may be useful here to separate out *form* from *content*. That is to say, the form of the lesson may be highly structured, and there will be some structure of content, in line with the demands of the National Curriculum. Beyond that, however, there is much potential for creative expression by both teacher and pupils, the task of the teacher being to inspire the pupils with the given material, encouraging them to draw on their own skills, imagination and creativity. *For many pupils the greater the overall structure and the clearer the task, that is to say, the tighter the form of the lesson and the safer the classroom because of a few, thoughtful rules, the more likely they are to feel comfortable enough to engage in any creative endeavour.*

The structure is provided by:

1. *Fundamental limits or ground rules.* For example:
   - whether in a group or the whole class, only one person speaks at a time, the others listen;
   - everyone remains seated unless addressing the whole class or fetching equipment;
   - everyone is treated with respect;
   - hand up in silence if anyone wishes to speak, be chosen, etc.;
   - walking only in classroom and corridors.

2. *Careful timing.* The teacher moves the lesson along crisply. This can avoid many potential points of disruption and often helps many pupils to achieve a little more.

3. *A clear leader.* The teacher remains in charge of the process of the lesson.

4. *Clear instructions and accessible tasks.* If pupils understand what is required of them and can achieve, they have less motivation to disrupt.

Rewarding good behaviour

It is not always easy to appreciate effort in the field of behaviour since it is easier to judge achievement: a pupil may be making a huge effort, even though it falls far short of perfect. It is helpful, therefore, to notice even small improvements, particularly with pupils who are frequently in trouble for behaviour. Without this attention they are likely to give up hope, while feeling increasingly angry with teachers and the school system. One boy on permanent exclusion from Year 9 summed it up like this, 'I know I shouldn't want them to give me a good mark when I'm only doing the same as all the others, *but it's so hard for me*, and they don't even seem to notice. But as soon as I do the least little thing, they're on me. I think they're collecting information to get me out.' With greater support and more frequent praise for good behaviour, he may have been able to adopt such behaviour more often.

Schools have a variety of reward systems – commendations, year or house marks and so on. Individual teachers may also develop their own systems. One which rewards without setting up sharp competition between pupils minimises conflict. The pupil must also *want* the reward for it to be of any use.

It can also be useful at times, while setting target behaviour, to focus on rewarding any improvement in behaviour measured against a child's own standards, rather than against those of the class in general. Expectations need to be realistic so that rewards can be given wherever possible. The pupil whose behaviour is consistently though perhaps unobtrusively 'good' also deserves rewarding.

Consistent sanctions for poor behaviour

It is usually helpful to maintain the inevitable law of cause and effect: X behaviour results in Y sanction. Pupils are then fully aware *before* they act of the consequences to be expected. Responsibility is thus placed squarely on their shoulders. If they knowingly infringe a rule, they know exactly what to expect and can blame no one but themselves. Rather than a personal vendetta between teacher and pupil, it is the impersonal working out of a system. It is not mere whim, but is safe and leaves them the choice of inviting the consequences or not. On the other hand, if pupils are punished without a warning and without knowing they are infringing a rule, resentment is likely from some.

One maths department maintained the rule that if a 60 minutes (or 90 for older pupils) a week homework target was not met, pupils would automatically receive a detention. The pupils timed their homework themselves, and parents or guardians countersigned the time stated. Knowing they would receive detentions for lesser amounts, the vast majority of pupils nonetheless reported very exactly the minutes they actually spent working, even if it was below the limit. Very rarely was there any disagreement or resentment shown regarding the detention: it was a simple fact and there was no point in arguing or getting upset about it. If a pupil had been absent or there were unusual circumstances, the spirit rather than the letter of the law was upheld and the rule was not enforced, though this was rare.

A clear beginning to a lesson and a speedy start

If you have some preparation to do yourself – gathering your thoughts, getting out books, setting up a video and so on – it is useful to set the class a short task while you do so. This may serve as revision, it may practise a certain rule or form the basis on which the lesson is built. For example:

> In pairs you have three minutes to remember at least five points from last lesson. Whisper so you don't give anything away to your neighbours and take notes in your rough books if you like. You can look things up. Put up your hand if you have a question. Okay, starting, now.

For another class it may be appropriate to ask pupils to list the major events from a certain chapter, for example, or finish some work from the previous lesson.

A class may take some time to settle for the first couple of times you use this approach, but they will soon learn. Obviously the general idea can be adapted, depending on the age of the pupils, and tasks would need to be varied frequently. Timing tasks very exactly can help focus the mind. It also can lead to a slicker, more dynamic lesson. Working in pairs ensures that pupils who might have great difficulty alone can be helped to achieve some result, especially, perhaps, if the teacher has drawn up the seating plan. Depending on the nature of the task, the information might, for example, be fed back to the whole class, or be used in a writing activity.

The aim is to avoid any time wasted in which disruption can occur or enthusiasm can wane. Thus the teacher can note in the register who is present once the pupils are working, perhaps, rather than taking it right at the beginning of the lesson. Pupils can get bored having to wait until there is silence in order for the register to be taken: it is a waste of time. Again, questioning the essence of the activity is useful. What is the purpose of taking the register: to know who is present or to impress the class that the teacher is in charge?

Ending the lesson and leaving the room

The end of one lesson is, in a sense, the beginning of the next since it is often the last experience pupils have of a teacher before the next lesson and it can shape expectations and set the tone for the following meeting. There are, of course, other elements which play their part: when the lesson takes place in the day, for example, or individual and class experience so far. Nevertheless, it is worth considering how to achieve an ordered close and exit from lessons.

- Leave enough time to close calmly. Some teachers find it helpful to have a brief ending activity, maybe for only five minutes, separate from the main focus of the lesson. Depending on the subject, this might entail a puzzle, a quiz on the topic covered that day as an exercise in consolidation, or a relevant passage read.
- Have a procedure for collecting up books, completed work, etc.
- Have some closure, a gesture, a phrase, which formally closes the lesson.
- Have a procedure for leaving the room, such as back row first, by table, or those on the left. This is to be done quietly or in silence, after carefully replacing chairs under tables.

9

Training in how to sit quietly and listen

This is covered in Chapter 6.

Disruptive behaviour: getting an understanding

Behaviour is generally termed disruptive when it disrupts the teacher's plans, upsets other class members, or in some way disturbs the process of teaching and learning in the classroom. In other words, the behaviour is *inappropriate* in the context of the classroom and is unacceptable since it detracts from the education of the other pupils. The question remains of how to deal with such behaviour and the pupils exhibiting it and, above all, how to encourage desirable behaviour. General prevention techniques are discussed above and in subsequent chapters. This section focuses on managing the individual in a way which is, in the long term, likely to produce least disruption and, therefore, minimal conflict.

It is possible to trace a line of cause and effect: if a human being is in difficulty he or she will frequently create difficulties for others as well as for him or herself. If a child in your class habitually causes you problems, he or she is not the problem (even though it may feel like that) – he or she *has* a problem. This difference in perception can of itself alter your way of handling a situation and, therefore, the outcome.

Some pupils are simply too sad, too anxious or too angry to learn. Indeed, the three emotions are often all present and may come to the surface unexpectedly. Thus a pupil who is anxious or sad may suddenly become very angry. Anger may be easier to feel than sadness or fear.

I would like to emphasise that it is not for a teacher to probe into any personal difficulties a pupil may have since the former's role is to teach and he or she is neither therapist nor social worker. However, a working understanding of a pupil's behaviour can often be helpful since it may suggest ways of managing the pupil effectively so that he or she can at least cope, and at best succeed, in school.

Disruptive or reasonable? A way of considering disruptive behaviour

It could be said that all behaviour is 'reasonable' if seen from the particular thinking of the person responsible for it. That is to say, behaviour that is totally unreasonable in a classroom could be said to be 'reasonable' if seen from the pupil's viewpoint, even if it could never be permitted. I am not suggesting that disruptive behaviour should be sanctioned. Far from it. *The point I am making is that understanding the thinking behind undesirable behaviour may provide a key for relating to the pupil in such a way*

that he or she is more likely to adopt acceptable behaviour in the future.
Rather than assuming that the pupil is determined to make your life as difficult as possible and is simply bad, it can thus be useful to ask *why* he or she is resorting to disruptive behaviour: for example, habit; lack of alternative skills; preferring to disrupt than appear stupid; frustration at not being able to do the work; attempting to gain peer approval because of poor self-esteem; the need to feel 'powerful' in some way; desire for attention; for a specific reason, as with the girl with the scraps of paper mentioned earlier; as a protest against authority.

It is often useful to consider what the behaviour might be saying. It is unlikely to be random and will be communicating something about and doing something for the pupil. It may, perhaps, illustrate and confirm his or her world view or perceived position in it. Thus it will in some way help the pupil make sense of the world. It may be a deeply entrenched belief resulting from earlier experiences or may have been triggered by a specific incident. Sometimes it is almost as if the pupil has a particular script of a play illustrating his or her stance in life. The undesirable behaviour is the cue for the teacher to follow on in a way the pupil expects according to that script. If the teacher does so, the pupil's self-image is confirmed. The self-image is usually a troublesome one or else the behaviour would not be regularly disruptive. If the teacher follows the script offered and confirms the pupil's self-image and world view the undesirable behaviour has been successful and has been reinforced.

Specific learning difficulties: dyslexia and dyspraxia

Dyslexia
I enter the world like everyone else
in my clear box.
As time passes
people start to emerge
and indulge in life's pleasures.
I can see the light shining above
like a door of hope,
yet here I am tied
down by invisible cords.
Stupidity imprints itself
in my brain
as I strain ...
The box closes itself upon me,
smothering,
and tears stain the crystal bottom
of the tomb.
The others crowding:
Stupid! Stupid!

Dumbo! Thicko!
Slow-
coach!
Am I the only one?
I cry for help.
Sleep my only rest
from torment.
But even here the echoes screech:
Stupid! Stupid!
Dumbo! Thicko!
Slow-coach!

Mikaela Davies, aged 10

Not all pupils with specific learning difficulties (SpLD) will resort to disruptive behaviour or become involved in conflict with teachers, but some will and the true nature of their difficulties may be hard to ascertain. Indeed, the extent to which young people and adults are able to hide and divert attention away from some learning difficulties is impressive. For example, one man in his fifties with dyslexia had managed to hide from his own daughter, then an adult, that he had a very low reading age and could write little beyond his name! Suffice to say here that, if a pupil is consistently misbehaving, one avenue to investigate thoroughly is that of a possible specific learning difficulty. This is the case *even if the common mythology in the school is that he or she is simply disruptive or lazy and more experienced teachers tell you the same.* One 14-year-old girl in a maths class I worked in was considered just that. Observing her avoidance strategies and what she could and could not do, it became clear that she was dyslexic. This was found, in fact, to be the case and she was given help.

Pupils learning English as a second language may also be dyslexic and/or dyspraxic. This is useful to remember since poor literacy skills may be attributed to the fact the pupil is not working in his or her mother tongue. This may not be so. For example, a 12-year-old girl orally fluent in Arabic and English had great difficulty with written English due to dyslexia. Since she was a second language learner, however, it was easy to assume her difficulty in producing written work was due to using English rather than because of a SpLD. Pupils may have difficulty with reading English not because it is a foreign language to them but because they are dyslexic.

Unfortunately misdiagnoses concerning pupils with SpLD are not uncommon and it is not surprising why. Many teachers are not made sufficiently aware of the pointers which may indicate SpLD, nor of what these difficulties really mean for the pupil in the classroom (see Appendix I for information). Add to this the smokescreen of withdrawn or disruptive, maybe clowning, aggressive or abusive behaviour and the fact that pupils who disrupt lessons are invariably behind with and experience difficulty in doing work anyway since they miss out on instructions, do not finish tasks and may miss fundamental concepts. It is a question of the chicken and the egg: which came first, the disruptive behaviour, or the difficulty with work? Obviously not all disruptive behaviour is due to a learning difficulty; it is, however, always worth carefully checking this out as a possible cause or a contributing factor.

Example A

One primary-aged boy with a then undiagnosed literacy difficulty clearly illustrated the link between difficulties with work and disruptive behaviour when I observed him while the class were doing maths. He sat with his work before him. He would look at it for a short time, try something and, as soon as he hit a difficulty, he would stand up and start wandering around the class. Then he would begin chatting with one friend, take someone else's ruler, hit another on the head, and so on, gradually moving round the class and back to his seat. Then he would sit down, look at his work for a while, and the process would begin again. It was clear to an observer intent upon him that, rather than fail at the work, be stuck and get the feelings he had associated with this, it was safer and more comfortable to wander round the class. Even if he were told off for this, it was better and *made more sense* to him to be rebuked for something he did 'wrong' than for not doing and not being able to do his work. Yet, part of him would be trying to please, trying to be the same as the other children in the class, trying to be 'okay', and so he would keep returning to his task, each time to be faced with the same implacable difficulties.

This kind of behaviour is not uncommon: for many it is preferable to be considered naughty, lazy or the class clown rather than slow, 'thick' or unable to do a particular task. It can also feel better, too, since you are not 'failing' in quite the same way: you have more control over what you do (disruptive behaviour) than over what you cannot manage to do (work). It is, therefore, perhaps a relatively empowering strategy to disrupt and generally avoid the failure associated with work and, in that context, is very reasonable. For the rest of the class and the teacher, of course, it is totally unreasonable and is clearly unacceptable.

Example B

A boy in Year 8 with specific learning difficulties was in regular trouble with teachers for disrupting lessons. He was highly articulate, particularly in confrontations with teachers, and this made it harder to appreciate his literacy difficulties. He found it very difficult to focus on his work, not to get distracted in lessons by general bustle and not to get drawn into trouble by friends. The less structure in a lesson the more difficult he found it not to disrupt. He would often have angry outbursts in class, often telling teachers what he thought of them, and associated with a group of pupils who encouraged his disruptive behaviour. He received a little special needs help and then always behaved perfectly, being cooperative and hardworking. In other words, when he received the help he required and could achieve, when school was relevant, met his needs and gave him something positive, he behaved as a model pupil. For the rest of the time, his behaviour seemed to say, 'I don't like you or your school. I don't want to be here!' He reported that, after two months at the school, during which time he was never sent out of class for disruptive behaviour, he decided it was not for him. Not surprisingly, he started to be sent out of class for disruption and confrontation with teachers from then on and was permanently excluded during his second year.

A new approach: offering a different self-image

The strategies outlined earlier and in subsequent chapters for maintaining order, helping pupils achieve and building relationships obviously apply when dealing with pupils who often resort to disruptive behaviour and/or all too frequently become involved in conflict. Additional strategies may be needed in dealing with a pupil's particular script which the teacher may regularly be invited to play out. It is as if the pupil sees the world in a particular way with him or herself in it playing a particular role. The teacher is invited to take a role which fits in with the script. Thus if a pupil views him or herself as an outsider, his or her behaviour is likely to reflect this in some way. Either the pupil will appear withdrawn and quiet, excluding him or herself from the community of the class, or the behaviour will invite the teacher to exclude the pupil by sending him or her out of the class.

Taking the role offered and helping to confirm the pupil's self-image reinforces the disruptive or angry behaviour. It is, in a way, also 'safe' since it confirms the pupil's world view and challenges nothing. However, the pupil's strategy for making sense of the world is in itself destructive since it gets in the way of learning and leads to conflict. In addition, the pupil may continue with increasingly extravagant behaviour until a limit is set.

In gaining an understanding of the pupil's behaviour and possible script, it is often helpful when away from the class to:
- consider dispassionately the pupil's behaviour: what is it saying; how does it appear to an uninvolved observer? Behaviour is often quite literal;
- consider whether there is a pattern to the behaviour. What triggers it?
- ask yourself how *you* feel on the other end of the behaviour;
- try out the pupil's body posture for a few minutes to feel what it is like in his or her shoes. How does he or she sit, stand, walk? From this position, how does the world look? How would you regard learning, school, authority figures in general and teachers in particular? How comfortable do you feel? How confident? How would a teacher's instruction or reprimand sound from here?

Once you can see a pattern of behaviour and can get an idea of how it might feel from the pupil's position, it is often easier to find strategies to deal with the behaviour a little more satisfactorily. At the very least you may feel better about it. Very often the pupils' behaviour is such that we end up feeling how they feel. For example, if a pupil feels angry, frustrated, powerless and so on, his or her behaviour may be such that the teacher ends up feeling angry, frustrated or powerless in response. Understanding this can often provide the key to managing the behaviour more effectively, sometimes by refusing the role offered in the script.

An alternative approach which does not confirm the self-image, consistently maintains firm boundaries and which presents the pupil with alternative ways of viewing him or herself may be of use. Also, a balance must always be struck between the smooth running of the lesson for the rest of the class and the needs of an individual. A teacher's aim is to facilitate the learning and educational development of all pupils. Sometimes introducing an alternative self-image for a pupil helps in achieving this.

Let us consider what is needed in more detail:

1. An understanding of the behaviour: what exactly is it saying? This involves an understanding of the pupil's script and of the part offered to the teacher. It is not necessary to know in detail about the pupil's home life or past experiences since his or her behaviour and body posture speak for themselves and provide the key to understanding enough with which to work.

2. An understanding of your own feelings. How do you feel about the pupil? Is this how you usually feel about pupils? Is this a kind of behaviour which triggers particular feelings in you? Or could it perhaps be how the pupil might feel? For example, most teachers, even those who were usually very patient, felt extremely angry and frustrated about a certain boy in Year 7. In time it was discovered that he had difficulty hearing. It seemed that, feeling angry and frustrated at not being able to communicate easily, he behaved in ways which invited similar feelings in others.

3. An ability to stand back and not take things personally; this can be difficult since the pupil's behaviour can at times feel like a very personal attack. This perception can be strengthened if the pupil behaves more acceptably in other lessons, but not in yours.

4. A sense that it is the pupil's behaviour that is unacceptable, rather than the pupil him or herself, and that behaviour can be changed.

5. An awareness of at least one area in which the pupil can already succeed and gain praise, for example, attendance, punctuality, one subject area in which he or she manages with less conflict and so on.

6. Work and behaviour tasks which can be achieved.

7. Consistent reinforcement that the pupil is fine, though the behaviour may need changing in very specific ways.

8. Persistence and patience.

(A detailed plan for helping a pupil to change is included in Chapter 7.)

The first three points enable the teacher to think independently, that is to say, to perceive the pupil's behaviour outside the script assigned. As long as the teacher is feeling personally targeted, or thinks that the pupil is aiming to make his or her life difficult, then the teacher is part of the script. Once able to stand outside the script and view the behaviour and what it is saying about the pupil's world view and self-image, the teacher is in a position to apply boundaries and sanctions in a way that does not confirm that self-image. The pupil may need to be sent from class, kept in or excluded, whatever sanctions are appropriate. The approach throughout, however, will remain consistently one that is free from blame, even though it is made clear that the unwanted behaviour is totally unacceptable and the pupil's responsibility. His or her actions may be *described* in detail, but not *interpreted* since interpretations are likely to fit in with the script. Every opportunity is taken to praise anything praiseworthy and to create opportunities where praise is likely.

With some pupils it might be appropriate to tell them they no longer need to behave in the old role and can now take on a new one. They may need help in constructing this.

Sometimes it can be quite threatening for a pupil's world view to be challenged in this way and his or her behaviour may at first become more extreme for a while or he or she may use avoidance tactics of some kind. The teacher needs to weigh up the choices: if the previous behaviour is unacceptable, confirming the script does not work. Therefore, a different approach which challenges the pupil's world view may be more effective in the long run. Obviously a whole-school approach is desirable, though this may not always be possible.

Examples

Each case is, of course, an individual one which calls for its own particular strategy. It is helpful for as many teachers as possible to be included in a consistent approach to discipline. Where appropriate, parents or guardians may also be involved.

Example A

I heard a lot about a boy in Year 7, W, with whom I was to work, some time before I met him. Three teachers and the head related to me aspects of his undesirable behaviour and how it affected them and the class. His disruptive behaviour invariably led to some kind of conflict with the teacher. In addition, he frequently became involved in fights with peers. I noticed that, quite independently, in talking about him all four of them said at one time or another, 'He's impossible.' This alerted me to a possible script along these lines, that W's deep belief about himself was that he was unmanageable, 'impossible'. Since one of W's difficulties was relating to peers, it was agreed that I should do a structured activity with him and two classmates in the library so that he would have the opportunity of building working relationships that could be transferred to the classroom. Within half an hour, to my horror I heard myself say to W, 'You're impossible!' This is not an approach I habitually adopt with pupils and I was astounded: even though I was aware of his script, I was nonetheless drawn in and had confirmed his world view on our first encounter!

After discussion, W's teachers adopted a consistent approach in which they attempted to make a distinction between W and his behaviour. Rather than interpreting ('You're impossible!'), they began to reinforce the fact that W was fine, even though his behaviour needed changing in very specific ways. Real effort was made to establish and reinforce the idea that W was easily manageable, and okay. He was given achievable targets and was praised and rewarded whenever possible. His form teacher, who was also one of his subject teachers, gave time to developing a one-to-one relationship with him, overseeing his progress and praising liberally where praise was due. Over time, W began to care about her opinion of him and he began to try to please.

W was also given help in establishing peer relationships. In all lessons he was seated with one of three other pupils who had all agreed to sit next to him, and any group work was also with them. This immediately minimised conflict with peers in class. It was hoped that, having established more secure relationships with a few peers, W would be able to extend this to some other members of his class.

Example B

D was an adolescent in Year 10 who was in trouble for insolence with most of his subject teachers and with those who had brief dealings with him in corridors, the playground and so on. When I did a role play with him of a recent incident I understood why. I took the role of the teacher telling D to stop shouting in the corridor. He said nothing but avoided eye contact, his head bowed, slouching, his hands in his pockets. His whole posture seemed to be saying, 'I think you're rubbish with all your poxy rules!', or something to that effect. I felt instantly angry and, in a real situation would have found it difficult not to express that anger to him in no uncertain terms, thereby confirming his belief that teachers were unreasonably and unjustly angry with him.

After getting an insight into D's script, I suggested that we swapped roles so that he would be the teacher and I would adopt his posture. In a few minutes he was amazed at how angry he was, as the teacher. Up until then he had had no idea that his anger against the school system was expressed so openly through his provacative body posture. He had quite unconsciously been offering teachers the cue to get angry with him so that they expressed the anger he felt, while also confirming his view that authority figures became unjustly angry with him. Once aware of his anger and of what he had been doing, D had a choice: to continue his silent insolence and reap the inevitable consequence of regular trouble, or to try a different approach. We practised what he might do instead. We also considered the teachers' point of view, how they had a job to do and carried that out as best they could. Although aware, D still had his habit of insolent body posture to contend with and this would inevitably take time to change, even if he persisted. At a meeting of his teachers we discussed his physical response to correction so that they could also understand the script being offered them. This gave them, too, more choices in dealing with D.

Example C

Within two weeks of joining the school, H had alienated all his classmates and teachers. He randomly lashed out at the former and ignored most of the latter's instructions. In the playground he stood on the edge of things, watching the others play or engage together. It seemed as if his behaviour was confirming a script along the lines of, 'I'm alone. No one wants me. I can't fit in.'

Patient efforts were made to counteract H's world view. He was seated next to two or three pupils who were less intimidated by him and whom he rarely troubled. Realistic behaviour targets were given which he could achieve. Understanding the dynamic that had been set up by H's behaviour, teachers were better able to manage his unacceptable behaviour in a way which nonetheless accepted him as a person. Since H also had learning difficulties, special effort was made to ensure that he could manage to achieve some work tasks every day. For these, too, he was praised and rewarded, in an attempt to help build his self-esteem. Eighteen months later he seemed much more settled and was accepted as one of the class. He occasionally got involved in fights with one or two classmates and sometimes had conflict with teachers but, overall, he had made great improvements.

Example D

The following is an example of how a teacher skilfully managed to settle a boy comfortably into the class in the morning in such a way that he was less likely to resort to disruptive behaviour. She did this by taking a few moments to relate warmly with him, clearly believing in his willingness to 'be good'. Indeed, the boy subsequently had a 'very good day', not surprising considering the kind of relationship established from the beginning.

A six-year-old boy, S, with considerable behavioural difficulties, poor spoken language and few skills in positive relating with peers enters the classroom. The children are sitting on the mat waiting for the register to be taken. As the boy approaches, the teacher moves towards him, bends down so she is at his level, smiles, looks into his eyes and welcomes him warmly into the group saying, 'Good morning, S, sit down.' She speaks with feeling, her full attention on him, as though he is uniquely special. He sits down, quietly. After a short time he starts to crawl towards the nearest child. The teacher says, 'Sit down on your bottom, S', repeating this two or three times until he complies. Then she says, again with feeling, 'Good boy, S!'

Even though this concerned a primary-age child, the process is also relevant to secondary teachers who would adapt their approach to the age of the pupil. Let us look in more detail at these interchanges: what exactly is the teacher doing?

1. She goes up to S, moves to his level and greets him: she is *meeting* him not only physically, but, with the warm smile and good eye contact, also emotionally, as one human being to another, with respect. He may not be able to do the work set as the other children can, he may not be able to behave in the ways requested, but for that moment it does not matter: he is valued *for himself* rather than for what he can or cannot do, he is welcomed unconditionally. From the start there is a positive relationship in which the teacher is clearly directing the process, with the expectation that the time spent together will be pleasant.

2. When he starts crawling she *reinforces the desired behaviour* ('Sit down on your bottom'), rather than what is to be stopped ('Don't do that'). It is usually the case that, if you tell people not to do something, they tend to remember it in the positive. For example, telling a class, 'Don't forget to do your homework' may result in some of them registering, 'Forget to do your homework' and is not as effective as the positive, 'Remember to do your homework.' If the teacher had used the form 'Don't do that', in this case she may have been unwittingly reinforcing the undesired behaviour: a confusing message which could undermine any sense of emotional security and safety built up.

3. When the boy does as asked the teacher immediately rewards him with heartfelt praise: her warm response makes it an attractive proposition to do what she says another time in order to win such praise. She is also helping to change the boy's perceptions of himself: sometimes he does things right, sometimes he is 'good'. *It is the way we think about ourselves and the world that shapes behaviour. It is at the level of thinking that real change is, therefore, ultimately possible.* By handling the incident in this way the teacher enables the boy to feel good about himself for sitting down, without feeling bad about himself for crawling in the first place. New behaviour is reinforced without the need to tell him off.

   If this approach is followed it is more likely that, in time, the boy's self-esteem will increase and his level of fear and alienation will decrease. His behaviour would, therefore, be acceptable more and more frequently. Boundaries would be imposed and self-esteem built at the same time. Conversely, if he were told off on each occasion that his behaviour was in some way undesirable (and this could be many times each day), his self-esteem could only be eroded and his fear increase, along with his isolation, a deep sense of always being 'wrong' and a general demoralisation. All this would, of course, be likely to result in more anti-social behaviour.

Difficulties

It can be helpful to consider what might stop us from managing similar situations to our own satisfaction. Once aware of potential difficulties we are more likely to avoid them, if possible. In some cases it might be useful to understand why a particular strategy did not work with a pupil so that we can, if necessary, refine our technique. Understanding difficulties can sometimes help save us from demoralisation.

Pressure of work and emotions

We may, for example:

- simply have too many other demands to be able to give the time to an individual: there are another 30 or more pupils all with their own needs;
- be caught up solely in teaching the next part of the curriculum, rather than in teaching young people;
- be tired, feel ill, irritated or be suffering from stress;
- not like the pupil in question;
- feel extremely angry for all the trouble caused in the past by this particular pupil;
- dread the pupil, our heart sinking whenever he or she enters the classroom;
- feel rushed, and so on.

Entrenched views and family role

Not all attempts to manage pupils with difficulties are successful; there is no panacea. M, for example, was a 14-year-old who was considered by both teachers and parents to be lazy. He spent most lessons slouching over the desk and produced little or no work. M was, in fact, both dyslexic and dyspraxic. He found writing very painful and slow and had a spelling age four years earlier than his chronological one, although his spelling was phonetic and his writing legible. The emotional impact of his difficulties was severe: his body posture had a look of despair about it. M considered himself to be lazy, bad and the problem of the family. After a relatively short period of one-to-one sessions, M had managed to write a full sheet of A4 answering an English GCSE question, probably the most he had ever written and finished at one go. This counteracted directly his script as lazy and bad. After this, M failed to come to any further sessions: his need to remain as the problem in his family may have been too compelling without much more comprehensive support, for example, family therapy, which was not possible.

It is important to remember at times like this that, as teachers, we have not necessarily done it all wrong and failed completely. Sometimes the weight of habit and need to maintain a role might be too great for the pupil to risk change. He or she might not have sufficient reason to step into the unknown of new behaviour. It might not be the right time, or there may be insufficient support. In some cases, the pupil may have a psychological problem which is not easily helped, even with interventions such as family therapy or child psychotherapy. However, the long-term effect of attention, time and care can never be assessed. At some level it is never wasted.

Cover work with supply teachers

Many teachers who do supply work are highly skilled and effective teachers who face a particularly difficult task. This is because they often do not even know the names of the pupils they teach, they may well not be experts in the subject and the work set may be less engaging than that possible when the subject teacher is present. In addition, the classes they teach are often angry and/or disappointed since their habitual teacher is absent. *Those pupils who are most likely to disrupt are usually those who are least able to manage change effectively.*

Pupils with specific learning difficulties and some second language learners frequently fare particularly badly in these lessons since the teachers are often unaware of their difficulties and, consequently, may have unrealistic expectations. Cover work tends often to be based on literacy, comprehension, written questions and answers and such like, and this may be difficult without help, extra individual explanation, pair work, or some other support.

Some schools use a system whereby pupils with specific learning difficulties carry a card stating briefly in which aspects of work they need most help, for example, copying from the board, writing down homework, understanding instructions, organising written answers. This alerts the supply teacher to a pupil's particular needs. If the pupil can achieve, he or she is less likely to disrupt the class and come into conflict with the teacher. Not all pupils will wish to carry such a card, but many find it helpful.

In setting cover work, departments may also consider that a large volume of writing is often overwhelming for pupils with learning difficulties, specific learning difficulties, and others, for example, second language learners, since many write very slowly and/or with considerable effort. Consequently, cover work for these pupils is generally preferable if it requires only an answer to be written, rather than the full question and answer in a sentence. If the task is too daunting, many will not even attempt it or will give up easily, particularly without the presence of their usual teacher, and will easily be led into or resort to some kind of disruptive behaviour. This is all the more likely because of heightened anxiety due to having a teacher they do not know, or do not know well.

Owning authority

It can be difficult at times to show, with conviction, that you really have the right to be in charge. There can sometimes be a fine line between owning your authority and remaining clearly in charge without resorting to an overbearing, controlling attitude which is likely to invite aggression from certain pupils. Here I would like to consider two areas in which owning authority with ease can be useful:

1. Starting off: entering the classroom or approaching the class with confidence.
2. Remaining in charge: realistic, compelling instructions.

Starting off: entering the classroom or approaching the class with confidence

Intention and preparation

Having thought through procedures in detail and being very clear of your aims and intentions can add to confidence.

You are on your way to teach your most dreaded lesson and/or class. Or it may be the first time you have met. How and where do you want the meeting to take place? If you are going to a room where the class has just been taught, can you arrange with the previous teacher for the pupils to leave the room and line up outside so that you can get individual eye contact, a greeting and a relatively controlled entrance? Or will you make that contact in some other way? How?

- What is your intention for the lesson?
- Do you have a procedure ready for gaining pupils' attention outside the classroom, for their preparation and for an orderly entry?
- Do you have a seating plan?
- Do you have an immediate activity for the class to begin while you sort out equipment, etc., or are you able to open the lesson immediately?
- How do you intend to gain attention when entering the room or approaching the class in the corridor? That is to say, how can you develop an authoritative (neither an overbearing nor confrontative) physical presence?
- How will you gain attention and get the pupils working on an activity in which you wish them to be involved before they create some unwanted activities of their own?

This kind of preparation is in addition to that in which we choose the content, tasks and general shape of a lesson. It is considering how we can make contact, get things going and capture attention and interest. It is a time in which we decide what will work for us, what we can put across wholeheartedly and with greatest ease; what we want and what we cannot accept; where we draw the line and what our sanctions are if needed. The clearer we are about our choices if things do not go according to plan, even though we expect they will, the more confidence we can have when entering the classroom.

Developing a dynamic physical presence

It is possible to approach a group or walk into a room and stand in front of a class without being noticed, or, at least, being studiously ignored, by a number of pupils. It is equally possible to enter and stand in such a way as to draw attention to yourself like a magnet. While appearing confident, this stance is non-confrontational and relaxed.

As you approach the classroom or, perhaps, the class approaches the door, what do you feel? Is there a sense of dread in your lower abdomen, overall tension, a muddled head, slight panic? Or do you feel calm, energised, relaxed and in charge? What happens to your breathing? What is your body posture?

For many of us all this will vary, depending on how prepared we feel, which class it is, when it is, how we are feeling in general and so on. What can sometimes be useful is to know certain skills that we can apply on those occasions when, for whatever reason, we are feeling vulnerable, insecure, unconfident, or simply ill or tired. Considering our physical posture and breathing can be helpful at such times.

As always, there are many ways into this and no single right way. Some might find it easiest to think of someone who would manage the given situation with ease, grace and enjoyment and then to take on that person's manner of moving, standing and sitting. The model can be from any walk of life or, indeed, a fictional character. The key point is to enter into the target body posture wholeheartedly, that is to say, to enter into role.

Another approach would be to be aware of your physical presence before, during and after you or the class enter the classroom. Before entering the room, you can imagine gathering your energy up around you like a cloak, sending it out ahead of you. It is not a question of flinging open the door and slamming it behind you to announce your arrival, which could appear as a challenge, but rather a matter of consciously projecting your energy forward with focus. Some pupils will thus be aware of your presence just *before* you arrive.

When in the classroom, notice two key areas: your contact with the ground and your chest, which includes your breathing and your voice. When anxious, many people tend to have poor contact with the ground, hovering from foot to foot, or will have their weight very unevenly balanced. Others may have their toes curled, gripping desperately at the floor. Stand evenly, feeling the support of the ground. Relax your shoulders by feeling the elbows are heavy and soften any tension in the chest. With the mouth closed, do some pretend yawns. This relaxes the throat and diaphragm. Remember to keep breathing.

From such a physical stance it is easier to respond in a relaxed way. It is also easier to think and choose, before rushing in with a usual pattern of response you may not particularly want. From this solid, relaxed and calm position you can reach out with your voice and eyes to any point in the room in order to gather attention to you. You come across as neither supplicant nor aggressor, rather as a relaxed, commanding presence.

As with any training, best results are obtained by relaxed practice at times outside the situation itself. A growing awareness of how body posture and breathing can influence your communication and feelings can thus be usefully developed and reinforced at your leisure.

Voice

The voice can be a powerful tool for teachers. It can convey warmth, approval, disapproval, enthusiasm, fear, anger and so on. At times of stress and high anxiety, in particular, we may be worried it might let us down, revealing all too clearly our insecurity of the moment. What we intend being a calm but commanding instruction to 'Be quiet', 'Sit down', or 'Come here', turns out to be far more feeble, squeaky or wrathful than we would wish. We feel exposed and undermined, let down by our voice. Yet we can use it too in a way that can help build our confidence and sense of personal power.

The first point is about structure. That is to say, if the chest and throat are relaxed and we are breathing with some comfort, our voices can flow more easily. Trouble often arises when there is considerable tension across the chest, shoulders and throat. This can inhibit voice production. To have a relaxed chest and powerful voice the legs, feet and diaphragm must be relaxed, and we must be breathing easily.

The second point concerns where we focus. Often when aware we have to make a loud sound we concentrate on our throat itself and on the 'target', the person or people we are addressing. This can limit our voice considerably, especially if our throat is tense. If, instead, we imagine our voice starting from the lower abdomen and flowing out through us, beyond those we are addressing, to infinity, the effect can be startlingly different. Rather than limiting ourselves we are facilitating the flow of energy within the voice to continue out from us. Another image might be that of a dart sent from a blow pipe. We are the pipe and we shoot out the energy dart with ease. It is less a question of volume here and more one of intensity.

Presentation

What do your clothes and footwear say about you? Do they increase or decrease your sense of confidence and inner authority? Do they support the image you are wishing to project? Are they likely to help you to be noticed and to appear as a commanding presence? If it is the first time you are meeting a class, will your appearance help or hinder the formation of a cooperative working relationship, with you in charge?

Remaining in charge: realistic, compelling instructions

The unexpected

A brilliant flash of lightning is followed shortly by a crash of thunder. A few pupils give pretend screams. About half the class rush to the windows.

As the storm continues the lesson is in a complete shambles. What do you do? What instructions can you possibly give that will be a) heard, and b) carried out? How will you deliver these instructions in a way as to ensure the desired result?

The unexpected is surprisingly common in teaching: you have based a lesson around a video or tape only to find the equipment is broken; a bee enters the classroom and proceeds to alight on various pupils amid general uproar; there is a dental check and the class arrives in small clusters over a period of some twenty minutes, completely disrupting your carefully planned lesson in which timing was to have been of the essence, and so on. You have the responsibility to take charge and make things happen. Just how do you exercise that authority convincingly?

Sanction the inevitable, on your own terms

Frequently, as in the example of the thunderstorm, it can be useful to sanction the inevitable, but on your own terms. It is, of course, possible to say, 'Back to your seats at once' and to be obeyed instantly, but this is likely only if you feel convinced yourself of the pupils' compliance. If you lack conviction, they will be unlikely to respond. Another approach is, therefore, *to take charge of what is already happening*, adding a time limit, or another aspect you wish to introduce, before giving the new instruction. For example, 'You have 30 seconds before I ask you all to sit down, so have a good look.' Then, 30 seconds later, you can say with conviction, 'Your time's up. Back to your seats *now*!'

Since this acknowledges the need of human curiosity to watch something unexpected or new, like a storm, it can meet with less resistance, while nonetheless being defined by the teacher.

Similarly, if a pupil is rushing out of the room in anger, the teacher has various choices. To say, 'Go back to your place and sit down immediately!' might be unrealistic, especially if the pupil is in a rage. Indeed, he or she might not even hear such an instruction at such a time. The outcome would also partly depend on the relationship already built up. In any event, it would be difficult for a pupil to comply and still save face. If the pupil did not obey, the teacher could be left appearing ineffective in the eyes of the class. Physically attempting to bar the way is unwise since an angry person whose way is blocked is likely to become violent. The dilemma is, therefore, how to maintain a sense of authority in front of the class, as well as in the eyes of the individual concerned?

Once again, sanctioning the inevitable but on your own terms can prove useful. Consequently, the teacher might say something along the lines of, 'Go and stand outside for a few minutes. You can come back when you're calm. I shall inform X [year head or other management figure who needs to know a pupil is out of class]. I'll see you later today to sort this out.' To the rest of the class the teacher might add something like, 'I'll deal wth

him/her later. Enough time wasted, now on with the lesson!' This implies the teacher is supremely in charge, remains unruffled by the incident, and is choosing to deal with it later in order not to waste teaching time. It also makes it clear that such incidents are reported and will be followed up, and, of course, they must be.

Instructions and inner conviction

Giving instructions occupies a considerable part of any teaching day and much has already been written about it. However, I would like to touch briefly neither on the words used nor on ways of ensuring attention, but on the thinking and body posture of the speaker. That is to say, I am concentrating on *how* we may appear neither 'diffident' (p. 14) nor 'over-bearing, or brash, or domineering' (p. 98), as Marland (1975) suggests. What thought process and stance will enable us to appear relaxed, calm and authoritative when we are feeling none of these? Ultimately, it is our inner conviction which results in instructions being carried out. I have used exactly the same words to the same class with different results because I felt differently about the possible outcome.

Let us consider the kind of thinking that might underlie instructions given in a classroom. For example:

- 'I don't think they're going to pay any attention to this.'
- 'Oh no! They look in a stroppy mood ...'
- 'Everything's organised and I know what I'm doing.'
- 'I'm at the end of my tether with this lot. I don't know what I'll do if they ignore me again.'
- 'I really like this class.'
- 'This is awful. Aaagh!'
- 'They'd better watch out today. One squeak of dissent and I'll have the lot of them.'
- 'I'm feeling great. What a beautiful, sunny day.'
- 'Oh no! J's back!'

We may be familiar with some of these or something similar and we may find that there is often a connection between the thinking attached to an instruction and its outcome. If we go into a classroom expecting a struggle, that is usually what we get. If we go in feeling very vulnerable and diffident it is more difficult to establish ourselves as being in charge than if we feel calm and at ease.

The question, therefore, remains: what helps cultivate a sense of inner conviction that our instructions will be carried out? Here I would like to note some elements regarding our manner that can be helpful in getting instructions across in a powerful way:

1. A sense of inner authority, that is to say, no doubt that you can manage *well enough*. This includes a deep belief that you have the right to

give instructions and that they will be fulfilled. Experience may be useful in this, but only if we can learn from it.

2. A relaxed physical presence that appears grounded and calm. A strong, though not necessarily loud, voice. A steady, though non-intrusive gaze.

3. A clear alternative of what to do if instructions are not carried out, without expecting this to be the case.

4. Congruent body language to show you mean what you say. For example, if pupils are slow leaving class at the end of the day, start closing windows, locking cupboards and so on, to get across the idea that everything is over. Quite simply, actions do speak louder than words and usually it is what we do and our *manner* that will be noticed more than *what* we say.

Teaching points

Dance and drama

The powerful potential of using body posture to assume different character traits and how to take on a role can be explored at many levels in both subjects. Parallels can then be drawn with real life and how these skills could be usefully employed to 'manufacture' confidence, for example.

Careers

The use of body posture can be successfully examined when teaching interviewing techniques. How to develop a dynamic though non-confrontational physical presence could be of considerable use when seeking employment and when carrying out job interviews.

This chapter has dealt with:

Elements that help create ordered procedures and a calm environment
- Preparation: the lesson begins outside the classroom
- Entering the classroom, preparing for and beginning work
- Asserting limits: rules and expectations
- Rewarding good behaviour
- Consistent sanctions for poor behaviour
- A clear beginning to a lesson and a speedy start
- Ending the lesson and leaving the room
- Training in how to sit quietly and listen

Disruptive behaviour: getting an understanding
- Disruptive or reasonable? A way of considering disruptive behaviour
- Specific learning difficulties: dyslexia and dyspraxia
- A new approach: offering a different self-image
- Difficulties

Owning authority
- Starting off: entering the classroom or approaching the class with confidence
- Remaining in charge: realistic, compelling instructions

Teaching points
- Dance and drama
- Careers

CHAPTER 2

Improving Behaviour through Building Confidence and Self-esteem

… Now doesn't exist because you don't completely accept who you are right now … Nothing is ever enough if you don't accept yourself right this moment as complete.

Lynn V. Andrews, *Star Woman*

… The basic premise of my work is that we each have something very special and unique to offer and express in the world … Through building self-esteem and other related techniques I encourage people to increase their awareness of their strengths and to learn to accept their limitations and areas of weakness. In accepting our weaknesses we can have something tangible to change … if we choose.

Kaleghl Quinn, *Stand Your Ground*

When pupils are involved in work and are succeeding they have little need for poor behaviour. If they feel good about themselves in school they are more likely to cooperate with teachers and support the ethos and aims of school life. This is easy enough to understand, but the question remains as to how you help pupils succeed when their needs are so diverse. This chapter acknowledges that diversity and looks at some techniques for helping those children who may experience difficulties in learning. These techniques will usually benefit all pupils. It also considers ways of minimising demoralisation and resentment. The chapter includes four sections:

1. Helping pupils succeed.
2. Avoiding demoralisation.
3. Constructive criticism.
4. Building confidence and self-esteem.

Helping pupils succeed

What is needed for achievement

There are obviously many different levels of achievement possible in school. For some it may entail passing 'A' levels, for others learning to read, learning a skill, or managing to sit relatively still and listen for five minutes, and so on, depending on the pupils, their age and the particular situation. There will, however, be some common elements usually required in order for any kind of achievement.

Some of these are to be found in the Venn diagram below. In essence, we are considering how pupils can be interested and motivated, feel good, and even better, when they do achieve, have an environment in which creative work is possible and tasks which they can manage.

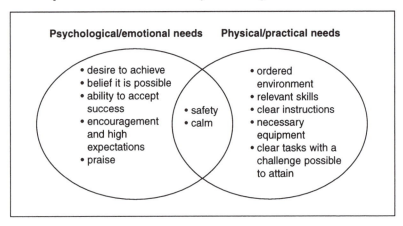

Figure 2.1 General requirements for achievement

Let us consider some of the details these elements might include in practice.

Emotional sphere

Emotional safety
- Support, encouragement and praise from the teacher.
- Constructive rather than 'labelling' criticism.
- Clear boundaries and structures regarding behaviour so pupils know what is expected of them.
- A consistent policy on disruptive behaviour so pupils know the consequences of breaking rules.
- Not being bullied by peers.
- An assurance that they will be taken seriously if they have a difficulty or concern and will be respected.

A desire to achieve
- A reason for learning and achieving, e.g. a thirst for knowledge, a qualification that is needed, a 'reward', an interest in the subject, etc.
- Work that is interesting, relevant and engages the pupil.
- An enthusiastic teacher.
- A desire to please the teacher and get praise.
- A desire to please parents or other significant people.
- A cooperative agreement with the teacher based on good will.
- A desire to feel the satisfaction of achievement.
- Opportunities for creativity and independent learning so that the pupil feels empowered by the learning process.

A belief success is possible
- Being able to succeed: work and expectations for behaviour are of an appropriate level.
- Encouragement.
- Seeing some measure of improvement, for example, working through a book, being able to write more; comparing past and present efforts.
- Sufficient self-esteem to believe success possible.

An ability to accept success
- A self-image which allows success.
- A peer group, family or carers and friends who support success.

Practical sphere

Physical safety
- Not being physically bullied.

A calm, ordered environment
- Routine procedures, for example:
  - having pupils prepare for the lesson outside the classroom;
  - a procedure for entering the class, sitting down and preparing to work;
  - a clear beginning to the lesson;
  - a strategy for giving things out and packing away;
  - a procedure for leaving the class.
- A seating plan.
- A quick start to a lesson.
- As little to-ing and fro-ing as possible.
- Clear rules and expectations.
- Rewards for good behaviour.
- Consistent sanctions for poor behaviour.
- Training in how to sit quietly, listen, etc.

Relevant skills
- The development of these should be included systematically in the National Curriculum. In particular, the development of concentration, thinking and reasoning are important since, without these, learning is impossible. Sufficient oral work before written tasks can help pupils think and reason. It is also much easier to write clearly when ideas are worked out first.

Work at an appropriate level
- The key element here is that the pupil can generally succeed most of the time (for some pupils with very poor self-esteem it is helpful to succeed all the time at first), otherwise she or he is, in effect, consistently learning to fail.

Help when needed
A number of these aspects will be considered in different sections of the book. Here we would like to focus on two areas many pupils find taxing. Strategies targeted at these pupils will improve and streamline teaching methods in general. Those pupils who are capable of more independent work will also benefit from the structural and organisational techniques offered. The areas covered are:
- making success possible;
- help with organisation.

Making success possible

A structure for written work

There are many elements involved in making success possible. In assessing past work set, we can usually deduce that, if a piece of work has been poorly done by some of the class, then we may still have work to do in making the exercise more accessible. The temptation is to blame the pupils for not listening, not trying hard enough and so on, rather than questioning the task itself or the clarity of our instructions.

A common oversight is to expect pupils to structure large and even relatively small written tasks independently. The assumption is often made that the pupils will have been taught how to compose and structure written assignments at primary school. Whether they have been taught or not, most will probably not know how to do so or will lack the confidence to try out their skills. Even pupils in Years 10 or 11 may not have some basic techniques at their fingertips. The result is that, while some pupils may manage, many will struggle, some will do poorly and others will not even attempt an assignment, leading to an erosion of confidence and enthusiasm and the possible growth of resentment and anger. For example, one pupil in Year 8 with specific learning difficulties (SpLD) had been told for a holiday homework task to 'Do a project on a famous artist'. Not surprisingly, many in the class were filled with consternation, and not only those with SpLD. Access to libraries might be restricted for many and those without assiduous and helpful family, friends or carers with time to spare had a formidable task indeed.

A structure and guidelines of some kind could have been immensely helpful. For example:

1.Write briefly under as many of these headings as possible.
Birth date and place.
Family members and early life.
Education and art training.
Places in which he or she lived.
Main kinds of painting, e.g. landscapes, still life, portraits, abstract.
Why he or she is famous.
Personal response to the painting, likes and dislikes.

2. Sketch two paintings and say why you have chosen them.

(If you would prefer to approach this project in a very different way and have clear ideas about this, or wish to add more information, please do so.)

The advantage of this kind of structure is that pupils know the kind of information to look for and when they can stop. Those who feel inspired by the subject will probably add much more anyway, while those who feel very lost with a general title will at least have some guidelines. When training a class for this kind of written task the teacher could, before setting the homework, supply pupils with some basic facts about an artist's life. The class could then construct the outline of a project in groups so that by the time individual pupils face the task at home they would have a much clearer idea of the demands made and how to meet them.

The standard of work in the class as a whole is likely to be higher than for a totally unstructured project. Consequently, the pupils' satisfaction and sense of achievement will probably be greater. For most pupils it is the case that the more satisfied at producing work they feel, the more work they will do and the less they will disrupt. Being able to fill an empty page with writing is an empowering thing to do and pupils can grow in confidence with each task they complete. Conversely, *those who fail to manage a task can lose confidence daily*. The ideal, therefore, is to teach to each pupil's strength, while strengthening any weaknesses – a particularly formidable task with 30 or more pupils per class! However, a given structure and practice in how to set about organising material and ideas can help in this.

A structure for oral work

In many instances this is also necessary since pupils often lack the grounding in verbal skills to be able to explore issues satisfactorily. The assumption is often made that, because it is just talking, everyone can do it. However, discussing a particular issue may require a special kind of questioning or technique in which the pupils may not be skilled. For example, a class of Year 6 pupils were given the task in small groups to discuss some old artefacts and to discover what they might have been used for. The pupils had neither pen nor paper to record ideas and had not been given any further instructions. Not surprisingly they foundered, and very soon started chatting about other things. Clearly they needed more structure and skills in brainstorming ideas. The teacher could have carried out a similar brief exercise using a different artefact with the whole class. For example:

- the pupils are first encouraged to really look at the item: is it large or small, heavy or light; what is it made of; is it in good or poor condition?
- these and other useful questions to think about are put on the board: for example, was it used for indoor or outdoor work; was it used on its own or was it part of a larger machine?
- the class then brainstorm possible uses, accepting all suggestions and the teacher writing them on the board;
- using the information gathered earlier, pupils decide which uses might be possible.

It is only after such preparation that pupils would have been ready to tackle the exercise independently in small groups. With the questions left on the board and the example of brainstorming followed by discrimination, they would have had a structure as a guideline. This would have generated much more discussion to the point and a more satisfactory result. One or two members of the group could have been given the task of scribe for the brainstorming exercise. The likelihood of disruptive behaviour would have been minimised and pupils would have been left at the end feeling much more positive and satisfied than they clearly were in the instance I observed. Such preparation is, of course, particularly important if a written exercise is to follow oral work.

When these Year 6 pupils entered secondary school a few months later they would not magically acquire the oral skills necessary to perform verbal tasks of a similar nature. Some might of course learn them at home, but many would not do so even much later on in their school career – such skills need to be specifically introduced by teachers into the learning process.

Help with organisation

The process of writing

As with oral tasks, there are several stages involved in writing, whether it is imaginative or factual. For many pupils the task of writing will seem too difficult without some help through these stages. If the teacher illustrates the process and practises writing using these stages with the whole class, pupils will have clear guidelines to follow. If pupils can frequently work in rough it liberates them from the need to get everything 'right' and they often produce more work of a higher standard. If the subject is interesting and relevant and the writing task seems to have a point, many pupils will stay on task most of the time if they can manage. Help with the process of writing will make this more possible.

The stages involved in writing are as follows:

1. *Talking or thinking through.* Very often this stage is omitted. *It follows general discussion on a topic and relates specifically on the written task.* It is frequently important since the clearer the thinking involved the sharper any written work will be. This stage could be done in pairs or alone and may be linked to the one below so ideas are not forgotten.

2. *Spidergram.* Brainstorm ideas or note down different aspects of relevant information. If this is done in the form of a spider with the title as the body and a new leg for each section, it is much easier to sequence according to meaning than if written in a linear fashion.

3. *Sequencing.* This involves numbering the ideas/information in the most logical order for writing.

4. *Writing.* Since each idea or point is written in order, it is often more approachable than tackling a whole essay at once. Writing one or two sentences for each numbered 'leg' helps many pupils organise information well enough to get it down on paper. Thus the pupils are helped to tackle writing in small chunks, rather than being faced with the daunting prospect of a whole blank page, no ideas and all the possible mistakes they could make.

5. *Checking.* Encourage pupils to read through once from the beginning to check for meaning. Is this what they really want to say? They should also read through once from the bottom up to check spellings. Reading from right to left in this way helps to make each word appear in isolation. Thus pupils are less likely to see what they expect to see and more likely to notice mistakes. It is useful to separate concern for correct spellings from the process of writing text so pupils are not inhibited by the fear of spelling something wrongly. Key words could be supplied where relevant.

Although some may consider such a structure as this to be

'spoonfeeding', many pupils will nevertheless need this much guidance in order to achieve. Some will require similar structures for a considerable time, others only until they have assimilated the process for themselves, while yet others might need it little.

Example

With pupils in Year 7 a teacher illustrated how effective adequate preparation, attention to process and a structure can be in helping pupils with a relatively low level of literacy skills organise ideas and achieve well with a written task. The class had read and discussed a passage about someone escaping from a prisoner-of-war camp. The teacher wrote some key words on the board and gave the class the task of writing about an escape from prison. She elicited from class members a spidergram of ideas which could be included. Again using class suggestions, she wrote three possible opening sentences that pupils could use if they wished. The class, therefore, had structured information to use, some key words and spellings given, an opening and a subject they had already spent some time considering. In other words, the teacher had helped with the first two stages outlined above. Pupils needed only to sequence, write and check their work. They could work in pairs if they wanted. Those who wished could write something completely different without using these supports. All pupils were working on a rough draft, so 'mistakes' were allowed.

C received special needs help for literacy difficulties. He had also missed work through disruptive behaviour in the past, particularly through storming out of class in a fury. He was sitting next to F who was a second language learner with good oral skills in English but more limited written ones. C immediately started to panic, put up his hand and told the teacher that he could not do the work. The teacher approached and suggested C and F worked together, first copying the spidergram from the board on to their paper. Then they could decide which ideas should come first and number the legs of the spider. This would give them the organisational structure for knowing what should come next. They were to start with the three sentences given. C soon put his hand up asking for a spelling, but was told to look on the board where key words were written. He soon started referring to the board himself. Both boys worked steadily and at the end of the lesson had written a whole side of A4 at a level better than anything they had achieved previously.

Revision and learning

Importance of a system

In Chapter 3 there is a description of different ways of thinking and learning using our senses of sight (visual), hearing (auditory) and feeling (kinesthetic), in other words using different representational systems. An awareness of such systems has direct application in the classroom since it touches upon the heart of much school work, namely, learning.

If a pupil knows which is his or her strongest representational system, he or she can employ this in learning. If the pupil is unaware, he or she may unwittingly employ the least successful strategy and fail, or manage but with unnecessary difficulty. An example will clarify my point. Although I found much school work relatively easy, there was one aspect in which I consistently failed: learning 'by heart'. This was because, misunderstanding the task, I employed my weakest representational system for the job. Since we would be called upon to recite a poem learnt 'by heart', I believed I had to learn it by saying it aloud. Consequently, I would look at a line or two, say it out loud and then close my eyes, while repeating it over and over, *listening* to the words. Using this technique I managed *not* to learn considerable amounts of poetry, including poems I really loved and wanted to know! Had I *looked* at the poems, thereby using my primary representational system, and had linked the words to images in my head, I would have had greater success. I might also have written the poem out using my second system (kinesthetic), perceiving the words as I did so.

When learning foreign languages I soon realised I could remember little or nothing unless I saw it written down. I would write new words in a book and read them over from time to time. Consequently, I learnt to speak foreign languages first and foremost by reading (visual), secondly by writing new words down (kinesthetic) and only thirdly by listening and speaking (auditory). Helping pupils, therefore, to understand their own process and individualise their method of learning can be of great value. Fitting the right kind of learning technique to the task is also helpful.

Pupils who have a kinesthetic primary representational system often find greater difficulty with literacy skills than those with either an auditory or a visual one. This is simply because it is easier to recognise and remember words by sound or visual image than by how they *feel*. Imagine, for example, trying to spell 'cough' or 'difficult', or even 'one' or 'top', if you are relying on how they *feel* rather than on how they look or sound! Reading would also seem extremely difficult and confusing.

If pupils were aware of their major representational system and, therefore, of how they would tend to set about a task, they could be taught to employ other methods to compensate if necessary. They could be encouraged to strengthen their weaker systems, while using their major one as appropriately as possible. Making a link between one system and a stronger one can be extremely helpful. For example, if a pupil has a poor auditory system but a strong kinesthetic one, he or she could successfully embark on playing the piano by relying on feeling the movement of the hands and the spatial relationships between notes. His or her auditory system could thus be developed. If the pupil had poor visual skills, reading music might be introduced very gradually after some success has been achieved by playing by touch.

Pupils with a highly developed kinesthetic representational system may well find difficulties in other aspects of school life, since they may be more attracted to *moving* and *doing* rather than sitting still and listening. Since many teachers will have managed the academic demands of school life with some ease, there is likely to be a high percentage of teachers with a primary visual or auditory representational system. Consequently, pupils with the kinesthetic as their major system may feel less connection with a greater number of teachers than their peers. In some cases this disaffection and lack of contact in school may lead to disruptive behaviour. Chapter 3 considers how teachers might redress this balance.

Curriculum demands may leave little time for considering and teaching skills concerned with the *process* of learning. However, some consideration of this process can ultimately save time and lead to greater achievement. If teachers suggested a range of learning techniques, pupils could choose those which they found most useful.

Finding the best way
These techniques can be useful in a number of subject areas, including those which require a body of information to be learnt as well as those, like modern languages, in which learning particular words is important.

• Primary visual representational system
These pupils will be able to learn by *looking* at notes, spellings and so on. They could be encouraged to perceive by using different colours and the position on the page to help memory. For spelling, for example, they could thus write each syllable in a new colour. They could take 'photographs' by looking at what they need to learn before closing their eyes and 'seeing' it on the inside of their eyelids. Or they could put whatever needs to be learnt inside a picture or shape which they draw or imagine, so that the target information is set in a visual context. In other words, they would have a visual association to trigger memory.

If their second strongest representational system is auditory, they could look at their colour-coded notes and so on while reading aloud or listening to information on tape. If their second most powerful system is kinesthetic, an emphasis of writing out what they then look at could be of help. Or all three systems could be employed by looking at a spelling or information, then writing it while sounding it out or reading it later.

• Primary auditory representational system
These pupils will learn most easily through sound. For learning spellings it would be helpful for them to sound out the words while looking at and writing them. They could tape words in this way to listen to while reading, writing or simply while relaxing. Listening to information in their own voice can also be of benefit.

Tapes could be used for larger chunks of revision too, pupils being encouraged to tape summaries and key points at the end of each topic that needs to be revised. In this way, they would build up a body of taped information for revision, notes being backed up by the more significant auditory input. Pupils could then draw diagrams or jot down notes from the tapes, thereby involving all three representational systems.

• Primary kinesthetic representational system

These pupils will find learning easier if 'doing', movement or feeling is included in that process. For spelling they will probably find it helpful to rewrite the word many times while integrating visual and auditory components to strengthen these systems.

Clearly, for larger amounts of material, rewriting is too arduous. In these cases, writing out key points could prove helpful. If these were written as a spidergram or in some other diagramatic form, the pupil could move his or her finger around the page from one set of key points to another to aid memory. As in all learning, repetition would be necessary. The pupil might need to retrace the movement in order to 'unlock' each section and recall the relevant information. Calling their second most powerful representational system into play would also be of help either by using tapes or teaching pupils how to look and perceive, using colour coding, pictures, diagrams and so on.

Organisation of material

At the end of each section of work it can be of great help if teachers help pupils organise material so that it is easy to handle when reviewing it during revision. This could be done by taking ten minutes to brainstorm from the class as a whole the most significant points in the section just covered. These could be written down on the board and copied (making sure that those with difficulty copying from the board were able to finish or were provided with copies), written out by the teacher and given out to the class next lesson, or pupils could be encouraged to put them on to tape.

Training and practice

As in the case of written tasks, pupils may well need practice with the *process* of revision with support in class. Teachers can help greatly in this by dividing work that must be revised into small sections and incorporating short revision sessions regularly into lessons. In this way pupils not only learn content but also the process of how to revise: in short sections frequently, rather than in rambling marathons.

1. The teacher selects a small amount of information which is to be learnt.
2. Pupils are given ten minutes to learn the information by their preferred means: reading it over quietly to themselves, writing it out, drawing diagrams with or without colour, questioning and answering with a partner, etc.
3. Pupils are then asked to write down what they remember or are asked to answer questions.

4. The pupils are given time to check their answers.

It is important that these sessions are not viewed as tests, but rather as experiments in learning. Consequently, pupils are not graded as a result of these revision sessions. If the teacher wishes to know how well pupils are learning material, papers could be taken in anonymously. If the emphasis is on the interest of the material rather than on the importance of remembering, greater success is usually achieved. This is because the pupils are then trained to focus on the material itself rather than on the need to remember.

Help with copying down information, homework instructions and so on

This is an area in which many pupils with SpLD, some second language learners, those with slow handwriting or those with poor eyesight fall behind, lose heart, give up and may turn to disruptive behaviour and conflict in order to divert attention from their 'failure', while also unburdening themselves of some of their frustration and anger. Certainly pupils with SpLD often find handwriting an arduous and slow task. Some can experience great difficulty transferring information from a distance to their books. Thus copying from a sheet on their desk may be easier than from the board, though still arduous. Pupils who are easily distracted by other class members also have frequent problems with copying from the board since, in moving from board to book, their line of vision may well encounter many distractions. They are thus more likely to be able to hold their concentration on work which is on their desk or nearby rather than across a room.

- It would greatly help pupils with such difficulties if they were given copies of notes written on the board.
- The same goes for homework instructions since many pupils arrive home with incomplete or muddled written instructions so that they cannot even attempt the work.
- For some pupils writing out a question sheet with answers is such a daunting task that they do not even make an attempt to start, since writing in itself is so slow and taxing it can simply seem too much. If it were a matter of just writing the answers, more pupils would be able to attempt work, and disruption and conflict would be minimised.

'Unpacking' a text

As with written assignments, when faced with a new text, many pupils will panic and will not know where to start. Again the assumption is often wrongly made that by secondary school pupils should know how to read a passage and answer questions on it. Some will, but many will not. Consequently, it would help many achieve more if time is spent training in the techniques of how to approach a text. Such practice can be done on different texts in stages, each of which may need to be practised for some time before passing on to the next one, depending on the experience of the class. For example:

1. Dissection of a text

(a) A passage is read through by the teacher with the class looking at the text. Any words or phrases that are not understood are explained. There is general discussion about the meaning of the text as a whole.

(b) In pairs or small groups pupils are asked to discuss the main point made in each paragraph. They might wish to underline or note down the key words which illustrate this point.

(c) There is class discussion to check all have understood the main points.

2. Comprehension with the whole class

(a) As 1(a) above.

(b) There are a number of questions about the text which are answered from members of the whole class together. During this the teacher points out some guidelines which can help pupils through a text. These might be elicited from class members:

- Answers to the questions are usually to be found in order in the text. That is to say, the answer to the first question is usually to be found near the beginning of the text, the answer to the second a little later, and so on.
- Key words in the question are often found in the text, indicating more exactly where to look for the answer.
- At the end of the questions there might be more general ones asking for an opinion or a view requested on the passage as a whole.

3. Comprehension in pairs or small groups

(a) As 1(a) above.

(b) In pairs or small groups pupils discuss the answers to comprehension questions, using the guidelines given previously.

(c) There is whole-class discussion to check all groups have understood the questions and the technique.

4. Individual comprehension in class

(a) As 1(a) above.

(b) Pupils discuss the answers as a whole class, using the guidelines.

(c) Individuals answer the questions in writing in class.

(d) The answers are discussed in class.

5. Individual comprehension at home

(a) As 1(a) above.

(b) As 4(b) above.

(c) Pupils answer the questions in writing at home.

6. Individual comprehension with less support
(a) As 1(a) above.
(b) Pupils write the answers without discussion.

7. Comprehension in test conditions
(a) Pupils read through the paper and answer the questions on their own.

Helping pupils manage time

Pupils may need help with time in a number of ways. For example, working out a precise revision timetable with a class can be extremely useful, rather than assuming individual pupils will know how to do this for themselves. Tight timing of certain exercises may also accustom pupils to get down to work with speed. This could involve instructions giving five minutes to discuss a point, for example, or ten minutes to write down some answers, and so on. The latter exercise could be completed in pairs so that those with literacy difficulties could work with someone as scribe, or they could be given a task which they could complete in the time.

Many minutes are wasted in classes since pupils take a long time to focus on their work. This is, in part, due to a different perception of time. I have watched numerous pupils putting very little effort into written work until the teacher says, 'Pens down. Time to hand in your work now please.' At that point, these pupils start working furiously, only to be told off a little later, of course, for not handing in their work! It may be helpful for some of these pupils to be given warnings and encouragement at various points. For example, the teacher might say to the class, 'You have 15 minutes before lunchtime. Work steadily and you can finish in time.' Another warning might be given with, say, five minutes left. This might prompt some pupils to tackle more work, while helping others to develop their own internal sense of timing.

Giving a structure as described earlier in this chapter can also help with timing, making it easier for some pupils to make a start. Timing can be introduced directly into the written exercise, for example, by allowing, say, ten minutes for discussion and thinking, five minutes for brainstorming, five to sequence, fifteen to write, five to check, as appropriate.

Avoiding demoralisation

There are many ways in which individual pupils may become demoralised by their experience in school. Here we will focus on just a few major areas in which demoralisation is common. This is to be avoided since it is demoralised pupils who are likely to turn to disruptive behaviour and conflict with teachers since the school, in their eyes, has failed them. As a result, they sometimes have little or no interest in trying to make school work for them any more; they lack motivation to behave well and disrupt in protest.

Correcting work

When pupils do a piece of work, what do you look for: what they can do and have done, or what they cannot do and have not done? Perhaps you look for both, but which do you consider more important, if either, and how do you report this information back to the pupils? Do you give lavish praise, adding what could be improved, or vice versa? Or is your approach different still?

It is easy, in our eagerness to do our job 'properly' and *teach*, sometimes to forget to acknowledge what has been done. A mother reported to me once how surprised she was when her teenage children got angry with her when she told them how to do things properly. Recently they had cooked some pizzas for lunch and when she had told them that it would be better next time if they cut the tomatoes differently they were furious with her. She was confused since she had been trying to help; she considered it her job as a mother to teach her children how to do things. It may well have been that her children were trying very hard to do something for her, to give her a gift, to do something *right*. They did not want to learn a better way, they wanted an acknowledgement for what they could manage now, for what they had done. It may sometimes be similar with some of the pupils in our classes. Maybe, at times, we underestimate the extent to which young people really want to please and gain praise. *Even when their behaviour gives no hint of this and they appear not to care.*

How would it feel if everything you did was corrected? If there were always red marks of correction on every letter you wrote, every idea you jotted down? How would it be if there was always the ideal of perfection ahead, just out of reach or far, far away, but never tangibly within your grasp? Maybe it would be helpful, just occasionally, to accept a piece of work *just as it is*, without correcting or improving it in any way, accepting it as *good enough*.

This is not to say that we could not note what next needs to be learnt and ensure that the pupil soon has the opportunity to do so. The difference is that we would here be separating out recognition of what has been done and what the pupil can achieve from what he or she next needs to learn. It is not a question of not teaching, simply one of choosing the most appropriate time in which to do so. It can be deeply demoralising for many if they can never rest a while, consolidate and enjoy their achievements without being shown the next hurdle they have to jump, the next mountain they must climb. If, as teachers, we can trust that young people, by their very nature, tend to learn if the environment is conducive to doing so, the information or skill has some relevance to them, they are interested by the subject matter or process of learning, and they are relaxed enough in order to concentrate, then perhaps we too can relax a little and sometimes allow a short period of triumph before moving on. This is particularly relevant for pupils with SpLD who may themselves be deeply frustrated at their own inadequacy at expressing ideas as they would like on paper and whose confidence is at rock bottom.

Just a tick may not be enough to help sustain a pupil's interest in working. Having put in considerable effort, he or she might expect some evidence that the teacher has noticed and taken that effort seriously. Plenty of ticks and positive comments might be more helpful. If the teacher believes the work is below standard for that pupil, then the comment can reflect this in a positive way: for example, 'Good ideas, but I sensed you had some difficulties with this task. Let's talk about it.'

In the courses she ran, training assertiveness group facilitators, Anne Dickson (1982) insisted that feedback was always balanced: for every positive point there was a specific learning point, and vice versa. This is a useful model and one which pupils can themselves also be encouraged to develop in assessing their own work. Many pupils will require more encouragement than this, particularly at first, and the balance could best be changed to, for example, two or three positive points for each learning point.

A report by Black and William (1998) which looked at 600 international studies involving over 10,000 pupils, claims that individuals achieve more when given feedback and encouragement rather than marks out of ten, since many are demoralised by the latter. Obviously the present exam structure requires a marking system. However, it is interesting to question the use of marks for pupils on a daily basis. Teachers can, of course, always keep records separately. For pupils who do well, marks can be satisfying, confirming and rewarding, but comments could perhaps serve as well. For pupils who are trying hard yet achieving poorly, marks may serve only to dispirit. For pupils who have missed work for whatever reason, a low mark may give the message that catching up is too hard a task. A constructive comment, on the other hand, could help pupils achieve more since it could point out specific steps for improvement. If both comments and marks are given, the latter is more likely to be remembered and compared.

Homework

There are many reasons why homework can be a source of demoralisation for some pupils. These might include the following:
1. Pupils not understanding what is required for homework and therefore not being able even to attempt it.
2. Pupils not writing down the full instructions and therefore being unable to do the task set.
3. Having no one at home to help with homework, while others in the class appear to get help and support.

4. Having nowhere quiet or lacking an appropriate space in which to work.
5. The homework 'disappearing' once it is handed back to the teacher with little or no comment; either it is not marked at all, is marked only after a long time or is just given a tick.
6. The work being returned covered with marks indicating mistakes of one kind or another (spelling, punctuation, etc.), while there is little mention of the content or acknowledgement of the effort taken.
7. The task being very boring and time-consuming without having any apparent relevance to class work.
8. Some pupils not having ready access to books which would be useful or necessary to complete the homework.

Again it may be helpful to consider what it feels like 'from the other side'. If you cannot do your homework once or twice because you had time to write down only half the instructions it is probably not too difficult to deal with, but if it occurs regularly, or nearly always, it is hard to continue trying. It is much easier to give up the attempt rather than experience the frustration, sense of failure and maybe panic at not managing. The accumulation of failed attempts can lead to demoralisation; if you have little confidence to start with it may not take long. Giving up before you start can be an easier way out, especially if you are without support at home.

During his first term in secondary school, a boy spent four hours working on a model for science. He waited impatiently for his next science lesson, eager to show his teacher how hard he had worked and how well he had done. When the lesson eventually came the teacher was anxious to get on with the work for that day and collected all the models in quickly, putting them on a shelf without comment. The boy looked crestfallen. This kind of treatment was particularly shocking for him since he had recently come from primary school where he would probably have had a very different experience on producing such a piece of work. There he may well have shown it to the class and explained how he made it. He might have shown it to the whole school in assembly and would have received much praise for his efforts. Considering the response he received in secondary school, I wonder if he ever spent four hours on a science homework again?

Suppose you had spent a long time on an essay for English. You do not find writing your ideas down easy and you usually make a lot of spelling mistakes. The essay topic was one in which you are particularly interested and so you had made an extra effort, expressing your opinions on the subject and showing your knowledge in the area. When you get your work back it is peppered with red ink indicating spelling mistakes. There is the comment at the end, 'Good, but careless spelling'. How do you feel?

Clearly some of these reasons for demoralisation, notably 3, 4 and 8, are outside an individual teacher's influence. A school could take the issues up by providing an after-school homework club which would also help children who are finding difficulty in carrying out homework tasks (1 and 2 above), but this may not always be possible. So what can we do as teachers, given all the other demands upon us? How can we use homework as another means for building our pupils' self-esteem, confidence and interest in work, thereby minimising the chance of demoralisation and consequent challenging behaviour in class? How can we help our pupils to feel that their work is valued, that they are valued?

One place to start is to ensure instructions are clear, that the homework is relevant to the lesson and introduces nothing new that may not be understood. What is the aim of the homework set? Is it to reinforce the content of the lesson, to research a coming one, to practise skills, to encourage self-expression, to fulfil a need because you have to set something? In what ways will it contribute to the pupils' education? Will it enhance their interest in the subject? Is it an enjoyable task? Is it a possible one? Is it easy for them to gain a sense of satisfaction in completing it? If it is research, do the pupils have adequate skills to carry out the work and easy access to resources? If it is written work do those pupils who need it have sufficient structure to be able to succeed? If a number of pupils produce poor homework or one pupil does so consistently, then the homework task itself should perhaps first be questioned. Is it appropriate? Is there enough guidance? Are instructions clear? As mentioned in the section above, it is also helpful to provide a written set of instructions for those who have difficulty in copying from the board.

Obviously we will not always respond in the exact way a pupil hopes; for example we may not enthuse over a piece of work as much as he or she would like. However, we can aim to acknowledge effort whenever we perceive it. It is always a difficult area: what may have taken hours to achieve, may in fact seem to be very little and it is easy to miss the huge effort entailed. The system outlined in the previous chapter in which, for maths, pupils have to complete 60 minutes' homework a week (or 90 for older pupils) can help in this respect. It is interesting that some pupils who persistently fail to do homework in other subjects reliably complete their weekly work when this system is employed. This may be due in part to the nature of the subject, but perhaps also to the degree of control they have over when and how they work. In addition, the tasks are generally clear since they require working in the same way as in class and there is never the problem of writing down only half the instructions. Some pupils do not manage their full quota one week since they did not understand the maths set on a particular card or they were unaware that equipment was needed and did not have this at home. Nevertheless, the completion rate of homework is particularly high, with many pupils doing more than is required. Everyone knows where he or she stands, the pupils are trusted and respond well.

Not all subjects would adapt to this model and, indeed, if each subject could be completed at some point in the week it could prove extremely difficult for all but those with exceptional organisational skills. However, some aspects of the scheme could perhaps be adapted with positive results. It could, for example, be possible for children to write down how long they spent on a piece of work and to have this signed by a parent or guardian. Effort might be easier to spot and difficulties also recognised. Although some might 'cheat' on this, most pupils most of the time would not and could gain from genuine acknowledgement of their time and effort.

Unfinished work

If pupils cannot finish a piece of work they miss out on the satisfaction which can be gained at finishing a task. If this happens frequently, after a while they can also cease to believe it possible to finish. Allowing all pupils to complete an exercise is obviously very difficult without a totally individualised scheme of work since pupils work at very different speeds. This can be partially addressed by having the main body of work which all should be able to achieve, followed by at least two extension sections. Different pupils will be expected to finish different tasks. In this way all pupils can complete their own work load. The structured approach and support with the various stages of writing outlined above can also help pupils finish written tasks.

If, however, a piece of work is of an inappropriate level and a pupil has great difficulty with it, insisting that he or she finish that work before being allowed to move on to a more interesting task can also lead to demoralisation.

Failure

This is, of course, a major cause of demoralisation and a constant challenge for every teacher is to help all pupils achieve in their own way, feeling both valued and valuable.

The change from primary school

A boy on permanent exclusion from Year 8 commented, 'It was all right in primary school, but in secondary school they treat you differently.' Of course pupils are treated differently, you might say, they are older – although only six weeks older at first! At times the dramatic change from primary to secondary might thus be a little abrupt. If we consider that those pupils who are most likely to disrupt lessons and invite conflict with teachers are those who feel least sure of themselves and most frightened, then it is easy to deduce that it is these same pupils who find the change from primary to secondary most difficult and frightening and who are least equipped to adapt. Consequently, they are more likely to resort to extreme kinds of disruptive, frightened and, therefore, often aggressive behaviour.

During his first week in secondary school a boy with literacy difficulties was given as a punishment the task of writing an essay 500 words long. He had never written that much in one go in his life before! He was bound to fail the punishment, thereby running into even more trouble with his teacher. The degree of panic and frustration he probably felt can only be imagined. He resorted to more extreme behaviour and was found later that term climbing out of a classroom window, a kind of behaviour he had never needed to exhibit in primary school since the environment was less frightening. Some pupils never quite recover from that change from primary to secondary and, starting off on a poor footing, their school career goes from bad to worse. They are usually among the most vulnerable pupils, even though their manner may appear aggressive, and they usually find themselves early on in conflict with teachers. Quickly stepping into the role of 'bad' pupil, they often find it difficult to behave well, particularly when feeling frightened, confused and angry at the change from primary school.

If there were greater liaison between primary and secondary schools, and if secondary teachers dealing with pupils in Years 7 and 8 knew more about the ethos, expectations and approaches used by their primary colleagues, some of the harshness of the changes could perhaps be softened and some pupils would fare much better in their new school. It would naturally follow that there would also be less disruption and less conflict with teachers and a general improvement in behaviour.

Not being listened to and perceived injustice

It is a common complaint from pupils who have been excluded that most teachers do not listen to them. Obviously, if a pupil has done something to disrupt a lesson it is probably inappropriate to listen to an explanation at the time since the lesson has to continue. However, considering the ill-will and demoralisation generated among pupils, it could perhaps be constructive to make it clear that you could listen to them after the lesson, at the end of the day, or in break, for example, to sort things out. Although this might take a few minutes extra at the time, *in the long run*, it could save future disruption: if a pupil is left feeling angry because he or she feels unjustly treated, the next lesson with that pupil is likely to present more difficulties. In time, some pupils are so demoralised by the injustice they perceive in the authority structure of schools that they do not even attempt to explain their position to teachers.

Sometimes teachers may make hasty judgements; with large classes there is not always time to sort out what to adults may seem trivial. However, if pupils are blamed for something they did not do, or did do, but with a good intention, the sense of injustice can linger in some pupils and, especially if there are several such incidents, can lead to resentment, cynicism and demoralisation. Leaving the door open to discussion at a later time can usually help.

The significance of relationships is discussed further in Chapter 3.

Public humiliation and making comparisons

Any kind of public shaming tends to encourage resentment and demoralisation. The more pupils are allowed to save face and maintain their dignity intact, the more likely they are to cooperate, work and change behaviour if necessary. Comparing pupils, classes or year groups publicly can also often lead to demoralisation. This is the case even if it is intended to spur pupils on in a spirit of competition, since many are easily discouraged. This may be for a number of reasons. For example, the task of improving may appear too great, pupils are unclear as to what *exactly* is expected of them in order to improve, they may already be trying hard; if the whole group is criticised because of a few, those who are working well may feel powerless to influence their less conscientious peers and so on. If pupils are told often enough that they are a poor class, bad singers, or not as good as someone else, they are likely either to believe it or to stop trying.

Rather than playing pupils off against each other, pupils and classes can compete against their own record. For example, they could be given praise, a very specific learning point, even more praise, another specific learning point, extra praise, and so on. If the subject were singing, the class Year 7, it could go something like this:

1. 'Good singing this morning. Well done.'
2. 'Now this time I'd like you all to open your mouths wide to let the sound out.'
3. 'Fantastic. Well done!'
4. 'Now imagine the sound is flowing from the centre of your body up through your chest and out of that wide open mouth.'
5. 'Amazing singing! The best so far.'
6. 'Now one more time, as sweetly as you can make it.'

The exact wording would obviously depend on the age of pupils addressed and the particular class. The point is that comments in the vein of 'Not very good – you're all still asleep this morning' or 'Not as good as ...', which aim to spur on, tend to discourage rather than encourage many pupils. It is, after all, the teacher's job to analyse *how* pupils can improve and communicate it to them in a way they can utilise. Generalised dissatisfaction is not helpful enough. Learning points, therefore, need to be very specific and constructive if they are to be of any positive use at all. The more praise given, the more some pupils will be able to respond positively to the learning point made.

Nurturing motivation

'Joy in learning' is a key point put forward by W. Edwards Deming (1994) as a necessity for an improvement in education, namely, that students learn best when they enjoy it. It is an interesting concept which would suggest the need for discussion concerning a shift in the ethos and structure of our education system far beyond the remit of this book. However, it is worth considering how a teacher, working within the current system, can encourage pupils to *enjoy* learning. There are, as Marland (1975) notes, the two major motivating factors of achievement and the relationship with the teacher. A third aspect to be considered is that of independence, that is to say, the degree of responsibility pupils may have towards their own learning. As a result of the structure of schools, many pupils tend to have less influence over their learning in secondary school than they did in primary. With a number of different periods in a day pupils have to stop and start, changing from one subject to another when the bell dictates rather than according to their interest level or pace. This creates a contradiction since at the very time when pupils are growing into young adults and are eager to exercise more of their own independence there is less room for it within the learning process. This can lead to frustration, demoralisation and conflict. It is, therefore, helpful if the individual teacher can create opportunities for students to have some influence over how learning takes place.

Many of the strategies in this book deal with ways of training pupils to study effectively. The aim is for them to become as independent in their learning as possible through mastery of the relevant skills. The teacher remains in charge of the overall process and within that the pupil has the chance to make decisions and take responsibility for his or her own study. Rather than the teacher exhorting pupils to learn, he or she sets up activities so that pupils take a very active part and *cannot help but learn since the process is interesting and enjoyable*. Collaborative group work is one technique which can provide variety and can be effective in nurturing motivation and reducing conflict, *if it is carried out with sufficient thought and planning*.

The use of cooperative learning through team or group work as developed by Latzko (1997) is one model which can be adapted for different subjects and ages. Latzko himself has worked in colleges in America and has found that team work together with lecturing enhances his students' learning. Preparation for working in a team and relevant guidelines are advisable and are discussed in Chapter 3.

Group work, for example, could be used instead of individual written questions and answers on a text and is often more engaging. The teacher divides the class into groups of between three and five pupils, depending on the task, age and pupils concerned. Each group member has a particular role, for example, scribe for taking notes, spokesperson to report to the whole group, facilitator to encourage participation by all, timekeeper and messenger who can ask the teacher for help. All are responsible for contributing ideas and for decision making. The teacher can mix up groups and rotate roles for different lessons as appropriate.

The text could be read by the teacher at the beginning to ensure all basic concepts are understood. The range of tasks then set could vary. Groups could be asked to choose what they consider the main points of the passage, backing up their choice with reasons, or could be asked to find out something specific to the passage, again providing reasons how and why. Or they could be asked to set two or three questions on the text. These could either be given to another group to answer or could provide the basis of a whole-class discussion. The teacher would add material and questions if important points were being missed. It would be in the pupils' own interests to whisper so they did not give away vital clues to another team.

Some pupils may become anxious with this kind of exercise unless there is a summing up where the main threads, the 'right' answers, are drawn together by the teacher. This may take the form, for example, of points being written on the board, or a brief review and notes handed out next lesson. The notes could both reflect the discussion and state information necessary for coursework or examinations. Without this consolidation, group work can be too vague and frustrating for some and loses effectiveness.

Refining the process

It can be useful to bear in mind the fact that pupils are very different both from each other and from teachers. That is to say, as teachers we need to employ a variety of teaching techniques to engage our pupils. We may, indeed, frequently use approaches which are quite different from those *we* found useful when studying. The question is what might excite the pupils' imagination or spirit of enquiry? What might get them really involved in the subject? What will get them to learn?

Not every pupil will find all lessons scintillating, of course. Indeed, some tasks will be mundane and will require perseverence to complete. However, even then the cooperation of the class can be maintained by the nature of the relationship with the teacher, and by the fact that pupils can succeed and that the material and tasks are interesting enough of the time.

If pupils are not succeeding it is an indication that we, as teachers, need to be doing something differently: relating differently to these pupils, providing other work maybe, or putting work across in a new way. Or maybe all three. We need constantly to be questioning and refining our process of teaching, using pupil success as our feedback. Inspectors aside, how would the *pupils* rate our performance? What would *they* get out of our lessons? Thinking along these lines, we can maintain our own level of motivation and success as teachers.

Constructive criticism

Giving criticism to pupils

As teachers we can obviously give criticism to pupils in many different ways, some extremes of which appear below. When feeling stressed, angry or pressurised for time it is easy and only human to snap out a criticism. Yet it may also be useful, as professionals, to consider how criticism could unwittingly provoke resentment and unwanted behaviour or how, on the other hand, it could be used to foster a willingness to work and desirable behaviour.

Imagine you are a pupil who is handing in a piece of homework three days late. What might you feel in the four situations below? Would you be likely to get your next homework assignment in on time? Would you put effort into future work for this teacher? Would you want to cooperate with this teacher?

1. *Teacher*: Oh, thank you. [No criticism voiced.]
2. *Teacher*: Oh, so we decided to give it in at last did we? It must be my lucky day! [Indirectly aggressive.]
3. *Teacher*: What do you think you're doing handing it in today? It was due in on Tuesday! I can't mark it now. It's too late. You're always late. (*Throws the book down on the desk in front of the pupil.*) [Directly aggressive and labelling.]
4. *Teacher*: Thank you, J. It's good you've finished it and handed it in. But I want it on time in future, or you'll get a detention. Unless you have a real problem and sort it out with me. Is that clear? [Constructive criticism.]

How would you feel and respond on the end of each of these approaches? Let us consider them briefly. Although people are very different, some common responses are likely.

1. Failing to mention the fact that the work is late places no boundary on the pupil for not meeting deadlines. It may well happen again since there are no apparent consequences for lateness.
2. Indirect aggression is often thinly veiled by an attempt at humour. Such an approach is difficult to answer and can leave the person addressed feeling angry at not being able to respond effectively. Thus the pupil may end up feeling anger or resentment towards the teacher. This may well lead to conflict in the future. *It also gives the pupil the opportunity of feeling angry and blaming the teacher rather than facing up squarely to his or her own inability to finish the work on time.*
3. In the case of direct aggression and labelling criticism some kind of confrontation is likely either immediately or at a later date since the pupil may well feel angry at being spoken to or shouted at in such a manner. Unless highly motivated, most pupils would not bother to

hand work in late in future if they had not managed to complete it on time. Although they might make an effort to meet deadlines in order to avoid such a response, it is at the cost of the relationship. As in point 2 above, some pupils are more likely to feel angry and indignant at their treatment than to acknowledge their fault in handing work in late.

4. Many pupils are likely to find this approach, constructive criticism, more helpful since a clear boundary is set for the future, their effort is acknowledged, and there is neither an element of blame nor an attempt to interpret their behaviour. If they have a difficulty with completing work in future the teacher appears approachable and reasonable.

Constructive versus labelling criticism

The essence of the labelling kind of criticism (point 3 above) is blame. It labels the behaviour as the critic interprets it, rather than merely describing what is happening. The label is, of course, highly subjective and often reveals as much or more about the critic than the person criticised! Conflict is likely since the one criticised often feels angry at the misinterpretation placed on his or her actions.

Equally important is the fact that the thrust of the criticism itself is often lost as the discussion is diverted by the 'red herring' of the aggressive manner in which the criticism is made. In a sense, it hands the pupil criticised a way out since he or she can feel outraged at the *manner* of the criticism without facing the message about the behaviour. Thus it is an effective technique for unloading anger and provoking conflict and/or resentment, though a much less effective one for facilitating a change in behaviour in future.

The concept of constructive criticism is very different since it is free from blame. The teacher is not placing the other in the category of 'bad' and, by implication, him or herself in that of 'good'. Instead, the teacher is pointing out something which is unacceptable in the pupil's behaviour, or something which is unhelpful to him or her in his or her efforts to achieve something. The results are, therefore, frequently quite different. Giving constructive criticism can be a very caring thing to do since it shows enough concern to bother.

Separation of past from present and future

The essence of this approach is to focus on the present and future change, rather than on blame for the past, however recent. Often we get it the other way round, concentrating on what has been done wrong or omitted rather than on what is desirable from now on. This separation of past from present and future is of great help in this area. To the two pupils pointing at each other and shouting, 'He did it miss!' we can then say, 'I'm not concerned with who did it. What I'm interested in is how we can make sure this never happens again. How do you think we can make sure it never happens again?' If appropriate, the culprit can tell a teacher privately later.

Owning the statement

This technique does not blame the other person for the emotions *we* experience and, therefore, models a responsible attitude towards our own feelings. It also claims our authority and power without allowing the pupil the satisfaction of being able to 'make us angry'. Thus it is more powerful to say, 'I feel very angry when you ...' rather than, 'You make me angry when you ...'

It may also help avoid a confrontation to own our feelings, for example, 'I feel quite angry about yesterday, but we'll focus on today now.' Having expressed the emotion, albeit in neutral terms, we are less likely to act out the feeling. In other words, having *said* we are angry, we are less likely to *behave* in that way towards someone. The advantage of this is that he or she, in turn, is more likely to answer us verbally, rather than by acting out in response to us. Thus this approach can often improve the lines of communication with pupils, avoid an escalation of aggression and lead to an improvement in behaviour.

Separating the person from the behaviour

This underpins the whole concept of constructive criticism. It focuses on criticising not the *person*, but the *behaviour*. The pupil is not 'bad', 'lazy' or 'aggressive', but the behaviour may be 'inappropriate', 'unhelpful' or 'aggressive'. The more specific the description of the behaviour (without interpretation), the more helpful it can be. Labelling tends to entrench behaviour in the person since one is confused with the other; whereas constructive criticism helps to create a distance between the person and his or her behaviour so that the pupil can more easily see exactly what he or she is doing. When behaviour and identity are linked this is more difficult to do. Also, as mentioned in Chapter 7, it is easier to change a specific kind of behaviour than to change oneself! In addition, being 'bad', for example, will mean very different things to different people. A clear and specific description of behaviour is more accurate and, therefore, more helpful. It is also much more likely to win the cooperation of the pupil and avoid conflict than a labelling approach.

Constructive criticism can thus enable the teacher to build a pupil's self-esteem while 'telling him or her off'. For example: 'I don't like the way you shout out, but when you finally get down to work it's often very good. Listen quietly, jot down any questions you have and ask me at the end.'

Focus on new behaviour rather than old

The emphasis is always on the new behaviour to be adopted rather than on the old behaviour to be stopped. Stopping talking is much harder than sitting quietly or listening quietly, and so on, because it is *not doing*, rather than *doing*.

Giving constructive criticism

The process of constructive criticism

*   Make a time to talk, *if necessary*. This may be a couple of minutes taken after class, in break or after school. This is not essential, but has the advantages of not detracting from a lesson and helping the pupil 'save face'. Without an audience, pupils are likely to be more receptive to constructive criticism.
*   Own the statement you make. Not, for example, 'You make me mad', but 'I feel angry when you ...', or 'I find it unacceptable in class when you ...' Without this approach, you are admitting the pupil has power over you, the power to *make* you angry.
*   Describe the other's behaviour in a *specific* way: 'when you frequently shout out while I'm explaining something to the whole class'. This is different from (mis)interpreting and generalising: 'when you try to disrupt my lesson by calling out all the time'.
*   Ask for a change in behaviour: 'I would like you to sit quietly from now on, put your hand up if you have a question and I'll come to see you as soon as I can.' (This is often missed out of aggressive and labelling criticism, the emphasis there being on blame, rather than asking for a specific change. Pupils may not always be sure *how* to stop doing whatever it is they are doing, that is to say, *what to do instead*. Thus having a specific behaviour that you request as an alternative can be very helpful. There may be various reasons why they are doing whatever you want them to stop. If they are calling out during instructions, for example, this may be to gain attention, or it may be out of anxiety at not understanding, fear of getting things wrong, etc.)
*   State the consequences if there is no change: 'otherwise I'll send you out /give you a detention if you call out'.
*   If appropriate, share problem solving: 'What would help you to sit quietly at that time?' This gives the pupil greater responsibility and the opportunity to question what he or she does indeed need in order to behave differently.
*   End with some positive statement about the other's work, the relationship, etc., as appropriate: 'The calling out is a pity because once you get down to work you usually do it very well.'

The person giving constructive criticism has opened the way for a real meeting to take place. It still might not, but it is more likely. Certainly it feels very different on the receiving end of this than if the same criticism is given in a different way, as, for example, below.

Labelling criticism

You make me angry when you try to disrupt my lesson by calling out the whole time. I'm not having it, do you hear? From now on you get sent out/have a detention as soon as you open your mouth. Do I make myself clear?

This opens up the possibility of red herrings and continued conflict – for example, 'I don't call out the whole time' – or resentment – 'That's not fair! I was only asking X about the work!'

Constructive criticism

I feel angry when you call out when I'm giving instructions to the whole class. In future I'd like you to sit quietly while I'm explaining to everyone. If you have a question you can put your hand up and I'll come to you as soon as possible. Otherwise I'll give you a detention/send you out of class if you call out. This calling out is a shame because your work is usually good once you get down to it. What do you think would help you to be able to sit quietly?

Thus, using constructive criticism, a few minutes spent with pupil J who has come 15 minutes late to the last two lessons might go along these lines:

Hello, J, come in. Please sit down. I'll come straight to the point and then you can put your side of things. I'm very concerned that you've come 15 minutes late to my last two lessons. I'd like you to be on time in future with everyone else. Then we can get down to some good work together. Otherwise I shall keep you in to make up the time you've missed, and you'll already owe me 30 minutes. If you have a particular problem with getting to class on time we can look at that now and see what can be done. I don't want this to get in the way of your work which is otherwise very good. Usually I enjoy having you in the class. Do you have a particular problem with getting to class on time?

Managing criticism from pupils constructively

A pupil may well make an aggressive criticism directly or indirectly. Sometimes it might be appropriate to ignore such comments, not considering them worthy of an answer. At other times, however, it is easy to respond in a similar vein, or at least with another aggressive comment. This could lead to an immediate escalation of the incident if the pupil responds aggressively in turn, or could pave the way for a confrontation at a later date. It may also sour relations with the whole class. Stepping outside the limitations of either a passive or an aggressive approach could give more choice. It may reveal some misunderstanding or old resentment on the pupil's part or may provide the opportunity for building a more positive relationship with a pupil.

Taking time

For this it is necessary to create a gap between the pupil's remark (or another's criticism) and ours, *a gap in which we can choose our response*. This may seem quite difficult to do, especially in front of a class! Often we feel compelled to have an instant reply, an immediate answer. However, these are more likely to be our learnt responses from the past and may not necessarily be our first choice in the present. It is simply a question of retraining and patience. Moreover, pausing for a moment before replying can appear powerful, since it seems to be a considered, rather than a purely emotional response. This gap can be created by breathing deeply, shifting our body posture and relaxing (see Chapter 5 for a fuller explanation).

Choosing when and how

Having given ourselves time, what, then, are the choices? Some remarks may be ignored or passed off with the comment that they are irrelevant to the lesson. Others may demand attention for one reason or another, in which case there is a choice, depending on circumstances: *do I deal with this here and now, in private now, or later in private?* It is obviously undesirable to hold up a lesson and, if the remark is made during free time in the corridor, for example, then there is still the 'audience' of other pupils to contend with. Seeing a pupil in private, even for just a couple of minutes, robs him or her of the opportunity of 'playing to the gallery' while making it easier for any real meeting to take place. Without an audience it is often easier for the pupil to save face.

Response

Thus a remark along the following lines might be useful:
 Pupil E (with an exaggerated, pretend yawn): Oh, boring!
 Teacher (looking steadily at E without smiling, calmly): We don't have time for discussion now, E, tell me at breaktime.
 Pupil E: No, it's all right, Miss.
This may be sufficient since the teacher has, while treating E with seriousness and respect, made it quite clear that she is in charge. Yet, since she was not aggressive in her response and refused to take up the bait, that is to say, she related to the *process*, that E had something to say to her in particular, rather than getting emotionally involved with the *content*, it is more difficult for E to respond aggressively. If this had been one of several similar

incidents, the teacher might like to continue as follows, before carrying on swiftly with the lesson:

Teacher: No, E, I shall expect you at 11.20 promptly, please.

If E had some specific points to make, this could provide useful feedback for the teacher who might wish to respond by a change in lesson format as a result. If E was making only the generalised criticism of 'boring', it may have been just for the sake of complaining.

The following kind of criticism is quite common. Having a choice of responses without getting drawn into the content in class can be useful. Ignoring such comments is, of course, always one option. Others might include something like this:

Pupil: You're only telling me off because I'm black/a boy/a girl/X's sister/Y's brother, etc.

Teacher: No, that's not the case at all. Come after school, then you can tell me why you think so.

Teaching points

It can be helpful if pupils are encouraged to adopt an attitude of constructive critical appraisal towards their work. This might include their noting at times a strength and a weakness in some pieces of work. The rule is that there must always be at least an equal number of strengths and weaknesses, or three strengths to one weakness, as noted earlier.

Building confidence and self-esteem

The approach suggested throughout this book and the techniques described earlier in this chapter can help build confidence and self-esteem. Some points not covered specifically are outlined below.

Measuring progress

For most people it is important to see regular progress following effort in order to maintain enthusiasm and confidence. Without this it is easy to lose heart and interest, particularly if work requires considerable effort. Thus, once again, it is those pupils who are most insecure and likely to resort to disruptive behaviour who most need regular reassurance of achievement. Some strategies which can encourage this follow.

A review of progress

Make time for pupils once a term or twice a year to compare two similar pieces of work done towards the beginning and end of this period. Encourage them to notice improvements such as those in presentation, in amount completed, kind of answer given and so on. If the comparison highlights a falling standard, then this review can be used to pinpoint two or three specific steps needed to make improvements in future. Those pupils with poor organisational skills (often pupils with SpLD and others) may lose books and worksheets so that this comparison over a period of time is difficult to achieve. Yet it is often these pupils in particular who need such proof of progress. It may thus be helpful for the teacher to keep representative copies which cannot be lost.

Use of textbooks

The ideal would probably be for pupils to be able to take textbooks home for study and work at home. This seems rare today due to lack of resources. If books cannot be taken home, perhaps a time could be made during a homework club, for example, when pupils could have access to them, or several reference copies could be available in the library. The advantages of textbooks are numerous:

- pupils can see their progress through the book;
- books can be used to help with revision;
- pupils who are interested in the subject can read ahead and grasp concepts, etc., which can foster an independence of learning;
- textbooks can seem 'safe' for those who do not instantly grasp all the information in the lesson since they can rely on reading things over later, in their own time;
- textbooks require less organisation than numerous worksheets.

If it is not possible to use textbooks, many teachers use a series of worksheets in an attempt to create a similar body of knowledge. Then it is helpful to ensure two points:

1. All pupils have all the worksheets used, even if they have missed lessons. Since those with poor organisational skills will find this most difficult, teachers may need to supervise the collation of relevant material.

2. All pupils have all the information needed on the worksheets. If it is important to finish the worksheet in order to have all the necessary information, then those who find work difficult may well have insufficient records when it comes to revision. Thus starting off with a disadvantage they will inevitably fall further behind and will lose confidence and enthusiasm.

Cooperative relationships between pupils

This point is dealt with in the subsequent chapter on relationships.

*Opportunities to have a role, excel in some area or have some
responsibility*

For some pupils it will be of great importance to be given a particular task
to carry out. However insignificant this may seem to an adult, it may be the
first time they have been trusted sufficiently with a helping role and it may
therefore help with their confidence and self-esteem. With the opportunity
to show a different aspect of themselves in the school setting, they can
sometimes begin to feel more comfortable there: the greater investment
pupils have in school and the more they can get out of it, the less they will
need or want to disrupt. Obviously tasks will vary depending upon the age
of the pupil.

Guided choice

Being able to make a choice can be empowering. Providing opportunities
for pupils to make informed choices whenever possible will help build their
independence and confidence for the serious career decisions they need to
make during their time in school.

This chapter has dealt with:

a review of what is needed to succeed on both the emotional and practical level

Helping pupils succeed
- What is needed for achievement
- Making success possible
- Help with organisation

Avoiding demoralisation
- Correcting work
- Homework
- Unfinished work
- Failure
- The change from primary school
- Not being listened to and perceived injustice
- Public humiliation and making comparisons
- Nurturing motivation
- Refining the process

Constructive criticism
- Giving criticism to pupils
- Constructive versus labelling criticism
- Giving constructive criticism
- Managing criticism from pupils constructively

Building confidence and self-esteem
- Measuring progress
- Cooperative relationships between pupils
- Opportunities to have a role, excel in some area or have some responsibility
- Guided choice

CHAPTER 3

Developing Relationships with Pupils

> Good relationships are in fact created largely by technique.
>
> Michael Marland, *The Craft of the Classroom*

The value of working at relationships

Cooperation, respect and, as Robertson (1981) calls it, an 'authority agreement' (p. 44), in which pupils acknowledge a teacher's right to be in charge, are usually gained by three major attributes:

- efficient teaching skills enabling pupils to succeed;
- interesting material and varied, relevant activities which involve pupils;
- positive relationships with pupils.

This chapter is concerned with the third point above, namely how to cultivate positive relationships with pupils. Undoubtedly, communication and the teacher–pupil relationship lie at the heart of teaching. Thus the important role constructive relationships can play in minimising conflict and encouraging desirable behaviour should not be underestimated. This entails not only the way in which we, as teachers, treat pupils but also how we think about them, in other words our expectations and beliefs regarding young people. At times, positive communication between teachers and pupils can break down completely, resulting in outright hostility and conflict. Techniques teachers can use to establish rapport and initiate a positive relationship with pupils are included in this chapter. The importance of fostering cooperative relationships between pupils is also considered.

Communication breakdown: a cycle of mistrust

Fear, anxiety and mistrust are the breeding grounds of anger and aggression. The safer the classroom and the greater the trust existing between pupils and teachers the less conflict is likely. Trust is possible only when communication is clear and open between people, that is to say, when people have the time, the will and the skills to talk and listen to each other. This does not always happen between pupils and teachers and it is made all the more difficult when there is a backlog of resentment, negative expectations and assumptions since these can undermine the will of both pupils and teachers to try to reach a more peaceful resolution through skilful dialogue. Each conflict left unresolved adds to that wall of resentment, which ultimately cuts off communication.

If pupils have had several, or indeed, many experiences when they have tried to explain their innocence and teachers have not listened, then why should they continue to bother? If pupils lack adequate communication skills and have at times got into more trouble because of trying to explain their position inappropriately, why try at all? Maybe it is easier to get angry or be rude than to feel powerless if no one listens and will not believe you. By the time pupils reach secondary school most, if not all, will have had experiences when teachers or some other significant adult misinterpreted their actions and told them off for something they either did not do at all or did by accident while attempting to do something helpful. Very soon some pupils will think there is no point in trying to talk to teachers. This can happen early on in a school career and, by Year 7, negative expectations and assumptions can be deeply entrenched.

Since the teacher is in charge in the classroom, the onus is very much on him or her to find ways of getting through to pupils in order to open up the lines of communication which at times close due to this cycle of mistrust.

B, a girl in Year 9 on temporary exclusion, put it like this:

> I can get on with some teachers, the ones that treat me with respect. But some teachers are so *rude*, they treat you as though you're still little. And they're so patronising. I've tried explaining things to them, but some of them just don't want to listen. I don't have any time for them. Once you're an adult it's easier, because adults have to listen to other adults, but they don't to children. They just tell you what to do …

Unfortunately I was unable to speak to her teachers who were said to be 'at the end of their tether' with her. Most of them, I suspect, would have said something very similar about her, for example:

> I can get on with some pupils, the ones who treat me with respect. But some pupils are so rude, they treat you as though you're rubbish. And they're so insolent. I've tried explaining things to them, but some just don't want to listen. I don't have any time for them. Adults are a different matter because they tend to listen more. These pupils just think they can do what they like …

I quote B because her comments are typical of many I have heard from pupils on temporary and permanent exclusion, usually because of disruptive behaviour and conflict with teachers. It seems as if, in many instances, communication in any real sense has broken down between the pupil and some or most teachers. Usually there are one or two teachers towards whom the pupil does not feel so angry and resentful. These are the ones who, they say, 'listen' and 'treat me with respect'. The power balance within schools has shifted and pupils, on the whole, no longer respect teachers just because of their position. Consequently, techniques which ignore the importance of maintaining a positive teacher–pupil relationship tend to alienate rather than subjugate a number of pupils in any class.

As we have seen earlier, the pupils who are most likely to disrupt lessons and respond aggressively are those who, despite an often arrogant veneer, are least sure of themselves. They tend to have a backlog of rage and unleash it readily. Since their sense of self is often fragile, a real or perceived attack on that self is often met with aggression: feeling powerless, they vehemently reject any treatment which they interpret as aiming to put them into a subservient position. A *perceived* attack may include incidents in which, for example, the pupil feels sure that he or she is unfairly treated, or that the teacher has not listened sufficiently well and treats him or her without respect.

It is not a question of who is to blame, since this is little more than a red herring when communication has broken down. Both parties may be doing their best to manage in the ways they know and with the skills available to them. The fact is that these strategies may frequently lead to misunderstanding and conflict. The issue is rather how can it be possible for lines of communication between teachers and pupils to stay open more of the time? Since teachers are the professionals, the responsibility lies with us to extend our repertoire of communication skills in order to make some kind of reconciliation more likely. How is it possible to create an atmosphere of mutual respect and cooperation for a common task, namely that of the pupils' learning?

Obviously it is never possible to change other people, however desirable that may seem. Nonetheless, it is possible to speak in ways in which it is *more likely* that most pupils would calm down and *less likely* that they would respond aggressively. This in no way entails a lowering of standards of discipline, which remain high: rather it is the *manner* in which pupils are addressed which differs. Thus the teacher remains firm, yet respectful.

The role of the school and the body of teachers taken as a whole should not be forgotten. However skilled in non-conflictual communication an individual teacher may be, he or she is nevertheless a teacher. A pupil who has a store of anger and resentment towards school because of past experiences or towards authority figures in general is likely to expect all teachers to be the same. Consequently, it may take some time before a pupil is able to perceive an individual as just that, rather than as merely another teacher 'trying to get me mad', as B put it. Each interaction that avoids outright conflict and improves communication between a teacher and pupil will probably make relationships a little easier for the staff as a whole. Conversely, each incident of open conflict after which a pupil is left angry and resentful is likely to create further difficulties for colleagues.

Towards a solution

In the field of human relationships there are no watertight solutions, merely guidelines and probabilities. With a large class to contend with, it might seem an unnecessary burden to have to consider the feelings of a pupil who disrupts and appears aggressive and insolent, *except that, in the long run, it will probably benefit the whole class since disruption will be reduced and it will save the teacher considerable time, effort and trouble.* The aim is to improve the quality of everyone's life.

The role of expectation

How we expect someone to behave often influences how we perceive and interpret his or her behaviour and there is evidence to suggest that a positive attitude towards pupils is associated with fewer difficulties with discipline, for example (see Hargreaves, Hester and Mellor 1975).

A teacher giving instruction on a new swimming stroke did so with an unclear explanation and inadequate demonstration. The pupils struggled across the pool as best they could, clearly not understanding the instructions any better than I had from the side. When they had finished, the teacher told them off for not listening properly. That adults are innately 'right' and children and young people innately 'wrong' is a common enough assumption in some societies (psychotherapist Alice Miller illustrates this well – see Appendix II). When I started running workshops for adults who at the end of each session were to fill in an evaluation form not only on the aptness of material and clarity of handouts but also on my 'performance', I suddenly understood to what extent I had held this assumption while teaching in schools. If the pupils carried out instructions poorly I thought *they* had not listened or had misunderstood, whereas if adults did the same I questioned the clarity of *my* explanation! Pupils as young as Year 1 have told me that they have been reprimanded for not listening properly when they had done so but were still unable to understand instructions. The teacher assumed they were at fault rather than understanding that his explanation was inadequate for some. The implications of such assumptions could be far-reaching, resulting in more disruptive behaviour, demoralisation among pupils and conflict with teachers.

If we expect a pupil to cause us trouble he or she is more likely to do so. If we expect a difficult lesson we are more likely to get one. We will communicate our expectation in many ways, verbally, through body language, and unconsciously. Psychotherapist David Mann (1997) gives an example of how, when he began to think more positively about a client in between sessions, the latter, up till then friendless, immediately managed to form a friendship. Fortunately, we are not obliged to *like* all the pupils we teach. However, if we monitor our assumptions and expectations we can perhaps use them to the advantage of ourselves and our pupils.

The potential power of communication

It is easy to feel demoralised by the apparent immensity of the task of communicating positively when confronted by a belligerent adolescent or younger pupil who appears to care little about your opinions. However, the power of such communication and of persistent and consistent kindness, respect, firmness and a steady separation between acceptance of the person and disapproval of unwanted behaviour, should not be underestimated.

Robertson (1981) gives an example of how teachers changing their behaviour towards a pupil and being non-aggressive and calm helped to promote change in the pupil. He also mentions a project by Graubard and Rosenberg (reported by Gray 1974) in which seven pupils aged 12 to 15 who were considered 'incorrigible' were taught to relate in new ways towards teachers. By communicating differently with their teachers, the pupils elicited different responses, and after the five weeks of the project the teachers all related more positively towards them. The power of communication is, I believe, often overlooked and we rarely exploit its full potential for positive change, frequently focusing too much on the content to the detriment of the process, that is to say, our manner. Yet skilful communication can considerably improve relationships and, therefore, behaviour in schools.

Example A

A girl in Year 8 had brought badges into school the day after they had been banned. She had been away and had not known of the ban. A boy in the class had asked to look at the badges. The teacher saw them and took them away, even though the girl tried to explain that they were hers, that she was trying to get them back from the boy in order to put them away, and that she had been absent the day before. The teacher said that he was going to confiscate the badges. The girl was angry, swore at the teacher and was later suspended as a result. Relations between the two were soured and, in future, the pupil was particularly uncooperative and disruptive in lessons. Being sworn at by a pupil did nothing to enhance the teacher's status in the eyes of the rest of the class, even if there were repercussions, and his self-esteem and confidence were eroded. Since the relationship was damaged for the future and would remain so unless steps were taken to improve it, both had in fact suffered from the transaction.

It is never, of course, appropriate for a pupil to swear at a teacher, but she did so in response to what she considered his provocation: he had not listened to the fact she had been away, thereby implying she was lying, and had confiscated the badges when she had, in fact, been *trying to put matters right* by getting them back in order to put them away so they would cause no more trouble. Thus her attempts to take some personal initiative and sort things out herself were frustrated. Other pupils later told her she should have kept quiet at that point and later secretly taken them back from the drawer in which confiscated items were kept. However, her sense of justice would not allow this and she spoke up. Unfortunately, lacking any alternative communication skills and having a backlog of anger against authority figures in general and teachers in particular, she swore. Thus it was her inappropriately expressed indignation at a perceived injustice that was punished by suspension.

Unravelling such situations from the pupil's point of view we get a very different perception than from that of the teacher: in effect, both are working from assumptions about the other which lead to misunderstanding. Such misunderstandings are compounded with time. Yet how else could the teacher have handled the situation in order to make a happier resolution possible?

The above approach can be said to rely on the assumption that the pupil is wrong, has some kind of 'bad' intention and should simply do what he or she is told. As we have seen, this can lead to difficulties in the short and long term. A different set of assumptions would lead to a very different kind of approach. For example, if the teacher were to assume that the pupil's intentions were 'good' and that she deserved to be listened to, in this and many other instances there may be another kind of transaction. Thus the teacher would not assume that the pupil was lying when she said she had been absent the day before and did not know badges were banned. He might say that he had no time at present to go into the matter but would listen later on. Meanwhile he would look after the badges since the girl might get into trouble with other teachers. When they met briefly at the end of the day he would hand them over. At that meeting he would listen to the girl's explanation and briefly point out his own position as teacher, obliged to enforce the school rules. He would also warn the pupil that if he saw her again with badges he would confiscate them immediately.

Example B

The last two boys were leaving class at the end of the day. As they left, they knocked over two chairs. The teacher called them back and asked them, politely, to pick up the chairs. They protested that they had not knocked them over on purpose. She assured them that she was clear it was accidental, but that she was nonetheless asking them, politely, to pick up the chairs they had accidentally knocked over. One boy wavered and said to the other that they had better do it. The other, R, refused and started to walk towards the door. The teacher asked him once again politely to stay and pick up a chair. As he carried on to the door, she warned him that, if he just walked away now, she would phone his mother, since there had been a history of difficulties and the teacher had agreed to inform her immediately of further problems. R walked out.

Half an hour later the teacher phoned R's mother only to find him alone at home. His first enthusiastic response on the phone waned as he realised who it was and why she had rung. The teacher gave him the opportunity to sort the matter out there and then on the phone in which case she would not contact his mother. R agreed and apologised. She praised him for doing so and asked him, in future, to carry out her reasonable requests promptly. He agreed to do so.

What may start out as a small incident may frequently develop into a more serious confrontation since the teacher's power is being tested. If the teacher had ignored the fact that the boys had knocked over the chairs, albeit accidentally, in future they may have felt justified in acting in a similar fashion again. They may well have 'tested' the teacher regarding other boundaries too, and a number of progressively serious contests of will could have ensued until the teacher reinforced a firm boundary.

By picking up on the incident the teacher was reinforcing her expectations of behaviour: mutual politeness and a responsibility to tidy up after oneself without blame. She did this without jeopardising the relationship since she remained polite and fair, acknowledging that it was an accident and giving R a clear choice with a definite consequence if he refused. Later she gave him another chance, which he wisely took. Thus she was persistent in reinforcing the boundaries she had set, consistent in her expectations of polite, reasonable and fair behaviour. Whenever possible she offered R a choice, thereby giving him the opportunity to be powerful within the framework she set up, while carrying out the consequences she had warned him would follow. When he apologised and agreed to comply in future she praised him.

At the end of the episode R had been given an experience to show the teacher meant what she said and would persist until he complied with the standards of behaviour she set. Since she had remained polite and understanding throughout, it was difficult to escape into the 'red herring' of indignation and blame over her manner, and R was left facing the stark consequences of his behaviour. Also, because she had been kind and polite his reaction was one of resignation rather than anger or resentment. He acknowledged that she had 'won'. The teacher had thus reaffirmed her authority without conflict and without damaging, and maybe even improving, the relationship. Future dealings with R would be that much easier.

There are some significant differences between the way in which the teachers handled these two incidents. In the first example the teacher's manner added fuel to the conflict. In the second, her manner made reconciliation more possible. In this she:

- had a positive assumption about the pupil's motives;
- listened to the pupil;
- gave him the opportunity to explain himself;
- gave him the chance to choose a way out and take personal responsibility;
- gave him a second chance;
- adhered to the spirit rather than the letter of the law.

Example C

I observed two teachers who taught the same class. The first, teacher F, had qualified relatively recently, the second, teacher G, was more experienced. F's approach was to praise the class and individuals frequently, while making it clear what his expectations were for behaviour and that they were to be upheld. He avoided outright confrontation with two pupils by focusing on the work that needed to be done, rather than making a large scene out of minor infringements of rules which did not disrupt the flow of the lesson. At the end, he called the two pupils back and asked them to see him for a couple of minutes immediately after school. In this brief meeting he voiced his displeasure at their behaviour, encouraging the pupils to choose one specific way in which each would behave differently next lesson. Having secured this agreement, he could refer to it easily in the lesson should either forget. If they succeeded, or succeeded in part, they would receive considerable praise.

This strategy was designed to help pupils become more aware of their patterns of behaviour, to have some power over change by choosing very specific, small alterations in behaviour and to cooperate in the process. Thus the teacher was not attempting to manage their behaviour as such, but was encouraging them to take responsibility for it and to experience a sense of power by being able to make gradual, small changes.

G's approach was very different and he criticised the class and individuals frequently. The behaviour of the two pupils mentioned above deteriorated rapidly and the teacher soon gave each an ultimatum or he would send them out of the class. The pupils accepted the 'challenge' and were sent out. Some time was taken from the lesson while there was open verbal hostility between the pupils and the teacher.

Both teachers had interesting material and exercises for their classes to do. Both had high standards of behaviour which they maintained, the latter at the expense of two 'casualties'. The experience of being in the two lessons was, however, very different because of the varying approaches used: everyone in F's class, including the teacher, seemed to enjoy him or herself considerably more. There was less conflict. The difference in approach falls into three categories: expectation, focus and communication skills.

1. F expected the lesson to run smoothly and had confidence that he could win over those pupils who might attempt to disrupt. G, on the other hand, seemed to expect a battle and was intent on crushing the least dissent before it took hold.
2. F focused on getting the work done and on the positive aspects of the pupils' work and behaviour. G noticed the least misdemeanour and focused on poor behaviour rather than the issue of work.
3. F gave the class polite requests and plenty of praise. G adopted a confrontational style, gave orders, told pupils off and praised rarely.

It is not, as we see from this last example, always simply a question of experience. Indeed, it may well be that those people who are considered 'born teachers' merely have acquired through life experience those expectations, focus and communication skills which make for peaceful relationships in the classroom. The fact is, however, that those of us who are not 'born teachers', and I was certainly not among their ranks, need not despair since these techniques can be learnt alongside any other teaching skill. As a rule of thumb, questions to ask oneself might be, 'How would I feel as a pupil in my class? Would I like to be spoken to in that way? Would it help motivate me or would I feel resentful? How would I feel if I had difficulties with the work? What qualities did I like in my teachers?' Obviously, everyone is an individual. However, we might get some very interesting answers to our questions.

It is easy as a teacher to be a zealot, so intent on teaching skills and content, as well as keeping up with administrative demands, that we lose sight of the human element, the *people* we are teaching. Obviously to be enthusiastic about our work is a great talent. If we ourselves are demoralised and bored, however can we inspire interest, enthusiasm and eagerness to work in others? It may nevertheless be helpful in our desire to do our job 'properly' to remember that we are first and foremost people, and only secondly teachers. If there can be some meeting, however brief, at that human level as well, it may make a fundamental difference as to how we are perceived by our pupils and how they perceive themselves. This need not undermine the fact that we are in charge, since we are unquestionably so, but we can exercise this power with respect and firmness.

If, as adults and teachers we have the greater experience, the information to get across, the right answers, the power to praise or criticise, the ultimate control of what happens in the classroom, the powerful end of the relationship, then how can we help our pupils to feel valued human beings? Some of our pupils probably will since they earn our praise easily, they feel valued at home, and can do what is required in the structure of a school. But not all. If you are always younger, told off frequently, never in charge, never 'right', it may be quite easy to feel demoralised from time to time. The years of childhood and adolescence can seem endless when seen from the midst of them and for some it may be easy to give up hope. Meeting our pupils as human beings before we rush into teaching them can perhaps help those who cannot meet all or many of our demands at least to feel valued for themselves. It may be simply a brief word, a warm look, but it can make a considerable difference, as seen in the example of S in Chapter 1.

Teacher not friend

Friendship is a relationship between equals, therefore, teachers and pupils can never be friends as such, since the former holds the power and responsibility and can make judgements which affect the latter. The teacher may be kind, caring, considerate and friendly while maintaining the distance conferred by authority. Keeping this balance can at times be difficult and it can be easy to try to be liked, to care too much or be too dependent on a pupil's success or change. This distance is important since pupils can feel betrayed if a teacher appears as a friend one minute while telling them off or referring them to a higher authority the next.

Adolescents, mothers and fathers

Question: Why did the teenager cross the road?

Answer: Because his parents told him not to.

The joke would, of course, apply equally to adolescent girls. It is generally the case that, during adolescence, young people are trying to find their way in life and this inevitably involves testing out their will. As part of growing up, conflict with their parents is common as they reject received values in order to become more separate. Since teachers are working in *loco parentis* it is to be expected that some of the rebellion aimed at parents will come their way. Sometimes gender is relevant: pupils who are having difficulty with one or other parent may act particularly rebelliously with a teacher of that gender. All the more reason never to take it personally.

Cultural differences

There are many cultural differences regarding attitudes to gender and styles of speaking which can lead to misunderstanding. Even though pupils may be using English words, if their manner and style of speech differ from that of the teacher, conflict can sometimes be more likely as a result. Norms of politeness, for example, are culturally based and misunderstandings can easily take place, particularly when people are using the same language but different codes of courtesy. The possibility of conflict arising from linguistic mismatches of this nature requires a separate study and is beyond the scope of this book other than to highlight it as a potentially difficult area.

Speaking to everyone and establishing rapport

As mentioned in Chapter 2, people have different ways of operating when thinking, these differences corresponding to the three principal senses of vision, hearing and feeling (kinesthetics). In other words, people think in one of three main representational systems. Internally, some will generate visual images, some will have physical sensations and some will have an internal dialogue or hear sounds.

One of the ways of assessing a person's representational system is by noticing the kinds of predicates (verbs, adverbs and adjectives) that she or he uses to describe personal experience:

- Someone with a visual representational system will tend to use words such as look, see, show, focus, perspective, view: 'I can see what you mean'; 'Let's focus on this'; 'How would you view the problem?'; 'It looks good to me.'

[a] Someone with a kinesthetic representational system would favour grasp, handle, feel, smooth, rough: 'I feel that's very important'; 'I get the sense you're not with me'; 'I get the feeling it's pretty tough at the moment.'

- Someone with an auditory representational system might choose sound, ring, resonate, hear: 'It sounds good to me'; 'It doesn't quite ring true'; 'I can hear what you're trying to say, but …'

Bandler and Grinder (1979) have used this information in relation to communication and propose that speaking in the same representational system as another tends to improve rapport, whereas using a different one can increase the likelihood of conflict. As the authors note:

> If you want to get good rapport, you can speak using the same kind of predicates that the other person is using. If you want to alienate the other person, you can deliberately *mis*match predicates. (p. 15)

Consider for a moment the fact that, in any class, there will be a spread of pupils working primarily on one of each of the three representational systems. Unless deliberately using words from the other two systems, a teacher will probably be operating in only one of those channels, thereby having less contact with a large proportion of pupils. For example, if the teacher says something like 'Today we're going to look at reasons for the Russian revolution', it is probable that those with a visual representational system are much more likely to get involved in the work than those with a kinesthetic or auditory one. By repeating the initial sentence with differences during the introduction, or using a variety of representational systems in general, the teacher is likely to attract more attention. She or he might add, 'We'll be listening out for any clues as to why the revolution took place in Russia at that particular time. We'll try to get a feel of what it was really like to be there.' Suddenly the teacher will start speaking the subtle 'sublanguage' those using a different representational system will be able to hear, see or hold on to.

If as teachers we want to connect and to establish good rapport it might be helpful to develop versatility in all three channels, so we can truly meet and therefore communicate with all our pupils. Take, for example, the following interaction:

Pupil: I don't know how to do it. I'm a bit out of my *depth*. I guess I just *feel* it's too difficult.

Teacher: I don't *see* what the problem is. Can you *say* it a bit more *clearly*?

The pupil is unlikely to feel the teacher is really in touch with his or her difficulties. Conversely, the latter cannot see the way forward. Mutual frustration and a sense of not quite meeting on the same path of communication, of not quite speaking the same language, are likely to ensue.

How could it be different? The teacher might make a link with the pupil. For example:

> *Teacher*: I don't *see* what the problem is. Can you *show* me where you're *stuck*?

Or she or he could answer totally in the pupil's representational system:

> *Teacher*: I don't get a *sense* of what the problem is. Can you *point out* where you're *stuck*?

This is not merely a question of splitting hairs, but a technique which can facilitate the learning process both directly and indirectly.

Speaking in a range of representational systems can help pupils to listen and understand and to feel understood since you are using their own 'sub-language'. Thus it can have a positive influence on motivation. It can help in the establishment of rapport with a class as a whole and with individual pupils. At times of potential confrontation it might add an extra sense of understanding which could avert greater conflict. Misunderstanding and, therefore, conflict is easier when two or more people are speaking different 'sublanguages' since each feels less well listened to and less understood, while finding it harder to understand the other. Relationships with colleagues and parents can be improved as well as those with pupils.

With individual pupils

When talking with a pupil who has consistently caused discipline problems and with whom you feel a good rapport is not established, taking care to speak in his or her representational system, or in all three if unsure, may sometimes swing the balance in your favour. This is not a panacea, of course, but if the pupil perceives that you are speaking the same language and feels well listened to, who knows, it might form the fragile foundations on which some new kind of relationship can be built.

Resolving conflict between pupils

The negotiating skills described in Chapter 6 can be of use in helping to resolve conflict between individuals or groups of pupils, as can an awareness of representational systems. Conflict may have arisen, in part, due to the fact that pupils are speaking a different 'sublanguage' and, therefore, misunderstandings are more likely. It can be useful to encourage pupils to see, feel or listen to the situation from the others' position.

Initiating contact: the first meeting

It is interesting that much of the time most of us are probably not consciously aware of eye contact at all, even though we will be responding to it unconsciously, and it is of major importance in establishing contact on meeting. Consequently, conscious use of it can be of help to teachers, especially during those first few meetings with a class, the significance of which has been well recorded in educational debate.

Let us assume that, when meeting a new class, the teacher is likely to want to appear relaxed and calm and to be in charge of the process as well as the content of the lesson. He or she will probably wish to make the whole class forcefully aware of his or her presence early on in order to define the situation in favourable terms and make a quick start. I would suggest that relaxed eye contact with each individual *as soon as possible* would be helpful in this. A second's meeting may be sufficient, more may seem intrusive.

Obviously there are many circumstances which could make this difficult. However, it might be possible during a written exercise to go round the class making or confirming a seating plan in order to learn names and make that initial personal contact. Or if the class lined up outside the classroom each pupil could say his or her name on entering so that the teacher could greet everyone individually. Or it might be possible during the course of the first one or two lessons to ensure some other specific contact with each pupil. There may well be cultural differences which would, of course, need to be respected but which might make it difficult to gain eye contact from some pupils.

What we are doing here is attempting to establish a personal relationship right from the beginning by meeting each pupil, not just a class. *We* are initiating the contact and are, therefore, in charge of the process. Pupils who seek attention through disruptive behaviour often initiate the first real pupil–teacher meeting by some disruptive act, thereby putting the teacher in the position of reacting rather than initiating. The teacher can sometimes pre-empt this by giving attention first, on his or her terms, and by giving it for the pupil him or herself, not in response to undesirable behaviour. I am not suggesting that this, on its own, is all that needs to be done, but it can be a helpful element, a long-term investment for the future relationship. Just as a pupil whose name you know is more likely to follow out an instruction than one who is unknown, so a pupil with whom you have had positive eye contact is more likely to take notice of your words than one who has not yet met you in that way. Already he or she has some investment in dealing with you. If all the pupils have met the teacher then he or she will be really present for them in the room. As Marland (1975) writes: 'the second greatest motivation (that is, after achievement) is the pupil's relationship with his teachers' (p. 14). Quite simply, the sooner that relationship begins, the better.

When working with adolescents referred for short-term intervention because of difficulties at school, I try to meet them at the door, introduce myself and welcome them by name, while stretching out my hand to shake hands. It is interesting that even the most downwardly staring young person has so far responded, shaking hands and glancing, however fleetingly, into my eyes. Contact has been made; the process has been speeded up; we have met. I have clearly indicated I am in charge of the process of the meeting yet have shown a degree of respect and equality totally baffling to most adolescents, though nonetheless intriguing. I am not suggesting that we set about shaking hands with the classes we are about to teach! I give the example merely to highlight the potential benefits of *initiating positive contact on your own terms* as early as possible, in whatever way feels most comfortable to you. Although there are specific communication skills which can be acquired, we can only carry them through *in our own way*.

If we feel anxious or intimidated we may be reluctant to initiate such contact since we may be concerned that our lack of confidence would be conveyed in our gaze. If so, stay with what you can carry through *with conviction*. It may be that you take care instead to make contact the way Marland suggests, addressing sectors of the classroom, as if speaking personally to a different individual in each group every time.

When making individual eye contact as an introduction, the intention is to welcome the pupil. If, however, it is to get across in the eyes the message 'I'm in charge!', this could be seen by some as a provocation and could spark off aggression. The process itself indicates the teacher is in charge. Within that structure he or she can relax into meeting the pupil.

What is true for first meetings is to a lesser extent relevant at the beginning of each lesson. If, when the pupils enter the class, the teacher is busy shuffling papers, looking through books, writing on the board or is in some other way engaged, his or her presence in the room will be felt less than if immediate eye contact is made. Although this may not be significant when a firm, long-standing relationship has been built up, it may be if this is not the case. Any necessary organisation can be done after making contact with the class in order to minimise potential disruption.

Facilitating cooperative relationships among pupils

There are many advantages to promoting cooperative relationships. For example:

- the greater the cooperation between pupils, the less conflict is likely between them;
- in an atmosphere of relative harmony, one potential source of anger which could be directed towards a teacher is eliminated;
- pupils can help and, therefore, could also hinder each other learn. If the former, more pupils can succeed and will have a greater investment in making school work for them. Behaviour will improve.

Working with a newly formed class

A little time spent working directly on relationships may save time in the long run since it can help peers to support one another. Using Circle Time can be valuable in this respect (see Bliss and Robinson 1995 and Moseley 1993). The suggestions below could also be adapted in many ways as appropriate for different ages or different subject areas. For example, introductions or other exercises could be conducted in a foreign language. Pupils could be asked to seek out a group of their peers not by name but by using terminology relevant to the subject: chemical formulae, names of countries, for example. Or pupils could be set mathematical problems with the aim of finding classmates whose problem when solved had the same answer as their own.

Getting to know names

With younger pupils, e.g. Year 7
The aim is for pupils to say their own name to the class and to learn the names of some of their classmates.

Pupils sit in a circle. The teacher has a ball the size of an orange made of crinkled silver foil. He or she rolls the ball to someone in the circle saying his or her name. The pupil who receives the ball does the same and so on until all pupils have said their names. Then the game changes, the person rolling saying the name of the person to whom he or she is rolling the ball. Pupils may need to repeat their own names from time to time as reminders or can wear clear labels. The teacher may need to ensure that all receive the ball at some time.

With older pupils
An alternative introduction for older pupils is to give each a card with the names of three or four members of the class whom they have to find to form a small group. Pupils thus have to move around asking the names of those they meet and introducing themselves. Once they have found their group they identify each member. Each group then introduces itself to the rest of the class.

Making eye contact

Pupils are asked to walk slowly around the room in silence simply looking at each person they meet. After a short time they are to do the same, but when they meet someone they are to smile and say 'Hello'. Finally, they are to walk round in silence and must look serious, that is to say, without smiling at those they meet.

For most pupils this last instruction usually ensures that they inevitably smile and laugh whenever they look at someone. This exercise provides the opportunity not only to really look at each other, but also to meet through eye contact. Some pupils will avoid this since there are different cultural expectations regarding eye contact.

Exploring differences and similarities

The class as a whole brainstorm the differences present between them and the teacher writes them up on the board. These differences may include age, colour, race, gender, interests, size, abilities in different areas, experience and so on. The idea is to note differences, many of which will be obvious anyway, in a spirit of acceptance. That is to say, before starting the process the teacher and class will discuss the concept of differences and that they signify merely a difference rather than something which is 'better' or 'worse'. All contributions are to be general and not personal.

After brainstorming it can be pointed out that, despite differences, the pupils also share many similarities. These, too, could be brainstormed. For example, pupils share a similar age, they are in the same class, they are all in school with X years to go. Another similarity is that they all have the same choice of making school work for them so that it is, in general, a positive experience, or making school not work for them so they have a difficult time.

Getting the most out of school

A follow-up exercise in small groups would be to have pupils decide what they need to do in order to make school work for them. The ideas can be collated from the groups, the teacher asking pupils to be specific if points are too general to be practical. The completed list can be displayed in the classroom as the pupils' intention to get the most out of school.

How pupils can support each other

Obviously class members can help or severely hinder their peers' progress in class. The aim of this exercise is to get pupils to be aware of how they can help each other work more effectively. If it is agreed early on that most pupils are in favour of supportive, helpful relationships in the class, more pupils will feel supported in discouraging disruptive behaviour in future from some class members.

Pupils brainstorm in small groups all the ways in which they can help each other and then ideas are shared, the teacher acting as scribe on the board. Later the summary of ways pupils can help can be displayed in the classroom, referred to as necessary, and updated when appropriate.

Resolving disagreements or conflict

Without adequate verbal skills pupils are more likely to resort to name-calling, teasing or violence if some disagreement arises. Although some pupils will have learnt such verbal skills at home or in primary school, many will not. Also there will be differences in approach stemming from a variety of cultural and other value systems. Consequently, it can be helpful if common strategies are worked out collaboratively before the situation arises.

What happens if there is a disagreement in or out of the classroom? How can pupils sort it out verbally, rather than fighting? The class can brainstorm together or in small groups possible resolutions, tracing likely consequences for each. The optimum methods for resolving conflict are then agreed upon and become part of the class code. They could be practised in small groups during PSE or drama lessons, pupils using the technique of breathing, shifting their position and relaxing as a means of creating a gap before rushing into a habitual response. This technique is explained more fully in Chapter 5. Even though, in the heat of the moment, pupils may sometimes forget skills for resolving conflict peacefully, some will remember some of the time. In addition, peers can remind them and the model will stand as an example of how conflict can be resolved as amicably as possible.

Preparation for cooperative work in groups or teams

Pupils will be required to work together in groups in various situations during their school life, and probably after. Some preparation is usually advisable in order to minimise conflict and ensure the highest degree of collaboration.

As preparation, pupils may be asked to brainstorm what they think is needed for a team to work together well. To do this they could think of the different examples of teamwork they know. Are they effective or ineffective teams? What makes them effective? From this guidelines could be drawn up, the teacher adding any crucial points which might be missed.

General guidelines might include:
- each respects another's right to speak;
- each respects another's contribution;
- only one speaks at a time while the others listen;
- each takes equal responsibility for the team's work;
- all have an equal right to vote on issues;
- each sticks to the role assigned for that particular lesson.

More specific guidelines could be drawn up for conflict resolution. For example:
- rules or precedent may at times be used to help resolve conflict;
- decisions should be put to a vote, the majority decision being final;
- if voting proves inconclusive, a coin is tossed;
- all have to accept the decision once taken.

Pupils can also brainstorm the particular roles which could be helpful in teams of three to five members. These might include: scribe to take notes, spokesperson to report back to the whole class, facilitator to encourage participation by all, timekeeper, messenger to ask the teacher for help.

Towards the end of each lesson involving group work, members review the team process stating one way in which they worked together well and one learning point for next time. Blame or personal remarks are not allowed. The teacher may like to add guidelines as appropriate.

It is easy to underestimate the power of relationships in teaching. What some may consider a personality clash or a fortunate match of personalities may well be more accurately described as a clash or concordance of communicative styles. While personality appears set, how we communicate can be altered as new skills are acquired. A relatively small change in approach can, in time, result in considerable differences. Thus a little time and thought directed at creating positive relationships with pupils can only improve learning, minimise conflict and benefit all concerned.

This chapter has dealt with:

The value of working at relationships

Communication breakdown: a cycle of mistrust

Towards a solution
- The role of expectation
- The potential power of communication
- Speaking to everyone and establishing rapport
- Initiating contact: the first meeting

Facilitating cooperative relationships among pupils
- Working with a newly formed class

CHAPTER 4

Teaching, Conflict and Power

Only the respect of the led creates a leader.

Ricardo Semler, *Maverick*

Education must begin with the solution of the student-teacher contradiction, by reconciling the poles of contradiction so that both are simultaneously teachers and students.

Paulo Freire, *Pedagogy of the Oppressed*

A major source of conflict in schools is disruptive behaviour. If a pupil feels unfairly treated and angry of the way in which a teacher has handled conflict, further disruptive behaviour may ensue. Thus, minimising conflict can lead to an improvement in behaviour, while better behaviour inevitably leads to less conflict. Handling an incident effectively can help improve relationships in the classroom.

This chapter examines the ingredients that make conflict more likely in the classroom illustrating, therefore, what might also help to avoid, reduce or defuse it. The question of power relations is also considered in relation to teaching and conflict.

A teacher's choice: to take up the challenge, or not?

J, a Year 9 pupil, throws open the classroom door noisily, stamps in ten minutes late to the back of the class, fishes in his bag for a book and throws it with a thud on to the desk before pulling out a chair, crashing it on the ground and sitting down heavily. The rest of the class had been working quietly.

Variations on this provocative, aggressive display are not uncommon. Obviously there are many possible responses and teachers will deal with it in their own way. Much depends on the kind of relationship, if any, already established. There are no magic formulae for all situations, only general guidelines, a way of thinking, and many possibilities. Most responses will probably fall into one of the three categories:

1. aggressive;
2. passive;
3. neutral (home position).

Aggressive response

An aggressive response might be to shout angrily at the pupil to get out and come back in properly. This might have the desired effect. It might, however, precipitate a heightened conflict.

Meeting aggression with an aggressive response often leads to a greater confrontation which may be time-consuming. Before answering in such a way a teacher would be advised to be very confident of his or her ability to gain the psychological advantage and would preferably be absolutely sure that the pupil would do what he or she was asked. If not, there would need to be procedures in the school which could provide adequate support. When feeling tired, stressed or unconfident it is very easy to respond aggressively to an initial provocation without assessing the nature and possible vehemence of the struggle which might develop.

It is worth remembering that the teacher's focus in such situations is split, since his or her main aim is to get on with the lesson and manage the rest of the class effectively. A pupil behaving in a disruptive way, however, is possibly more focused since he or she need pursue only one aim which may satisfy several needs. Supposing J, in the scenario above, wanted to provoke the teacher because he was angry from an incident in an earlier lesson. By such provocation he may also be avoiding work, creating a scene, impressing some peers and feeling powerful. Since the pupil is more focused he immediately has a psychological advantage. The teacher may, of course, have other advantages as, for example, the sense of being part of a team and of being supported by a clear discipline policy and sanctions within the school.

An approach to challenging behaviour has been considered in greater detail in an earlier chapter. Here I would like to make the point that meeting aggression with aggression can lead to greater conflict at times. There is, of course, a wide range of possible responses. Usually in any group there are two people who have dealt with a similar situation in very different ways, and they have both been successful since, *ultimately, it comes down to our own sense of conviction.* There are, however, many choices, many subtle shades of relating, each with their own outcomes.

An aggressive response may be totally appropriate at times, as long as you are sure that you will 'win'. It is perfectly possible to be commanding, maybe even angry, and yet remain *respectful*. Respect is of the essence. It is often useful to hold in view the overall, long-term relationship. What, *in the long run*, will improve the relationship between you and establish the pupil's acceptance of your authority? How can you best gain his or her cooperation and respect? The relationship with the whole class is also to be considered. Although pupils like teachers who can keep order, they do not like injustice or disrespect shown by a teacher.

Passive response

Responding passively, the teacher might do nothing for fear of provoking trouble and might simply tell the pupil the work to be done. Although this might not invite an immediate escalation of conflict as is possible in the point above, neither would it make clear to the pupil, nor to the rest of the class, the kind of behaviour that is required. Seeking attention and a boundary, the pupil might continue with some other disruptive behaviour, redoubling his efforts in order to elicit a response, or might regularly enter the classroom in the same way. At times, ignoring unwanted behaviour can be effective, but it depends on the relationship already established between the teacher and pupil and the determination of the pupil to be noticed.

Neutral response

Making a neutral response the teacher might, for example, greet the pupil, approach him and explain the work to be done, acknowledging his anger and saying he can talk to him or her about it later. The focus would be the work the pupil needs to be doing, rather than the behaviour he should not be exhibiting. The aim would be to get J involved in the lesson and cooperating as quickly as possible so time would not be wasted.

When J had calmed down sufficiently, perhaps at the end of the lesson, or earlier if appropriate, the teacher would ask him to see him or her for a few moments at a specific time to discuss how they could work better together. It is important that this point is made so the rest of the class, and the pupil himself, know that this kind of behaviour has a clear consequence: seeing the teacher. The content of this discussion is best kept private, if possible, partly to save time during the lesson and partly to help the pupil save face.

At this brief meeting the teacher would say that he or she found the pupil's entrance unacceptable and would ask him to come to class on time and quietly in future. Sanctions if the pupil were to behave in a similar way again would be made clear. The teacher might also mention that the pupil seemed angry and that if he was angry with him or her then they could sort it out. Perhaps the teacher had unwittingly done something the pupil resented during a previous lesson? The pupil, after all, has the right to be angry, but not the right to disrupt lessons.

This third approach disarms the pupil by redefining the situation, refusing his script and assigning him the role you, the teacher, have chosen. The teacher would be focusing on his or her main aim, teaching the whole class, and would not be waylaid by the red herring of disruptive behaviour. The possible anger behind the pupil's aggressive stance would be acknowledged and the pupil offered a chance to air his or her grievances in private, the teacher again reaffirming the code of class behaviour at this time. The rest of the class would be aware that the behaviour was being tackled, but it would not take time from the lesson.

In a sense, the teacher is addressing those aspects of the pupil which remain calm and which can sit down quietly and take part in a lesson, confident that the pupil is capable of that. This can set a boundary and help the pupil feel safe. *The more opportunity a pupil displaying disruptive behaviour has to save face, the more likely he or she will be to accept a way out.* Any further unwanted comments or behaviour can be met and passed over with the phrase that the lesson is not the place and that the question of how they can work better together can be dealt with properly later.

The pupil has gained the possibility of special time with the teacher and has been treated with respect. It will be pointed out during the meeting that, if the pupil has a grievance in future or wishes to talk with the teacher, the way to do so will be to ask directly for time together, *not* to misbehave in class. Having given the pupil an alternative strategy for seeking attention and expressing anger, the teacher will have added to the pupil's overall communication skills. Rather than being diminished by the experience, the pupil can then grow in self-esteem while being told very firmly that the 'acting out' kind of behaviour is totally unacceptable and will be met with inevitable sanctions.

Faced with such neutral behaviour, a would-be aggressor cannot be aggressive in the same way. There is no one to fight, since the teacher will not do so and there is no one to intimidate, since the teacher is not open to intimidation. The situation is safe, since a boundary has been set, and the aggressor's need for attention has been met with the agreement to meet in private. Potential conflict is defused. Many would-be aggressors will calm down with this approach and the relationship for the future can be built in a positive way.

Teachers have considerable power at their fingertips: the way in which they relate to pupils usually influences the result of an interaction, since most of the time most people respond differently, depending on how they are treated. Since some pupils are used to being treated in certain ways and are entrenched in their behaviour, a new approach can sometimes take a little time to take effect. However, it is nevertheless the case that there is much potential for teachers developing skills that can help manage conflict constructively.

Reducing and managing conflict: it takes two to tango

For conflict to be fuelled it requires an aggressive 'invitation', a provocation of some kind, and then a response which is either 1) aggressive or 2) passive.

1. If there is an aggressive response, then a struggle will ensue either verbally or, ultimately, physically until one party 'wins', the other backs down or there is another intervention which ends the confrontation. Playground fights would often be an example of an aggressive response to provocation, with neither side backing down and the conflict being interrupted by teachers.

2. If there is a passive response, the provocateur is likely to exploit the opportunity by further aggressive acts or words either at that time or at a later date. This usually occurs, for example, in a case of ongoing intimidation or bullying. It may also be the case that someone responding passively may at some point have had enough and will suddenly unexpectedly answer in an aggressive manner.

People can move easily from passive to more aggressive roles and many do so frequently each day. For example, meekly accepting harsh criticism from a boss or colleagues (passive), someone may later snap angrily at a friend or family member (aggressive). This is behaviour and habit, not an innate characteristic: habits can be changed, skills learnt, propensities shifted. Some people are more entrenched in one role than another so that their habitual response tends to be passive or aggressive. This applies to some pupils and, in considering how to manage and avoid conflict it is, therefore, helpful to examine the underlying stance of a passive or aggressive response.

Underlying an aggressive or passive response

Both responses are based on a lack of confidence, fear and poor self-esteem which might be a temporary or more permanent feature of thinking. Thus although the behaviour is so very different, both responses share a common basis. Neither includes a sense of flexibility or choice. This view of aggression contradicts the way in which someone acting aggressively is often presented in entertainment and the media. However, a brief consideration of real incidents will establish that people who have adequate self-esteem and who feel secure and confident do not need to intimidate others. The pupils in our classes who most frequently act in an aggressive way generally do not feel good about themselves and are usually fearful and insecure, even though this may be masked by apparent bravado.

The neutral alternative: the home position

The alternative approach is to make a neutral response to aggression from what I shall call the home position, since it is based on a sense of calm and security. This is one which is relaxed and non-confrontational, being neither aggressive, nor passive. It thus refuses either role assigned in the would-be aggressor's script and follows a script of its own. As a result, conflict tends to be defused or totally aborted and *the aggressor cannot be an aggressor in the same way since this depends on the other person taking on an aggressive or passive role*. Without this, conflict tends to dissolve.

The home position:

- sets a firm boundary but without personal antagonism or blame;
- considers the process of an incident rather than getting caught up in content;
- is flexible rather than intransigent;
- attempts to build self-esteem and give praise wherever possible;
- does not take rudeness or a refusal to carry out a request as a personal insult;
- seeks a solution in which the long-term relationship between parties is taken into account;
- is consistent and persistent in enforcing sanctions;
- is confident;
- shows respect towards the other;
- allows the other to 'save face';
- gives the other an opportunity to make amends;
- allows the other to exercise some personal power wherever possible;
- includes a relaxed body posture and breathing.

Power relations and teaching

Teaching is based on a relationship of power. Today, the earlier balance of power in which the teacher was definitely in charge with the potential for overtly aggressive behaviour has been eroded. In its place there is sometimes a confusion of power relations. Not all pupils accept the power structure of a school and some may question a teacher's authority in many ways. Examples of actual violence towards and intimidation of teachers by pupils are not unknown. The falling status of teachers together with increasing demands and common, sometimes very public criticism erodes self-esteem among the teaching profession and facilitates a retreat into powerless ways of thinking.

It is all too easy when faced with a pupil who behaves in a consistently disruptive way to feel stuck and powerless, particularly if school sanctions are undermined by a lack of parental support, as is sometimes the case, or even parental intimidation. With the sheer weight of other demands, it can be easy to feel that all choices regarding such pupils are used up and nothing can be done. It is also easy to take the 'bait' in teacher teasing and, as Robertson (1981) calls it, to find oneself 'the victim of malicious teasing' (p. 88).

Yet since the teacher is, ultimately, in charge and has to maintain order, there is pressure on him or her to switch into a more aggressive mode, using any verbal opportunity to 'defeat' the pupil, put him or her down, perhaps, or humiliate him or her in some way. The teacher may use criticism, shaming, humour or sarcasm, anything to hurt the pupil and establish superiority. That is to say, it is all too easy for the teacher to slip from the extreme of feeling powerless and passive to that of responding aggressively. Although an aggressive response may help the teacher to win the particular battle, he or she may well lose the war with such methods. Not only will he or she be likely to destroy any tenuous hopes of a future cooperative relationship with the pupil in question, but the latter is likely, as a result, to feel even more disenchanted with the school system in general, thereby storing up more difficulties for the teacher involved, other colleagues and, ultimately perhaps, society at large. Such conflict tends to be highly stressful. It further erodes the self-esteem of both parties, while continuing to damage the relationship with the pupil in question and, usually, also that with the rest of the class.

It may be that a teacher feels powerless in relation to a particular pupil, a whole class, the school structure, or the current trend of education policy. Thus it is often very easy as a teacher to become entrenched in ways of thinking that you have no choice and can do little with pupils who disrupt lessons. From this position an aggressive response is likely at some point. This is often perceived as weakness. As Robertson (1981) writes: 'The experienced teacher will avoid bullying, shouting, sarcasm and other such methods, as these really only reveal one's own insecurity' (p. 34).

Developing a relaxed, non-confrontational response to conflict or disruptive behaviour can, therefore, be of great use.

Ways of developing the home position

Ways of thinking

1. Consider the pupil is on the same side in an endeavour to learn, that is to say, is not the enemy.
2. Be aware that the pupil *has* a problem rather than *is* the problem.
3. Notice situations and words which trigger your own anger.
4. Develop techniques to manage anger and learn different ways of responding.
5. Manage stress and develop relaxation.

6. Err on the side of the spirit rather than the letter of the law.
7. Consider how you would like to be treated if you were the pupil in question. How would a close friend of yours wish to be treated in a similar situation?

On the spot

1. Take up and maintain a relaxed body posture and breathing.
2. Avoid standing directly opposite, since this is the fighting position.
3. Stand back or to the side and be aware of the *process* of what is happening.
4 Do not become involved in the *content* of what is being said.
5. Focus on the learning that should be taking place rather than the behaviour which should not. 'We're going on to do an experiment with weights now. Listen carefully at the back so you know how to make your experiment work well.' This tends to be more effective than 'One more word at the back and you have a detention!' The latter can come across as a challenge which is often met. In addition, it obliges the teacher to carry the threat through even though the 'word' might in fact have been about the work in hand. Bad feeling, arguments and confrontations can easily be generated by such ultimatums.

Using body posture and breathing

One of the most effective ways of creating sufficient time to choose a response which is based in the home position and is, therefore, less likely to lead to an escalation of conflict is to ensure a relaxed body posture and breathing. If a pupil behaves in a challenging and provocative manner the teacher's body posture and breathing are likely to change unconsciously to one suited to an aggressive or passive response. This will be a learnt response which has become entrenched as a habit. The body posture and breathing support, maintain and often fuel particular ways of thinking, feeling and, consequently, acting. *Thus the quickest way to change unwanted behaviour and ways of communicating is to interrupt the flow of a habitual response by breathing freely and shifting into a different, relaxed position.* This requires:

- the will to change;
- an awareness of how breathing and posture alter in response to an aggressive challenge;
- a way of breathing freely and shifting to a different, more relaxed posture;
- practice.

A technique for using breathing, relaxation and a different position to interrupt a habitual response so choice is possible is in the next chapter.

Times when conflict is more likely

Some of the most common general elements relevant to the classroom which make conflict more likely between teacher and pupils or between class members are included below:
- the other is perceived as an opposing force, an 'enemy';
- there is an underlying insecurity or anxiety that the other can cause harm, take something away or somehow damage us or our standing;
- there is a history of unresolved conflict and unhappy experiences in the past, a cycle of mistrust;
- perceived or real injustice.

One or both parties:
- are unsure about their own resources;
- are out to 'win';
- want a fight;
- lack the resources or communication skills to find a more peaceful solution;
- want to hurt the other;
- want the same thing and are fighting to see who gets it, or want to take something from the other;
- habitually speak and respond aggressively;
- feel under pressure and are stressed;
- are angry or resentful about a related or even an unrelated issue;
- dislike the other;
- have no interest in forming or maintaining a positive relationship;
- are unaware of alternative ways of behaving which might defuse or avoid conflict.

Between pupils

As far as conflict between pupils is concerned, this is most likely to take place when:
- pupils are moving about the room, into or out of it and jostling can occur;
- pupils are not busily engaged in work;
- there is a disagreement about whose turn is next, e.g. on the computer;
- there is a disagreement about how a collaborative activity should be done;
- the conflict is brought in from the playground, started earlier, or is ongoing;
- one or more pupils are very angry;
- one or more pupils feel pressured and stressed;
- one or more pupils are unable to do the work.

Between teachers and pupils

With the presence of some of the elements predisposing conflict outlined above, conflict between teacher and pupil is most likely when:
- a teacher perceives a pupil as answering rudely or appearing insolent;
- a pupil perceives the teacher as being unfair or rude;
- a pupil arrives late;
- a pupil fails to hand in or complete a task;
- a pupil refuses to carry out a request;
- a teacher asks a pupil to stop some disruptive behaviour;
- a teacher asks a pupil to do something he or she does not wish to do;
- there is bad feeling on one or both sides from an earlier incident;
- a teacher is investigating a conflict between pupils or some other incident;
- a teacher is reprimanding a pupil;
- a pupil does not understand or is unable to do the work.

This analysis highlights the need for measures which prevent or minimise the likelihood of conflict arising in the first place as well as those to reduce any escalation should it arise.

Prevention techniques

Prevention techniques include the following:
1. An environment, rules and procedures which make disruptive behaviour difficult and desirable behaviour easy.
2. Consistent, firm boundaries, with clear sanctions and rewards.
3. Work which is attainable by all so some success is always inevitable.
4. Skills for teachers and pupils in resolving conflict constructively, in finding alternatives to conflict and in talking about old disagreements to clear the air.
5. Ways of building pupils' self-esteem, giving praise and showing appreciation wherever possible.
6. Maximum opportunity for the exercise of choice, personal initiative and independence.
7. Strategies for understanding and managing anger constructively, both one's own and that directed towards one.
8. An acknowledgement that positive, cooperative relationships have a role in reducing conflict; skills to build such relationships.
9. Ways of managing stress.
10. Building trust by listening to pupils and allowing them opportunities, in private, to voice difficulties and grievances.

Teaching points

There are several areas in the school curriculum when the issue of conflict can be discussed in various ways. Certainly it is the case that, if there is an ethos in the school and in the classroom suggesting that conflict can be resolved peacefully through negotiation it can only help to minimise aggressive and violent incidents. If the mechanism of conflict and the dynamic between aggressive and passive responses are discussed, then it is easy to analyse what has happened should an incident occur or merely be threatened. *If it is understood that aggressive behaviour indicates insecurities and fear existing in the aggressor, then any status given a would-be aggressor is fundamentally eroded.*

Obviously more is needed than for pupils simply to understand about conflict. They will also require alternative skills, primarily communication skills, in order to *talk* about difficulties and maybe resolve them, rather than resorting to violence. Some of these skills are presented in Chapters 3, 5 and 6.

The points below aim merely to suggest some areas in the curriculum which readily lend themselves to work on conflict.

Conflict in the curriculum

English

Much literature provides an opportunity at different levels for discussing how conflict emerges, the relative roles of 'victim' and 'aggressor' and investigating possible constructive, alternative solutions. For example, *Romeo and Juliet*, *West Side Story*, *Across the Barricades* and *The 18th Emergency*.

Drama or PSE

Based on literature or on the outline of a situation it is possible to explore the dynamic between 'victim' and 'aggressor' through drama. Incidents of attempted or actual bullying from the pupils' own experiences can be investigated, looking for alternative solutions from the home position. The internal weakness of the 'aggressor' can be highlighted.

Humanities

Considering the reasons for international conflict will illustrate that aggression is often started by a country in response to *internal* problems. That is to say, an external show of might is usually an attempt to unite a country experiencing severe difficulties at home. Parallels can of-course be drawn with individuals who resort to aggressive behaviour.

This chapter has dealt with:

an explanation of choices in response to provocative behaviour: passive, aggressive or neutral (home position)

A teacher's choice: to take up the challenge, or not?
- Aggressive response
- Passive response
- Neutral response
- Reducing and managing conflict: it takes two to tango
- Underlying an aggressive or passive response
- The neutral alternative: the home position

Power relations and teaching

Ways of developing the home position
- Ways of thinking
- On the spot
- Using body posture and breathing

Times when conflict is more likely
- Between pupils
- Between teachers and pupils
- Prevention techniques

Teaching points
- Conflict in the curriculum

CHAPTER 5

Anger

Anger is actually energy just doing its job.

Emaho, *The Fire Dance*

... a little fear goes a long way in influencing behaviour, sometimes in quite subtle ways.

Daniel K. Oestreich and Kathleen Ryan, *Driving Fear out of the Workplace*

Why consider anger?

There is little doubt that anger invites conflict. When angry, pupils are also unlikely to cooperate and are very likely to disrupt the class. They are unlikely to learn. Considering the issue of anger is, therefore, extremely important for teaching. If you can manage angry pupils and your own anger confidently, your teaching skills will be greatly enhanced and life will simply be much easier. This chapter explores anger and ways of feeling more confident at dealing with it. It also includes techniques for helping pupils understand more about anger and the responsibility they have for expressing it in constructive or destructive ways.

- P, Year 10, stands up, furious, and swears at the teacher. His chair falls as he storms to the door, slamming it behind him.
- A pupil in Year 7 is jostled in the queue outside the classroom. She turns round and pushes the boy nearest her hard against the wall.
- In a corner of the playground two boys are locked in combat, their faces flushed with rage.

There is plenty of anger in our schools, often just below the surface waiting for an insignificant incident to trigger it off. And it is not only to be found among the pupils.

The youth stands there, a picture of insolence, refusing to leave the room. You are in charge and have a class to teach. At the end of an exhausting week a class is persistently noisy when you are trying to get across some important information. Two pupils are constantly baiting one another, and so on. As a teacher, too, there are often numerous daily opportunities for feeling angry and there are many ways of expressing it.

Sometimes you might lose your temper and regret it later since you had been gradually building a delicate trust with a pupil at whom you have just shouted. At other times a pure expression of anger might be appropriate and very effective. Or you might use a show of anger in order to get across the gravity of a point. When facing the anger of pupils directed towards you it might be difficult not to reply in kind. Thus there are times when it could be useful to have a choice of response: meeting anger with anger or using an alternative strategy. In addition, when mediating in a quarrel between pupils a deeper understanding about anger may provide the key to a more satisfying resolution. If pupils themselves understood more about anger they, too, could have more choice about it.

Points to consider when dealing with angry pupils

- What might be the teacher's aim when a pupil is angry? In the classroom it is probably most useful to continue teaching the class with the least possible disruption, while making it clear that the incident will be dealt with later.
- If the teacher responds angrily it can sometimes be seen as showing that he or she perceives the pupil as a threat of some kind. A calm response which acknowledges the pupil's anger but refuses to be waylaid from the purpose of the lesson indicates that the teacher has supreme confidence in his or her authority and can take it all in his or her stride.
- It is usually helpful to keep in mind the *process* of the interaction, rather than being immersed in the *content*. For example, if a pupil makes a rude comment to a teacher it is easy for the latter to respond to the content of what has been said. This is likely to develop into further conflict which may help no one, neither the pupil in question, the teacher, nor the class. If the teacher refuses to take the bait, however, and responds only to the fact that the pupil has spoken in an unacceptable way, it may be possible to return to the lesson more quickly. *That is to say, the teacher is firm, but does not take the content personally. He or she notes the fact that the pupil is angry, making it clear that, athough angry, the pupil never has the right to be rude or disrupt lessons.* Any grievances could be explained properly at a set time outside lessons, since only then could they be dealt with adequately. The teacher would return swiftly to the lesson. If the pupil made subsequent, inappropriate comments, the teacher could brush them off with a 'Not now, at … please'. If the pupil persisted so that teaching and learning were seriously affected, appropriate school sanctions, such as sending to a withdrawal room or detention, would need to be applied. Whatever happens it is useful for the next

lesson if it is made absolutely clear to the pupil *before* this that:

1. rudeness and disruption to lessons are unacceptable;
2. if angry, a pupil can make a time to see you to talk about it and you will respect that right and will listen;
3. if the pupil is polite it is easier to hear the message;
4. if the pupil is rude in class or disrupts the lesson again specific sanctions will follow.

Thus it is not anger itself which is unacceptable but the manner and place of its expression.

Expressed clearly and appropriately, anger can be a constructive force. One way of expressing it clearly is to put it into words rather than act it out. It is still possible to be extremely angry with a pupil and treat him or her in a respectful way. This provides a model for pupils, emphasising the need to remain respectful even during disagreements.

- Remember the possibility of responding in an aggressive, passive or neutral way, as outlined in the previous chapter. Standing directly opposite an angry pupil is unlikely to be helpful. Breathing freely, shifting your position and relaxing makes a neutral response easier.
- A pupil may well carry anger from one lesson to another, from one teacher to another. Although it is important to remember that teachers are teachers and neither counsellors nor social workers, it may sometimes be useful to listen to pupils' grievances at an appropriate time. Elizabeth Kubler-Ross (1970), who has worked for years with very sick and dying people, has found in her research that patients' anger and rage diminished when they:

1. were respected and understood;
2. were given attention and time;
3. were understood rather than judged;
4. were able to maintain their dignity;
5. felt they had the right to have an opinion;
6. had the opportunity to be heard;
7. were able to 'ventilate some rage';
8. had the maximum opportunity for control in an overall situation over which they had no control.

It was useful if those dealing with them:

1. did not take personally angry outbursts directed at them;
2. could put themselves in the other's place and assume his or her anger was reasonable, even if inappropriately expressed, wondering where it might come from, rather than condemning it.

- Much of the above is relevant to pupils who are frequently angry. Their anger is not 'wrong', though how and where they express it may leave much to be desired. The teacher's role is, primarily, to teach. This may sometimes require listening to a pupil's angry outbursts outside lessons and providing him or her with the skills to talk about anger at an appropriate time, rather than to act it out in lessons. Above all, the pupil is treated with respect and allowed to save face in class, while it is made clear that lessons cannot be disrupted.

- A pupil's anger against the school, authority figures and/or particular teachers may be so great that he or she will not at first turn up to a private meeting or will not cooperate during one. Patience may be required in order to build up trust and to get a dialogue started.
- Outside school some pupils will be used to anger being expressed through physical and/or verbal aggression and it may take them a little time to adjust to a different kind of communication.
- Recovery: after an angry confrontation it is helpful to check your breathing, return it to normal and relax.

Choosing to keep your temper – a technique

Having a choice is often useful since it can increase a sense of self-esteem: you were not out of control, you chose to express your anger at the time, to postpone it and sort it out later, or not to bother at all. *In order to choose, time is needed, a gap in which you can think and choose.* Thus, a habitual response may be halted and reassessed before being discarded or applied.

Technique

1. Breathe, since when angry or becoming so the normal pattern of breathing changes. Take breaths deep within the body so the lower abdomen expands. No more oxygen is taken in than usual (or over time you can hyperventilate) but the feeling is that it is taken deeper within the body.
2. Shift the posture from one which may be associated with anger, and relax. Being aware of wriggling the toes can help in this. If you are directly opposite the pupil you may wish to step a little to one side.
3. Give yourself an internal commentry: for example, 'X has just stood up angrily and sworn at me. Shall I shout back angrily, calmly send her out or carry on with the lesson, telling her to come and talk to me directly after school?'
4. Consider possible consequences of the alternative responses. What do you want? What is wise? What best shows that your authority is unruffled by this? What will least disrupt the whole class?
5. Take a few more breaths, relax, and choose.

Often we feel obliged to respond instantly, but there is no reason why this should be the case. Usually taking some time to think in itself helps defuse a situation which could otherwise deteriorate as a result of immediate and hasty reactions.

Changing a habit takes time, effort and practice. Relapses may occur; some attempts may fail. Patience is, therefore, helpful.

Helping pupils to manage their anger

It may be appropriate to work with an individual pupil or small group who find difficulty with their anger specifically on the issue of managing it: choosing to keep their temper, as described above, and calming down. (It can be useful if you have used the techniques yourself since then you know how they work and can get them across with greater conviction.) Much of the information and many of the exercises given below for use with whole classes in subject areas could also be adapted for group or individual work.

Many pupils are frightened by their own anger and dislike sudden outbursts in which they feel out of control. Understanding what anger is and learning that it is possible, with practice, to choose a different kind of behaviour can, therefore, be a relief for some. Discovering that they have a right to anger alongside a responsibility to manage it constructively in school and in society can come as a revelation to many: often they have been told not to be angry at all. Anger suppressed in this way can frequently burst out inappropriately or with inappropriate force, when someone appears to overreact to a relatively insignificant incident.

One way of expressing anger is to stop communicating with those towards whom the anger is directed. If a pupil expresses his or her anger in this way it may take some time to establish a dialogue and this will be possible only when the pupil trusts that anger can be expressed verbally without punishment, he or she has the skills in order to do so and believes that there is a point to the whole exercise.

Helping pupils to choose to keep their temper

The technique described above for choosing to keep one's temper can be used with pupils. The idea of different consequences resulting from the different ways they behave is very important since this incorporates the concept of personal responsibility. A number of pupils may resist the idea that they have any control over their anger, stating that others 'make them angry'. This can be countered by discussion about the fact that people are angered by different things. *Therefore, it is not the stimulus which creates anger, but the individual's response to it.* Numerous examples from their school life might be useful here since different teachers and pupils will become particularly angry in response to different situations at different times, some rarely becoming angry at all. *Choice and, therefore, control are possible if breathing and body posture are changed appropriately.*

The new behaviour needed for providing time to choose to keep one's temper can be practised by recreating situations in which a particular pupil would usually respond angrily. The teacher, or other group members, could then remind the pupil of the different stages of behaviour needed: breathing, shifting posture and relaxing, moving away from a position of direct confrontation and so on. Practice of the desired behaviour outside the real situation can be useful since it helps pupils experience the new technique in a way mere talking about it cannot. In a supportive situation, therefore, they can be aware of the difficulties encountered in changing a habit which might have seemed relatively straightforward in discussion.

Helping pupils to calm down and recover

Talking about strategies for calming down from anger and practising them if appropriate is also important since otherwise pupils may remain angry during one lesson after another, their sense of anger and injustice deepening by the year. Some points which may be helpful in learning to calm down and recover from anger:

- Anger does not have to be expressed at the time, in the situation, to the person with whom you are angry.
- The expression of anger can be separated from the message. In other words, an angry outburst may contain a criticism, complaint or comment. The latter is different from the anger which is our emotional response to the situation. Consequently, it is possible to express anger, which is, after all, ours, on our own or with support but separate from the incident when it was triggered. Later we may choose to make the criticism, complaint or comment to the other person, without the overlay of our angry response.
- Running, swimming as fast as possible, punching a punch bag, playing football are all (safe) ways of expending anger energy. If it is not expended but held in the body as muscular tension, we can feel tired as a result. Moreover, any past, lingering anger may burst out inappropriately in response to an insignificant trigger in the present.
- After energetic release it can be helpful to find emotional release. This may be by talking to a friend or someone sympathetic about the incident in which you felt anger. If this is not possible then you may choose to write about it, do a drawing or painting about it or speak into a tape recorder.
- After talking about or exploring the incident it might be the case that another feeling or feelings emerge as the anger subsides. These feelings may include sadness, emotional hurt, fear or a sense of inadequacy, and the experience may be quite painful.
- Someone who can be supportive and listen can be very important in helping people to work through anger. If, at times, it is a teacher who is in this supportive role it is helpful to remember that he or she is a

teacher and that the aim is to enable the pupil to function adequately in school and to succeed within a school environment.

- A concept from martial arts can be useful in recovering from anger and is also often acceptable to many young people. Martial arts embrace the idea of the *hara* or *dan tien*, the body's movement centre which is to be found three or four finger breadths below the navel in the centre of the body. When concentrating on this area, a person can be said to be 'centred'. He or she will be relaxed and his or her energy will be extending out. Movements made while concentrating on this centre will be more powerful and flowing. This counteracts the Western idea that strength is about muscular tension. On the contrary, strength is about relaxation and the concentrated extension of energy. It is with such strength that a person experienced in the technique can chop a brick in two with the edge of a hand. When angry, or indeed fearful, a person usually tenses and becomes 'uncentred'. Consequently, consciously 'centring' is another way of helping a pupil to relax and calm down or to stay calm.

- There are various ways of helping pupils to become aware of and focus on their centre. If they practise doing so at peaceful times, then it will be easier to remember and do so after an angry incident. One way of centring is to imagine a sphere expanding and contracting at the 'dan tien'. If it is difficult to 'see' images, it is possible to imagine a sound or a feeling expanding and contracting in this area. Another way of centring is simply to think of something you love, or to imagine yourself doing something well. (Thinking of something you hate or imagining yourself doing something badly will have the corresponding effect of uncentring.)

- When physically 'centred', or balanced, a person is less easily unbalanced emotionally.

- Pupils may also appreciate guidance in channelling their anger creatively. Often they have a strong sense of justice which has been offended by incidents in school. Since such a sense is, in itself, an admirable quality, how could they use it to promote positive change? Some pupils, for example, might like to write to their MP about certain issues or get involved in local environmental campaigns. Others might wish to concentrate their anger energy into school work, to prove a point, perhaps. Or there may be a responsible role they could adopt in the school which would help bring about positive change.

Teaching points

The following ideas and exercises can be used with whole classes in different subject areas and with groups and individuals. The information about anger might also be relevant to teachers themselves in dealing with angry pupils, since the deeper their understanding of the subject the more equipped they will be to deal with it confidently.

A quiz on anger for use with pupils

This could be incorporated in several subject areas. For example, PSE, biology, if the physiological aspects were emphasised, or a modern language if it were translated. The quiz can be adapted to suit various ages and can form the basis for longer discussion. It could be answered individually, in pairs or in small groups, before general discussion. Comments in addition to information earlier in the chapter are below.

---

1. What is anger?
2. Can another person make you angry?
3. Is anger always bad?
4. Can anger become a habit?
5. What are some of the emotions that anger may mask? For example, fear, hurt, insecurity, fear of failure, a sense of inadequacy, etc.
6. Is getting angry good for your health?
7. Is bottling up anger good for your health?
8. Is it possible to manage your anger without either exploding from time to time or bottling it up?
9. Do people often get angrier when a present situation reminds them of a similar one in the past?
10. Can talking to someone sympathetic outside the situation help with your anger?
11. Can physical exercise help you to calm down after an angry incident?
12. Do you want to be ignored or taken seriously when angry?

(This quiz is in Appendix III and can be photocopied to use with pupils.)

Comments on anger

- Anger is a response to a real or imagined attack of some kind or to frustration, real or imagined, of a desire or need. The attack may be physical or emotional. Adrenalin floods through the body providing it with extra energy to fight, flee, shout or grab, and so on.
- No one else can ever *make* us angry. We can *become* angry in response to someone's words, action or expression. It is, therefore, ultimately always our responsibility. However provocative someone else may be, if we take up the challenge and become angry then it is *our* anger. Anger is never inevitable, another response is always possible. For example, we

may get angry at something that another person might consider insignificant, remaining perfectly calm throughout, and vice versa.

- Anger for a just cause can be channelled creatively to help bring about positive change. It can motivate someone to strive for a particular goal. Anger *per se* is not bad, it all depends on *how* it is used. All too often it is used destructively against others and the self. *Saying* we are angry can often make it easier to *act* more calmly. Not talking about anger makes it more likely that we will act in an angry way: somehow we will show our anger, even if it is by avoiding or ignoring someone with whom we are angry.

- Anger can very easily become a habit. Indeed, if it has been successful in the past in helping us to get our own way or if we have no alternative skills, that is to say, we know no other ways of expressing ourselves, it is likely to do so.

- Anger may mask all of these emotions and more. Although anger is often expressed in a powerful way, the emotions underlying it usually indicate a sense of powerlessness: jealousy, rejection, abandonment, frustration, failure and so on. Often when we are angry we simply wish to hurt someone else, presuming this will help us to feel better. In the long term it usually does not do so.

- Getting very angry very often is generally not good for your health since it uses up considerable energy and increases wear and tear on the body.

- Bottling up anger is also bad for your health since holding on to unexpressed anger is also tiring and stressful.

- It is possible to manage one's own anger differently, with time, practice and patience. Since an angry response is often, partly at least, habit, all that is needed is to instil alternative habits. This is not necessarily as easy as it sounds and involves six aspects.

1. An on-the-spot technique for choosing whether to respond angrily, to explode on the spot or to breathe, stand back, relax and deal with it later. Our anger will have its own body posture and breathing style that maintain and fuel angry emotions. If we change into a different posture, for example, one which is calm and relaxed, we cannot remain as angry.

2. Techniques for releasing anger tension in the body safely and calming down: running, swimming, football, a punch bag, etc.

3. Emotional support: someone to talk to.

4. Doing something creative, since anger is often associated with feelings of powerlessness. This can be anything: mending a bike, tidying a room, making people laugh, drawing a picture, deciding what you will do or say in a situation.

5. Communication skills which make it easier to express anger verbally, when appropriate, rather than acting angrily.

6. The more long-term task of building self-esteem so that confidence

for dealing with situations increases and less incidents are considered to be threats or attacks. Consequently, the potential number of angry responses decreases. Learning to stand and move in a relaxed and centred way can also help in this.

- If there is a reason for anger in the past which is unresolved and remains simmering at some level, then another incident which is a reminder of that original situation is likely to be met with additional anger. In the present this may well appear to be an overreaction.
- Many people find that talking about their anger to someone who is sympathetic can be extremely helpful, since in explaining to someone who will listen it is often possible to become clearer about the issues involved and the real source of anger.
- Many people also find that some safe physical exercise helps them to dissipate some of the tension from anger and to feel calmer. After dispelling some of the anger tension in the body, centring can help return us to a state of calm.
- Most people will probably wish to be taken seriously when angry. Since anger is often about giving a show of power when feeling powerless about something, an 'audience' is required for best effect. If someone who is angry is ignored, he or she is likely to act in an increasingly angry manner, for a while at least.

Exploring anger through the curriculum

Obviously, anger would need to be included within the confines of the National Curriculum. Teachers of subject areas not mentioned specifically may still find opportunities for touching upon the subject, if relevant, and can use earlier techniques for managing individuals.

English

There are many ways in which anger could be included in an English curriculum. Poems dealing with it could be studied and pupils could write their own about how it feels to be angry.

Pupils could write imaginative stories which involved someone angry or could describe real incidents. They could then write alternative endings: one in which a character dealt with his or her anger destructively by acting it out in some way, and one in which it was handled constructively by changing the body posture and breathing, gaining understanding and expressing it verbally. The aim would be to illustrate the fact that a destructive result to anger is not inevitable. Another way of approaching this theme would be to read a passage or story which involved a character getting angry. Leaving the passage unfinished, ask the class to write endings to the scene. This could also provide a starting point for discussion on the subject, highlighting the differences in people's approaches.

Some literature could act as a resource for the subject. The character of Othello, for example, illustrates how underlying his anger and aggression there are self-doubts, insecurities and fear. Again it could be instructive to write an alternative ending to the play in which Othello was able to manage and deal with his anger constructively by voicing his feelings and fears and building his own self-esteem and confidence!

Drama, English, PSE

In these subjects pupils could get into small groups which have been set scenarios involving anger. The rule would, of course, be no physical violence permitted. The groups have the task of working out at least two different scenes in which anger was dealt with differently. Discussion and analysis about what made the difference and what led to a more comfortable resolution could ensue.

A more structured way of getting the same point across would be to have a few pupils acting the scenario in front of the class, who would suggest different approaches the players could take. Both techniques could underline dramatically the element of choice and personal responsibility in handling anger.

Dance

In this subject area the body posture of anger and its effect on emotions and thinking could be explored effectively. Also the technique for antidoting it by relaxation, breathing deep within and shifting position could be highlighted. The relationship between anger and movement, peace and movement could be considered.

Pupils could be asked when standing to get into positions which for them seemed to express anger. This could be repeated sitting down. Doing these two exercises with closed eyes initially can be useful since pupils are less inhibited or distracted by others. While in the positions of anger pupils could be asked to notice any changes in their breathing, any tension, and how the posture affects their feelings and thinking. Would they need to move in order to stop feeling angry, for example? Common visual features could be noted as well as the internal experience regarding breathing, emotions and tension. The relationship between posture and feelings could be underlined. It could be pointed out that, since it is possible to 'simulate' anger by getting into an angry body posture even for just a few minutes, it is also possible to avert or postpone anger by changing postion and breathing differently. There is a fluidity involved which is rarely recognised.

The static postures could be extended into movement: how, without touching each other, could pupils move in angry ways? How does it feel? How does it affect their breathing? The same could be done for peaceful feelings. In this way a dance could be constructed, contrasting the qualities of anger and peace.

Music

If the department involved pupils composing and performing their own pieces they could create some conveying anger and peace to accompany dance. Otherwise pupils could be involved in selecting suitable music, concentrating on the emotional power of the works.

Humanities

The contrasting ways in which anger is viewed in different cultures or at various times throughout history could be explored. This could lead to a discussion concerning varying expectations and taboos about anger in the class, depending on cultural, gender and individual differences.

Modern languages

The different ways of expressing anger in a different language, including variations in body posture, could be considered. Again the aim would be to get across the idea that anger is variable and depends upon the individual expressing it and not the stimulus.

Art

By painting, drawing, sculpting and creating pottery on the subject of anger, pupils could learn that art is another medium for expressing it constructively.

Biology

The physiological aspects of anger, including health risks and ways of managing and dissipating it, could be studied.

One of the most effective long-term methods of managing anger is to help pupils build self-esteem and confidence and learn communication skills which will enable them to express feelings and opinions verbally and more appropriately, rather than acting them out. These subjects are dealt with elsewhere in the book.

This chapter has dealt with:

Why consider anger?

Points to consider when dealing with angry pupils

Choosing to keep your temper – a technique

Helping pupils to manage their anger
- Helping pupils to choose to keep their temper
- Helping pupils to calm down and recover

Teaching points
- A quiz on anger for use with pupils
- Comments on anger
- Exploring anger through the curriculum

CHAPTER 6

Skills

If we are not open to what the other person is telling us, genuine rapport is hardly possible ... Learning is a result of listening, which in turn leads to even better listening and attentiveness to the other person.

Alice Miller, *For Your Own Good*

One of the main reasons we make such a mess of things is that we simply do not have the skills.

Anne Dickson, *A Woman in Your Own Right*

This chapter considers the need for teaching and modelling specific communication skills as a means of reducing conflict and improving behaviour. It focuses on negotiating and listening skills.

Many pupils lack a variety of communications skills. Often it is easy to make the assumption that they are wilfully insolent or rude. This may at times be true; yet at other times they may simply lack a range of alternative responses from which to choose. They are bound by habit to the few ways of responding they have acquired. Unless specifically taught new skills, most pupils will continue with familiar behaviour and patterns of communication which may provoke and fuel conflict. Without alternatives, they have no choice. As we have seen in earlier chapters, experiencing a sense of having no choice erodes self-esteem and fosters powerless kinds of thinking which can in turn lead to an aggressive response. A vicious cycle can thus be established which can be broken by teaching relevant skills and modelling alternative ways of communicating. This need not be time-consuming. In essence, the aim is to illustrate that there are many possible ways of responding and everyone has the responsibility of choosing for him or herself. Such responsibility is also empowering.

Examples

'When I'm an adult I'll go up to someone afterwards and ask them what their problem is and sort it out ...' Z, a 15-year-old on temporary exclusion, had no idea that asking someone, 'What's your problem?' is likely to come across as an attack and will probably receive an aggressive response along the lines of, 'What do you mean, I've got a problem?' She firmly believed that this was an adult way of talking about a disagreement, calmly, in a manner that would sort out an earlier altercation of some kind.

Similarly, D, mentioned in Chapter 1, was totally unaware of his insolent body posture when a teacher was telling him off. Neither pupil was conscious of the fact that what he or she was doing was likely to provoke an aggressive response from most people. Although no one can make another angry, it is nevertheless true that certain kinds of response are provocative and many will respond angrily, unless they are very aware of what is happening and choose to respond differently.

Only when the roles were reversed with the two pupils above and I played their behaviour back to them did they understand: they both felt angry. Up until then they were merely repeating behaviour they had learnt, without realising how they came across and without any alternative communication skills from which to choose. However differently they might wish to come across, it would be difficult for them to do so unless they:

1. want to change;
2. are aware of what exactly they are doing at present which can help provoke conflict;
3. have some new communication skills to adopt;
4. practise.

Consequently, it can be very helpful, if appropriate, at times to reflect back to some pupils who are in regular conflict with teachers just how they do come across. This could best be done in private by a teacher with whom they have established a more positive relationship and could take place in time otherwise taken up by detention or 'telling off'. Alternative skills, that is to say, how else they could stand and speak and so on, could be explored. The idea is to convey that the pupil *always has a choice* and could always choose a route which would minimise conflict. (Some communication skills to work on with pupils are included in Appendix IV.)

Negotiating skills

The more pupils are equipped with adequate communication skills the less likely they are immediately to resort to violence or verbal abuse with peers or teachers. They have the means to *talk* about differences rather than *fight* about them. Frustration and anger can be expressed verbally rather than being acted out. This is as true for 5-year-olds as it is for 15-year-olds (see Appendix V for an example). Principled negotiating provides an approach which is highly practical and easy to convey. Teachers could use this to:

• help pupils sort out an argument among themselves, not by interfering in the content of the dispute, but by providing a means by which pupils could talk about it;

• talk to individual pupils, thereby modelling the approach.

The skills could also be conveyed more directly in some subject areas.

The essence of principled negotiating

1. Rather than seeing the other person as an opponent, he or she is considered to be *on the same side*: both are seeking a fair solution to a shared problem. This assumes that, if there is conflict, then both parties are adversely affected by it.
2. The long-term relationship is considered to be important. Therefore a short-term victory which damages the relationship is no victory at all.
3. The aim is to relate to the other person separately from the problem. Thus it is possible to relate warmly to him or her while remaining firm on the issue.
4. The approach is one which looks for what is in common, simply different or complementary, the interests, rather than what is the area of conflict, the position taken up by both sides. Interests tend to be needs, fears, concerns or desires. Often people are wanting the same general goal, for example, to manage in school, but have very different ways of interpreting that, often getting stuck in one approach, one position.
5. The technique involves thinking creatively about possible solutions before deciding what might be practical or not.
6. If possible, use some kind of objective standard, precedent, common practice, a rule, etc., since this helps people to save face and goes beyond the personal.

Helping pupils sort out disagreements

L was a boy in Year 8 who was frequently getting into trouble with teachers. He associated with a group of boys with whom he played at break times. In lessons, however, one of this group, G, had the habit of taking L's pen off his desk and keeping it until L started to tell a teacher. L tended to get extremely angry at this since he had literacy difficulties anyway, and G taking his pen seemed the last straw. Consequently, he was sometimes sent from class for disrupting the lesson concerning the pen. If he tried ignoring G's behaviour, the latter simply kept the pen. If he kept hold of it the whole time, G would take something else off his desk, returning it just as he told a teacher so that L was usually told off for disrupting the lesson. After some time, L told a teacher about his predicament. He felt totally powerless to change the situation, since everything he attempted had met with failure.

G, L and the teacher met briefly after school. The teacher explained that he was there primarily to help them sort out the difficulty.

1. The teacher ensured that G and L were sitting alongside one another and not opposite, so that it would be easier for them to focus on the common problem they both faced. He then asked G if he could concentrate on lessons when taking L's pen and if this was helping his learning. G answered that he did not concentrate well because he was thinking about the pen. The teacher pointed out that, although L was getting into trouble over the incident, G also had a problem with it. In fact, they shared the same problem. The question remained, what to do about it?

2. The teacher asked G how he thought the friendship with L might be affected in time if he continued to take his pen. After some consideration, G said he thought they would stop being friends.

3. The teacher asked how they felt about each other. They replied that they both liked each other, L adding that he was very angry about the incidents with the pen.

4. Since L was left feeling powerless on these occasions, the teacher thought that the underlying issue might be one of power, G trying to feel more powerful in lessons at L's expense. The teacher put forward this idea and asked G if he sometimes did not understand and found the work difficult, in other words, if *he* felt powerless. This was, indeed, the case. Thus it was established that both boys had a common interest: both wanted to feel powerful in lessons. The question remained as to *how* they could *both* achieve this.

5. The boys thought about what they might do. G said he would stop taking the pen, or anything else. The teacher asked what he would do instead in order to feel powerful. After some thought, G suggested that he sit next to L and that they work together whenever possible. In this way they would probably both get more work done and feel they could better manage in class.

In this example it was not necessary to call on any precedent or rule, since the boys had come to their own agreement without it. If G lapsed into old behaviour, L need only remind him that he was not doing that any more and, if need be, tell the teacher who had helped them sort the issue out.

During the meeting, the teacher had directed the boys through the major points found in principled negotiating. If they had got stuck, he could have given more explanation or examples, or given them time to think about it, coming back together another day. Throughout, he was endeavouring to find a common language and common ground even though, at first, there seemed to be none.

Modelling the skills: principled negotiating with a pupil

As the Elton Report (1989) indicates, appealing to a pupil's reason is a particularly effective technique for dealing with those exhibiting disruptive behaviour. Principled negotiating techniques are, therefore, ideal for this and model an approach the pupil might emulate in future.

What then, might such an approach entail?

Preparation

This may be as little as five minutes' thought but it is extremely helpful. Be clear of:

- your intention, for example, to communicate: listen, speak and 'meet' the other;
- your aims, for example, to find ways you can coexist cooperatively in the classroom, remain in charge and motivate the pupil in question;
- what to do if your aims are not reached, for example, involve the year head and write home to parents requesting an interview.

Approach

The idea is to separate the pupil from the problem, his or her behaviour, perceiving him or her as a 'co-seeker for a fair solution to a common problem'. By this we are assuming that the behaviour is also a problem for the pupil, since it interferes with learning and the relationship with the teacher. That is to say, he or she is losing two major areas of motivation: achievement and teacher praise. Attempt to remain warm and open to the pupil, while remaining firmly opposed to his or her behaviour.

Environment

It might be helpful to make the seating or standing arrangements as equal as possible. If sitting, chairs are alongside one another, some feet apart but turned to half face each other. In other words, pupil and teacher are not opposite. This is important since it reinforces the approach: opponents are often face to face, while co-workers are alongside one another.

Opening

An opening that might establish this approach would go something like this:

> Hello, Lisa, please take a seat. I'd like to start by saying that I've been quite angry with you in the past and you've seemed quite cross with me at times. So I suggest we put our anger aside for the moment and spend a little time looking at what's really going on. Let's try to get a sense of what's going wrong in our lessons together and see if we can come up with something that sounds better for us both. Would you like to start or shall I?

(If the pupil's primary representational system is known then the language would be targeted to meet it. This example is if it is not known.)

Direction

The teacher continues to direct the meeting and is, therefore, unquestioningly in charge of the process.

Interests

The teacher introduces the idea of 'interests', that is to say, what each might expect to get out of his or her position. For the teacher, general, rather than personal statements are probably advisable, for example, 'Any teacher wants to help every pupil learn as much as possible.' Although many pupils would not use personal information given at such a meeting for gossip, malicious teasing or disruptive behaviour at a later date, some might. The teacher could help the pupil to explore what she wants to get out of her position of behaving as she does. She may well say she does not know, she 'just does it'. It might then be up to the teacher to talk in general terms about reasons for behaviour. For example, 'People are different, but I might do something like that in order to avoid the work, impress my friends, just to be different, or because I was angry ...'

The pupil may well not be consciously aware of what she is doing or why she is doing it, since it may be a pattern set a long time previously. Or she may not want to admit anything to the teacher and has the right to privacy. It is not necessary for the teacher to know the reason for the behaviour in order for the pupil to change and it may be helpful to state that. The teacher is neither counsellor nor social worker. He or she is simply attempting to find an opportunity for new behaviour through the tool of negotiation. The pupil may get very angry, perhaps, if one point hits home hard. She may not be accustomed to talking about feelings and motivation.

With many pupils, voicing possible reasons for their behaviour can be helpful. First, it is a question of *talking about* behaviour rather than *blaming* them for it. Second, it can convey a sense of order and safety: their behaviour is not random and chaotic; in a way it has its own reasoning. This can sometimes help pupils begin to communicate about the issues. For example, one 14-year-old boy I worked with sat during the first session answering my questions while staring fixedly ahead without looking at me. Only when I suggested that the behaviour he was describing gave me the impression that he was very angry with the teachers and the school did he really start to 'communicate'. He looked directly at me and said, surprised at the discovery, 'Yes, I am angry.'

It may be helpful to break the meeting there and continue another day, if that is possible, giving the pupil time to reflect on what it means to her to behave in a disruptive manner and making it clear that the purpose of the next meeting is to find a solution to the shared problem.

Towards a solution

In creating options for mutual gain, teacher and pupil consider ways in which they can 'coexist' with greater harmony in the classroom, and then choose which seems the best, drawing on precedent or objective standards if possible. That is to say, they would work out the basis for an 'authority agreement' between them, a 'contract' in which *both* gave something and *both* could gain. Ways in which the pupil could continue to experience the benefits the earlier behaviour produced but in a constructive way would be considered, along with positive reasons for change.

Alternative strategy

The teacher needs to be clear as to what he or she would do if the negotiation did not produce a positive result and this may best be communicated to the pupil so she could make an informed choice.

Ending

The teacher ends the meeting by summarising the conclusions reached and ensuring he or she and the pupil are clear of the situation. The agreement may be written down and a follow-up meeting arranged.

Review

Afterwards, the teacher could review the meeting when alone, considering both positive and learning points. If the interview did not produce a constructive result it does not necessarily follow that the technique is unhelpful, but simply that, in this case, the aim was not achieved. Another time it might be different.

Having interviews along these lines with the aim of reaching some negotiated 'solution' is, of course, only a part of potential change, only a small beginning. The pupil may well need a very detailed, step-by-step plan for change, since the detail of *how* to do so is often crucial. A pupil will also need ongoing encouragement and support from an adult who is important to him or her. All this is discussed in the following chapter.

My experience of talking to young people in similar ways is that they are usually amazed. They come into a meeting with an adult expecting to be 'told off', their body posture already defensive for protection, and rarely giving any eye contact, either because they are scared or angry, or both. What generally happens is that, during the interview, fleeting eye contact becomes established as the pupil gradually realises she or he is not going to be blamed or verbally attacked in some way, that she or he is being part of a dialogue rather than being *talked at*, that the teacher is listening. When and how much eye contact develops depends on many factors: the degree of conflict existing, the approach, the pupil's general level of disaffection, cultural norms and so on. However, usually the pupil relaxes at some point, shifts his or her position and breathes more freely.

Often we expect young people of 13 or 14 to make fairly serious choices as to what options they wish to take; we expect those of 16 or 18 to have clear ideas and make firm decisions about their path in life. However, how much opportunity for choice, for exercising decision-making abilities and for taking responsibility have we truly given them during their daily life in school?

It may seem a little far-fetched that, by talking and behaving differently to a pupil and by working out new ways of behaving in a problematic situation, a relationship can be changed. However, since it is through the way we communicate and behave that misunderstandings and conflicts arise, our communication and behaviour also hold the key to a resolution. It is through them that we show whether we trust, like, dislike, care for, love, feel indifferent towards or even hate others.

Teaching negotiating skills

This could be done directly with individuals by providing a model and practice. Also it could be conveyed to a group or whole class.

The idea that there is always a range of possible responses could be fruitfully explored in several subject areas, thereby introducing alternative communication skills to a whole class. A number of examples follow.

Tutorial time and drama

Examples from pupils' experience could be analysed from this viewpoint and possible alternative responses explored, based on principled negotiating.

English and drama

Dialogues from literature could be reworked exploring the ways in which characters might respond differently to each other, depending on the approach taken.

History

There could be discussion about how certain scenes from history could have been very different if the individuals concerned had had wider, or indeed, narrower repertoires of communication skills.

Listening and teaching

We expect our pupils to listen to us attentively, but just how well do we listen to them? Do we model attentive listening? Do we help our pupils to aquire skills in active, attentive listening? Let us consider the implications of all this for teaching.

The significance of listening for communication and learning is not always emphasised sufficiently. As far as relationships and communication are concerned it is fundamental. Without it there is no sense of other people, nor of other points of view beyond our own internal one. It is essential for the emergence of empathy, a sense of justice and compassion. It is also often particularly important in regard to minimising or reducing conflict. Indeed it is difficult to resolve conflict without each side listening carefully to the other. Yet it is at such times that the ability to listen to others abandons many of us. When angry, people tend to be too busy with their own thoughts and feelings to listen at all, or are especially prone to listening out for whatever will fuel anger, or to interpreting what has been said in that way. In dealing with two or more pupils in conflict, therefore, asking each to *listen* to what the other has actually said and is saying is, perhaps, a first tentative step towards encouraging empathy and a more peaceful resolution.

Listening is, of course, also crucial for learning.

Potential problems of poor listening

- Pupils fail to understand instructions and miss the content of lessons and are, therefore, more likely to find work difficult, to underachieve and to get involved in disruptive behaviour.
- Over time, pupils may cease to expect to hear and a process will be established and reinforced, namely that of *learning not to listen*. Certainly it is the case that some children who suffer intermittent hearing loss through glue ear when young are disadvantaged not only by missing out on hearing language and by feeling isolated, but frequently also by the habit of not listening, of being physically but not emotionally present, of living in a dream world.
- Pupils are more likely to respond aggressively to peers since poor listening cuts an individual off from others and he or she is more likely to misinterpret and jump to wrong conclusions.
- Similarly, pupils are more likely to respond aggressively to teachers.
- A common complaint made by pupils who are in regular trouble with teachers is that the latter do not listen to them. This leads to growing resentment and anger against individual teachers and the school system as a whole.
- Since listening carefully to someone tends to help the person feel valued and respected, the effect of teachers and pupils not feeling listened to adequately by the other can be to reduce confidence and self-esteem which, in turn, increases the likelihood of conflict.

Advantages of adequate listening

- Pupils will more easily become engaged in work, will better understand instructions, will be more likely to become interested in content and will be more able to achieve. Listening skills develop with practice.
- Pupils are likely to be less hasty in their reactions and will be able better to appreciate another's point of view.
- Communication is likely to improve between teachers and pupils and within a class itself.
- Teachers and pupils will gain in confidence and self-esteem.

Obstacles to pupils' listening

- External distractions: traffic noise, interruptions, other pupils, etc.
- Internal distractions include thoughts and feelings about personal life: breaktime, hunger, thirst, tiredness, fear of failing at work, anger with the teacher, the school or a peer, daydreaming, etc.
- The teacher failing to engage the pupils, uninteresting content or delivery of material.
- Lack of motivation: little interest in school or academic learning.
- Hearing difficulties, including earlier intermittent hearing loss through glue ear.
- A habit of poor listening.

Techniques for promoting attentive listening

1. Content which is interesting and made as accessible as possible to the listener.
2. An engaging delivery by the teacher and an interesting tone of voice is more likely to gain pupils' attention.
3. If the teacher is able to use language targeting different sensory channels, as explained in Chapter 3, more pupils will probably listen.
4. Appropriate timing: when and for how long. Pupils are more likely to listen well when they come to it fresh. If they have just sat quietly listening for half an hour in assembly it is unlikely to be the best time to expect them to sit and listen again: a change in activity is required. (The frequent placing of assembly first thing in the morning at a prime learning time is perhaps not the best timetabling.) In general, listening activities need to be punctuated by frequent breaks or changes of activity, depending on the age and attention span of pupils.
5. The environment of the classroom and the position of the speaker in relation to the class can facilitate or hinder listening. Attention will wander if the speaker's words are not easily audible; this refers not only to those of the teacher, but also to those of peers talking to the class. Over

some time, if a pupil does not expect to hear, he or she will probably cease attempting to listen. If the speaker is not easily visible this may also increase the difficulty for some children of listening attentively.

It seems to be the case that a major factor in many people thinking they are being listened to well is if they have eye contact with the listener, although cultural norms differ. Certainly looking at the speaker can help the listener to focus on what is being said. It is also significant, perhaps, that, for many pupils, times of sustained listening outside school are usually accompanied by pictures, that is to say, television. Their experience of listening is often, therefore, inextricably linked to that of watching.

6. A minimal number of potential distractions. Obviously there are many distractions the teacher can do nothing about: thunderstorms, parents inspecting the school, the noise of traffic, an urgent message from the head, building works next door, etc. There are some distractions, however, which can perhaps be avoided or minimised. For example, the method of encouraging pupils to prepare mentally, physically and emotionally for the lesson before entering the classroom can help to avoid some distracting behaviour. It may also cut down on internal distractions, some of the wandering thoughts, that pupils bring with them.

A major and very common distraction is anxiety about the immediate future: 'What am I going to say next? Am I going to get it right? What is it I have to do?' and so on. At the very least this kind of thinking might result in a shower of unnecessary questions. A very clear example of such distraction is apparent when pupils have to read aloud in sequence round the class. As most who have experienced this know, waiting to read is generally taken up with working out which bit you will get and practising, while the time after reading is occupied largely with calming down, relief or embarrassment, depending on how things went. There is little space for actually *listening* to what is being read. If reading aloud is the skill to be practised that is one thing; if the intention is for pupils to listen and take in the content, then a different technique is probably more effective.

The clearer instructions are from the start and the more the teacher reassures pupils as to what exactly will be required of them, the greater the number of pupils who will be able to listen. The guided, focused listening mentioned subsequently may be of use to some pupils since they know very specifically what to listen out for. Obviously, pupils actively engaged in listening are less likely to disrupt and are more likely to understand subsequent tasks.

7. If pupils are trained how to *listen*, not merely to *hear*, their capacity to pay attention to the speaker will be increased. They will be able to focus more actively on the speaker rather than on their own associated thoughts, sensations and feelings provoked by his or her words.

The approach outlined in earlier chapters will help teachers to listen attentively to pupils. The following exercises involving listening skills can help pupils to develop their skills.

Training to listen

What is needed

Brainstorm with pupils what they do to listen well. How do they feel when really listening? What do they notice if other people are listening attentively to them or someone else? This can be done as a whole class or in pairs or small groups first before pooling ideas. A list of five or six key points could be drawn up for the class to use as guidelines. The following could be added if they are not included:

- a body posture and eye contact conducive to attentive listening;
- an awareness of possible distractions and how to refocus;
- practice.

Body posture

What kind of body posture will facilitate and maintain active listening? Left to their own devices, many pupils will slouch across the desk, swing back on their chairs, gaze out of the window, sit askew and so on. These are not necessarily postures which will aid concentration since they are often associated with chatting, resting, and daydreaming. What is required is a posture which fosters and maintains concentration.

Listening is an active process which requires alertness. Therefore, a posture which is still, upright and alert will probably be helpful. Looking towards the speaker and being able to see his or her face is likely also to help focus attention. Thus if one pupil is addressing the rest of the class at some length, he or she will need to be seen. For listening, pupils could be asked to adopt the position they would use if what they were about to hear was extremely interesting or was of such vital importance that they had to listen fully in order to catch every word. This could be their listening position and, in time, it would be associated with the activity of focused listening. If practised in Years 7 and 8, it would gradually become an automatic posture which would inevitably facilitate listening.

Recovering from distractions

The first point in dealing with distractions is noticing that you are distracted; the second is returning your attention to the original focus. The first point may come about as the result of a teacher or classmate drawing the pupil's attention back to his or her work. It may also come about when the pupil notices the distraction. A teacher can reinforce the listening training by frequently asking the class if they are in their listening position and if they are indeed listening with attention. The aim is, over time, to encourage the pupils themselves to check their own performance: 'Am I in the listening position? Am I listening?'

Once the pupil notices that his or her attention has wandered, he or she can bring it back in line. Body posture will be useful in this since it will have shifted or slumped out of the listening position as the attention was lost. Reinstating the habitual position will facilitate the activity of attentive listening.

Practice

The exercises given later in this chapter could be used to practise listening. The idea is to sharpen auditory focus at will by brief, but frequent practice. Regular reminders to pupils about how they are listening and about their listening position also helps to keep the issue alive and practised.

Teaching points: using listening in teaching

Intention and focus

Using intention and a focus for listening can help develop concentration. This idea is already in use in some modern language and English listening exercises, with the pupils being asked to listen out for the answers to certain questions before, for example, a dialogue is played or a passage is read. However, its application could be extended to positive effect.

In giving verbal instructions concerning work, for example, a teacher could sometimes ask pupils to listen out for three or four particular points. These could then be recapped, class members supplying the answers. In this way, pupils would be primed to listen with extra care and the instructions would be repeated. Pupils with specific learning difficulties often find it difficult to remember a number of instructions given at one time. A visual back-up is often useful and can benefit other pupils too.

Some of the exercises below, particularly those in the recall section, also use intention and a focus to sharpen listening skills. Since pupils are listening not merely for themselves but with the intention of passing on the information they often listen more attentively and may wish to jot down notes. Some pupils may find such exercises daunting and for these it may be helpful to build up the skills gradually and provide visual prompts such as multiple choice items that could be ticked.

Preparation for written work

For many pupils written work can be facilitated by adding an extra layer of preparation. Supposing, for example, a Year 8 science class is set for home-work the task of writing up an experiment done that lesson. Some pupils will succeed well. Many will struggle. Some will fail. Something similar to the following exercise could help.

The class is divided into pairs. The task of one from each pair is to listen without interrupting, though essential prompting could be helpful. The other is to describe the experiment, as he or she will write it for homework. A schema for this will already have been given: for example, aim, method, in a number of clear stages, result and conclusion. At the end, the listener can add any points missed, ask for clarification, and so on. The teacher could intervene as required, summarising briefly at the end. The whole exercise need take no longer than five or ten minutes. As pupils learn the procedure, less time is often needed. In the following lesson roles could be reversed.

Preparation of this nature can greatly help pupils' confidence with writ-ten work. What may have seemed clear in their heads is less so when called upon to talk about it. This difficulty would otherwise have arisen at home when faced with writing down the information when it was too late to ask a peer or the teacher for help. For many pupils a rehearsal of this kind which separates out thinking and explaining from writing down can be extremely helpful. Clarification of thought is required at an oral stage sep-arate from the task of writing.

The pupils listening have the task of attending in order to notice any mis-takes, omissions or confusions. Listening in this way can also make it eas-ier for them to do the written work while training their listening skills. Such an exercise requires active participation by all pupils. Similar exercises could be adapted for many subject areas and different ages.

Recall and assimilation of information

Listening exercises can be used in helping to get new information across in many ways. For example, after reading a passage together, the class is split into groups of three. In turn, each pupil retells a piece of the information read. The first relates the beginning, the second relays the middle and the last takes the end, the teacher making the divisions clear, depending on the text. The others listen, adding, at the end, any omissions and prompting if the speaker is stuck. Pupils usually listen eagerly in such situations and considerable discussion about the information is frequently generated. By the end of the exercise most pupils are likely to have a greater grasp of the topic and remember more about it than if the passage had simply been read. This can also be, of course, effective preparation for written work.

An adaptation of this exercise is to have the pupils working in pairs, one recounting the first half and the other the second. In each case, the pupils have a copy of the passage for reference.

Consolidation and revision

When, for example, a topic has been completed, pupils work in pairs. One talks about an aspect of the topic and the other listens. The latter has a checklist of key points supplied by the teacher and has to listen carefully to notice if all points are covered. Using the checklist, he or she corrects mistakes and fills in gaps in knowledge. Roles are then reversed. The pupils could add to the checklists, keeping them for future reference.

Developing resources for listening

If it is possible within the school, building a resource of tapes for pupils to listen to can help in developing listening skills. These may be fiction or information on specific subjects. Pupils may tape some of them themselves for others to use explaining topics, giving information or, as mentioned above, providing notes for revision.

Pupils who may be more confident orally than writing or reading, pupils with specific learning difficulties, for example, or some second language learners, may benefit considerably from a taped resource such as this. Since their oral skills are more advanced than their written ones they could also do taping for other pupils to use. If appropriate in the school, second language learners could also tape in their mother tongue for pupils arriving with little or no spoken English.

This chapter has dealt with:

Negotiating skills
- The essence of principled negotiating
- Helping pupils sort out disagreements
- Modelling the skills: principled negotiating with a pupil
- Teaching negotiating skills

Listening and teaching
- Potential problems of poor listening
- Advantages of adequate listening
- Obstacles to pupils' listening
- Techniques for promoting attentive listening
- Training to listen

Teaching points: using listening in teaching
- Intention and focus
- Preparation for written work
- Recall and assimilation of information
- Consolidation and revision
- Developing resources for listening

CHAPTER 7

Facilitating New Behaviour

> Man can live three weeks without food, three days without water. But he can't live three minutes without hope.
>
> Rabbi Hugo Gryn, *Guardian* 20 August 1996

This chapter looks at the nature of change and suggests a detailed programme to adapt as necessary in order to help a pupil change his or her behaviour in positive ways.

Anyone who has ever endeavoured to change an aspect of behaviour, an entrenched habit of some kind, will probably appreciate just how difficult that can be. Yet so often we exhort pupils to turn over a new leaf, to try harder, to be different in some way without spelling out the detail of just *how* that is possible. At the time the pupil may sincerely wish to change, but when a similar situation next arises he or she slips back into the old, undesirable behaviour. Desire alone, however sincere, is often insufficient: more is needed if change is to be lasting. Indeed, there are at least four ingredients vital for change: a genuine desire to change; detailed knowledge of how to do so, that is to say, what to do instead; practice; and perseverence.

The models suggested can be used, modified and adapted to suit individual pupils. They can be employed by anyone: class and subject teachers, form tutors, year heads, head teachers, classroom assistants and support staff. It may sometimes be helpful if someone not directly involved in regular reprimanding can be the main person responsible for support. At times a teacher could thus act as the main support to a pupil in a colleague's class. Peer counselling can also be helpful (see Cowie and Sharp 1996).

Pupils who disrupt lessons often take up considerable time out of class in detentions, receiving reprimands, and so on. Such times could be used instead to implement a similar approach to the one outlined below.

What may help a change in behaviour

1. A reason. This may be positive, for example, the pupil will gain something he or she wants from the change in behaviour; or negative, the

pupil wishes to avoid an undesirable consequence of the old behaviour. Or it may, of course, be both.

2. Desire and will. The pupil really wants to change and has the determination, energy and will to try out new behaviour and to persist in his or her efforts.
3. Sufficient self-esteem to try.
4. A belief that change is possible. Without realistic hope, there is no point in trying.
5. Some inevitable success. Few people will be able to maintain efforts to change without some early success. The less self-esteem a pupil possesses the more early success is necessary: without signs of progress the belief that change is possible is quickly eroded. Since success is so essential, expectations and targets need to be realistic if they are to be met and may well include some desirable aspect of behaviour the pupil already achieves, for example, punctuality, good attendance.
6. Support, encouragement and safety. Support can be given by regular attention from someone already significant to the pupil or who may become so. Emotional safety can be provided by support, acceptance of an occasional lapse into old behaviour and encouragement of the new role adopted. Very firm boundaries can add to a sense of safety. That is to say, a consistent approach is used in which the inevitability of certain consequences following certain actions is highlighted and carried through.

   Some level of emotional safety is important because without it change is unlikely. In many cases change can be challenging and frightening and the risk involved may seem daunting. When frightened, people tend to hang on to the familiar; it is not a time to try out new behaviour. Consequently, the safer the emotional environment around a pupil in school and, indeed, at home, the more possible change will be.
7. A new self-image or role as someone who *already* exhibits the new, target behaviour, rather than as someone stopping the old behaviour. The pupil might think of a person he or she knows and likes or admires who would easily behave in an acceptable way in the given situation. The person chosen does not need to be known by the teacher and could, indeed, be a fictional character.

   Change is especially challenging when a person's self-image is based on a deep belief, or world view, which manifests in a particular kind of behaviour. If, for example, a pupil believes he or she is impossible then he or she will be unlikely to give up the role of an 'impossible' pupil unless there is a new role to move on to. People do not move into a void: it is too frightening.

   There usually needs to be another image with which pupils can identify sufficiently as a substitute for the old one. A pupil might, therefore, find it helpful to adopt a more positive image: that of someone who can gain the teacher's praise, manage the work, help others, run well, make friends and so on. The assumption and acceptance of a new role helps develop the behaviour required.

8. A change in world view or underlying belief system may sometimes be helpful if the behaviour stems from these beliefs and is deeply entrenched. The medium for change is school activity. By endeavouring to form a positive relationship, by giving constructive rather than 'labelling' criticism and by facilitating achievement, the teacher can, at times, gradually challenge underlying beliefs which may hinder the pupil's progress and willingness to change.

9. Time to develop alternative habits. This is crucial. Despite understanding, awareness and a desire to change it can take time to overcome the inertia of habits which may have lasted for years. Although the decision to change can be instantaneous, instilling a new habit in place of an old one inevitably takes time. An appreciation of this can avoid a complete loss of heart when old behaviour is repeated.

10. An awareness of what might be lost by a change in behaviour and what might hinder change. It is often useful for a pupil to be aware of what is holding him or her in an old behaviour and what he or she might lose by becoming a more successful student.

11. A substitute or alternative for whatever benefit the original behaviour was supplying. For example, if the undesirable behaviour was gaining teacher attention, then the attention is given for the target behaviour instead; if it gained peer approval then that needs to be provided in a different way, perhaps by being given a specific role or task in the class which gains approval; if the unwanted behaviour was a means of avoiding work because of learning difficulties, then help is provided, or work which can be achieved is supplied when help is not available.

12. Perseverence, patience and practice.

13. An opportunity to develop positive qualities or strengths which are, at present, often employed in the unwanted behaviour.

14. Something else to do instead, a new habit.

Specific requirements for the process of change

1. An awareness of the current pattern of undesirable behaviour, particularly of the trigger, that is to say, *whatever immediately precedes the unwanted response*. A teacher might be helpful in pointing this out. For example, he or she might notice that the pupil in question hits another member of the class whenever angry, or when he or she gets stuck with the work, or when there is a change in routine, and so on.

2. An awareness of the internal response to the trigger: what the pupil feels, thinks, sees, and his or her body posture immediately before the

unwanted behaviour. This is the warning signal indicating that such behaviour is imminent, unless the pupil chooses differently. As one pupil with specific learning difficulties described his experience: 'When I look at all the questions on the page and think I have to write them all out *and* all the answers I feel all knotted inside. It's just too much. I don't care what I do after that.' Typically he would create some pretext and storm from the room. His warning signal was, therefore, feeling knotted inside. Learning to recognise this, he could then begin to create moments of choice, as described in Chapter 5 and outlined below.

3. Skills for creating a moment of choice. This disrupts the automatic progression into the unwanted behaviour, the undesirable habit. Instead, a gap is created in which it may be possible to introduce an alternative behaviour.

Over time, the new behaviour will become habitual, with occasional lapses. For many people the most effective way of creating this moment of choice is to breathe, shift their body posture and relax. This is because the unwanted behaviour will be associated with and facilitated by a particular breathing pattern and body posture. By altering these it is easier to try out new behaviour which will be linked to and facilitated by a different way of breathing and posture.

For example, once the pupil above feels 'all knotted inside' he can learn to create a moment of choice by taking a breath deep within, shifting his position and relaxing. This can give him time to decide to carry on as before, becoming angry, causing some kind of scene, storming out of class and getting into trouble as a consequence or to try out a new strategy: for example, telling the teacher it is too much work, covering the page so he sees only one question at a time, writing the answers only and explaining to the teacher later, and so on. The point is he is no longer stuck in only one kind of behaviour feeling there is no way out. He has a choice.

4. Alternative behaviours in response to the trigger situation: *what he or she could do instead*. Thinking back to a role model can be useful here: what might X do and say in such a situation? It is often useful to have two, three or more possible alternatives to the unwanted behaviour. This reinforces the fact that the current way of behaving *is in no way inevitable*. Many other responses are possible. Some pupils may need encouragement even to consider a different kind of behaviour as a possibility.

5. Practice outside the actual situation is helpful. What would it feel like to carry out these new behaviours? Which feels most comfortable? How would X stand, sit or walk in this situation? How would he or she look? How would he or she sound? Try it out.

6. Small, specific, attainable targets.

7. Definite acknowledgement for achieving a target, some kind of reward, if appropriate. Rewards tend to be more difficult to devise in secondary school. They may come simply in the form of a regular letter back to parents acknowledging the fact that the target has been reached, in the form of a visit to the head for praise rather than a reprimand, or in that of a commendation or good conduct mark if the school has such a reward system in place. Or it may be some kind of privilege. To be effective a reward must be desirable to the pupil. Sometimes this can be difficult to ascertain since the pupil *apparently* 'doesn't care'.

(A sheet which can be photocopied for use with pupils is to be found in Appendix VI.)

Rather than focusing on stopping poor behaviour, the emphasis may be more effectively placed on concentrating on developing the desired behaviour: on instilling a new habit. For example, rather than thinking about not talking in assembly, a pupil would be given specific things to listen out for or to notice during that time and a new body posture to practise.

Example A

One Year 8 boy, F, started to get into trouble with a number of subject teachers for calling out and making 'clever' comments to the teacher which, though often very humorous, were extremely disruptive to the smooth running of the lesson and led to frequent confrontations and conflict with his teachers. He had quickly gained himself the role of class clown. He had no undue difficulties with work. At times he had shown himself to be a very efficient organiser and leader.

The intervention was discussed and agreed between the pupil, year head and form tutor who informed subject teachers. If possible, a meeting with all subject teachers would have been called to discuss a strategy, but this was impractical in this case. The form tutor saw the pupil regularly and the year head reviewed progress weekly.

Conflict arose when F was reprimanded for calling out and, consequently, it was this behaviour which was targeted for change. In speaking to him it seemed that his role as clown fulfilled a need to make an impact on his peers. He did not like the consequences of his behaviour, detentions, letters home and meetings with the year head, but his need to exercise his wit and be noticed by his classmates was stronger. The question emerged: how could he develop his abilities and gain attention in a positive way, one which avoided conflict and other undesirable consequences? How could he change his role of class clown into something that would enhance, or at least not hinder, his own learning and that of his peers?

It was agreed that he would take a report card to those lessons in which he had created difficulties with three specific targets: 1) punctuality, 2) finishing his work and 3) listening quietly to the teacher and others, making only relevant contributions when invited to speak. The subject teachers needed merely to tick or cross the relevant boxes. The first two points he invariably achieved without difficulty. Some success was, therefore, assured. The third outlined the target behaviour. At first he was to achieve three ticks in a lesson at least twice a week, reporting briefly to his form tutor who was his main support at lunch-time for praise and encouragement, then building up to all targets met in one lesson a day. This was gradually increased over a term until four out of the five daily periods were to be incident free. The initial target was set so that he could easily achieve and even surpass it on occasion.

The trigger to his calling out was considered. There seemed nothing specific, but his unwanted behaviour occurred mostly at the beginning of the lesson before he settled down to a particular task. There were several strategies concerning this point discussed with his teachers: that pupils might at times be given an initial task as a focusing and settling down exercise; that the teacher might ensure individual contact with F, greeting him, making eye contact and having a brief, positive interchange at the start of a lesson (presenting the report card provided a natural opportunity for this); that F might sometimes be given a specific task to do, such as handing out books or going to fetch the video recorder.

Thinking more about the trigger situation, F reported to his form tutor that he felt at times what he described as 'bored and restless'. This then was to be his warning signal. Whenever he started to feel this he would need to breathe, relax, shift his position into the new posture mentioned below, look at the teacher and focus on what he or she was saying, or get on with his own work, as appropriate.

F's body posture which accompanied his calling out was taken into account. He was not sure how he would be sitting at such times, although there would probably be a particular body posture which belonged to and, therefore, facilitated the calling out behaviour. (If it had been possible for another teacher to observe F in lessons this could have been of great value in noticing this.) F was able, however, to recreate how he might sit when listening to instructions and when writing. There was a notable difference, the former involving his sprawling back and twisting to the side with one arm hanging down over the back of the chair. In the latter he leant over the desk. It was suggested that he find a new listening posture that allowed him to be relaxed, attentive and ready to work, and he did so. In this he sat more upright and square to the desk in front.

F carried his own report card for his personal comments on progress made. The targets on this were: 1) to think of his intention for the lesson before entering the classroom; 2) to give in his teacher report card; and 3) to take up and maintain his new listening posture as much as possible at the beginning of a lesson. Whenever he remembered he was to check his posture and return to the listening position if he had moved out of it. If he chose he could show this card to his form tutor, but it was not obligatory since it was for his own satisfaction and for developing self-awareness.

The question of replacing his role as class clown was also addressed. F was given the responsibility of helping class members prepare for a talk they were to give on a subject of their choice. This meant that two pupils a week rehearsed their talk in front of F and the form tutor who gave useful feedback. F also compered the talk in tutor time, introducing the speaker and subject. It was hoped that, for a time, this would give him the experience of having peer attention and using his wit in a way which facilitated learning in the class, thus helping him develop a new self-image. It was pointed out to him that, with this new role, he might no longer need to be a clown.

It was tempting at first to make this helping and compering role dependent upon F achieving his targets. This idea was rejected, however, since the aim of his taking on this role was to demonstrate that he could gain attention from the class and entertain without sabotaging lessons. *It was important that he had the opportunity of using positively a skill he had previously used with negative results.*

F's parents were involved insofar as they were regularly informed of his progress and supported his efforts to change. They also helped him to find a drama club where he could further develop his performing skills. Attendance at this was dependent upon his meeting his targets.

The issue of F's angry response to a reprimand was also addressed directly in the meeting with his form tutor and year head, since some incidents of this would probably occur during a period of change. His habitual response had been to argue back with the teacher in some way, endeavouring to point out that his comment had been relevant, had not been time-wasting and so on. In his attempt to get the last word he had sometimes been sent from the room, which he left angrily, slamming the door.

The report card system often helped prevent the situation developing into one of conflict. If F made some inappropriate comment, the teacher need only refer to the card, for example, 'Remember your report card', or 'I still have your report card, remember', and F usually quietened down. Rather than being told off as such he was in these instances being given a choice: to continue with his comment and fail in meeting his target, or to back down. Usually he chose the latter.

This intervention with F was successful and his behaviour in class improved gradually over the term. However, even though he wanted to avoid detentions and saw the reason for change it still took time to replace one habit, one way of operating, with another.

It is all too easy to expect change to be immediate and total. This is unrealistic. The decision to change can be instantaneous, but the process of carrying it out inevitably takes time because of the inertia of habit. It is after the first few failures, the early lapses, that hope is often lost and determination and perseverence are most needed. Consequently early targets are best kept easily attainable, increasing demands gradually. Support and encouragement are usually essential.

Example B

In talking to one 14-year-old girl, H, it seemed that the major potential obstacle to change was her self-image as 'tough', someone who 'stood up' to teachers. She was frequently in trouble for confrontations with staff, swearing at them, answering rudely and sweeping angrily out of class. She appeared very proud of her reputation in dealing with teachers. After talking to her it seemed there were three main issues to address:

1. her anger towards teachers for what she considered to be past injustices;
2. her lack of non-confrontational communication skills;
3. her need to maintain her tough self-image and reputation as someone who stood up to teachers.

H's year head asked her to choose one teacher with whom she was prepared to build a more positive relationship. This teacher agreed to see H for ten minutes a day for the next month. During this time she would:

• talk with H about any confrontations she had had with teachers, listening attentively to her anger;
• work out with H what else she might have done and said, and what the consequences of each choice might have been;
• help H to think of how else she could use her toughness in more positive ways. How else could she be proud of herself?

Subject teachers were asked to give H the benefit of the doubt during this trial period, whilst still maintaining boundaries.

H was motivated to try to improve her behaviour. Since her friends went to the school she did not want permanent exclusion. Consequently, she attended most daily meetings. She did not reform overnight, but a month later was in trouble less frequently than before, having consistent difficulties in only two subjects. She was beginning to see that there was a correlation between how she behaved and how teachers treated her, that is to say, she began to take some responsibility for her actions and to acknowledge that she had more power to influence an interaction with a teacher than she had previously believed. She had started attending a karate class to maintain her tough image.

Some common issues which might undermine change

Some of these issues might lie outside the school's or an individual teacher's control, some will not. A teacher can only do his or her best, referring on to relevant agencies where necessary and facilitating change where possible.

It is useful to be aware of potential obstacles to sustained change for two main reasons:

1. to avoid wherever possible such obstacles when drawing up a programme of change for a pupil;
2. if change is not sustained to check if there is an underlying issue which needs to be addressed.

Such obstacles may include one or more of the following:

• Poor attendance. Frequent absences help pupils escape from the difficulties created by and resulting from their own behaviour. Also they have less investment in making the school community work for them and are less likely to form a strong enough relationship with a teacher or peer to provide adequate motivation or support for change.

- Lack of parental support. If parents show little interest in a pupil's progress or openly disagree with the school's approach it can make change more difficult to achieve.
- Peer group pressure and expectations are too strong. Change is jeopardised if the pupil in question values peer approval for the unwanted behaviour above other potential gains and if it is not possible to create new avenues for peer approval of more positive behaviour.
- Force of habit. If a habit is deeply entrenched then change will require substantial support over a longer period of time. The focus will need to remain on developing a new habit rather than on stopping the old one. If it is possible to avoid the exact situation in which the old habit occurred, then that is extremely helpful.
- Reliance on a particular self-image. If a pupil is dependent on status attached to a certain role he or she has adopted, for example, as tough, or a troublemaker, change is difficult *unless the pupil has another, equally appealing image to take on or can transfer the original image to another area of his or her life where it is constructive.* In the example above H did the latter by taking karate lessons.
- Inadequate support or lack of continuity. Pupils endeavouring to change may require very frequent, regular support. Once a programme has been set up, five minutes daily is probably more helpful than half an hour a week. A brief meeting at lunchtime can sometimes rescue the afternoon if the morning has brought little success. Instant praise and instant encouragement are thus important. Changing the person who is the main source of support can present difficulties unless there is adequate preparation for this since the pupil may need time to build up trust and liking.
- If nothing is important enough to the pupil, in other words, if he or she *really* does not care what happens to him or her, then change can be severely hindered. The way through this may be to provide the opportunity for the pupil to form a positive relationship with one person. His or her approval may gradually become significant and the pupil may wish to earn extra time with this person, that is to say, the pupil may come to care.
- If the pupil is set on leaving the school then, unless this decision can be reversed, he or she has no investment in change.
- Sometimes a pupil may need to remain a problem at school in order, in some way, to stabilise the family unit. He or she may need to be a unifying element as scapegoat, masking other difficulties in the family.
- If a pupil's emotional turmoil is greatly due to an ongoing situation outside school, change is unlikely *at that time* since concentration will be difficult and there is insufficient overall safety to risk changing.
- If there is insufficient success, many pupils may lose hope and give up.

- If the pupil, and often also the teacher, expect change to be instant and total or not at all, it is easy for both to become disillusioned at an early stage.
- If the part of the programme for change which is involved in developing some positive aspects of behaviour is reliant upon good behaviour, that is to say, is used as a potential reward. In the example of F above this would have been the case if his helping the form tutor and compering the class talks had been considered his reward for not calling out and disrupting lessons. Since the compering was intended to give him the opportunity for using wit and gaining attention in a positive context, it would have been counterproductive to make this reliant upon the kind of acceptable behaviour it was aimed at promoting.
- If there is no help given as to *how* to change. Often more is needed than simply *talking* about what the pupil *should* do. Even if he or she comes up with alternative behaviour in the discussion this may well not be sufficient. Changing entrenched behaviour usually requires more than agreement and an intellectual appreciation of the situation. It also requires:
  1. recognising the trigger for the unwanted behaviour;
  2. skills for creating a moment of choice;
  3. new behaviour to substitute;
  4. practice until the new behaviour becomes automatic;
  5. support and encouragement throughout.

Skills for creating a moment of choice are, in particular, frequently omitted.

Teaching points: introducing the idea of choice

For Year 7 pupils the following 'Just suppose ...' exercise can help introduce the idea of choice about actions. It reinforces the distinction that behaviour is separate from who we are, that behaviour can be chosen. Consequently, change is possible – it simply requires a different choice and the skill and perseverence to carry that choice through. This could take place in, for example, PSE, English or drama.

The teacher starts off by suggesting a possible scenario. For example, 'Just suppose X jostles Y when lining up for lunch. What could Y do?' For some scenarios, pupils could volunteer to take roles, without actually hitting each other, of course. The class suggests what Y could do. The consequences of each line of action are traced and discussed, including how participants might end up feeling. For example, Y hits X back: what might happen next? Y tells a teacher, ignores the jostle, and so on.

Potential scenarios could come from pupils themselves and could become more complex. Alternatively, an episode from a story could be used as the starting point, or an incident from the news, or history. The exercise can, of course, be adapted for older pupils.

Follow-up exercises could entail an exploration of *how* you take up a new behaviour. *How* do you remain calm rather than immediately assuming that someone who jostles you in a queue is meaning to hurt you, so you do not instantly hit them back and get into trouble? *How* do you get on with your work instead of chatting to a neighbour?

What might be suggested, discussed and practised here are the specific requirements for the process of change outlined above.

- The pupils identify the trigger for the response, and what they might feel, see or hear prior to that response, in other words, their internal signal that the unwanted behaviour might follow. They have already explored alternative responses.
- Next come the skills for creating enough space to choose a different behaviour from the habitual one: breathing, shifting position and relaxing. It is at this point that determination and will can be particularly helpful: the pupil decides on the desirable behaviour anew. Each time he or she does so, the next decision will be a little easier.
- Then comes the alternative behaviour which has been chosen.
- Finally comes reflection on how they might feel about the consequences of this behaviour as opposed to those following their former behaviour.

All this can be practised: instead of instantly hitting back, a pupil might breathe, step back, relax, decide and then ask why the other pupil jostled him or her. The class watching can prompt and help. The pupil who has been playing the role of the one chatting can, once she or he notices the old pattern, breathe and shift into a position which is attentive for work. In this body posture chatting will be less likely.

Once issues have been discussed and explored in such a way, there is a quick reference point whenever the unwanted behaviour occurs. These exercises can be easily adapted for use in small groups or with individual pupils.

This chapter has dealt with:

What may help a change in behaviour

Specific requirements for the process of change

Some common issues which might undermine change

Teaching points: introducing the idea of choice

CHAPTER 8

Cultivating Calm:
Managing Stress Peacefully

Stress can be avoided only by dying.

Hans Selye, The Stress of Life

'I've got enough to do. Why tackle stress?'

Stress often seems to create its own momentum in which the more stressed we are the more stressful situations we encounter. Work seems more effort and it is much easier to get into conflict with others. In response to this we become more stressed: it is a vicious circle often fuelled by tiredness. When stressed it is more difficult to work creatively, to have a sense of humour, to see things in perspective, to carry out the approach outlined in this book. Over time, stress can also undermine our health. In contrast, when relaxed it is possible to get more out of work, to work to greater effect, to improve relationships with pupils, to help their learning and, in general, to experience a better quality of life.

Although tackling stress might require a little extra effort in the short term, the long-term gains can be considerable. This chapter looks at ways of minimising stress and working with a greater sense of calm.

What is stress?

Stress is an individual's response to any stimulus, or stressor, the body's response to change. As such it is a perfectly natural process inevitable in life, and *it is not necessarily damaging*. Indeed, stressors which we consider benign have less harmful results (*eustress*) than those which we look on as a problem (*distress*), even though the physiological process is similar. That is to say, it is *how we perceive a stressor, as good or bad, our perception of events, which seems to determine the degree of damage we experience*. Thus our attitude is extremely powerful in this context.

Here we will use the term 'stress' to signify distress suffered and 'stressor' to signify the stimulus.

Why some people suffer more from stress than others

It seems to be the case that the more stressful jobs are those in which the highest demands are made and in which the individual has little control. This may remind you of many teaching posts! However, since the harmful effects of stress depend largely on our perception of events, that is to say, our attitude to what happens, some people suffer more from stress in a similar kind of work than some of their colleagues. The significant factors which seem to influence the degree of susceptibility or resilience to suffering from stress are noted below:

- *Control* – how much control people have in work or how much they *perceive* themselves having.
- *Confidence* – viewing change or potential difficulties in a way which does not necessarily mean they will be a problem. People with this approach tend to take an optimistic view with confidence in their own resources to meet new experiences. Change is not immediately regarded as a threat, burden or problem, but rather as an opportunity to be met.
- *Commitment* – people feel supported and find something meaningful in their work or life.

Thus we find that the crucial elements seem to be:

- a confidence in one's own resources;
- a sense of being supported and doing something which has meaning;
- being aware of the control and choices one does have in a given situation. Being aware of having a choice and some control is an antidote to feeling powerless and makes it easier to practise types of non-conflictual communication.

Pupils and stress

If teachers suffer from the ill effects of stress, then so do pupils since they often have what may seem to them as large demands and very little control over their day-to-day experience in school. Many feel insecure about their ability to meet these demands and they may have little or no support system. *In other words, they find themselves in those conditions in which people are likely to experience considerable stress.* Thus those who tend to perceive any change or difficulty as a major problem or threat, lack support, have poor confidence and have little commitment to school or learning are most likely to suffer stress. In addition, they are growing up, a state of constant change, which for some will be highly stressful in itself, especially at times. Trying to become independent, some may not use support which is offered by their family or friends.

It is a vicious circle since, when stressed, pupils are generally less able to manage change effectively and are more likely to respond at such times by acting out with disruptive behaviour and/or aggression. That is to say, they are likely to become major sources of potential stress for teachers. The change to a new school, a new class or new teacher, a supply teacher, a change in routine and so on, may all trigger off excessive stress in some pupils who then turn to some kind of disruptive behaviour.

Example

I met one Year 8 pupil with specific learning difficulties in early December when he was on temporary exclusion from school for consistently getting into trouble with many teachers for aggressive outbursts and disruption to lessons. Throughout our three meetings he sat on the edge of his seat like a tensed spring ready to uncoil at the slightest provocation. The muscles in his neck and face were taut, his hands were clasped tightly. I then saw him three months later shortly after he had been permanently excluded from school. He was a different person, sitting back in his chair in a relaxed manner without any of the tension he had displayed earlier. On all occasions he had spoken very clearly about his situation. Now, although he did not like having been expelled and felt particularly badly about letting some people down, he could not hide his relief: it was obvious in every aspect of his body posture. He had not wanted expulsion but, unaware of any other possibility, had found it preferable to the continual immense stress he had experienced at school. In such a state of tension it is no wonder that he had 'overreacted' in some lessons.

This young person is not alone: there are many children and young people in our schools suffering considerable stress for one reason or another. Although it is recognised that some pupils may become stressed when under pressure from exams, the fact that others are stressed at times or even throughout their school life is rarely acknowledged. The causes can be many: always being in a large group, not having their own 'safe' territory, rarely being surrounded by silence, being bullied, difficulties with friendships or with work and so on, not to mention possible difficulties outside school, and adolescence itself. It is frequently these distressed pupils who become major stressors for many teachers.

How to minimise potential stress for pupils

Obviously, if the causes of a pupil's stress lie outside school there is often little teachers can do directly, other than offering a safe place in which the pupil can feel supported and can succeed. For other pupils, however, it will be some element connected with school itself which becomes the major stressor. The techniques outlined in earlier chapters are designed to help such pupils by easing relationships and learning. To summarise, the most helpful approach will probably include the following:

- *Control* – allow pupils as much control as possible, that is to say, wherever possible to take responsibility for and gain independence in some aspects of their school life, behaviour and learning.
- *Confidence* – help pupils to grow in self-esteem, feel valued and develop increasing confidence in their ability to manage the unexpected, the everyday and new experiences.
- *Commitment* – help pupils to get something positive out of school so that they have an interest in developing themselves and their learning; fostering supportive relationships between pupils and between teachers and pupils.

An approach to minimising stress for teachers

At a school level

The organisation of the school can help minimise stress among teachers by devising a supportive discipline structure, an ethos and policy for learning which promotes ideas outlined earlier, good communication among the staff and with parents and pupils, an atmosphere in which teachers can feel personally supported and valued, additional training where appropriate, opportunities for teachers' experience and ingenuity to be incorporated in improvements, and as much individual control over workloads as possible.

Individuals

The individual teacher can perhaps begin to minimise stress in three ways:
1. immediately by giving attention to the process of getting stressed and reversing it;
2. in the longer term by beginning to look at his or her attitudes and working practices and by considering what he or she can, realistically, change;
3. cultivating calm.

Teaching can be divided into two major areas: first, administration, planning and marking, and second, the process of teaching and relating to pupils. If feeling overwhelmed by the workload rather than in control of it, there is a danger that a teacher might resort to an authoritarian approach in an attempt to control the pupils themselves rather than the process of teaching. This is likely to result in increased conflict and probably greater stress. Earlier sections of the book suggest ways of approaching the process of teaching and relationships with pupils which can not only improve the education of those in your classes and reduce conflict but also help minimise stress. The second point above can help cut down stress in the other area of teaching, namely, that of administration, planning and marking.

Reverse the process

Gather information

The first difficulty in dealing with stress is noticing that you are suffering from it. It is often easy to be so involved in the detail of the day that you become stressed without realising it, and only in retrospect do you notice your own symptoms of stress (a list of common symptoms is included in Appendix VII). Consequently, the earlier you notice your pattern of stress symptoms the better. Non-judgemental observation of present tendencies is the first part of change. With practice it is possible to spot the internal triggers which are your particular indicators of stress:

- How do you feel physically and emotionally right at the beginning of being stressed, or just beforehand?
- Are there any key phrases you catch yourself saying that might alert you to your state of stress? For example, 'I've got so much to do ...', 'I haven't time for that now ...', 'Just leave me alone ...', etc.
- What kind of thinking accompanies or immediately precedes your feeling stressed?
- Are there any particular situations or times in the week or term which you tend to find particularly stressful?

Check your posture: breathe, shift position and relax

Once you have spotted your own pattern of stress then frequently check to see how you are. It can be more difficult at times to ascertain emotional tension, but a quick check of your body posture and breathing can be done many times a day, at the end of each lesson, for example, as you collect up your books from the desk, wipe the board or walk through the door.

1. Notice any tension in your forehead, eyes, jaw, neck, shoulders, hands, hips, knees and feet.
2. Take a breath deep within you and as you breathe out feel or imagine a wave of relaxation sweeping over you from head to foot, taking with it all tension. Take two more breaths in a similar way.
3. Shift your posture so that you feel yourself standing or sitting in a relaxed way, supported by the floor or chair and yet upright, with the sense of having your head in the clouds and your feet firmly on the ground.
4. Think of an image, a word or two, a sound or a feeling which instantly helps you to feel calm, relaxed and able to manage with ease.
5. Carry on with the day.

The more frequently you check for stress and then relax the more time you will spend in a calmer state. Gradually that state, rather than a stressed one, will become the norm. Patience and perseverence are useful in this. If you forget to check and have been stressed for some time before you notice, relax anyway. 'Centring', the concept used in martial arts and explained in Chapter 5, is also useful in preventing and recovering from stress since it requires relaxation. It is impossible to experience emotional and mental stress at the same time as deep physical relaxation. Being relaxed and yet alert can help both concentration and efficiency.

Review attitudes and working practices

Control 1. Where external change is possible

Using time in your favour

Experience of time is very subjective. Waiting for a desired event can seem to take forever, while the event itself often speeds by. This subjectivity in relation to time could perhaps be used to our own advantage, so that we succeed in using it constructively rather than constantly battling with or feeling overwhelmed by it. Three points are helpful in this:

1. using intention;
2. planning and prioritisation;
3. dividing up time.

Once practised successfully, these techniques can, of course, be taught to pupils.

Using intention

The use of intention in a positive way can be a powerful tool. Often we are unclear as to what our intentions really are. We have them all the time but they remain unconscious. By becoming aware of this process we can choose to instil different intentions or keep the same ones, but as a conscious choice. This demands a certain self-honesty: 'What am I really about here?'

You may sit down to do some marking, for example, without being conscious of what you are in fact setting up. Just what is your intention?

- 'I'm going to finish this marking in half an hour exactly.'
- 'I've only half an hour to get through before I can go home.'
- 'I'll just do a bit of this marking before tea.'
- 'I suppose I should get some of this marking done.'

If we really listen to our own intentions and see them plainly for what they are, we may at times wish to change them. Sitting down to do some work with such a negative intention as in all but the first example is unlikely to result in much work being done. If we recognise the intention we have an immediate choice: to change it to one which will encourage work to be done, or to go and do something completely different for a while. Such an intention might be a signal that we need a break or a change of activity.

After that we could get back to work with renewed vigour and a positive intention. Otherwise we achieve little other than getting through time, rather than *using* it to our advantage, and are likely to end up feeling frustrated and resentful at work that takes so long! Of course, it might not be possible to complete everything in half an hour, but then a more flexible intention could be used: 'I'm going to complete as much marking as possible in this next half hour.' It is worth noting the difference between a positive intention ('I'm going to ...') and a sense of obligation ('I should ...', I ought to ...').

Intention can be used in this way in any situation. If there is a meeting, for example, it could be helpful to set out with a definite intention of getting through the agenda in a certain time. If you are listening to a lecture, the intention could be to retain the most important points made. If you are teaching a lesson it could be to get the material across effectively in a given time. To use intention effectively, concentrate very deeply for a few moments before beginning the task in question, on the way to a meeting or a lesson, for example, and then forget about it and become absorbed in the particular activity.

Our thinking is powerful, more powerful than we often give it credit for. It also strengthens with practice. If at first you notice little difference, then try it again until you do. It may take a little time to establish positive intentions in the place of unclear, masked and maybe unhelpful ones, but the more you use them the greater their effect will become.

Planning and prioritisation

Making a list of all that needs to be done can be helpful since it relieves us of the burden of having to remember everything, but it can also be extremely depressing. The list always seems so long and it is often difficult to know where to start. There may be a temptation to flit from one task to another without finishing any. The likelihood of this is often increased the more stressed we are and the cycle is thus worsened. A more helpful approach can be to categorise the list from the start by placing tasks under the following, or similar headings: 'To be done this week; next week; this half term; next half term; next term; this year; if it were a perfect world'.

You might find that things get shunted down the list as the time limit elapses. Some may even find themselves in the last category. This is an invaluable one since it very often highlights our creative desires, maybe also our unrealistic expectations or high level of demands on ourselves. If there is no time for tasks in this column then it is easy to feel deeply frustrated since what we really want to do as a creative contribution in our work is left undone. If we have high personal demands then it is difficult to maintain confidence and uncompleted tasks are likely to result in stress and self-blame. Conversely, if we concentrate on the final column without completing essentials to be done in the near future, again it is easy to lose confidence and suffer considerable stress since everything seems out of control, as we cannot meet everyday deadlines.

You will not do any less work if you categorise tasks in a similar list and the chances are you will do more. The significant difference is, perhaps, that you will worry less about what is not done and have more energy for the task in hand.

Once you have tasks planned in this way, at any one point you have only *this week's* agenda on which to focus. This minimises the likelihood of your running through the work in your mind several times *before* you finally get down to doing it in reality. The work needed for the current week can then be planned on a daily basis, setting *possible* goals for each day and spreading the load through the week. Adding a few items you have nearly completed and which can be crossed off early on can help make a promising start.

Prioritise: who needs this work doing – me, the pupils, my head of department, the school, the government? What are the consequences if you do not do it today? These may vary, for example, from having to face a class of pupils disgruntled because their work is not marked, to a complete overload tomorrow, to a row with your head of department. You then can choose your priorities. Once choosing you are taking responsibility for the consequences and accepting your own area of power within external constraints. Without conscious choice it is all too easy to slip into a mentality of helplessness: 'I have to do this. It's too much. I can't manage. It's their fault ...'

At the end of each day it is helpful *to focus on what you have done*, while acknowledging what still requires attention and carrying it over, if still relevant, to a later time. The temptation is to concentrate on what is left undone and blame ourselves for having failed. This achieves nothing but an increase in our levels of stress.

Dividing up time

Another way of working with time is to divide it up into manageable chunks and to persevere with your plan. Often we work at minimum efficiency simply because we fail to recognise the fact that we are able to work faster and better at some times than at others. If, for example, straight after school you hit an energy trough, then this is an unsuccessful time to try to plan tomorrow's lessons. Take a break, then think about tomorrow. If your concentration levels drop after 25 minutes then acknowledge this and build in a short break when marking so that you can always work at maximum efficiency. The break can be very brief, if that is enough to renew your energy and concentration. It is easy to persevere unproductively rather than resting briefly before returning to the task. Do *you* utilise the study skills that you encourage your pupils to use?

As we tell our pupils to structure stories and essays with a beginning, a middle and an end, so we can divide up both tasks and time. Rather than a mountain of amorphous work which seems to increase on each occasion we consider it, we can separate out tasks into more manageable chunks and allot portions of time to them. It can be helpful to intersperse work with other activities, for example: 'I'll tidy the room for ten minutes, have lunch, walk round the block and then have 20 minutes to prepare for this afternoon.' Without planning and taking charge of the time it is easy to spend the whole hour procrastinating or dashing unproductively from one chore to the next, missing lunch and starting the afternoon feeling resentful, tired, out of control and very stressed.

Once you have a plan of action work through it systematically. *Concentrate on one thing at a time.* If you have not finished a task in the time allotted make another decision. How much longer might it take to complete? Would it be best to do that now or later? Choose as you go along. Experiment with the idea of time outside of work. Try different approaches and see what is most effective. What is your best time for working? What helps you feel confident in the way you use time? What system serves you best? The concept of managing time by apportioning it out for specific activities can often help to develop a sense of being in charge and a conviction that, if you keep at something long enough, often enough, in small enough chunks, even the most enormous of tasks, even report writing, can be completed. Once we have truly refined our time management skills we can help our pupils greatly in their efforts to manage homework, revision and in answering exam questions.

Control 2. When all that can change is our thinking

There will always be some aspects of our work we cannot change. Yet even in these areas we have an element of control, that is to say, at the very least, a choice about the attitude with which we carry them out. Do you carry out what you have to do grudgingly, angrily, willingly ...? Do you continually feel oppressed by such tasks? Do you postpone them indefinitely until the deadline approaches, or do you just get them done? What attitude will help you most? What attitude causes you least stress? Simply acknowledging that the bottom line of control is choosing *how* you go about something can, in itself, often reduce stress.

Confidence: a change in thinking

Learned response

Are you most likely to perceive a change, a demand on your time and energy or a new task as a problem, a burden, a threat, or something else? Do you generally feel stressed by them or do you view them as opportunities?

We learned to react to new things and demands when we were very young. We will have a learned response which will seem natural to us. It is natural, however, only in so far as it is very familiar. In fact, it will be shaped to a large degree by how those around us themselves reacted and how they responded to our reactions during our early years: we learnt a reaction which was reinforced in some way. Consequently, as an adult, it is possible gradually to add alternative responses to our repertoire, if we so choose. Although we will probably have a usual way of responding, it can start to take a back seat at times.

If you have a habit of feeling stressed in response to change, demands or new situations, here is one way you can start developing a more relaxed approach.

1. Start to notice as early as possible when you are feeling stressed.
2. Ask yourself if this is, in part, due to an old pattern of immediately perceiving a change, a new situation or a demand as a threat, a burden or a problem.
3. Breathe, relax, feel your feet on the ground. Take a few steps back mentally from the situation. Review it from a different perspective. See how it sounds and feels from there. Is it really, *in the present*, such a burden, threat or problem?
4. How would it be if it were merely an opportunity? What might you lose? What might you gain? Who do you know who might consider it an opportunity? How would he or she sit or stand? Get into that position and see what it feels like. If you do not know anyone who fits this description, or if it feels more comfortable, get into the posture you imagine someone would have with that frame of mind. How is it to stand or sit like someone who faces opportunities rather than threats, problems or burdens? (Remember that all new behaviour inevitably feels a little strange.)
5. In this new posture ask yourself what new personal qualities you could employ or develop in taking this opportunity. Tell yourself that you could try out a new approach. Imagine how differently you could see things, talk about the situation or feel about it.
6. You may not want to change anything. Simply experiment with the possibilities: 'What if I were to ...'

Internal demands

One aspect of our thinking which often helps us perceive change as a threat, problem or burden is that of our internal demands. These are beliefs about the way we think we *ought* to behave which may be conscious or unconscious. We may, for example, be aware that we are a perfectionist, that we feel anxious if we are even a few minutes late, that we find it difficult not to win, or that we get upset if others are arguing, and so on. We may not, however, be aware that we have other demands driving us from the unconscious. These are not obvious, but when looking at the pattern of a life they may become clearer. The fact that we may never be satisfied with ourselves whatever we do, for example, may point to a belief that we have to be perfect or have to succeed. Internal demands of this nature can be about anything. For example: 'I must be good, perfect, brave, beautiful, entertaining, busy, calm, cheerful ...'; 'I must hurry up'; 'I must try harder'; 'I must do my best'; 'I must keep troubles to myself'; 'I must stand on my own two feet'; 'I must succeed'; 'I must get it right'; 'I must please others'; 'I must make it all right for everyone', and so on.

Such demands add an extra pressure on top of any external demands we are facing in our work. They keep us trying harder and harder, driven by the fear of not matching up to our own standards. Even if we attain approval or success in the world we may not be able to accept it fully since our internal demands tend to be relentless. This can cause a constant erosion of our confidence. It also contributes to our levels of stress. It is difficult to meet a demand as an opportunity if we are driven on by an internal demand that we *must* be something or other, since viewing a demand as an opportunity allows for experimentation, testing out and flexibility. Above all, it allows for the possibility of some degree of failure at times.

Again, we have usually formulated these demands at an early age in response to our situations in order to survive or flourish as well as possible. They may not be relevant to our current lives and may well contribute to our sense of stress. Here, too, it is a question of acknowledging these internal demands, accepting that they may have been of use in the past though may not be valid in the present. They will, of course, be a habit and, consequently, we will probably slip into familiar lines of thought. In time, with practice, it is possible to draw back and choose new ways more often.

What is true for teachers is, of course, equally true for pupils who will also often be driven by conscious and unconscious internal demands.

Inner authority

Our confidence in teaching is often linked to a belief in our own authority as a teacher, that we do, indeed, have the right to take charge of the class and make things happen in the lesson. Developing and maintaining a sense of inner authority can, therefore, be helpful in minimising stress. It is a gradual process and is promoted by certain ways of thinking about ourselves. This thinking includes four elements:

1. A belief that it is possible that pupils will listen and carry out the instructions you give – that they will accept that you are in charge.
2. A belief that you have the right as a teacher to make demands and be in charge of the process in the classroom and that this is necessary in order to maintain respect for all and to foster learning and achievement.

3. No *need* to be liked by the pupils. Obviously, if you are liked it is pleasing, but you are not *dependent* on pupil approval or this can cloud your judgement. You are likely to be popular if you enjoy teaching and being around young people, if pupils feel respected by you and each other in lessons, if it is safe to learn and demands and expectations are clear, if it is possible to succeed and if the content and/or process of the lesson is interesting enough of the time.
4. A self-image which enables you to take charge, make demands and take unpopular decisions if you think them necessary.

Commitment

This is closely linked to our sense of control since, in general, the larger a part we play in something and the more we have contributed to it, the more committed we are to it also. When decision making is at a distance, it is more difficult to feel responsible for and connected to our work. Being aware of the choices we make every day, while increasing our sense of personal power, can also help to develop greater commitment.

Another element that engenders commitment to work is the sense that it is worthwhile. Although on a large scale this may be difficult to assess, considering an individual's progress sometimes makes it easier to appreciate our contribution. Indeed, from the pupil's point of view the impact of a teacher can be very great, a fact we tend to forget as adults. Usually, faced with the whole class, we are largely unaware of the important role we play for individuals. Ask any parent, however. Think of your own experiences and those of friends and you can understand the huge importance of teachers when viewed through a young person's eyes. Consequently, we tend to underestimate the positive contribution we can make as teachers, focusing on what we cannot change, rather than on what we can and do achieve.

Cultivate calm

A benign circle: support, balance and recovery

Another factor which helps reduce stress is feeling supported. Develop a support system at school, with teachers from other schools, outside the workplace – wherever possible. A support system ensures that you can discuss concerns, air ideas and talk about incidents to help you unwind.

It can also be useful to support oneself by a balanced lifestyle, creating a balance of rest, exercise, food and interests not connected with work. This ensures that you go into potentially stressful situations with your resources in prime condition.

Developing strategies to unwind and recover from any stress you have incurred during the day is also useful since this prevents stress building up all term resulting in illness during the holidays. Any technique you enjoy which contributes to a balanced lifestyle can be of great benefit (some relaxation techniques are included in Appendix VIII). Viewing the world without undue stress will make it easier to apply the approach described earlier in this book in order to minimise conflict and improve pupils' behaviour. Choosing how we respond rather than responding from habit antidotes any kind of powerless thinking and enables us to adopt a non-confrontational yet firm stance whenever possible. Once we think and act consciously from choice we can feel increasingly empowered. As Paul Martin writes in *The Sickening Mind* (1997) in regard to stress management:

> What you are doing to alleviate your stress may be less important than the fact that you are doing something – anything – and thereby taking control of your predicament. Perhaps we should not agonise over which stress management technique we use. The best thing may be simply to get on with it and enjoy the benefits of being in control. (p. 145)

As in any field, focusing on the positive alternative, the new habit, is more beneficial than thinking of stopping the old. Consequently, the emphasis is best laid on how to cultivate a calm way of thinking and working rather than concentrating on managing stress as such (a checklist for cultivating calm is in Appendix IX). When calm oneself it is easier to instil a sense of peace in others. From a calm centre it is far easier to form positive relationships, teach peacefully and enjoy working.

This chapter has dealt with:

'I've got enough to do. Why tackle stress?'

What is stress?

Why some people suffer more from stress than others

Pupils and stress
• How to minimise potential stress for pupils

An approach to minimising stress for teachers
• At a school level
• Individuals

Reverse the process
• Gather information
• Check your posture: breathe, shift position and relax

Review attitudes and working practices
• Control 1. Where external change is possible
• Control 2. When all that can change is our thinking
• Confidence: a change in thinking
• Commitment

Cultivate calm
• A benign circle: support, balance and recovery

APPENDIX I

Specific Learning Difficulties (SpLD)

There are many theories concerning the definition of SpLD and a considerable body of literature dealing with it. Here I would like to point out that people with SpLD often have strengths in areas other than literacy, for example, spacial concepts, sensitivity to other people's moods. In a society and, therefore, in an education system based on literacy skills these other qualities are often overlooked or undervalued and the pupil with SpLD frequently ends up feeling that he or she is *wrong* rather than *different*.

For the teacher it is useful to recognise warning signs which might indicate SpLD and warrant further investigation and a referral to an educational psychologist.

Specific Learning Difficulties – Signs and Symptoms
by Gill Backhouse

Dyslexia and, to a lesser extent, *dyspraxia* are the specific learning difficulties most frequently associated with problems in learning to read and write. These conditions may, of course, co-occur. Although these difficulties are experienced by students of *all* levels of ability, their effects may be more notable in the pupil of average or above average ability, when a discrepancy between apparent ability and attainments in literacy can be obvious.

The manifestations of a specific learning difficulty will depend on a) its severity; b) how it interacts with the pupil's other intellectual and emotional strengths and weaknesses; c) how effectively – or otherwise – the student has been taught. By secondary transfer, therefore, a wide range of individual differences in symptoms exists. However, some common threads may be discernible, particularly if information about earlier development is available, alerting staff to the possibility of either dyslexia or dyspraxia.

Dyslexia

In the majority of cases, dyslexics' written language difficulties are rooted in subtle problems with the sound (phonological) system of spoken language. These may manifest themselves to a certain extent in their speech, but the major effect is on the acquisition of phonics.

Pre-school

- There is a history of language/literacy problems within the family (e.g. parents, grandparents, siblings, cousins).
- The child is late learning to talk; speech and/or language skills are noted to be immature for age; the child may have been referred for speech and language therapy.

At primary school

- The pupil has great difficulty with phonics for both reading and spelling.
- In less severe cases progress may eventually have been made with reading, but spelling has remained immature and below the expected standard. In the more severe cases, reading and spelling progress has been 'arrested' at a very early stage. Spelling may be described as 'bizarre' since the target word could not be deciphered (e.g. *stmck* for mistake, *splich* for ship).
- The pupil has an uneven profile of attainment – his or her speaking and listening is better than reading and writing, and maths and science (also technology, art and IT) is better than English.
- The pupil's adjustment and behaviour, confidence and self-esteem has gradually deteriorated.

At secondary school

- The pupil has persisting literacy difficulties; dislikes reading – especially *aloud* – and reading is slow and effortful. Spelling may be immature or 'bizarre'; there are particular problems with multisyllable words. He or she has difficulty copying notes from the board, writing to dictation, producing any written work.
- The pupil's attainments in maths, science, technology, art, IT, etc. are significantly better than in language-based subjects.
- The pupil's oral contributions in class are notably better than his or her written work; staff are convinced the pupil 'could do better'. Note that it is not uncommon for mildly dyslexic pupils to be perceived as poorly motivated. Although they 'survived' at primary school, their fragile literacy skills are insufficient to cope with the greater demands of the secondary curriculum.
- The pupil has severe problems with learning a second language – especially French.
- The pupil may have difficulty expressing him or herself and have word-finding problems; articulation may be generally unclear and multisyllable words mispronounced; he or she may have difficulties learning new vocabulary for science, etc.
- The pupil is anxious/withdrawn or frustrated/aggressive/'acting out'; he or she has low self-esteem.

Further information

British Dyslexia Association
98 London Road
Reading
Berkshire RG1 5AU

A list of centres offering specialist SpLD teacher training courses is available from:

The Royal Society of Arts Examination Board
Westwood Way
Coventry CV4 8HS

Recommended reading

Ott, P. (1997) *How to Detect and Manage Dyslexia*. London: Heinemann

Dyspraxia

This is sometimes known as 'clumsy child syndrome' and its main effect on the development of literacy skills is on handwriting. Specific difficulties in *planning and executing a sequence of voluntary movements* may also result in difficulties with speech production, and a range of fine and gross motor skills.

Pre-school

* The pupil has a history of delayed development of motor skills at the pre-school stage – walking, feeding, dressing, etc.

At primary school

* The pupil has poor fine motor skills – cutting, sticking, drawing, handwriting; fastening clothes and shoes.
* The pupil has poor motor coordination – generally clumsy; has difficulties with PE, changing clothes, learning to catch a ball.
* The pupil's adjustment and behaviour, confidence and self-esteem have gradually deteriorated.

At secondary school

* The pupil's handwriting is poorly-formed or illegible; complains that writing makes his or her hand/arm 'tired' or ache.
* The pupil has difficulty developing fast, efficient keyboard skills.
* The layout of the pupil's written work and maths; execution of diagrams, etc. is of a low standard.
* The pupil is accident-prone, is poorly coordinated and has low self-esteem.

Further information

The Dyspraxia Trust
8 West Alley
Hitchin
Hertfordshire SG5 1EG

Recommended reading

Ripley, K., Daines, B., Barrett, J. (1997) *Dyspraxia: A Guide for Teachers and Parents*. London: David Fulton Publishers.

(© Copyright of this section: Gill Backhouse, Chartered Psychologist, Department of Human Communication Science, University College London)

Examples: Pupils' experiences of SpLD

The following extract also helps to convey the kind of experiences some pupils with SpLD may have.

What I remember most is a feeling which permeated the whole of my early life. It was a sense, right from the beginning, when I started to socialise with other children, that I was in some way different ... At the time, of course, I couldn't understand what it was that made me different ...

So even in my own world, I was an outsider.

I also became distanced from other children at playgroup and playschool because they bullied me. They could sense something odd about me, I suppose, like small children can, and so they started to tease and bully me, which got progressively worse as I got older.

From *A Little Edge of Darkness*,
by Tanya Faludy and Alexander Faludy (1996)

Imagine you are in a training session with a group of colleagues. There is a discussion on a topic about which you feel fairly confident and you make several good contributions. After this, the trainer hands out questions for all to answer in writing. You look at the paper but find it hard to concentrate. Around you everyone has already started writing furiously. You begin to panic, feeling left behind. You take a deep breath and look at the first question. It seems to make sense and you know the answer, but as you go to write it down what seemed so clear in your head slips away. You copy a bit of the question to introduce the answer and feel the familiar ache in your fingers and arm you always get when writing. There's so much to get down. It's impossible. You glance at your neighbour. He's still working fast and seems to be on Question 8! Now you really panic: your breathing is shallow, your hands sweat, you feel very sick. The words begin to swim and jump as you stare at the paper. 'Just another two minutes to finish off', the trainer announces. 'Don't worry if you haven't quite finished.' But what if you haven't even started? Will anyone find out? Will the trainer ask people for answers? Why am I so stupid? Why can't I just do it? Everyone else can. I know the answers, at least, I think I do ...

Imagine the situation is complicated by the fact that you have experienced such feelings in similar situations for the past seven years. (A pupil is likely to start feeling different and a failure as soon as starting literacy work at school in reception, if not before.) Indeed, the panic really starts as the papers are given out, or as you approach the classroom or the school gates, or when you wake up each school morning.

It is not surprising, therefore, that some pupils with SpLD may adopt alternative strategies in an attempt to hide their difficulties and avoid facing them and the feelings they evoke by truanting, disruptive behaviour, clowning around or getting angry. It is not surprising that these pupils may sometimes appear to overreact, answering the teacher rudely, hitting a classmate, storming out of class and so on.

Some common areas of difficulty

There is a broad spectrum of difficulties under the umbrella term of SpLD, ranging from mild to severe. Here I would like to focus on some general difficulties which are common and can often cause particular problems in schools. Some of them may not always be easily identified as part of SpLD.

Emotional legacy

However mild or severe the SpLD may be, by the time a pupil reaches secondary school, the emotional impact is usually considerable. This is particularly so if the difficulties are undiagnosed since the confusion and sense of being stupid can be greater. However, even when SpLD is diagnosed, the emotional legacy is not to be underestimated and can make learning more difficult and relationships more volatile.

The emotional legacy of SpLD may include:

- *fear of failure*, of being found out;
- *shame* for not being able to manage, for being different and apparently stupid;
- *confusion and self-doubt* since sometimes you can do something, and sometimes not;
- *frustration and anger* at apparently being so 'stupid', at not being able to do the same as others, at not being able to express yourself as you would wish;
- *dread* of school and of any written work;
- *exhaustion*, since it is so much effort to concentrate and write;
- *despondency* – there seems no hope and what may have taken a huge effort to do is often not even noticed;
- *poor self-esteem.*

Concentration difficulties

Many pupils with dyslexia find concentration difficult in a number of different ways. This can be exhibited as a difficulty to:

- listen to a speaker if there is any background noise;
- follow instructions on a page if the layout is at all confusing;
- remember instructions, especially if given orally;
- focus on work in hand rather than daydream;
- focus on own work rather than being distracted by other class members.

In some cases it seems as if a pupil with dyslexia lacks an extra 'skin' which usually helps to shut out unwanted distractions and allows individuals to stay firmly where they are without being pulled off course by others. Consequently, pupils can be distracted by their own thoughts or by other people, and may easily daydream or be drawn into disruptive behaviour.

Organisational difficulties

Again, these can range from the general to the specific. Pupils with dyslexia may find great difficulty in bringing to lessons relevant equipment, books and homework. They may lose important notes and find organising a large piece of work extremely problematic. Answering an essay question is also a challenge since it requires ordering and sequencing thoughts and material coherently, on paper. Consequently, training in techniques for structuring written work is particularly important from as early an age as possible.

Reading

Some pupils with dyslexia are voracious readers. One ten-year-old dyslexic girl I taught had, for example, read J. R. R. Tolkien's *Lord of the Rings* nine times!

Reading difficulties, therefore, may not show up particularly in primary school. Difficulties may still arise, however, in some contexts since, although skills may be excellent for general purposes, they may be inaccurate for the specific and the detailed. Thus problems may be experienced when answering questions for comprehension or from a specialised text when getting the 'gist' of the passage is insufficient.

Writing and copying

The physical effort required to write by some pupils with SpLD is tremendous. They grip the pen with intense pressure and suffer considerable aching in the arm and shoulder. Progress is, therefore, often slow and the result unsatisfactory. Many are ashamed and angry at their writing ability.

Teachers can help by encouraging the pupil to adopt and maintain a relaxed body posture while imagining that the movement for writing comes from the lower abdomen (the *hara* or *dan tien* movement centre of martial arts) rather than from the fingers.

One reason copying from the board is so difficult for pupils with SpLD is that there are so many distractions between the board and their paper that concentration is difficult. Keeping their place is also problematic. Often the teacher rubs off some of the writing before they have finished in order to let the rest of the class continue. (The pupils with SpLD are unlikely, of course, to admit they are so far behind and end up with very inadequate notes.) Writing from dictation is, of course, even more difficult.

Spelling

This is often considered the major difficulty a pupil with dyslexia faces. As we can see from the above, however, it is frequently not the only one. If pupils can express themselves fluently and can organise material into a coherent answer they can succeed even with poor spelling, as long as their mistakes do not interfere with meaning. If, for example, they spell phonetically, then as soon as their work is read aloud it will make sense. Those who use bizarre spellings, however, face greater difficulties since their work will remain largely incomprehensible. The teacher can help by encouraging pair work and work with a tape recorder so that the pupil can learn to structure and order material and thoughts and can get some satisfaction from contributing ideas without being stuck all the time with the task of spelling.

What the teacher can do

1. Question his or her assumptions about a pupil. This can be a complex process at times. For example, pupils of average or above average ability with moderate to mild difficulties may be difficult to spot, *especially if their performance is not particularly poor in relation to the rest of the class*. It is easy to consider them lazy or careless. On the other hand, the poor performance of a pupil of lower ability may be attributed to slow learning rather than SpLD. Listen to parents. Does the pupil dread school?
2. If in doubt, thoroughly investigate the possibility of SpLD and refer to an educational psychologist.

3. Write clearly on the board and worksheets.
4. Ensure the layout of worksheets is logical, clear and uncluttered.
5. Ensure pupils have homework instructions written down.
6. Provide written copies of notes, where necessary.
7. Sometimes accept one-word answers and taped work.
8. When marking, consider the content of the work separate from the presentation and spelling.
9. Ensure structural support for written work is used regularly with the whole class (see Chapter 2).
10. Encourage pair and group work for some written activities.
11. Include regular help with revision, including information put on tape.
12. Give pupils a list of essential words which must be known and spelt for your particular subject area and topic.
13. Ask a pupil with SpLD how else you could help. Tell him or her what you expect regarding behaviour. Work out an agreement for mutual cooperation.
14. Be encouraging and constructive wherever possible, giving praise for a piece of work first and retaining learning points for a later date.
15. If possible, find ways in which a pupil with SpLD can achieve and succeed other than those connected with written work.

Cultural Attitudes Towards Children

Basing her theory on childrearing practices, Alice Miller (1983) describes a very negative attitude towards children in German society in the first four decades of this century. The fundamental aspects of this attitude, which she calls 'Poisonous Pedagogy', include a belief that parents (and in this context also, therefore, teachers acting in *loco parentis*) deserve respect simply because they are parents (teachers), whereas children are undeserving of respect simply because they are children. Parents (teachers) are always right merely because of who they are and children are, by analogy, wrong.

Since adults were treated in this manner themselves as children, they must uphold these values or would be forced to face the pain they experienced when young when receiving such treatment. Thus negative attitudes towards young people are passed on from generation to generation, unless adults have the opportunity, support and courage to acknowledge their early experience.

In his work with dysfunctional families and co-dependency in the USA, John Bradshaw (1988) believes that a similar view of children to that outlined by Miller is widespread in America and lies at the heart of problems for many people today.

I would suggest that a deep negativity towards children and young people also lies in the fabric of English society, following on from the Victorian view that children should be seen and not heard. Like all pervasive attitudes, such negativity can be difficult to pinpoint while immersed in it. Thus, for example, I was aware of my assumption that if pupils did not understand my explanation they had not listened properly only when I worked with adults and realised that, in contrast, I then readily assumed responsibility for an inadequate explanation!

On the contrary, Miller proposes that children require physical and emotional support from adults. This includes:

1. Respect for the child.
2. Respect for his rights.
3. Tolerance for his feelings.
4. Willingness to learn from his behaviour.

Quiz on Anger

1. What is anger?

2. Can another person make you angry?

3. Is anger always bad?

4. Can anger become a habit?

5. What are some of the emotions that anger may mask? For example, fear, hurt, insecurity, fear of failure, a sense of inadequacy, etc.

6. Is getting angry good for your health?

7. Is bottling up anger good for your health?

8. Is it possible to manage your anger without either exploding from time to time or bottling it up?

9. Do people often get angrier when a present situation reminds them of a similar one in the past?

10. Can talking to someone sympathetic outside the situation help with your anger?

11. Can physical exercise help you to calm down after an angry incident?

12. Do you want to be ignored or taken seriously when angry?

Communication Skills

These are some examples of how you could work with pupils on communication skills for specific interactions with teachers. Adapt as necessary since these are merely an outline. If possible, they would be read through, discussed and practised with the pupil. The aim is for pupils to understand that they do have responsibility and choice regarding their behaviour: how they speak to teachers usually influences the outcome.

What to do on the spot

A teacher tells you off and you think it is unjust or you are angry at the teacher's manner. Try to do the following:

- Take a breath deep within yourself.
- Stand/sit differently.
- Feel your feet on the ground.
- Choose

  a) Shall I say something now? Remember the teacher is less likely to listen with the class/friends watching and a lesson to teach.

  b) Shall I accept what the teacher says now, and see him/her later to sort it out? The teacher is more likely to listen when there is more time and no audience.

  c) Shall I shrug it off and get on with my life? After all, everyone makes mistakes sometimes. Can I do this without lingering resentment? Can I do this without acting angrily next lesson?

If you decide to say something now
Remember:

- if you remain polite you stand more chance of getting your message across. Once you're rude, the teacher will ignore *what* you're trying to say and get angry with *how* you're saying it.

If you ask to speak to a teacher later
Find a time when the teacher is not in the middle of doing something else, for example, at the end of a lesson or in the staffroom at break, and ask if you could see him or her for a few minutes privately, when convenient.

You will find your own words. Here are some examples:

- 'Excuse me please, Sir/Miss .../ Mr .../ Mrs ..., please could I see you for a few minutes privately when you have the time. It's very important.'

If asked what it is about you could say something like:
- 'I'd rather not talk about it now' or 'I was concerned/angry/upset about last lesson and I'd like to sort it out.'

Remember:
- if you wish to be treated like an adult, act and speak the way adults are supposed to. Use their language. Try it and see.

Preparation for the meeting

Questions to ask yourself
- What are you feeling – angry, upset, anxious or anything else?
- Is this because the teacher was unfair or because of the way he or she spoke to you?
- Do other people treat you like this? If so, who in particular?

If you are angry:
- Are you extra angry with the teacher because other people have treated you like this in the past?
- It can be helpful before speaking to the teacher to release some of your anger through exercise: running, swimming, playing football, etc.

Much conflict arises out of misunderstanding people's actions, words or intentions.
- What could the teacher have misunderstood?
- What could you have misunderstood?
- What would you like the teacher to do differently in the future?
- What could you do differently in future?
- What would you like the meeting to achieve? What might the teacher like it to achieve?

The meeting

- How you sit and stand can help you. Avoid sitting or standing directly opposite the teacher.
- Look at him or her when he or she is speaking.
- If you feel you are getting angry, breathe, change to a different way of sitting or standing, and relax.
- Listen while the teacher is speaking. *Really listen*, without thinking about what you are going to say next.
- Take your time.
- Stay brief and to the point.
- State your point of view and stay open to the teacher's position.
- Stay polite.

Here is an example:
1. Say what you are there for: 'I wanted to talk about what happened last lesson.'
2. Say what you are feeling: 'I still feel angry/ upset because …'
3. Describe what happened from your point of view: 'You told me off yesterday for talking and I hadn't said anything' or, perhaps, 'I was just helping X with his work.'
4. Why you think the misunderstanding occurred: 'It might have looked as if it

was me but it wasn't', or 'It might have looked as if I wasn't working too but I was.'

5. What you want out of the meeting: 'I wanted to clear this up so I'm not angry next lesson.'
6. At the end thank the teacher for his or her time.

Remember:
- there are many misunderstandings because of anger and prejudice on either or both sides.
- if you learn to speak to teachers in a way they can *hear* they will begin to *see* you differently.

APPENDIX V

Talking not Fighting

The following example, provided by two five-year-olds, illustrates how a would-be aggressor fails to be aggressive if the other refuses the passive role and will not respond as expected. The girl, S, had invited the boy, D, home to play after school. When they arrived, however, S started pushing D around. He complained loudly, S's mother intervened and S went upstairs to see her father. D started investigating the toys. When S returned she picked up a rubber snake and began trying to push it down the back of D's jumper. The scene proceeded as follows:

Boy: Don't!
(This was repeated on several occasions while he moved away and continued to play with a toy.)
Girl (chasing after him with the snake): It's poisonous and it's just touched you. You're dead now.
Boy: No I'm not. I'm, wearing a suit of armour.
Girl: No you're not.
Boy: Yes I am. It's invisible.
Girl: I can't see it.
Boy: It's invisible.
Girl: Where's your skin?
Boy: Underneath.
Girl (going to get a toy frog to help the snake chase the boy): You're the baddie and I'm the goodie and I'm going to kill you.
Boy (avoiding the snake and frog): You shouldn't do this. I'm your guest. When you come to my house, I'm going to make you the baddie then.
Girl (stepping back): It wasn't me, it was them [the frog and snake].
(She put the toys down, went over to where D was standing by the toy box, picked out a toy and both children started looking at it together and talking about it.)

D avoided the passive role in several ways and was able to do so only because of the sophisticated communication skills both children possessed. First, he ignored the snake and carried on playing. Once S increased the pressure by saying the snake was poisonous and he was dead, D resorted to a fantasy protection: he was safe from her attacks. Then, when the frog was involved too and he was cast as the baddie, he used reason, pointing out that guests should not be treated in this way and that she

158

could expect the same treatment when visiting him. This mention of the consequences of her actions gave S the choice: she quickly chose to make peace and initiated another, cooperative activity.

During this interaction D remained in the home position throughout. It is easy to imagine how this could have been otherwise. He could easily have returned aggression with aggression at which point S would either have flipped into passive role, or a fierce tussle would have ensued. If D had accepted passive role and run away screaming and frightened, S would almost certainly have redoubled her efforts since he would have confirmed to her that her actions were indeed scary. As it was, he indicated that he was not really threatened by her at all. Ignoring her did not work, however, since she wanted some acknowledgement of what she was doing. This he gave by the fantasy solution. Although he was not accepting the passive role up to this point he had nevertheless been reacting to her provocation, parrying her assaults. When he told her she was not behaving properly towards a guest and would receive the same treatment, he was taking charge and redefining the situation in his terms. She immediately complied. He had, however, given her a choice, that is to say, he did not disempower her, but left her the option of saving face. He also put a boundary on her behaviour by his last comments, adding a sense of safety to the situation. It is a tribute to the communication skills of both children that they managed to come to such an amicable resolution.

Changing Behaviour Questionnaire

This could be used as a basis for talking with a pupil about how to change behaviour.

Changing behaviour can be difficult for four main reasons:
1. The old behaviour must have given us something we wanted at some time.
2. We may not know what to do instead.
3. We may not know how to switch from the old behaviour to the new.
4. Habit.

Remember:
- new behaviour always feels strange because it is new.

The following questions may help you in your change.

Deciding

- Do you want to change some part of your behaviour?
- If so, why?
- What behaviour do you wish to change? (Be as clear as possible.)
- What do you get from this behaviour at present?
  - Something you want? How else could you get it?
  - Something you don't want?

The process

- What happens just before this behaviour you wish to change?
- How do you feel then?
- What could you do at this moment to change course?
- What other behaviour could you choose then?
- Is there someone you know or could imagine who would manage this new behaviour easily? What could you take on from the way they would do it? How would they stand, move or sit?
- Who could help you change by giving advice, encouragement and support?
- What could you do to encourage yourself if you slip back into old behaviour?

Remember:
- the way to create a gap so you can choose to try out new behaviour is to breathe, relax and shift your position.
- put effort into doing the new habit rather than into stopping the old one.
- practice and patience help.

Possible Indications of Stress

Part of the problem is simply noticing *as soon as possible* when you are experiencing stress in your life. The following may indicate this. Becoming aware of your own particular pattern of stress symptoms is a first step to dealing with it.

Lack of appetite.
Eating more than usual (whether hungry or not).
Putting on or losing weight.
Unable to get to sleep.
Waking early.
Feeling constantly irritable, or more irritable than usual.
Being unable to sit still and relax.
Bursting into tears easily.
Feeling bored most of the time.
Frequent headaches.
Being unable to enjoy a good laugh.
Feeling that you can't talk to anyone about your problems.
Being unable to concentrate.
Unable to enjoy yourself.
Inclined to panic easily.
Frequent heartburn or stomach pains.
Frequent diarrhoea or constipation.
Coordination impaired and reflexes slowed.
Forgetting instructions easily.
Feeling that everything has got on top of you.
Frequent feelings of dread.
Feeling tired most of the time.
Feeling uneasy much of the time.
Muscle spasms or twitches.
Tension in the shoulders, neck, back, legs.
Waking up tense.

Relaxation Techniques: Using Focused Imagination

Focusing imagination can be a handy and quick way of relaxing. It tends to involve both mind and body so can be very effective. It may take a little time to feel comfortable with it: explore, experiment and practise at peaceful times. You may prefer feelings, sounds or words to visual images. See what works for you: there is no right or wrong way to do it. After practising focused imagination, benefits can be gained very quickly. You may wish to put some of these ideas or some of your own on to tape.

Preparation

Sit, lie or stand as comfortably as possible. Be aware of your support – the floor, chair, bed – and connect with your breathing, without trying to change it in any way.

Crystal clear water

Imagine a stream of crystal clear water above your head; let it trickle through you. See it, feel it, hear it: use whichever sense comes easiest to you. As you imagine the water trickling through you, feel it taking with it any worries, anxieties, thoughts, tensions that you want to get rid of. See/feel/hear it moving down through you until it flows out through your feet leaving you relaxed and refreshed. You may like to go back to the top of your head to send down a second stream in case any tensions remain. When you have done this exercise a few times at your leisure you can, if need be, set the water running in your imagination and return to everyday life, knowing that it can continue to relax you whilst you carry on with your work.

(by Susannah McInerney)

Colour breathing

Imagine you are breathing in a colour of your choice. (Orange tends to be invigorating, blue and green calming, rose pink is nurturing.) Enjoy the colour. You may like to give it a particular sound, or associate it with a feeling, if this works better for you. Draw the colour deep within you: imagine it moving down through your body as you breathe in, and as you exhale imagine it seeping out through the soles of your feet. See/feel/hear the colour pushing out any tension from your body leaving you feeling invigorated, calm, nurtured.

Quiet place

Take an image which, for you, is very calming. For example, you could see the reflection of a full moon on a calm lake or a still sea. Any unwanted thoughts could be ripples gently moving out and dissipating quietly. Place the image between your eyes. Enjoy the peace. Expand this calm, if you want to, outside yourself – an inch, a foot, three feet – so you are constantly in a permeable bubble of your own calm. Another image might be a field of grass and flowers on a warm summer afternoon. Unwanted thoughts could fly away like bees. Imagine the image in the middle of your chest. Enjoy and expand this, too.

A place of power

Think of a place in the open air which for you feels powerful. It may be somewhere you already know; it may be an imaginary place. Include some water if you can, and sunshine, moonlight, stars, or a fire. Lie comfortably. Notice any sounds you can hear. Feel the breeze on your skin, smell the air. Feel warmth or coolness. Be aware of what you are lying on: rock, sand, earth, grass. Sense the power of this place of nature, the power of the mixing of the elements earth, water, fire and air. Know that you carry these elements within: their power is your power. Imbue yourself with the energy of that place. When you are ready, gently come back to the present, taking that power with you, refreshed and regenerated.

Roots

Imagine roots growing from your feet and right down into the core of the earth. See/feel/hear red earth energy travelling up those roots and into your body, anchoring you firmly on the ground, energising you.

Clearing breath

With your normal breath, inhale to the count of one, exhale to the count of two. Inhale to three; exhale to four. Keep your attention on the ebb and flow of the breath. Let any unwanted thoughts drift away; keep returning to the counting. If you lose count, start again at the beginning. Continue for as long as you like to create a break and clear your mind.

Checklist for Cultivating Calm

A relaxed, alert and calm attitude makes it easier to work efficiently and conveys a sense of peace and order to pupils. There are many ways of developing and maintaining such an attitude. These include:

- a balanced lifestyle – enough fresh food, rest and exercise;
- a support network;
- fun and laughter;
- awareness of body posture – using breathing and body posture to break habits, allow choice and reduce tension;
- relaxation;
- time spent thinking of only one thing at a time;
- daily quiet time;
- time spent in the open air enjoying nature;
- many people find meditation a highly effective way of reducing stress and cultivating calm (see bibliography for further information).

Bibliography

Andrews, Lynn V. (1986) *Star Woman*. New York: Warner Books.

Bandler, Richard and Grinder, John (1979) *Frogs into Princes*. Utah: Real People Press.

Black, Paul and William, Dylan (1998) *Inside the Black Box*. London: King's College.

Bliss, Theresa and Robinson, George (1995) *Coming Round to Circle Time* (video). Bristol: Lucky Duck Publishing.

Bradshaw, John (1988) *Bradshaw on: The Family*. Florida: Health Communications.

Cowie, Helen and Sharp, Sonia (1996) *Time to Listen*. London: David Fulton Publishers.

Deming, W. Edwards (1994) *New Economics for Industry, Government and Education*. Boston: MIT.

Dickson, Anne (1982) *A Woman in Your Own Right*. London: Quartet Books.

Elton, Lord and Education and Science Department of the Welsh Office (1989) *The Elton Report*. London: HMSO.

Emaho (1992) *The Fire Dance*. USA: Shailendra Publishing.

Faludy, Tanya F. and Faludy, Alexander F. (1996) *A Little Edge of Darkness*. London: Jessica Kingsley Publishers.

Freire, Paulo (1972) *Pedagogy of the Oppressed*. Harmondsworth: Penguin.

Galbraith, Paul (1997) *Meditate Rejuvenate*. Singapore: Media Masters.

Goleman, Daniel (1996) *Emotional Intelligence: Why It Can Matter More than IQ*. London: Bloomsbury.

Gray, F. (1974) 'Little brother is changing you,' *Psychology Today* (March).

Hargreaves, D. H., Hester S. K., Mellor, F .J. (1975) *Deviance in Classrooms*. London: Routledge and Kegan Paul.

Kubler-Ross, Elizabeth (1970) *On Death and Dying*. London: Tavistock.

Kuroyanagi, Tetsuko (1982) *Totto-Chan, The Little Girl at the Window*. Tokyo: Kodansha International.

Latzko, William J. (1997) 'Modeling the method. The Deming classroom', *Quality in Management Journal* **97**, 5, no. 1.

LeShan, Lawrence (1995) *How to Meditate*. London: Thorsons.

Mann, David (1997) *Psychotherapy: An Erotic Relationship*. London: Routledge.

Marland, Michael (1975) *The Craft of the Classroom*. London: Heinemann.

Martin, Paul (1997) *The Sickening Mind*. London: HarperCollins.

Miller, Alice (1983) *For Your Own Good: The Roots of Violence in Child-rearing*. London: Faber & Faber.

Moseley, Jenny (1993) *Turn Your School Round*. Wisbech: Learning Development Aids.

Oestreich, Daniel K. and Ryan, Kathleen (1991) *Driving Fear out of the Workplace*. San Francisco: Jossey Bass.

Ott, P. (1997) *How to Detect and Manage Dyslexia*. London: Heinemann

Quinn, Kaleghl (1983) *Stand Your Ground*. London: Orbis Publishing.

Ripley, K., Daines, B., Barrett, J. (1997) *Dyspraxia: A Guide for Teachers and Parents*. London: David Fulton Publishers.

Robertson, John (1981) *Effective Classroom Control*. London: Hodder & Stoughton.

Selye, Hans (1976) *The Stress of Life*. New York: McGraw-Hill.

Semler, Ricardo (1993) *Maverick*. London: Century Business.

Winnicott D.W. (1958) 'The antisocial tendency', in *Collected Papers: Through Paediatrics to Psycho-Analysis*. London: Tavistock.

Yogananda Paramahansa (1953) *Autobiography of a Yogi*. Los Angeles: Self-Realization Fellowship.

Index

Andrews, Lynn V., 29
authority agreement, 62, 111
Bandler, R., 72
Bliss, Theresa, 76
body posture, 3, 14, 17, 18, 20, 29, 23, 24, 26, 27, 57, 65, 85, 87, 95, 96, 100–3, 111, 116, 117, 124–126, 131, 134, 136, 141, 151, 155, 156, 160, 164
boundaries, 4–6,15, 16, 19, 30, 52, 53, 68, 82, 83, 85, 89, 122, 128, 159
Bradshaw, J., 152
brainstorm, 6, 77, 78, 116
British Dyslexia Association, 146
calm, 1, 2, 9, 23, 26, 30, 31, 74, 83, 85, 93, 96, 100, 101, 104, 106, 115, 131, 132, 135, 136, 142–5, 154, 163, 164
centred, 98, 101, 136, 150
choice, 17, 18, 22, 23, 25, 26, 51, 57, 58, 60, 61, 68, 69, 77, 80, 81, 84, 86, 87, 89, 91, 93, 95–7, 104–6, 111, 124, 126–8, 130, 131, 133, 137, 139, 140, 142–5, 154, 163, 164
Circle Time, 76
communication skills, 11, 62–71, 75, 83, 88, 90, 95, 96, 99, 100, 103, 105, 106, 112, 128, 133, 155–9
concentration, 32
confidence, 22, 24, 27, 29, 32, 33, 44–6, 58, 60, 66, 75, 84, 85, 92, 93, 99, 100, 102, 103, 11, 113, 118, 133, 135, 138, 141, 142, 147–9
contract, 111
cooperation, 2,14, 24, 50–2 54, 59, 61, 62, 64, 69, 75, 78, 79, 82, 86,89, 92, 95, 152, 159
Cowie, Helen, 121
creativity, 6, 7, 30, 31, 100, 107, 137
criticism, 29, 30, 49,

52–8, 61, 69, 70, 84, 85, 86, 107, 123
cultural differences, 71, 74, 76, 77, 103, 112
Deming, W. Edwards, 50
demoralisation, 20, 29, 42–8, 50, 61, 65, 66,70
Dickson, Anne, 44, 105
distress, 131
dyslexia, 10–12, 20, 146–8, 150, 151
dyspraxia, 10–12, 20, 146, 148
Dyspraxia Trust, 148
Elton report, 108
Emaho, 92
eustress, 131
expectations, 1, 3–6, 8, 9 19, 21, 30, 32, 35, 47–9, 62–6, 68, 69, 76, 79, 103, 122, 129, 130, 138, 143, 152, 158, 159
eye contact, 17, 19, 22, 73–76, 112
fear, 1, 10, 19, 35, 37, 48, 55, 62, 84, 90, 92, 96, 97, 99, 102, 111, 114, 122, 154
Freire, Paulo, 80
glue ear, 113, 114
Graubard, 66
Gray. F., 66
Grinder, J., 72
group work, 7, 50, 51, 78, 79, 96, 98, 112, 118, 131
Gryn, Rabbi Hugo, 120
habit, 10, 11, 20, 87, 96, 97, 100, 113, 121, 123–7, 129, 131, 141, 142, 144, 154, 160
Hargreaves, D. H., 65
Hester, S.K. 65
home position, 80, 82, 83, 85–7, 90, 91, 94, 159
Homework, 8, 19, 33, 40, 44, 45, 46, 52, 61, 118, 150, 152
independence, 31, 32, 34, 50, 59, 60, 89, 133, 135
instructions, 6, 7, 19, 22, 24–8, 32, 40, 46, 55, 56, 74, 114, 115, 142, 150, 152
intention, 3, 22, 48, 49, 67, 75, 76, 109, 117,

121, 126, 137, 138
Kubler–Ross, Elizabeth, 94
Latzko, 50
learning difficulties, 1, 13, 18, 21, 122
limits, 3–7, 14
listening, 7, 32, 38, 48, 61, 63–7, 72, 73, 78, 94, 97, 101, 105, 112–21, 126, 128, 138, 143, 155
literacy difficulties, 12, 13, 36, 37, 42, 47,107, 147
Mann, David, 66
Marland, Michael, 26, 50, 62, 74, 75
martial arts, 98, 128, 129, 137, 151
Mellor, F. J., 65
Miller, Alice, 65, 105, 152
misunderstanding, 64, 65, 67, 71, 73, 155, 156
Moseley, Jenny, 76
motivation, 7, 30, 50–2, 61, 70, 73, 74, 109, 110, 114, 129, 147
National Curriculum, 7, 32, 101
negotiation, 90, 105–12, 120
Oestreich, D. K., 92
peer counselling, 121
poisonous pedagogy, 152
praise, 7, 15–19, 30, 31, 43, 45, 49, 68–70, 85, 89, 109, 123, 125, 126, 129, 152
Quinn, K., 29
rapport, 71–3, 79
reasoning, 32
relationships, 2, 4, 17, 18, 19, 24, 25, 49, 50–4, 55, 57, 59, 61–6, 68–70, 73, 75, 77, 79, 80, 82, 83, 85, 86, 88, 89, 106, 107, 112, 113, 123, 128, 129, 132, 134, 135, 150
representational systems, 36–8, 71–3, 109, 114
respect, 7, 19, 62–4, 70, 74, 75, 81–3, 85, 93–5, 113, 142, 143, 153

responsibility, 8, 16, 25, 50, 54, 60, 61, 68, 70, 78, 92, 96, 99, 102, 105, 112, 126, 128, 135, 139, 143, 155
revision, 36, 38, 39, 42, 59, 118, 119, 140, 152
rewards, 4, 7,8, 17, 18, 31, 44, 89, 125, 130
Robertson, John, 62, 66, 86
roles, 2, 4, 5, 17, 20, 23, 27, 48, 50, 60, 61, 64, 78, 83–5, 90, 94, 97, 118, 119, 123–7, 129–31, 158, 159
Rosenburg, H., 66
RSA, exam board, 147
rules, 1, 3–8, 30, 31, 58, 67, 69, 78
sanctions, 1, 3, 4, 6, 8, 16, 22, 31, 81–3, 85, 89, 93, 94
script, 11, 14–18, 20, 83, 85
second language learner, 12, 21, 36, 40, 119
self-esteem, 1, 11, 18, 19, 29, 31, 32, 40, 54, 58, 60 66, 83–6, 89, 95 100, 102, 103, 105, 113, 114, 122, 135, 147, 150
self-image, 11, 14–16, 24, 31, 122, 126–9, 143
Selye, H., 132,
Semler, Ricardo, 80
specific learning difficulties, 10–13, 21, 32, 33, 40, 44, 58, 117, 119, 124, 134, 146–52
stress, 6, 20, 24, 52, 86, 88, 89, 100, 132–45, 161, 164
structure, 2, 6, 7, 13, 17, 32–4, 36, 42, 46–50, 70, 75, 135, 139, 151, 152
Supply, 21
Tagore, R. 1
targets, 8, 17, 18, 109, 114, 122–27
thinking, 32
trigger, 11, 14, 15, 92, 123, 124, 126, 131, 137
trust, 46, 60, 62, 89, 93, 95, 96, 112, 129